GUITAR HEROES

ART DIRECTOR Brian MacMullen
EDITORIAL DIRECTOR Lisa Purcell
DESIGNERS Hwaim Lee, Amy Pierce, Terasa Bernard
EDITORS Lori Baird
CONTRIBUTING WRITER Nancy J. Hajeski

COVER DESIGN Brian MacMullen

Metro Books
122 Fifth Avenue
New York, NY 10011

ISBN: 978-1-4351-1970-3

Printed and bound in China

10 9 8 7 6 5 4 3 2 1

GUITAR HEROES

FROM BLUES TO ROCK AND BEYOND

Jon Derengowski

METRO BOOKS
NEW YORK

CONTENTS

The Six-String Revolution   9

Blues and R&B   11

ELVIN BISHOP   12

BO DIDDLEY   14

PETER GREEN   16

BUDDY GUY   18

B.B. KING   20

ROBERT RANDOLPH   24

HUBERT SUMLIN   26

IKE TURNER   28

STEVIE RAY VAUGHAN   30

JOHNNY WINTER   32

Rock and Roll   35

DUANE ALLMAN   36

TREY ANASTASIO   38

BILLY JOE ARMSTRONG   40

CHUCK BERRY   42

DICKEY BETTS   46

ERIC CLAPTON   48

DICK DALE   52

DUANE EDDY   54

THE EDGE   56

PETER FRAMPTON   58

JERRY GARCIA   60

HENRY GARZA   62

BILLY GIBBONS   64

DAVID GILMOUR   66

WARREN HAYNES   68

JIMI HENDRIX   70

JOAN JETT   74

ERIC JOHNSON   78

JORMA KAUKONEN   80

MARK KNOPFLER   82

LENNY KRAVITZ   84

ROBBY KRIEGER   86

BRIAN MAY   88

GARY MOORE   90

STEVE MORSE   92

RICK NIELSEN   94

JIMMY PAGE   96

Pete Townshend

JOE PERRY 100
JOHN PETRUCCI 102
KEITH RICHARDS 104
FRANCIS ROSSI 108
RITCHIE SAMBORA 110
CARLOS SANTANA 112
PETE TOWNSHEND 116
ROBIN TROWER 120
DEREK TRUCKS 122
STEVE VAI 124
EDDIE VAN HALEN 126
JACK WHITE 128
NEIL YOUNG 130

Pop Music 133

SHERYL CROW 134
DAVE DAVIES 136
RAY DAVIES 138
JOHN FOGERTY 140
GEORGE HARRISON 142
JOHN MAYER 146
LIZ PHAIR 148
PRINCE 150
TODD RUNDGREN 152
STEPHEN STILLS 154
NEAL SCHON 156

The Edge

Folk and Country 159

JOHNNY CASH 160
BOB DYLAN 164
DON FELDER 166
VINCE GILL 168
BERT JANSCH 170
JONI MITCHELL 172
BRAD PAISLEY 174
BONNIE RAITT 176
RICHARD THOMPSON 178

Charlotte
Hatherley

YNGWIE MALMSTEEN   208
MICK MARS   210
DAVE MURRAY   212
VERNON REID   214
JOE SATRIANI   216
SLASH   218
ADRIAN SMITH   220
GLENN TIPTON   222
ANGUS YOUNG   224

Alternative, Indie, and Punk   **227**

MATTHEW BELLAMY   228
PETER BUCK   230
BUCKETHEAD   232
KURT COBAIN   234
GRAHAM COXON   238
BILLY CORGAN   240
ANI DIFRANCO   242
JOHN FRUSCIANTE   244
NOEL GALLAGHER   246
PAUL GILBERT   248
JONNY GREENWOOD   250
DAVE GROHL   252
CHARLOTTE HATHERLEY   254
JOSH HOMME   256
CHRISSIE HYNDE   258
JAMES IHA   260
MICK JONES   262

Hard Rock and Metal   **181**

NUNO BETTENCOURT   182
RITCHIE BLACKMORE   184
JERRY CANTRELL   186
PHIL COLLEN   188
C.C. DEVILLE   190
ACE FREHLEY   192
MARTY FRIEDMAN   194
JANICK GERS   196
KIRK HAMMETT   198
JAMES HETFIELD   200
TONY IOMMI   202
KERRY KING   204
ALEX LIFESON   206

JOHNNY MARR   264
MIKE MCCREADY   266
THURSTON MOORE   268
TOM MORELLO   270
DAVE NAVARRO   272
ED O'BRIEN   274
JOHNNY RAMONE   276
LEE RANALDO   278
ANDY SUMMERS   280
BERNARD SUMNER   282
PAUL WELLER   284

PACO DE LUCÍA   292
AL DI MEOLA   294
ALLAN HOLDSWORTH   296
STEVE HOWE   298
PAT METHENY   300
JOHN MCLAUGHLIN   302
LES PAUL   304
JOHN SCOFIELD   306
FRANK ZAPPA   308

Jazz, World, and Progressive   287
JEFF BECK   288
GEORGE BENSON   290

More Guitarists   310

Index   316

Credits   320

George
Benson

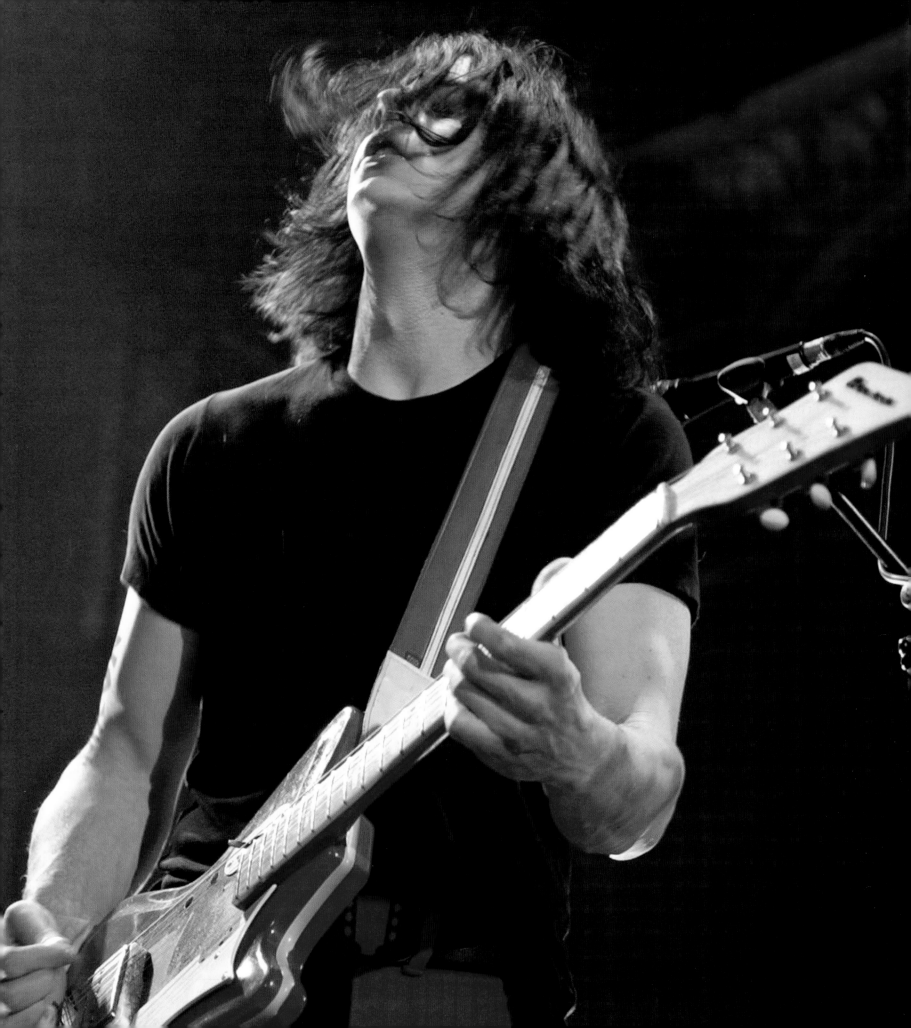

THE SIX-STRING REVOLUTION

At the start of the 1900s, the forefathers of modern popular music developed a common language—the twelve-bar blues—and adopted the guitar, one of the world's great ancient stringed instruments, as their weapon of choice. This exciting, new, adaptable, and personal style spread outward from the American South, taking root in every part of the globe, driving the genesis of rock and roll, and inspiring children everywhere there was a radio, a television, a music club, or a secondhand guitar store to pick up their first ax and play.

The first wave of guitar heroes with commercial potential embraced the electric guitar, invented in the 1930s and perfected in the wake of World War II's end. The pioneering virtuosos gave us just a hint of how the instrument would come to define contemporary music—and left blueprints for how to behave, how to live, and how to play to legions of budding musicians.

COMMON THREADS

Most of the guitar heroes in this book have a few things in common. Want to set yourself—or a child under your care—up for a lifetime of accolades and stardom? Having musical parents helps. Early access to a guitar, too, and ample exposure to the greats—Jimi Hendrix, B. B. King, Eric Clapton—all essential. To be sure, the earliest wave of virtuosos all trace their musical beginnings back to very early memories of the blues recordings that they heard on the radio or spun on vinyl in average living rooms in Nashville, New York, Manchester, London, Chicago, and Los Angeles.

Jack White

Practice is the other thing. Once the greats became hooked, they followed through and made good. Studies were ignored or abandoned completely, friends—all except the musical ones—left to the wayside, drugs and alcohol indulged with abandon . . . for focus, of course. The best young talents, by hook or by crook, got noticed—if they were lucky, by the very icons who drove them to play in the first place.

The life of a guitar hero isn't always tops. Divorce, financial instability, backstabbing and infighting, substance abuse, creative dry spells and irrelevance—all are potential obstacles to a carefree life of strumming and success. Some would say it all comes with the territory—and the best in this book would insist it's worth it, and anyway, they didn't choose the guitar—the guitar chose them.

LOOKING AHEAD, LOOKING BACK

The masters in this volume prove that there's no sound, emotion, or wizardry that can't be expressed with the help of six strings—and boundaries are certain to fall as the latest generation of geniuses cedes their reign to the new players, a class set to fully exploit the limitless possibilities of affordable, electronic recording and distribution.

At the same time guitar players need not shred or tragically self-destruct to qualify as heroes. A renewed interest in and reverence for clear, simple sounds and proper technique—even stripped-down, sometimes antique instruments—show no sign of slowing. Jazz, classical, historic, and world music is experiencing unprecedented levels of popularity, and it's likely some of the near future's most gifted talents will ignore the pull of trendy clubs, huge arenas, and radio airplay, opting for the hallowed traditions of craft and practice.

BLUES AND R&B

An undeniably American export, blues traces its roots back to the African-American communities in the South and their spiritual and work tunes. Coalescing into one definable sound around the dawning of the twentieth century, blues would further expand its boundaries with the advent of an electric style following World War II, ushering in some of the genre's most compelling and immortal voices.

Encompassing several distinct flavors, including Chicago, Delta, Jump, and Piedmont—named for the regions in which they developed—blues is truly the mother sound out of which rock and roll evolved. For almost every one of today's guitar heroes, all roads lead back to the blues.

ELVIN BISHOP

"The blues sprang out of the Mississippi Delta, and then it moved up to Chicago. It was the music that expressed the lifestyle that was going then with black people. And then the other music came in, you know, and kind of kicked blues out. It didn't really express the culture that was going on anymore. But I fell in love with the music as I first found it, and I've stayed in love with it."

—ELVIN BISHOP, 2008

E lvin Bishop (born October 21, 1942, in Tulsa, Oklahoma) is the guitarist behind the Elvin Bishop Group. Bishop has also gained fame as a collaborator with such well-known acts and artists as the Allman Brothers Band, B.B. King, and Bo Diddley.

Inspired early on by the Jimmy Reed recordings he heard as a young teen on the radio in Tulsa, Oklahoma, Bishop set his sights on the fertile 1960s blues scene in Chicago and moved there for college. As a student at the University of Chicago in the early 1960s, Bishop studied physics and moonlighted as an amateur musician, befriending local Paul Butterfield and playing in his Paul Butterfield Blues Band. The band created a stir due to the young ages of its members and the fact that, during early gigs on Chicago's very white—and very segregated—North Side, several of the bandmates were black. Today Butterfield's band is credited in part with introducing Chicago-style electric blues to previously unacquainted white audiences.

In 1968 Bishop broke off from the group to form his own project and, by 1971, a San Francisco–based Elvin Bishop Group was performing at the Fillmore East in Manhattan with the Allman Brothers Band.

Bishop navigated to mainstream success in 1976 with the hit "Fooled Around and Fell in Love," a track that featured Donny Baldwin and Mickey Thomas, both of whom would become members of Jefferson Starship.

Bishop's career has forged ahead, and the twenty-first century has seen the introduction of a pair of new albums: *Gettin' My Groove Back* in 2005 and Grammy-nominated *The Blues Roles On* in 2008, an ambitious project that enlisted the assistance of B.B. King and James Cotton, among others.

Elvin Bishop in concert, 1980s

essential albums

WITH THE PAUL BUTTERFIELD BLUES BAND

1965   *Paul Butterfield Blues Band*
1966   *East-West*
1966   *East-West Live*
1967   *The Resurrection of Pigboy Crabshaw*
1968   *In My Own Dream*

WITH THE ELVIN BISHOP GROUP

1969   *The Elvin Bishop Group*
1970   *Feel It!*
1972   *Rock My Soul*

SOLO

1974   *Let It Flow*
1975   *Juke Joint Jump*
1975   *Struttin' My Stuff*
1975   *The Best of Crabshaw Rising*
1976   *Hometown Boy Makes Good!*
1977   *Raisin' Hell*
1978   *Hog Heaven*
1981   *Is You Is or Is You Ain't My Baby?*
1988   *Big Fun*
1991   *Don't Let the Bossman Get You Down!*
1992   *Sure Feels Good: The Best of Elvin Bishop*
1994   *The Best of Elvin Bishop: Tulsa Shuffle*
1995   *Ace in the Hole*
1997   *The Best of Elvin Bishop*
1998   *The Skin I'm In*
2000   *That's My Partner!*
2001   *King Biscuit Flower Hour Presents Elvin Bishop in Concert*
2005   *Gettin' My Groove Back*
2008   *The Blues Roles On*

Awards and Honors

2009   Received the Blues Blast Award for Best Male Artist

Elvin Bishop onstage during a 1972 concert

ONE HIT WONDER OR CULTURAL TOUCHSTONE?

Bishop's best-known track remains "Fooled Around and Fell in Love." The hit song has Mickey Thomas on vocals—but it's Bishop's expansive, twangy R&B–flavored guitar that steals the show. Noted, too, is Bishop's audible slipup during his solo; critics agree that the decision to leave the flub in makes for an especially warm and honest recording.

Charting at No. 3, "Fooled Around and Fell in Love" has come to represent the sound of 1976. It regularly appears on compilations and sound tracks inspired by the period, and it has been given a prominent place in acclaimed 1970s-set films such as *Summer of Sam* and *Boogie Nights*.

BO DIDDLEY

"Everything, even music, was viewed and appreciated through color of skin . . . Even today, unfortunately people have the wrong idea by which someone's child can't play with other kids just because of their nationality or color of skin . . . But finally when I realized what was going on, that experience brought me a lot of pain. Man finally has to understand that we all live on this planet . . . living one relatively short period of time. And in that time living in hatred is nothing but complete madness."

—BO DIDDLEY,
REFLECTING ON THE
1940S AND 1950S IN AMERICA, 2004

Bo Diddley (born Ellas Otha Bates on December 30, 1928, in McComb, Mississippi; died June 2, 2008, in Archer, Florida), also know as the "Originator" for his prominent position at the conflux of blues and rock and roll, was a groundbreaking guitarist, both musically and technically.

Diddley's church in Chicago first exposed him to gospel and hymnal music in his teens; he went on to learn guitar and aligned himself with a number of bands in the early 1940s. By 1951 he had a permanent spot at a blues club on the South Side, which allowed him to network and form a band to help him record a handful of demos. In 1955 he released "Bo Diddley," which shot to No. 1 on the R&B charts.

A legendary performance on the *Ed Sullivan Show* would follow, along with a string of hits through the early 1960s. In 1963 he toured the United Kingdom, supported by a then barely known group called the Rolling Stones. The 1970s brought a number of high-profile collaborations, with Diddley appearing with B.B. King, the Clash, the Grateful Dead, and Les Paul.

A fiftieth-anniversary tour kicked off in 2005, and Diddley visited the United States, the Great Britain, and Australia. Diddley spent the last few years of his life active in Hurricane Katrina relief efforts. He gave his last performance in 2007 and died a year later after a long period of illness.

essential albums

STUDIO

1957	*Bo Diddley*
1959	*Go Bo Diddley*
1959	*Have Guitar, Will Travel*
1960	*Bo Diddley in the Spotlight*
1961	*Bo Diddley Is a Gunslinger*
1961	*Bo Diddley Is a Lover*
1962	*Bo Diddley*
1962	*Bo Diddley & Company*
1962	*Bo Diddley's a Twister*
1962	*Hey! Bo Diddley*
1963	*Surfin' with Bo Diddley*
1965	*Hey, Good Lookin'*
1965	*500% More Man*
1965	*Let Me Pass*
1966	*The Originator*
1967	*Boss Man*
1967	*Road Runner*
1968	*Super Blues*
1970	*The Black Gladiator*
1971	*Another Dimension*
1972	*Where It All Began*
1973	*The London Bo Diddley Sessions*
1974	*Big Bad Bo*
1989	*Pay Bo Diddley*
1992	*Who Do You Love*
1992	*Bo's Guitar*
1992	*This Should Not Be*
1994	*Promises*
1995	*The Mighty Bo Diddley*
1996	*A Man Amongst Men*
1996	*Mona (Drive)*
1998	*Road Runner Live*
2000	*I Am a Man, Volume*
2003	*Greatest Rock & Roll Show*

LIVE

1963	*Bo Diddley's Beach Party (live)*
1989	*Live at the Ritz*
1992	*Live (Fan Club)*
2005	*Vamp*
2007	*You Can't Judge a Book by the Cover*
2008	*Rock 'N' Roll All Star Jam*
2008	*In Concert*

Awards and Honors

1987	Inducted into the Rock and Roll Hall of Fame
1996	Rhythm & Blues Foundation, Lifetime Achievement Award
1998	Lifetime Achievement Award from the National Association of Recording Arts and Sciences
1998	Grammy Award for Lifetime Achievement
2003	Ranked No. 37 on *Rolling Stone*'s list of the 100 Greatest Guitarists of All Time
2003	Inducted into the Blues Hall of Fame

Bo Diddley in concert at the Kentish Town Forum, London, 2005

DIDDLEY'S GUITAR & THE BO DIDDLEY BEAT

Diddley is renowned for his collection of custom-designed—and oddly shaped—guitars, but no instrument is more famous than the "Twang Machine," an usual box-shaped ax originally constructed by Diddley and later commercially produced by Gretsch. The design resulted from an injury Diddley suffered on stage—normal guitars, he felt, were too bulky, and tended to collide with his body during performances. Another ax, the aggressive "Cadillac" model, is featured on the cover of *Bo Diddley Is a Gunslinger*.

"I play guitar like I play a drum," Diddley once proclaimed. The Bo Diddley Beat, based in rumba and African rhythms, drives many Bo Diddley compositions in place of the chord changes more common in modern pop and rock music. Many of his best known songs have their roots in older, more traditional folk tunes that Diddley ingeniously adapted and made new again. Diddley's beat and riffs have made their way into the repertoire of almost every blues and rock act to follow.

PETER GREEN

"I decided to go back on lead guitar after seeing Eric Clapton. . . . He had a Les Paul and his fingers were marvelous. It took everything away from me, like my birthday, Christmas; you forgot everything, just listen to this. All music that you'd ever heard was washed away by this group of guys that were letting Eric Clapton take the floor."

—PETER GREEN, 1999

Awards and Honors

2003 Ranked number 38 on *Rolling Stone*'s 100 Greatest Guitarists of All Time list

Peter Green (born October 29, 1946, in London, England) is a founding member of Fleetwood Mac. His unpretentious blues style bought immediate fame to the group, but the demands of success proved to be too much. After several jarring experiences with drugs, Green was forced to quit the band.

After beginning on the bass, Green's first major gig was in the Bluesbreakers, where he crossed paths with Eric Clapton, ultimately replacing him on lead guitar. His time with the band allowed him the chance to compose as well; a sampling of his work appears on 1967's *Hard Road.*

Fleetwood Mac debuted as Peter Green's Fleetwood Mac in 1968, named for two of Green's Bluesbreakers bandmates, Mick Fleetwood and John McVie. Both Fleetwood and McVie soon joined the new band. The band's initial record focused on the blues, but later releases would embrace a wider pop and rock sound, finding extensive chart success. Ever modest,

Green seemed uneasy about Fleetwood Mac's mainstream success, shrugging off suggestions by interviewers that it was his songwriting and composing that put the band on top.

By 1970 Green had grown disillusioned with fame and had discovered LSD. A diagnosis of schizophrenia followed. The change in his personality led to his departure from the band, and he spent most of the 1970s and 1980s as a vagabond, in and out of psychiatric care. He was able to record a few solo albums, but his personal problems prevented a truly complete musical reemergence.

In 1997 Green formed the Peter Green Splinter Group, entering a productive period of album releases; nine in total by 2004. Again, the effort ran aground after Green's departure—he claimed his medication interfered with his ability to contribute meaningfully to the group.

Green has been active again since 2009, playing concert dates in Europe as Peter Green and Friends.

GREEN'S STYLE

Even guitar great B.B. King has expressed his respect for Green's playing. His signature tone, courtesy of his Gibson Les Paul, is usually described as clear and mournful, best captured on "The Super-Natural," one of his most important recordings. The track's long, sustained guitar notes take on an almost humanlike wailing vibrato. In discussing his tone, Green revealed the pickup on his guitar had been rewired in the late 1960s, resulting in a one-of-a-kind instrument. Green always advocated a simple setup. During his Fleetwood Mac days he appeared with the Les Paul and a single amplifier; he eschewed extra equipment or effects.

Peter Green with Fleetwood Mac bandmates in 1969. From left to right: John McVie, Danny Kirwan, Mick Fleetwood, and Peter Green. Front: Jeremy Spencer

Peter Green in 1969 in concert with Fleetwood Mac

essential albums

WITH JOHN MAYAL & THE BLUESBREAKERS

1967	*A Hard Road*

WITH FLEETWOOD MAC

1968	*Fleetwood Mac*
1968	*Mr. Wonderful*
1969	*Then Play On*
1969	*English Rose*

SOLO

1970	*The End of the Game*
1979	*In the Skies*
1980	*Little Dreamer*
1981	*Whatcha Gonna Do?*
1982	*White Sky*
1983	*Kolors*

WITH PETER GREEN SPLINTER GROUP

1997	*Peter Green Splinter Group*
1998	*The Robert Johnson Songbook*
1998	*Soho Session*
1999	*Destiny Road*
2001	*Me and the Devil*
2001	*Blues Don't Change*
2003	*Reaching The Cold 100*

BUDDY GUY

essential albums

WITH THE JUNIOR WELLS BAND

1965	*Hoodoo Man Blues*
1966	*Chicago/The Blues/Today! Volume 1*
1966	*It's my Life, Baby!*
1970	*Buddy and the Juniors* (with Junior Wells and Junior Mance)
1970	*South Side Blues Jam* (with Junior Wells and Otis Spann)
1972	*Play The Blues*
1981	*Alone and Acoustic*
1998	*Last Time Around: Live at Legends*
1992	*Live at Montreux*
2000	*Every Day I Have the Blues*

SOLO

1967	*I Left My Blues in San Francisco*
1967	*Berlin Festival Guitar Workshop*
1968	*A Man and the Blues*
1968	*Coming at You*
1968	*Blues Today*
1968	*This Is Buddy Guy*
1969	*Hot and Cool*
1969	*First Time I Met the Blues*
1971	*In The Beginning*
1972	*Hold That Plane!*
1974	*I Was Walking Through the Woods*
1979	*Got to Use Your House*
1981	*Stone Crazy*
1982	*Drinkin' TNT 'n' Smokin' Dynamite*
1982	*DJ Play My Blues*
1982	*Dollar Done Fell*
1983	*Buddy Guy*
1983	*The Original Blues Brothers*
1985	*Ten Blue Fingers*
1986	*Atlantic Blues: Chicago*
1987	*Chess Masters*
1988	*Live at the Checkerboard Lounge: Chicago 1979*
1988	*Breaking Out*
1989	*I Ain't Got No Money*

Buddy Guy (born July 30, 1936, in Lettsworth, Louisiana) is best known for his indelible contributions to Chicago blues. Picking up the acoustic guitar at an early age, he soon found himself under the tutelage of Muddy Waters in Chicago. In 1957, he earned his first recording deal after competing against other guitarists in the Windy City.

After a steady stream of recording in the mid-1960s, Guy watched his career slow down while the careers of many of his contemporaries, who had captured the favor of their record companies, either through sheer determination or complicated politics, surged forward. Guy remained in the scene as a session guitarist, backing up other greats—even Waters himself—but it wasn't until the late 1980s that the public rekindled its interest in Guy's original recordings.

Guy continues to keep a hectic global touring schedule.

"If you don't think you have the blues, just keep living."

—BUDDY GUY,
ROCK AND ROLL HALL OF FAME
INDUCTION SPEECH, 2005

1991	*Damn Right, I've Got the Blues*
1991	*Buddy's Baddest: The Best of Buddy Guy*
1992	*My Time After Awhile*
1992	*The Very Best of Buddy Guy*
1992	*The Complete Chess Studio Recordings*
1993	*Feels Like Rain*
1994	*Slippin' In*
1996	*Live: The Real Deal*
1997	*Buddy's Blues*
1998	*Buddy's Blues 1978–1982: The Best of the JSP Recordings*
1998	*As Good as It Gets*
1998	*Heavy Love*
1998	*This Is Buddy Guy*
1998	*Blues Master*
1999	*Buddy's Baddest: The Best of Buddy Guy*
2000	*The Complete Vanguard Recordings*
2001	*20th Century Masters: The Millennium: The Best of Buddy Guy*
2001	*Sweet Tea*
2001	*Double Dynamite*
2003	*Blues Singer*
2003	*Chicago Blues Festival 1964*
2003	*Jammin' Blues Electric & Acoustic*
2003	*Live At the Mystery Club*
2005	*A Night of the Blues*
2005	*Bring 'Em In*
2006	*Can't Quit The Blues*
2006	*Live: The Real Deal* (with G. E. Smith and the Saturday Night Live Band)
2008	*Skin Deep*
2009	*The Definitive Buddy Guy*

GUY'S STYLE

Guy is recognized across generations of guitar pros as well as casual fans for his dynamic, unpredictable style and his flair for drama and stagecraft. Many of his favorite tricks have delighted audiences for their value as spectacle—never mind the music being played.

Inspired by the antics of Guitar Slim as a child, whose hypnotic, zany performances directly affected Guy's presentation, Guy has been known to pluck women or children from his audiences and ask them to strum while he frets.

As a technician, Guy's work, especially his early material, which fleshes out an intuitive and emotional style that deals in contrasts, extremes, and textures, is often called "pathfinding." Many popular rock and roll guitarists of the late 1960s and 1970s credit Guy for bridging the gulf between traditional blues and rock. His fearless and lengthy solos turned the common tradition of quaint, bite-sized pop tunes on its ear.

Among the scores of talented guitar artists to profess a debt to Guy are Jeff Beck, Eric Clapton, Jimi Hendrix, Jimmy Page, and Stevie Ray Vaughan.

Among his many accolades, Guy can count twenty-three W. C. Handy Blues Awards.

Awards and Honors

1992	Grammy Award for Best Contemporary Blues Album, for *Damn Right, I've Got the Blues*
1993	The Century Award, *Billboard* magazine
1994	Grammy Award for Best Contemporary Blues Album, for *Feels Like Rain*
1996	Grammy Award for Best Contemporary Blues Album, for *Slippin' In*
2003	National Medal of Arts
2003	Ranked No. 30 on *Rolling Stone*'s list of the 100 Greatest Guitarists of All Time
2004	Grammy Award for Best Contemporary Blues Album, for *Blues Singer*
2005	Inducted in the Rock and Roll Hall of Fame
2008	Inducted in the Louisiana Music Hall of Fame

Known to the world as "B.B. King," Riley B. King (born September 16, 1925, in Itta Bena, Mississippi) is considered one of the greatest blues guitarists of all time. His unmistakable command of the instrument as well as his intricate soloing techniques has influenced guitarists and songwriters of every style and background.

King began humbly as a boy with a $15 guitar. In his early 20s he moved to Memphis and became infatuated with the electric guitar, putting himself under the tutelage of older cousin Bukka White, a jazz player in his own right. Soon King established a recording contract with a Los Angeles–based label and was anointed with his nickname, based on his radio host personality— "Beale Street Blues Boy."

In 1949 King released a single called "Miss Martha King," which flopped. King began to network with a wide range of musicians, producers, and businesspeople with whom he

entered a prolific and successful period of recording and touring that would span through the end of the 1970s. King grew close to earnest producer Sam Phillips, who would go on to found Sun Records.

"Three O'Clock Blues," a Lowell Fulson cover, was King's first taste of the big-time in 1951; his career would truly take off during the decade. Recruiting a team of fellow musicians and dubbing themselves the B.B. King Review, King would roll out a parade of hit singles and tour the country almost non-stop for several years, performing nearly 350 times in 1956.

After a temporary lull in popularity and relevance in the 1960s, King's career surged when "The Thrill Is Gone," a song King recorded in 1969, quickly became regarded as King's crowning achievement for its masterful guitar playing. It has been widely acknowledged as one of the best songs ever recorded. King pushed ahead commercially and artistically

KING OF INFLUENCE

Commonly referred to as America's "Ambassador of the Blues," there is quite simply no other living practitioner of the art held in higher esteem. King has never been the speediest player, but the care he takes in hitting each note in its sweet—and sometimes wrenching—spot is obvious. Eschewing more complicated techniques like slide playing, or even fairly rudimentary chords, King's technique is defined by his bending and stringing of individual notes into vocal-like sounds and phrases.

King considers himself a devout bluesman, but with-out his influence an entire generation of guitarists—especially in rock and roll—would be bankrupt. Eric Clapton, Buddy Guy, and Stevie Ray Vaughan are among the most vocal virtuosos in King's debt. King, in turn, has had kind works for Clapton and Jimi Hendrix—and is responsible for carrying along the influence of his own idols, which include T-Bone Walker, Lonnie Johnson, Blind Lemon Jefferson, Elmore James, and Lowell Fulson.

"We all have idols. Play like anyone you care about but try to be yourself while you're doing so."

—B.B. KING

into the 1970s, playing with genres like funk and country. In the 1980s and 1990s King was as visible on the concert circuit as ever, though his studio releases slowed to a mere trickle. His collaborations with artists such as Eric Clapton and U2 kept him at the forefront of popular musical trends, even as he basked in his status as a living icon.

In honor of his eighth decade on earth in 2005, King released *80*, an album of duets with some of music's biggest names. At 80 years old he decided it was time for a farewell tour, kicking it off in 2006 in the UK—only to return to the road for major appearances in 2008 at Bonnaroo, the Chicago Blues Festival, the Grammy Nomination Concert, and the Kennedy Center Honors Awards Show. His most recent studio release is 2008's Grammy-winning *One Kind Favor*.

Now immune to such notions as retirement, in 2009 King toured with John Mayall and Buddy Guy.

Awards and Honors

1971 Grammy Award for Best Male R&B Vocal Performance, for "The Thrill is Gone"

1982 Grammy for Best Ethnic or Traditional Folk Recording, for *There Must Be a Better World Somewhere*

1984 Grammy Award for Best Traditional Blues Album, for *Blues 'N' Jazz*

1986 Grammy Award for Best Traditional Blues Album, for *My Guitar Sings the Blues*

1987 Grammy Award for Lifetime Achievement

1991 Grammy Award for Best Traditional Blues Album, for *Live at San Quentin*

1992 Grammy Award for Best Traditional Blues Album, for *Live at the Apollo*

1994 Grammy Award for Best Traditional Blues Album, for *Blues Summit*

1996 Grammy Award for Best Rock Instrumental Performance, for "SRV Shuffle," with Art Neville, Bonnie Raitt, Buddy Guy, Dr. John, Eric Clapton, Jimmie Vaughan, and Robert Cray

1998 Grammy Hall of Fame Award, for "The Thrill is Gone"

2000 Grammy Award for Best Traditional Blues Album, for *Blues on the Bayou*

2001 Grammy Award for Best Traditional Blues Album, for *Riding with the King*

2003 Grammy Award for Best Traditional Blues Album, for *A Christmas Celebration of Hope*

2003 Ranked No. 3 on *Rolling Stone*'s list of the 100 Greatest Guitarists of All Time

2006 Grammy Award for Best Traditional Blues Album, for *B.B. King & Friends: 80*

2010 Grammy Award for Best Traditional Blues Album, for *One Kind Favor*

B.B. King at the Grammy Awards in 2000, where he picked up a statue for Best Traditional Blues Album

essential albums

STUDIO

1956	*Singin' the Blues*
1958	*The Blues*
1961	*My Kind of Blues*
1962	*Mr. Blues*
1963	*Blues in My Heart*
1966	*Confessin' the Blues*
1967	*Blues Is King*
1967	*The Jungle*
1968	*Blues on Top of Blues*
1968	*Lucille*
1969	*Completely Well*
1970	*Indianola Mississippi Seeds*
1971	*B.B. King in London*
1972	*Guess Who*
1972	*L.A. Midnight*
1973	*To Know You Is To Love You*
1974	*Together for the First Time* (With Bobby "Blue" Bland)
1974	*Friends*
1975	*Lucille Talks Back*
1977	*King Size*
1978	*Midnight Believer*
1979	*Take It Home*
1981	*There Must Be a Better World Somewhere*
1982	*Love Me Tender*
1983	*Why I Sing the Blues*

B.B. King in concert in Deauville, France, 1989

"I was watching TV one night, and the lead singer of the Beatles—John Lennon—said he wished he could play like B.B. King. I almost fell out of my chair. And that started me to thinking, 'God, what am I doing? The greatest group on Earth, and the guy is saying that to me?' I tried not to let it go to my head. But I sure thought about it. That was like Jesus Christ coming down and saying, 'Yeah, B., you're pretty good.'"

—B.B. KING

1985	*Six Silver Strings*
1991	*There is Always One More Time*
1992	*King of the Blues*
1995	*Lucille & Friends*
1997	*Deuces Wild*
1998	*Blues on the Bayou*
1999	*Let the Good Times Roll*
2000	*Riding with the King*
2000	*Makin' Love Is Good for You*
2003	*Reflections*
2005	*B.B. King & Friends: 80*
2008	*One Kind Favor*

LIVE

1965	*Live at the Regal*
1969	*Live & Well*
1971	*Live in Cook County Jail*
1980	*Now Appearing at Ole Miss*
1976	*Bobby Bland and B.B. King Together Again . . . Live*
1990	*B.B. King and Sons Live*
1990	*Live at San Quentin*
1991	*Live at the Apollo*
2007	*Forever Gold: B.B. King Live*
2008	*Live*
2009	*Live At The BBC*

LUCILLE

One of the most storied guitars in the history of music, Lucille has been King's ax of choice since 1949. Though her form has changed over the years and he possesses several replicas, the original guitar's story is inseparable from the legend of King himself.

At a concert gig in 1949, King was performing in Twist, Arkansas. The venue had set up a barrel of burning fuel as a heating source, and two fighting men knocked it over—setting the entire place aflame. In the chaos, King escaped—but not before realizing that he had left his acoustic Gibson inside the concert hall. He braved the flames to retrieve his most important possession, making it out alive (two patrons were not so lucky). King later discovered that the men had come to blows over a girl named Lucille. King co-opted the name as a reminder about avoiding dangerous situations. Indeed, Lucille would come to protect King on several occasions; he cites her as a factor in his surviving multiple car wrecks.

Currently, Lucille is manifest in a Gibson ES-355 solid body. Gibson began mass-producing the B.B. King Lucille signature guitar in the 1980s, following up in 1999 with Little Lucille, a currently discontinued model based on their Blueshawk guitar.

Lucille has been the subject of numerous pop culture references and has made her share of appearances in public life. A King-autographed replica resides in the National Music Museum in South Dakota, and she has been given an audience with Pope John Paul II. Today, the name Lucille is shorthand for any number of capable, familiar, and much-loved objects throughout literature, film, and television.

Lucille onstage at a concert at the Seminole Hard Rock in Hollywood, Florida. Master guitarist B.B. King's favorite ax has become nearly as famous as the man himself.

ROBERT RANDOLPH

Robert Randolph (born December 20, 1978, in Irvington, New Jersey) is a pedal steel guitarist relatively new to the music scene, but he's already grabbed the attention of Eric Clapton, who contributed to Randolph's most recent album and was instrumental in conceiving his first tour with the Family Band.

Raised in suburban New Jersey, Randolph grew up in the shadow of New York City and had access to music venues of every size in Newark and other cities on the East Coast. Randolph's church, rooted in the Sacred Steel gospel tradition, exposed him to the steel guitar, and he absorbed the skill and technique of other players during services.

Randolph's first gig was opening for the North Mississippi Allstars, a rock-tinged blues band. During a performance at the Beacon Theater in Manhattan, Randolph met John Medeski, a keyboardist, who persuaded him to record with his band. Medeski Martin & Wood released the gospel record *The Word* in 2001.

Awards and Honors

2003   Gospel Music Association Dove Award for Urban Album of the Year

Randolph recruited a bassist and drummer and formed Robert Randolph and the Family Band, honing a funk-influenced sound. The band quickly gained a reputation for its energetic, participatory dance-filled live performances. Building on influences that include Stevie Ray Vaughan, Earth, Wind and Fire, and Sly and the Family Stone, the band has released three albums, even recording a version of the NBC theme song for network television broadcasts. Tour partners have included Eric Clapton, the Dave Matthews Band, and O.A.R. (Of a Revolution).

THE PEDAL STEEL GUITAR

The pedal steel guitar is an unusual, highly customizable setup with its roots in American country music. A type of slide guitar, the instrument also includes a set of levers and pedals. The guitar itself is arranged on a horizontal console, supported by legs underneath. A pedal steel guitar can have multiple necks with various tunings, but it's the pedals that give the instrument its versatility.

Pedal steel guitars have their roots in Hawaiian music, where traditional guitars were fretted with a comb or other tool, instead of fingers. The instrument went through a rapid period of development and advancement in the 1950s, when various technicians and musicians experimented with the addition of knobs, levers, and pedals to modify pitch and give the player an unprecedented level of control over its output.

The guitarist normally sits in front of the instrument, manipulating the levers with his or her knees and the pedals by foot. A slide, or steel, is used to fret the neck, and the player uses a free hand to pluck the strings.

Robert Randolph performing with the Family Band at the Gathering of the Vibes in 2001. The gathering of the Vibes is an annual four-day music and arts festival that celebrates the Grateful Dead and showcases a diverse variety of music.

"We didn't meet the queen, but we did wind up talking with Ringo Starr and Paul McCartney backstage, who came down to see the show and really enjoyed it. That was such a great moment, and it's always so amazing that a young artist can be appreciated by so many musical pioneers. That's really the ultimate highlight—that I've been given the chance to call up Clapton or Steven Tyler anytime and [ask] 'What are you up to today?' and 'What do you think of this idea?'"

—ROBERT RANDOLPH, ON OPENING FOR ERIC CLAPTON IN THE UK, 2007

essential albums

WITH VARIOUS ARTISTS

1999	*Sacred Steel, Volume 2: Live at the House of God Church* (with various artists)
2001	*Pulling up Atlantis* (with the Demolition String Band)
2001	*The Word* (with John Medeski and the North Mississippi Allstars)
2001	*Train Don't Leave Me: The First Annual Sacred Steel Convention* (with various artists)
2002	*Medicated Magic* (with the Dirty Dozen Brass Band)

WITH THE FAMILY BAND

2002	*Live at the Wetlands*
2003	*Unclassified*
2006	*Colorblind*

HUBERT SUMLIN

A protégé of legendary bluesman Howlin' Wolf, Hubert Sumlin (born November 16, 1931, in Greenwood, Mississippi) is an idiosyncratic guitarist lauded for his raw style.

A guitar player since the age of 8, Sumlin was an early fan of Howlin' Wolf, also known as Chester Burnett. An underage Sumlin snuck into one of Wolf's performances around 1941 and, after nearly getting kicked out, succeeded in striking up a conversation with the musician. In 1954 Sumlin eagerly took up Burnett on his offer to join his band as a backup guitarist—even though it meant Sumlin would have to relocate to Chicago.

Sumlin became lead guitar a year later and held the post for decades. Sumlin's contributions to Burnett's records of the early to mid 1960s are considered legendary; fellow bluesmen like Bob Margolin consider this period the one during which Sumlin truly came into his own, confidently establishing his own signature sound and style. Sumlin gradually grew comfortable as bandleader, reconfiguring members of Wolf's outfit as the Wolf Pack after Burnett's death in 1976.

Even after lung surgery in 2004, Sumlin continues to nurture his career, still playing guitar and promoting his latest work.

"You try to tell a story . . . you live the story. That's what I think that Wolf did and Muddy did. What they sung about, what they said. . . . It's in the way you say it and the way you sing it. You have to live it. I know I have and I know the rest of them have seen it. . . . It may be a little faster or a little classier but it comes down to you playin' the blues or you ain't."

—HUBERT SUMLIN, 1997

Awards and Honors

1988   Inducted into the Blues Foundation Hall of Fame
2003   Ranked No. 65 on *Rolling Stone*'s list of the 100 Greatest Guitarists of All Time

THE SUMLIN LEGACY

Sumlin is often cited as a "link" musician by contemporary (especially British) blues-based guitarists, responsible for bringing a American Southern acoustic style of playing to the acolytes of more recent electric blues, including Jeff Beck, Eric Clapton, Stevie Ray Vaughan, and Jimmy Page. The influence of Sumlin and Howlin' Wolf is frequently heard—and sometimes downright imitated—in tracks put out by Cream, Led Zeppelin, the Rolling Stones, and the Yardbirds.

It was Sumlin's mentor Howlin' Wolf who convinced him to start playing without a pick, encouraging him to soften his playing—no doubt out of concern, in part, that his own vocals wouldn't be heard during performances.

essential albums

STUDIO

1964	*American Folk Blues*
1974	*Kings of Chicago Blues, Volume. 2*
1976	*Groove*
1980	*Gamblin' Woman*
1987	*Hubert Sumlin's Blues Party*
1989	*Heart & Soul*
1990	*Healing Feeling*
1991	*Blues Guitar Boss*
1993	*Made in Argentina*
1994	*I'm the Back Door Man*
1996	*Blues Classics*
1998	*I Know You*
1998	*Wake Up Call*
1999	*Pinetop Perkins & Hubert Sumlin: Legends*
2004	*About Them Shoes*

Sumlin performs at the Beale Street Music Festival in Memphis, Tennessee, 2006

IKE TURNER

"If he have millions of dollars, I been there. If he's poor, eating out of the garbage can, I been there. If he have fifty women, I had that. If he lookin' for one, I been there, too. I've lived my life."

—IKE TURNER

and bandmate Willie Kizart's unintentionally distorted guitar licks, the result of a broken amplifier.

Turner met young singer Anna Bullock in St. Louis in 1957, and he quickly persuaded her to join the Rhythm Kings, bestowing the stage name "Tina" upon her. Ike and Tina claimed to have wed in Mexico the following year—a union that Ike would deny near the end of his life. The band's act rapidly morphed into a showcase for Tina's incendiary vocal talents, eventually dropping the rest of the Kings and going on tour as a pared-down Ike & Tina Turner. Popular success would elude the duo, and Ike's public perception took a nose-dive in the 1970s after Tina left to establish a wildly successful solo career, basing her embattled stage persona on the physical and psychological abuse she suffered at the hands of Ike.

Left in his former wife's increasingly long shadow and seemingly unable to reenergize his career on his own, Turner turned heavily to drugs, winding up in prison and eventually dying from an overdose.

Ike Turner (born November 5, 1931, in Clarksdale, Mississippi; died December 12, 2007, in San Marcos, California) was a pioneering rock and roll and blues musician, infamous for his dramatic and violent relationship with backup singer and, later wife, Tina Turner.

Originally trained on the piano, young Turner picked up the guitar after discovering the tunes of other greats, such as Elmore James and Muddy Waters. In 1951, with the band Jackie Brenston and His Delta Cats (later to become the Kings of Rhythm), Turner recorded "Rocket 88," a song historic for its synthesis of one of the earliest identifiable rock and roll sounds

Awards and Honors

1971	Grammy Award for Best R&B Vocal Performance by a Group, for "Proud Mary"
1991	Inducted into the Rock and Roll Hall of Fame
2003	Ranked No. 61 on *Rolling Stone*'s list of the 100 Greatest Guitarists of All Time
2004	Heroes Award, National Academy of Recording Arts & Sciences
2007	Grammy Award for Best Traditional Blues Album, for *Risin' With the Blues*

essential albums

WITH IKE TURNER & THE KINGS OF RHYTHM
1969   *A Black Man's Soul*

WITH IKE TURNER & THE FAMILY VIBES
1972   *Strange Fruit*

WITH IKE & TINA TURNER
1960   *The Soul of Ike and Tina Turner*
1962   *Dance with Ike & Tina Turner & Their Kings of Rhythm Band*
1963   *Don't Play Me Cheap*
1963   *Dynamite*
1963   *It's Gonna Work Out Fine*
1963   *Please Please Please*
1964   *The Ike & Tina Turner Revue Live*
1965   *Live! The Ike & Tina Turner Show*
1965   *Festival of Live Performances*
1965   *Ike & Tina Show 2*
1965   *Ooh Poo Pah Doo*
1966   *River Deep, Mountain High*
1966   *Ike & Tina Turner and the Raelettes*
1966   *Live! The Ike & Tina Turner Show*
1966   *Live! The Ike & Tina Turner Show, Vols. 1-2*
1968   *Outta Season*
1969   *Ike & Tina Turner in Person*
1969   *Fantastic*
1969   *Get It Together*
1969   *Her Man His Woman*
1969   *The Hunter*
1970   *Come Together*
1971   *Workin' Together*

1971   *Nuff Said*
1971   *Something's Got a Hold on Me*
1971   *What You Hear Is What You Get*
1972   *Feel Good*
1973   *Let Me Touch Your Mind*
1973   *Nutbush City Limits*
1973   *Live! The World of Ike and Tina Turner*
1974   *Strange Fruit*
1974   *Sweet Rhode Island Red*
1974   *Tina Turns the Country On*
1974   *The Gospel According to Ike and Tina*
1974   *The Great Album*
1975   *Sixteen Great Performances*
1977   *Delilah's Power*

SOLO
2004   *Here and Now*
2007   *Risin' with the Blues*

"ROCKET 88" & THE FAMOUS AMP

"Rocket 88" is on a short list of contenders for first rock and roll song ever recorded. Laid down in 1951 and produced by Sam Phillips, the song was conceived as an homage to a particular model of Oldsmobile and based on an earlier tune by Jimmy Liggins. The song met with significant and immediate success after its release, noted for its expressive, energetic percussion, piano, and saxophone—and its groundbreaking licks.

The single's now-famous distorted guitar is part of music legend. Accounts differ as to how it happened, but the Kings of Rhythm's amplifier was damaged on the road, either by rain or a spill off the back of the truck. Turner attempted a repair, but the amplifier still produced a fuzzy tone. Neither Phillips nor the members of the band disliked it, so they went ahead with the recording.

The amplifier is exhibited at Sun Records in Memphis, the studio where the track was put together.

Turner performing with the Kings of Rhythm during the Montreux Jazz Festival, in Montreux, Switzerland, 2002

STEVIE RAY VAUGHAN

"You know, there's a big lie in this business. The lie is that it's okay to go out in flames. But that doesn't do anybody much good."

—STEVIE RAY VAUGHAN

Stevie Ray Vaughan (born October 3, 1954, in Dallas, Texas; died August 27, 1990, in East Troy, Wisconsin) was one of the most talented and influential electric guitarists in the history of rock and blues.

Vaughan was born in Dallas, Texas, but spent his childhood on the move, living in more than thirty towns. His first guitar was a mere Sears toy, but when Vaughan was 8 his big brother, Jimmie, gave Stevie his old electric. His parents were fans of Western swing, a genre that left its mark on Vaughan, but he got hooked on the blues while still young, copying riffs and techniques of greats like Albert King and Buddy Guy.

Throughout his high school years, Vaughan began playing in a succession of bands, and by 1973 he had joined Marc Benno's the Nightcrawlers, which was already under contract to A&M Records—although its album was never released. Nonetheless some good came out of the connection; Vaughan began his songwriting partnership with Nightcrawlers drummer Doyle Bramhall.

By the end of the next year Vaughan was playing five nights a week with Austin band Paul Ray & the Cobras, honing his already impressive skills. After three years with the Cobras, Vaughan form the Triple Threat Revue, the band that eventually morphed into Double Trouble.

Double Trouble's appearance at the Swiss Montreux Jazz Festival in 1982 met with a mostly hostile audience, who found white men playing the blues less than "authentic." But there were two influential watchers that night—Jackson Browne and David Bowie. The blown-away Bowie invited Vaughan to join his Serious Moonlight Tour, a deal that fell apart. Vaughan did land up jamming with Browne that night at the after party, and Browne even offered Vaughan and Double Trouble free use of his Los Angeles studio. These sessions led to the release of *Texas Flood*, Vaughan and Double Trouble's debut effort. The album received critical acclaim and has since achieved Multi-Platinum status.

Couldn't Stand the Weather followed in 1984, gaining Vaughan recognition as on the charts and bringing him awards. But by the time the third LP, *Soul to Soul*, saw daylight, Vaughan was sinking into alcohol and drug addiction. By 1986 he was touring but missed several performance to check into a London hospital. He got himself clean and by the time *Live Alive* dropped, he was making a fresh start. His next effort, *In Step*, shot to the top, with a No. 1 single, "Crossfire," leading the way.

In 1990 Vaughan worked with brother Jimmie on the album *Family Style*, recording bluesy rock with a Western tinge. By that summer he was back on tour for *In Step*, with bookings for August 25 and 26 at Alpine Valley Music Theatre in East Troy, Wisconsin. Along with Double Trouble, Eric Clapton, Buddy Guy, Robert Cray, and Jimmie Vaughan performed with Vaughan. On the 27th Vaughan, along with three members of Clapton's travel group, boarded a helicopter to fly to their next gig. Just after liftoff on that foggy morning, the helicopter crashed into a nearby hill. All onboard died on impact.

Not yet 36, Vaughan died at the height of his powers, but his music lives on to inspire new generations of guitarists.

Awards and Honors

1988 Grammy Award for Best Traditional Blues Album, for *Blues Explosion*, with Sugar Blue, John P. Hammond, J. B. Hutto & the New Hawks, Luther 'Guitar Junior' Johnson, Koko Taylor & the Blues Machine, and Double Trouble

1987 Grammy Award for Best Rock Instrumental Performance, for "Say What!," with Double Trouble

1987 Grammy Award for Best Rock Instrumental Performance for "Pipeline," with Dick Dale

1991 Grammy Award for Best Contemporary Blues Album, for *In Step*, with Double Trouble

1991 Grammy Award for Best Contemporary Blues Album, for *Family Style*, with Jimmie Vaughan

1991 Grammy Award for Best Rock Instrumental Performance for "D/FW," with Jimmie Vaughan

1993 Grammy Awards for Best Contemporary Blues Album, for *The Sky Is Crying*, with Double Trouble

1993 Grammy Award for Best Rock Instrumental Performance, for his cover of Hendrix's "Little Wing," with Double Trouble

2003 Ranked No. 7 on *Rolling Stone*'s list of the 100 Greatest Guitarists of All Time

A Fender replica of Stevie Ray Vaughan's Number One guitar, complete with "SRV' stickers

essential albums

WITH DOUBLE TROUBLE
1983 *Texas Flood*
1984 *Couldn't Stand the Weather*
1985 *Soul to Soul*
1989 *In Step*

LIVE
1986 *Live Alive*
1992 *In the Beginning*
1997 *Live at Carnegie Hall*
2001 *Live at Montreux 1982 and 1985*

WITH JIMMIE VAUGHAN
1990 *Family Style*

NUMBER ONE AND MORE

Vaughan had an impressive array of axes, but none is so famous as his Number One. Vaughan used this Fender Stratocaster, which he bought in an Austin music shop in 1973, throughout his career, making it his main performing instrument. And Number One, also known as "His First Wife," makes appearances on all of his studio albums. The ax itself has become one of the most recognizable in the business—Vaughan's early attempts at customizing it were so poor that he resorted to covering up holes with stickers, including large, prismatic stickers that spelled out his initials. Before his death, Vaughan worked with Fender to produce the Stevie Ray Vaughan Signature model Stratocaster, first introduced in 1992. In 2004 Fender also came out with a limited-edition Tribute series that faithfully reproduced the battered Number One.

Other axes also made the grade: Yellow is a yellow 1959 Stratocaster now on display in the Las Vegas Hard Rock Cafe. Red is a 1962 Strat Vaughan picked up in Dallas. Main, a custom Strat that Billy Gibbons gave Vaughan, jumped to fame as the guitar Vaughan turned to film the video for "Couldn't Stand the Weather." In 1983 Vaughan picked up another custom Strat, Charley, made by Charley Wirz, a friend and owner of Charley's Guitar Shop in Dallas. During the final years of his life, Vaughan often used a butterscotch-colored 1961 Strat called Scotch.

In 2007 Fender introduced another Vaughan tribute guitar, styled after Lenny, a 1965 Stratocaster. In 2004 the original Lenny sold at auction for $623,500.

JOHNNY WINTER

essential albums

SOLO

1968	*The Progressive Blues Experiment*
1969	*Second Winter*
1969	*Johnny Winter*
1970	*Early Times*
1970	*Johnny Winter And*
1971	*Live Johnny Winter And*
1973	*Still Alive and Well*
1974	*John Dawson Winter III*
1974	*Saints and Sinners*
1976	*Captured Live*
1977	*Nothin' but the Blues*
1978	*White, Hot and Blue*
1980	*Raisin' Cain*
1981	*Ready for Winter*
1984	*Guitar Slinger*
1985	*Serious Business*
1986	*3rd Degree*
1988	*The Winter of '88*
1990	*The Winter Scene*
1991	*Let Me In*
1992	*Hey, Where's Your Brother*

Johnny Winter (born February 23, 1944, in Beaumont, Texas) is an esteemed blues guitarist frequently associated with his younger brother, Edgar.

Winter was born into a musically enthusiastic family—he tried out several instruments as a child before settling on the guitar on the suggestion of his father. A rabid consumer of blues on the radio, Winter cultivated an extensive record collection and began imitating the songs he heard, adding his own color after he had mastered a particular passage or solo.

With Edgar (like Johnny, born with albinism), Johnny Winter performed in a number of amateur bands as a teenager, laying down a series of early recordings that would gain attention only after he shot to fame. After a short stint in Chicago, Winter returned home to Texas, where he became a sort of regional celebrity. Intrigued by the blues scene in Great Britain, Winter made a trip there but failed to gain any traction.

On his return to the United States in 1968, however, Winter realized that he had been the subject of an effusive *Rolling Stone* profile. By December of that year after playing a "Super Session" jam concert with Al Kooper and Mike Bloomfield at the Fillmore East, Columbia Records immediately offered him a recording contract, paired with an unheard-of advance for the time. After a few successful albums, Winter began to consider himself less a singer and more a guitarist. Facing pressure to embrace a more rock-oriented sound, Winter withdrew from the public eye and struggled briefly with drugs.

Winter staged a resurgence in the 1970s, releasing several albums, including a release with his brother, 1976's *Johnny and Edgar Winter: Together*. In 1977 Winter was instrumental in convincing his record label to sign Muddy Waters—a decision that resulted in a heralded four-album collaboration between the two artists.

Winter continued to record in the 1980s, returning to the older blues and R&B songs that he has always considered his bread and butter. His critically acclaimed recent material is viewed as a "coming home," with streamlined production and Winter's guitar where it belongs: front and center.

1992	Scorchin' Blues
1998	Live in New York City '97
2004	I'm a Bluesman

WITH EDGAR WINTER
| 1976 | Together Live |

WITH MUDDY WATERS
1977	Hard Again
1978	I'm Ready
1979	Muddy "Mississippi" Waters

"I think the blues will always be around. People need it."

—JOHNNY WINTER

Awards and Honors

| 1988 | Inducted into the Blues Foundation Hall of Fame |
| 2003 | Ranked No. 74 on *Rolling Stone*'s list of the 100 Greatest Guitarists of All Time |

Winter performs in the Blues Tent at Memphis's Beale Street Music Festival, 2006

WINTER & THE MASTERS

Winter has always made a point of rubbing shoulders with the legends—and then turning them into friends. A 17-year-old Winter went to see B.B. King perform in Texas and breezily demanded a shot at the mike. Already conspicuous in the predominantly black setting, Winter's request was denied several times until he got the audience on his side. After providing his union credentials, King gave Winter his guitar. The resulting performance earned a standing ovation.

A coda to this classic story played out almost two decades later, when Winter assisted Muddy Waters with his Grammy-winning comeback album, *Hard Again*. The album's success launched a string of successful collaborations into the early 1980s, with Winter as producer and contributor—and steward of Waters's reinvigorated career. Waters has voiced his respect for Winters, crediting him with the best financial returns of his career and praising his skill at preserving and expanding Waters's classic sound for a new generation of fans.

Winter briefly billed his band as Johnny Winter And, shown here in the early 1970s.
From left: Rick Derringer, Bobby Caldwell, Johnny Winter, and Randy Jo Hobbs

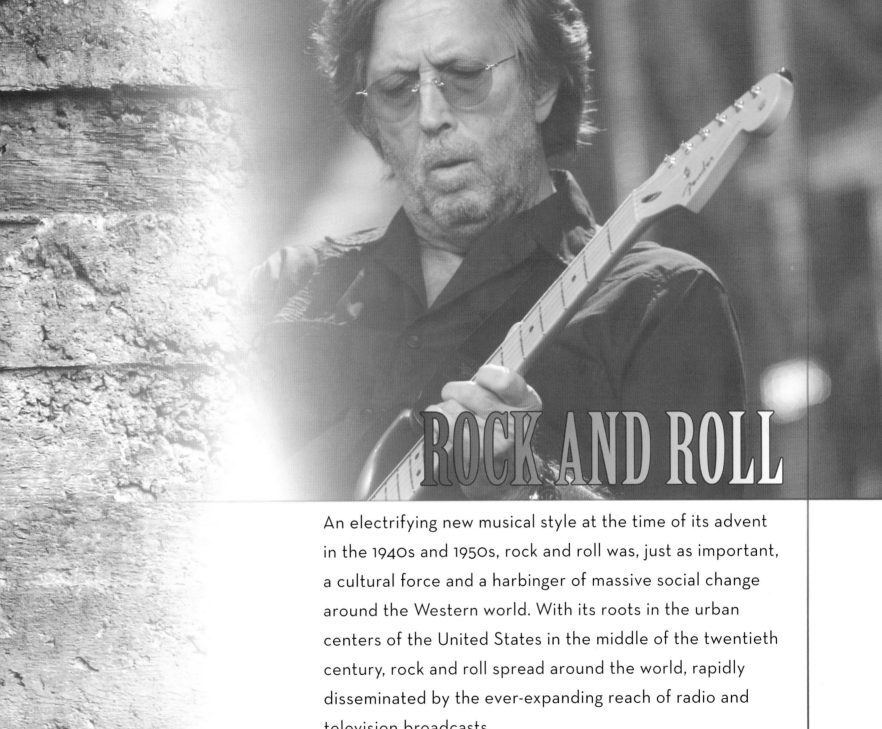

ROCK AND ROLL

An electrifying new musical style at the time of its advent in the 1940s and 1950s, rock and roll was, just as important, a cultural force and a harbinger of massive social change around the Western world. With its roots in the urban centers of the United States in the middle of the twentieth century, rock and roll spread around the world, rapidly disseminated by the ever-expanding reach of radio and television broadcasts.

Credited with flouting the rules, engaging the ears, brain, and body, and affecting widespread shifts in thought and values, especially among the young, rock has since come to encompass everything electrifying, fun, and even dangerous about popular music.

DUANE ALLMAN

"I'm hitting a lick for peace. And every time I'm in Georgia, I eat a peach for peace. But you can't help the revolution, because there's just evolution. I understand the need for a lot of changes in this country, but I believe that as soon as everybody can see just a little better, and get a little hipper to what's going on, they're going to change it."

—DUANE ALLMAN, WHEN ASKED, "HOW ARE YOU HELPING THE REVOLUTION?"

essential albums

WITH THE ALLMAN JOYS
1973   *Early Allman*

WITH THE HOUR GLASS
1967   *The Hour Glass*
1968   *Power of Love*

WITH THE ALLMAN BROTHERS BAND
1969   *The Allman Brothers Band*
1970   *Idlewild South*
1971   *At Fillmore East*
1972   *Eat A Peach*

Duane Allman (born November 20, 1946, in Nashville, Tennessee; died October 29, 1971, in Macon, Georgia) was an esteemed guitarist, famous for his work with the Allman Brothers Band and his numerous, generous appearances as a session musician on other albums, including his acclaimed slide work on Eric Clapton's classic "Layla."

Now revered as an American guitar god (ranking No. 2 on *Rolling Stone*'s list), Allman developed in his early teens, spurred on by his younger brother Gregg's influence, as well as a seminal show by B.B. King the brothers witnessed in 1959.

Allman dropped out of school in the early 1960s to devote himself full time to playing. With Gregg he put together a number of bands, which all fizzled out. The brothers' efforts finally paid off when they created the Hour Glass, their first group to gain label attention. After moving to Los Angeles the band put out two albums; Allman's masterful playing is evident even in these early tracks.

With any ax, Allman could turn out melodic solos, but a Taj Mahal record turned him onto slide guitar, the method with which he would emblazon himself into the rock pantheon.

ALLMAN BROTHERS BAND & LEGACY

After the brothers aborted the Hour Glass in 1968, Allman threw himself into performing as a session musician, contributing to a staggering number of recordings, including those of several R&B greats. Allman was legendary for surprising musicians in the studio, contributing a few licks or a solo, and continuing on his way. Even when he was paid for his work, Allman seldom signed a contract, leaving behind a legacy of impossible-to-trace contributions to an unknown number of albums.

Looking for something more, Allman concocted a lineup that included his brother and in 1969 formed the Allman Brothers Band in Florida. Later that year the band released its self-titled debut, following that up less than a year later with *Idlewild South*—the album that would bring chart success.

Allman's ascent to the top was quick. Fellow great Eric Clapton took an active interest in Allman and tried to poach him from the ABB; he was unsuccessful but persuaded Allman to contribute some of his best-known work to Clapton's *Layla and Other Assorted Love Songs*.

ABB's third album, *At Fillmore East*, came out in 1971. Allman only had a short time to bask in its warm reception—he died in a motorcycle accident in Macon, Georgia, in the fall of that year. The band released *Eat a Peach* after Allman's death; the album includes material started before his death.

Lynyrd Skynyrd's "Free Bird" is dedicated to—but not written about—Allman.

The original Allman Brothers Band, standing from left to right: Jai Johanny Johanson (drums, congas, timbales); Gregg Allman (organ, piano, vocals); Berry Oakley (bass guitar); and seated, Duane Allman (lead guitar, slide guitar); Dickey Betts (lead guitar, vocals); Butch Trucks (drums, tympani). A year after Duane's accident, bassist Oakley suffered a motorcycle crash three blocks from where Duane died. Oakley, too, died of his injuries.

Awards and Honors

1995	Inducted into the Rock and Roll Hall of Fame, with Allman Brothers Band
2003	Ranked No. 2 on *Rolling Stone*'s 100 Greatest Guitarists of All Time list

Duane Allman plays at one of the Fillmore East's last shows in 971. The Allman Brothers played this venue so many times that it earned the nickname "Bill Graham's House Band."

ALLMAN'S SINGULAR SOUND

Duane Allman's name is synonymous with Southern rock, the genre and sound he largely conceived in his short career. Crucial to the sound is Allman's pioneering work as a slide guitarist. Allman was famous for picking up an empty glass pill bottle after an illness and using it to play slide for the first time, turning even Eric Clapton onto the possibilities. Allman continued using the glass bottle, even for his most famous slide work on "Layla."

Allman brought several other idiosyncrasies to his playing, including a penchant for unusual open tunings. He also had a habit of playing a right-handed guitar, even though he was a southpaw, which gave his fretting hand a greater degree of control when bending notes or adding vibrato, whereas his weaker picking hand lent him a very light touch.

For most of his career Allman handled Gibson guitars, including a 1959 Cherryburst Les Paul and a 1968 Cherry SG.

TREY ANASTASIO

Awards and Honors

2003 Ranked No. 73 on the *Rolling Stone*'s list of the 100 Greatest Guitarists of All Time

"There's a real feeling between us. I don't feel like I'm performing at the audience. It's like a party. Or it's like some night in high school, where you blew off some plans and, instead, you and your friends stayed out all night. You went to the lake and watched the sun rise. It was a spontaneous bonding experience that you remember all your life. That's how I feel at a show when everything goes right. It's much more powerful than a planned-out show. When people have that experience, they're hooked."

—TREY ANASTASIO

Trey Anastasio (born September 30, 1964, in Fort Worth, Texas) is an American guitarist primarily associated with the band Phish.

A prolific guitarist, composer and singer, Anastasio has contributed to several solo and collaborative projects with dozens of musicians since Phish's breakup in 1994. Anastasio started honing his music skills as a child, playing drums and writing songs with his mother. At prep school as a teenager, Anastasio began developing as a songwriter, and some of his early compositions became a regular part of the Phish catalog. Post-Phish, Anastasio has been seemingly omnipresent. His

résumé consists of dozens of largely instrumental solo albums and guest appearances with a diverse range of artists.

His friendship and collaboration with Paul Languedoc, Phish's sound technician for nearly twenty years, has yielded a stunning collection of five custom electric guitars, designed and built by Languedoc. Known for a largely traditional style that eschews gimmicks and techniques like tapping and slid-ing, Anastasio has shared the stage with such heavyweights as Stewart Copeland, Dave Matthews, and Phil Lesh of the Grateful Dead—a band to which Phish is unavoidably com-pared for cultural, if not musical, reasons.

ANASTASIO'S STYLE

Anastasio's playing is based in technical precision and prowess, as well as improvisation. His understanding of music theory and his background as composer allows him to utilize a stunning range of demanding techniques not frequently deployed in popular music, including barre chords and pentatonic scales. Although he eschews theatricality for its own sake, Anastasio is known to rely heavily on such setup modifications as delay effects pedals and delay loops, often activating them on the fly and "quoting" his own guitar playing within lengthy, journeylike solos.

essential albums

WITH PHISH

1986	*Phish*
1987	*The Man Who Stepped into Yesterday*
1989	*Junta*
1990	*Lawn Boy*
1992	*A Picture of Nectar*
1993	*Rift*
1994	*Hoist*
1996	*Billy Breathes*
1998	*The Story of the Ghost*
2000	*Farmhouse*
2000	*The Siket Disc*
2002	*Round Room*
2004	*Undermind*
2009	*Joy*
2009	*Party Time*

SOLO

1998	*One Man's Trash*
2002	*Trey Anastasio*
2004	*Seis De Mayo*
2005	*Shine*
2006	*Bar 17*
2007	*The Horseshoe Curve*
2009	*Time Turns Elastic*

Phish bandmates, from left: keyboardist Page McConnell, guitarist Trey Anastasio, bassist Mike Gordon and drummer Jon Fishman, perform on stage at the Saratoga Performing Arts Center in New York, shortly before the band's 2004 breakup

PHISH

Phish started off as a four-man University of Vermont college band. After Anastasio was expelled from the school for an especially outlandish prank, he transferred to Goddard College, and the band began recording in earnest.

A series of experimental tapes led to the band's release of *Junta* in 1989, which garnered little attention. Led by Anastasio, Phish began fleshing out its legendary live concert tradition, heavily involving its growing audience. By 1991 the band had a record deal and released *A Picture of Nectar*.

During the mid-1990s the band's profile expanded exponentially, the result of heavy worldwide touring with several well-known acts such as Pearl Jam. Phish's unparalleled antics—including the occasional playing of other bands' material exclusively and an elaborate, extended game of chess between the band and the audience—inspired many curious fans to finally come onboard.

Phish spent the late 1990s as a perpetual fixture on the New England music festival scene, leading up to a New Year's Eve performance to mark the end of the millennium. That following autumn, the band announced a hiatus.

The group resumed touring in 2002, but the return to form was short-lived—Phish announced its breakup in 2004.

A 2009 reunion was paired with a string of high-profile events and the release of a new studio album in September of that year.

BILLY JOE ARMSTRONG

"I get on the bus, and my wife says, 'Did that bitch just tell you to fuck off? I'm gonna kick her ass right now.' I'm holding her back, while my child is naked, jumping on the couch: 'Hi, Daddy!' That was my whole life right there—screaming kids, punks telling me to fuck off, my wife getting pissed, my naked son waiting to get into his pajamas."

—BILLY JOE ARMSTRONG

essential albums

WITH GREEN DAY

1991	*1,039/Smoothed Out Slappy Hours*
1992	*Kerplunk!*
1994	*Dookie*
1995	*Insomniac*
1997	*Nimrod*
1999	*Warning*
2001	*International Superhits!*
2002	*Shenanigans*
2004	*American Idiot*
2005	*Bullet in a Bible*
2009	*21st Century Breakdown*

WITH PINHEAD GUNPOWDER

1995	*Jump Salty*
1995	*Carry the Banner*
1997	*Goodbye Ellston Avenue*
1999	*Shoot the Moon (EP)*
2003	*Compulsive Disclosure*
2008	*West Side Highway (EP)*

WITH THE NETWORK

2003	*Money Money 2020*

Billie Joe Armstrong (born February 17, 1972, in Oakland, California) is the front man for American rock group Green Day, among his several projects.

The youngest of six children, Armstrong was exposed to music by his father, an amateur jazz musician. After the death of his father in 1982, Armstrong began writing songs and indulging an interest in metal and punk. He formed a punk-inspired band called Sweet Children at the age of 15, securing gigs at the restaurant where his mother worked as a waitress.

Green Day was born in 1989 as a three-piece band with Armstrong's childhood friends. After a series of EPs and lineup changes, Green Day released its breakthrough album *Dookie* in 1994, which sold more than 15 million copies.

In addition to his work with the band Pinhead Gunpowder, a side project formed in 1990, Armstrong is an in-demand songwriter, backup vocalist, and producer for several other bands. Along with his wife, Adrienne, Armstrong started Adeline Records in 1997, the label which represents the Network, a band in which Armstrong is said to be the lead singer, but he has publicly denied the connection.

BILLIE JOE'S GUITARS

Armstrong's most famous guitar, known as Blue, was a gift from his longtime guitar teacher; the ax originally belonged to Santana's David Margen. Armstrong prizes this guitar for its rich sound and its flexibility, attributes that were missing from his first instrument, a red acoustic Hohner that his father gave him as a gift. Blue has made several appearances in Green Day's music videos.

Recently, though, Armstrong has grown infatuated with an ax he calls Floyd, the guitar he acquired in 2000. This 1956 Gibson Les Paul Junior went on to inspire Armstrong's custom line of Gibson Les Pauls.

Armstrong owes an obvious stylistic debt to the pantheon of punk rockers like the Clash, the Ramones, and the Sex Pistols. Musically, however, he cites his biggest influences as alternative bands Hüsker Dü and the Replacements, borrowing such elements as chord changes and incorporating them into his snappy, manic style.

Awards and Honors

1995	Grammy Award for Best Alternative Music Album, *Dookie*, with Green Day
2005	Grammy Award for Best Rock Album, *American Idiot*, with Green Day
2006	Grammy Award for Record of the Year, "Boulevard of Broken Dreams," with Green Day
2010	Grammy Award for Best Rock Album, for *21st Century Breakdown*, with Green Day

Armstrong, center, with Green Day drummer Tre Cool, left, and bassist Mike Dirnt, right, at Wembley Arena, 2009

GREEN DAY

Since *Dookie*, Green Day has transitioned into a decidedly American Grammy-winning powerhouse, selling some 22 million records in the United States alone. The band, whose name is a not-so-subtle adolescent nod to marijuana, remains at the top of its game with no sign of slowing down.

Not without controversy, the band has elicited raised eyebrows from an older generation of legends such as John Lydon of the Sex Pistols, who has suggested that the band trades on a legacy of punk music it hasn't earned. Peers have weighed in, too—among the band's detractors are Brendon Flowers from the Killers and Noel Gallagher of Oasis.

Green Day pulled off a reinvention of sorts in 2004 with *American Idiot*, coming off a period of less-than-ecstatic album reviews and sales. This album, an ambitious "punk rock opera," debuted at No. 1, enjoying marked success in Europe but sometimes rankling American musicians for its supposed capitalization on anti-American sentiments abroad.

Green Day released *21st Century Breakdown* in 2009. Another landmark album, it represents the band's biggest victory on the charts yet. In early 2010 the band was on tour in support of the record. Green Day's success has translated into a specialized version of the popular Rock Band video game, which will feature the band member's likenesses and playable versions of their best-known songs.

Billy Joe Armstrong fronting Green Day, live in Hamburg, Germany, 2005

CHUCK BERRY

"It amazes me when I hear people say, 'I want to go out and find out who I am.' I always knew who I was. I was going to be famous if it killed me."

—CHUCK BERRY, 2001

Charles Edward Anderson Berry—better known as Chuck Berry (born October 18, 1926, in St. Louis, Missouri) is an iconic figure at the junction of blues and early American rock and roll. His influence, whether or not explicitly acknowledged by other artists, is evident through several generations of guitarists and musicians and continues to shape modern music. Well known for his prolific output as well as his numerous legal skirmishes and indiscretions, Berry is a cornerstone of American musical history.

After marrying his wife, Toddy, in 1948 and holding several odd jobs as a Midwestern 20-something, Berry played guitar gigs to make ends meet. It was with his early act, the Johnnie Johnson Trio, that Berry first began to bridge the sounds of black and white music, bending his traditional blues sound to suit the popular white music of the day.

In 1955 Berry met Muddy Waters, long one of his idols. Waters put the young Berry in touch with Chess Records (also the one-time home of Buddy Guy), which signed him immediately upon hearing a country and western cover that he'd recorded called "Ida Red." Berry retooled the song with a full band (which included Johnnie Johnson), renamed it "Maybellene," and watched in awe as it shot to the top of the R&B charts, selling more than a million copies.

Berry's star continued to ascend through the 1950s. He became associated with other popular acts of the time, including the Everly Brothers and Buddy Holly, even starring in a few movies before the decade was out, appearing as himself and playing some of his hits.

By the 1970s Berry had achieved bona-fide legend status, continuing to record and travel the country performing. His preference for recruiting local bands to back him during performances lent his live performances an unpredictable—and sometimes erratic—quality.

Berry resides in St. Louis to this day and regularly performs at local restaurants and bars.

essential albums

STUDIO

1957	After School Session
1958	One Dozen Berrys
1959	Chuck Berry Is on Top
1960	Rockin' at the Hops
1962	Chuck Berry Twist
1963	More Chuck Berry
1964	St. Louis to Liverpool
1965	Chuck Berry in London
1965	Fresh Berry's
1967	Chuck Berry in Memphis
1968	From St. Louie to Frisco
1969	Concerto in B. Goode
1970	Back Home
1971	San Francisco Dues
1972	The London Chuck Berry Sessions
1973	Bio

1973	Sweet Little Rock and Roller
1974	Wild Berrys
1974	Flashback
1975	Chuck Berry
1979	Rock It
1981	Alive and Rockin'
1982	Retro Rock
1982	Chuck Berry

LIVE

1963	Chuck Berry on Stage
1967	Live at the Fillmore Auditorium
1972	The London Chuck Berry Sessions
1978	Chuck Berry Live in Concert
1981	Chuck Berry Live
1982	Toronto Rock 'n' Roll Revival 1969 Vols. I and II
1987	Hail! Hail! Rock 'n' Roll

Chuck Berry, still vigorous at 80 years old, performs at his concert at the Northfork Theatre in Westbury, New York, in 2007

SKIRMISHES WITH THE LAW

Berry butted heads with law enforcement early on as a middle-class high school student in St. Louis, Missouri. After a broken-down car stranded him far from home, Berry carjacked another auto and was quickly pulled over by police. He spent three years in a reformatory and was released on his 21st birthday in 1947.

More than a decade later, Berry was convicted under the Mann Act of hiring a young Native American prostitute to work at his music club in St. Louis. The press sensationally covered the ensuing trial because of its sexual and racial undertones. After an appeal, Berry was fined and imprisoned for five years.

In the late 1970s, Berry aroused the suspicion of the Internal Revenue Service, which had long pegged Berry as an income tax evader. Upon investigating payments he accepted for touring—usually in cash—the IRS found enough evidence to send Berry to prison for the third time. He served four months and promised to perform one thousand hours of benefit concerts.

"Rock's so good to me. Rock is my child and my grandfather."

—CHUCK BERRY

Above: Berry, second from right, with Taylor Hackford, far right, director of *Chuck Berry: Hail! Hail! Rock 'n' Roll*, with other R&B greats Bo Diddley and Little Richard

Right: Berry onstage in the 1998 Legends of Rock 'n' Roll concert at Wembley Arena

Berry in 2007

"JOHNNY B. GOODE"

What's the most famous guitar riff in the history of rock and roll? Easy—the throbbing, hard-driving opening to Berry's "Johnny B. Goode." Written in 1955 and released a couple of years later, this song tells of a poor country boy who makes it big through hard work and guitar talent—a bit of Berry autobiography. Berry took the opening, almost note-for-note, from Carl Hogan's version of the song "Ain't That Just Like a Woman" by Louis Jordan. "Johnny B. Goode" reached No. 8 on the Billboard charts in 1958, and nearly thirty years later had a prominent role in the hit move *Back to the Future*, in which Michael J. Fox's character famously plays the song at high school dance.

In 2005 the song ranked No. 42 on *Q* magazine's list of the 100 Greatest Guitar Tracks, and four years later *Rolling Stone* crowned it the No. 1 song on its 100 Greatest Guitar Songs of All Time. It also placed high—No. 7—on *Rolling Stone*'s 500 Greatest Songs of All Time list. Other Berry hits made the list: "Maybellene" at No. 18, "Roll Over Beethoven" at No. 97, "Rock and Roll Music" at No. 128, "Sweet Little Sixteen" at No. 272, and "Brown Eyed Handsome Man" at No. 374.

Awards and Honors

1985	Inducted into the Rock and Roll Hall of Fame
1985	Grammy Award for Lifetime Achievement
2002	ICON Award, BMI
2003	Ranked No. 6 on *Rolling Stone*'s list of the 100 Greatest Guitarists of All Time
2004	Ranked No. 5 on *Rolling Stone*'s list of the Immortals: the 100 Greatest Artists of All Time

Chuck Berry at the Long Beach Blues Festival, 1997

DICKEY BETTS

essential albums

WITH THE ALLMAN BROTHERS BAND

1969	*The Allman Brothers Band*
1970	*Idlewild South*
1971	*At Fillmore East*
1972	*Eat A Peach*
1973	*Brothers and Sisters*
1975	*Win, Lose or Draw*
1979	*Enlightened Rogues*
1980	*Reach for the Sky*
1981	*Brothers of the Road*
1990	*Seven Turns*
1991	*Shades of Two Worlds*
1994	*Where It All Begins*

SOLO

| 1974 | *Highway Call* |
| 1982 | *Night* |

WITH GREAT SOUTHERN

1977	*Dickey Betts & Great Southern*
1978	*Atlanta's Burning Down*
2002	*The Collectors, Number 1*
2006	*Official Bootleg*

WITH THE DICKEY BETTS BAND

| 1988 | *Pattern Disruptive* |
| 2001 | *Let's Get Together* |

Forrest Richard "Dickey" Betts (born December 12, 1943, in West Palm Beach, Florida) is a guitarist/singer/songwriter/composer and one of the founding members of the Southern rock group the Allman Brothers Band.

Betts played with several bands in the 1960s before hooking up with bassist Berry Oakley. One night at a club in 1969, Betts and Oakley jammed with two brothers, Duane and Gregg Allman—and the rest is history. The newly formed band did away with the typical lead/rhythm format, allowing both Duane and Dickey to weave intricate lead licks.

Betts composed several of the Allman Brothers Band's biggest hits, including "Revival," "In Memory of Elizabeth Reed," and "Blue Sky."

When Duane Allman and Berry Oakley were killed in motorcycle accidents in 1971 and 1972, the band staggered, but came back strong with Betts's biggest hit, "Ramblin' Man" in 1973. Betts also released his first solo effort, *Highway Call*, that same year. When the Allmans split up in 1976, Betts formed Dickey Betts and Great Southern. Its debut album featured the hit single "Bougainvillea," which Betts cowrote with actor Don Johnson.

The Allmans reunited briefly in 1978, long enough to produce the 1979 release, *Enlightened Rogues*, after which Betts put together the Dickey Betts Band.

In 1989, to mark their twentieth anniversary, the Allmans again went on the road, this time with Betts trading licks with Warren Haynes. Betts parted with the group for good in 2000—reportedly he was "suspended" for missing too many tour dates—and he took the Dickey Betts Band on the road. He renamed the group Great Southern in 2001 and later added his son, Duane, as lead guitarist. Although Betts has talked of retiring after more than four decades of performing, he continues to tour into 2010.

Awards and Honors

1995   Inducted into the Rock and Roll Hall of fame, with the Allman Brothers Band

1996   Grammy Award for Best Rock Performance, for "Jessica," with the Allman Brothers Band

2003   Ranked No. 58 on *Rolling Stone*'s list of the 100 Greatest Guitarists of All Time

The Allman Brothers Band line up for a group shot shortly after the death of Duane Allman. Front row from left: Berry Oakley, Butch Trucks, Gregg Allman, and Dickey Betts. In the back is Jai Johanny Johanson, far left, with an unknown man.

Dickey Betts and Goldie

"I'm not retiring from playing. I'm sure there will be some great special events that I'll be at in the future. But for now, I look forward to waking up tomorrow with nothing on my schedule."

—DICKEY BETTS, ON TURNING 66 IN 2009

THE DICKEY BETTS GIG BAG

With his distinctive voice and the soaring, lyrical blend of jazz, blues, country, and rock that informed his music, Betts's signature sound became synonymous with Southern rock. During his early days with the Allmans, he played a 1961 Gibson SG, which he gave to Duane to use as an all-slide guitar. Betts was also known for his Gibson Les Paul Goldtop, named Goldie, which he later painted red. He has occasionally played Fender Stratocasters and more recently has been using a red Telecaster with a pearl pickguard.

ERIC CLAPTON

Eric Clapton (born March 30, 1945, in Surrey, England), a three-time Rock and Roll Hall of Fame inductee, is revered as a groundbreaking blues guitarist, one of the world's best ever. Famous for his work with the Yardbirds, Blind Faith, and Cream, as well as his prolific solo career, Clapton was called an "immortal" artist by *Rolling Stone*.

Clapton got his first taste of guitar as a young teenager with a hard-to-manage Hoyer model. Infatuated early on by old blues recordings, Clapton taught himself how to play by imitating what he heard.

After brief stints in a couple of R&B bands, Clapton found his way into the Yardbirds, which found popularity with a sound based on that of greats like Buddy Guy, B.B. King, and Freddie King. No sooner did the single "For Your Love" become a hit, Clapton departed the band, replaced at different times by Jeff Beck and Jimmy Page.

In 1965 Clapton joined John Mayall & the Bluesbreakers for the second time that year, quickly gaining attention for his passionate playing. The next year Clapton formed Cream, a supergroup that also included bassist Jack Bruce and drummer Ginger Baker.

Cream became a sensation in England and the United States as well, where Clapton came to tour in 1967. The band's star burned out quickly, though—drugs and negative press ravaged the group, which recorded its last album and then dissolved in 1968.

A low-profile period followed for Clapton before he formed Derek and the Dominos in 1970. The album *Layla and Other Assorted Love Songs*, released that year, is considered Clapton's masterpiece, though it was not immediately received with praise. The process of its recording—featuring Duane Allman—is a cornerstone of rock legend.

Amid a storm of shocking deaths (Jimi Hendrix in 1970 and Allman in 1971) and a plague of drug abuse, the group soon fell apart. Clapton turned to heroin and alcohol in the 1970s; it wasn't until the early 1980s that he entered rehab.

> "I mean, the sound of an amplified guitar in a room full of people was so hypnotic and addictive to me."
>
> —ERIC CLAPTON, 2007

essential albums

Tina Turner, left, and Eric Clapton, right, team up at Wembley Arena, 1987.

WITH THE YARDBIRDS

1963	*London 1963: The First Recordings!*
1964	*Five Live Yardbirds*
1965	*For Your Love*
1965	*Having a Rave Up*
1966	*Sonny Boy Williamson and The Yardbirds (live)*
1971	*The Yardbirds Featuring Performances by: Jeff Beck, Eric Clapton, and Jimmy Page*

WITH JOHN MAYALL & THE BLUESBREAKERS

1966	*Blues Breakers with Eric Clapton*

WITH CREAM

1966	*Fresh Cream*
1967	*Disraeli Gears*
1968	*Wheels of Fire*
1969	*Goodbye*
1969	*Best of Cream*
1970	*Live Cream*
1972	*Live Cream Volume II*
1972	*Heavy Cream*
1983	*Strange Brew*

WITH BLIND FAITH

1969	*Blind Faith*

WITH DEREK AND THE DOMINOS

1970	*Layla and Other Assorted Love Songs*
1973	*In Concert*
1994	*Live at the Fillmore*

SOLO STUDIO

1970	*Eric Clapton*
1974	*461 Ocean Boulevard*
1975	*There's One in Every Crowd*
1976	*No Reason to Cry*
1977	*Slowhand*
1978	*Backless*
1981	*Another Ticket*
1983	*Money and Cigarettes*
1985	*Behind the Sun*
1986	*August*
1989	*Journeyman*
1994	*From the Cradle*
1998	*Pilgrim*
2000	*Riding with the King* (with B.B. King)
2001	*Reptile*
2004	*Me and Mr. Johnson*
2004	*Sessions for Robert J*
2005	*Back Home*
2006	*The Road to Escondido* (with J. J. Cale)

SOLO LIVE

1973	*Eric Clapton's Rainbow Concert*
1975	*E.C. Was Here*
1980	*Just One Night*
1983	*Time Pieces Volume II: Live In the Seventies*
1991	*24 Nights*
1992	*Unplugged*
1996	*Crossroads 2: Live in the Seventies*
2002	*One More Car, One More Rider*
2009	*Live from Madison Square Garden with Steve Winwood*

> "From the beginning, I knew intuitively that if nothing else, music was safe, and that nobody could tell me anything about it. Music didn't need a middleman, whereas all the other things in school needed some kind of explanation."
>
> —ERIC CLAPTON, 2007

Clapton, left, with former Beatles Ringo Starr, center, and George Harrison, right

CLAPTON'S SOUND, HIS LEGACY, HIS INFLUENCES

Clapton occupies a legendary crossroads between several generations of guitar players across a spectrum of styles and influences. Clapton has often spoken of his admiration for the legendary Robert Johnson, in his eyes, "the most important blues musician who ever lived." His 2004 album and companion DVD *Sessions for Robert Johnson* contain covers of many of Johnson's songs.

"Clapton is God" is indeed a rallying cry among the virtuoso's fans—casual and professional alike. This graffiti epitaph was photographed in a London subway station in 1967; since then, Clapton has been humbly validating its prescience. Other greats on record as looking up to Clapton include friend and collaborators Duane Allman, Eddie Van Halen, Alex Lifeson, John Mayer, and Stevie Ray Vaughan. Not afraid to acknowledge his own debts, Clapton holds Buddy Guy, Albert King, B.B. King, Freddie King, and Hubert Sumlin as crucial influences to his development as a musician.

Clapton is famous for the "woman tone" that he honed in his Cream days. It's a heavy, distorted sound, created with his Gibson SG and a counterintuitive combination of controls and amplification. Would-be imitators generally find Clapton's signature sound impossible to replicate.

A number of Clapton's axes have become famous and a select few have gone on to sell for nearly $1 million at auction.

John Mayer, left, with Eric Clapton, right, on *Good Morning America* in New York, 2007. Mayer, like many current guitarists, states that he admires Clapton.

Awards and Honors

1992	Inducted into the Rock and Roll Hall of Fame, with the Yardbirds
1993	Inducted into the Rock and Roll Hall of Fame, with Cream
1993	Grammy Award for Song of the Year, Record of the Year, and Male Pop Vocal Performance, for "Tears In Heaven"
1993	Grammy Award for Album of the Year and Best Rock Vocal Performance, for *Unplugged*
1993	Grammy Award for Best Rock Song, for "Layla"
1994	Appointed Officer of the Order of the British Empire (OBE)
2000	Inducted into the Rock and Roll Hall of Fame
2004	Appointed Commander of the British Empire (CBE)
2004	Inducted into the Rock and Roll Hall of Fame
2004	Ranked No. 4 on *Rolling Stone*'s list of the 100 Greatest Guitarists of All Time
2006	Grammy Award for Lifetime Achievement

Clapton with an award from *Melody Maker* magazine, whose readers named him Best International Musician in 1969. His 2000 induction into the Rock and Roll Hall of Fame as a solo artist made him the first musician inducted three times.

CLAPTON POST-REHAB

Against doctor's orders, Clapton threw himself back into his work after leaving rehab in the early 1980s, releasing a number of albums and collaborating as musician and producer with an extensive list of artists. *August*, Clapton's 1986 collaboration with Phil Collins, brought him a new level of popular success and led to a two-year tour with Collins.

Clapton saw more tragedy in the 1990s. Within one year, both friend and fellow guitarist Stevie Ray Vaughan and Clapton's young son, Conor, died. A grieving Clapton wrote "Tears In Heaven" in 1991. The song appeared on his album *Unplugged*, which captured six Grammy awards.

Married most recently in 2002, Clapton has spent the last decade putting on a large number of benefit, relief, and tribute concerts, performing and recording new work as well. Clapton's future plans include an extensive world tour through the first half of 2010; former Blind Faith bandmate Steve Winwood will join him for the European leg.

Clapton in concert at the Royal Albert Hall in London

DICK DALE

"I cannot retire, because there are too many people depending on me. . . . I'd love to just stop, but I can't, because too many wrong things will happen. So I will keep on playing. When I die, it's not going to be in a rocking chair with a can of beer in my hand, it'll be on stage in one big explosion of body parts."

—DICK DALE, 2004

essential albums

1962	*Surfers' Choice*
1963	*King of the Surf Guitar*
1963	*Checkered Flag*
1964	*Mr. Eliminator*
1964	*Summer Surf*
1965	*Rock Out with Dick Dale and His Del-Tones: Live at Ciro's*
1983	*The Tiger's Loose*
1993	*Tribal Thunder*
1994	*Unknown Territory*
1996	*Calling Up Spirits*
2001	*Spacial Disorientation*

Born Richard Anthony Monsour, Dick Dale (born May 4, 1937, in Boston, Massachusetts) is primarily responsible for the "surf rock" sound that he brought to prominence in the late 1950s and early 1960s.

Born on the East Coast, Dale's parents—a Lebanese father and a Polish mother—relocated the family to Orange County, California, in 1954. There Dale learned to surf and practiced several instruments, including the ukulele and the guitar. Inspired by the sensation and rhythm of surfing, Dale experimented with a reverb-heavy guitar sound that would come to define the surf rock period in the United States.

Dale's early playing was notable for adhering to Middle Eastern–inspired sounds and scales. Dale, a southpaw, also pioneered a reverse picking style, effectively handling a right-handed guitar backwards, reaching his fingers over, instead of under, the fretboard. Dale was so committed to this technique in his early days that he continued to use it even when afforded the use of a proper left-handed ax.

Dale formed the Del-Tones in the early 1960s, and the band soon recorded a series of hit songs, including "Let's Go Trippin'," a surf rock milestone, and "Miserlou," a track that continues to feature in current popular culture.

After a dormant period, brought on by changing musical tastes in the United States and a bout with cancer, Dale returned to recording in the 1980s, releasing several albums since. In his 70s and a committed vegetarian and martial artist, Dale continues to tour.

DALE'S RIG

Aiming for an overwhelming, reckless sound, Dale's legendry volume and energy initially proved too much for the equipment of the day. Dale worked directly with Leo Fender to develop an amp and speaker setup that could withstand the output Dale desired without—literally—catching on fire. Fender eventually recruited the help of James B. Lansing—the namesake behind the JBL speaker company—to produce a fifteen-inch speaker installed within a rubberized enclosure. Fender installed two of these new speakers side by side, necessitating the production of a more powerful transformer, too, which Fender oversaw. Dale could finally shred as loud and long as he wanted, with no risk of obliterating his equipment.

Crucial to Dale's sound is the fact that he normally plays a right-handed guitar upside down and backwards; this configuration allows for unorthodox stringing, especially when considered with Dale's preference for heavier-than-normal gauge strings.

Awards and Honors

2003 Ranked No. 31 on *Rolling Stone*'s 100 Greatest Guitarists of All Time list

Dick Dale plugs his ax into an amp. Dale's need for volume resulted in a new amp that could hold up to his shredding without blowing out or catching on fire.

DALE IN POPULAR CULTURE

Several of Dale's recordings, especially 1962's "Miserlou," have resurfaced and regained popularity in recent years. Based on a popular Greek folk song that has equivalents in several traditions and cultures, Dale's jangly, surf-inspired version appeared in the sound track to Quentin Tarantino's 1994 film *Pulp Fiction*. More recently the track has been sampled by the Black Eyed Peas in their single "Pump It," and it features in the video game Guitar Hero II.

Dick Dale, still "King of the Surf Guitar"

DUANE EDDY

Duane Eddy (born April 26, 1968, in Corning, New York) is an esteemed guitarist celebrated for his pioneering contributions to the birth of rock and roll. Eddy's early career was marked by overnight fame and comparisons to Elvis Presley. His 1959 debut album, *Have "Twangy" Guitar Will Travel*, enjoyed a lengthy stay on the charts, reaching No. 5. The LP is also notable for being one of the first stereo rock and roll recordings. His 1960 single, "Because They're Young," was a huge hit, appearing in the film of the same name, which featured Eddy as well. He leveraged this role into an acting career that spanned the 1960s; in the 1970s, he focused on producing.

Eddy's later collaborations explored a range of styles, including country and dance. His 1987 self-titled release featured a diverse group of musicians and producers, including John Fogerty, George Harrison, and Paul McCartney.

Into the 1990s and beyond, filmmakers have chosen Eddy's music for several high-profile films, including *Broken Arrow*, *Forrest Gump*, and *Natural Born Killers*, allowing Eddy to enjoy the acclaim of the music establishment and a legion of new fans as well.

In 2004 Eddy won the coveted Legend Award from *Guitar Player* magazine. After the inimitable Les Paul, Eddy was only the second musician to receive this accolade.

essential albums

1958	*Have "Twangy" Guitar—Will Travel*
1958	*Especially for You*
1959	*The Twang's the Thang*
1960	*Songs of Our Heritage*
1967	*The Roaring Twangies*
1979	*Duane Eddy*
1986	*Como Nunca*
1995	*Duane Eddy: His Twangy Guitar & the Rebels*
1995	*Rebel Rouser*
1996	*Space*
1998	*Mucho Mejor*
2001	*Movin' n' Groovin'*
2001	*Universal Sounds*
2004	*Guitar Man*
2005	*Monsoon*
2005	*Duane Does Dylan*
2006	*The Biggest Twang of Them All*

DUANE EDDY, FILM HERO

Eddy is a veteran actor of film and television. In the 1950s it wasn't unusual for musicians to appear—often as themselves—in films that featured their music. His first bit part was in *Because They're Young* alongside Dick Clark, who played a sympathetic teacher. Eddy segued into more visible roles in television, taking on a memorable role in the long-running *Have Gun–Will Travel*, an extremely popular American Western series. Eddy's other films include *Kona Coast*, *The Savage Seven*, *A Thunder of Drums*, and *The Wild Westerners*.

"Well I was the first one to actually . . . do an instrumental and be an artist with a guitar—which is pretty revolutionary back then, in the birthing days of rock 'n' roll."

—DUANE EDDY, 2005

EDDY'S SIGNATURE SOUND

The title of Eddy's 1959 release was no marketing gimmick—Eddy is the originator of "twang" in rock and roll, a sound inspired by his own Western upbringing—his family moved to Arizona when he was 13. Eddy and producer Lee Hazlewood achieved the deep sound by running the lowest notes he could play through an echo chamber. The sound became legendary, and everyone from the Beatles to Bruce Springsteen has paid homage to it.

Unafraid to take risks, Eddy broke further ground in the early 1960s and pushed his work into the realms of film sound tracks. He also dedicated whole albums to exploring disparate sounds and themes—country and surf all appear in Eddy's repertoire. Eddy also put out an instrumental album-length tribute to Bob Dylan.

A guitar player since the age of 5, Eddy has relied on a Gretsch Chet Atkins 6120 for much of his career.

Awards and Honors

1986	Grammy Award for Best Rock Instrumental, for *Peter Gunn*

Duane Eddy attending the Nobody's Child fund-raiser for Romanian orphans, 1990

THE EDGE

David Evans (born August 8, 1961, in London, England), better known as "the Edge," is the lead guitarist for U2. Born to Welsh parents, Evans was raised with his brother, Dik, and sister, Gill, in Dublin. As teens Dik and Dave both responded to an advertisement posted on their school's bulletin board seeking musicians for a new band, and the group that formed—the Edge on guitar, Bono on vocals, Adam Clayton on bass, and Larry Mullen Jr. on drums—would eventually become one of the world's most popular and successful rock acts.

The Edge's renowned sound inspires awe among casual fans and master guitarists alike. A unique style of delay, achieved through the use of various amps and other electronics, resulting in the "shimmering" sound so prevalent on U2's most acclaimed albums, marks his clean, straightforward technique.

MUSIC RISING

Following the lead of his bandmates and other high-profile peers, the Edge has found a new role as philanthropist. Founded in 2005 by the Edge along with music producer Bob Ezrin and Gibson CEO Henry Juszkiewicz, Music Rising is a campaign dedicated to preserving the musical culture of the Central Gulf region by assisting musicians whose instruments and livelihoods were devastated by the hurricanes of summer 2005. The Edge has made several visits to New Orleans and the surrounding region to champion his new cause, including a few appearances to show off a custom-made, limited-edition Gibson guitar created just for the campaign.

essential albums

WITH U2

1980	*Boy*
1981	*October*
1983	*War*
1984	*The Unforgettable Fire*
1987	*The Joshua Tree*
1988	*Rattle and Hum*
1991	*Achtung Baby*
1993	*Zooropa*
1997	*Pop*
2000	*All That You Can't Leave Behind*
2004	*How to Dismantle an Atomic Bomb*
2009	*No Line on the Horizon*

LIVE

1983	*Under a Blood Red Sky*
2007	*Live from Paris*

Awards and Honors

2001	Grammy for Record of the Year, for "Walk On," with U2
2001	Grammy for Best Pop Performance by a Duo or Group with Vocal, for "Stuck in a Moment You Can't Get Out Of," with U2
2001	Grammy for Best Rock Performance by a Duo or Group with Vocal, for "Elevation," with U2
2001	Grammy for Best Rock Album, for *All That You Can't Leave Behind*, with U2
2003	Ranked No. 24 on *Rolling Stone*'s list of the 100 Greatest Guitarists of All Time
2004	Grammy for Best Rock Performance by a Duo or Group with Vocal, for "Vertigo," with U2
2004	Grammy for Best Rock Song, for "Vertigo," with U2
2004	Grammy for Best Short Form Music Video, for "Vertigo," with U2
2005	Inducted into the Rock and Roll Hall of Fame with U2
2005	Grammy for Album of the Year, for *How to Dismantle an Atomic Bomb*, with U2
2005	Grammy for Best Rock Performance by a Duo or Group with Vocal, for "Sometimes You Can't Make It on Your Own," with U2
2005	Grammy for Best Rock Album, for *How to Dismantle an Atomic Bomb*, with U2

The Edge performing during U2's 2005 tour. He was also inducted into the Rock and Roll Hall of Fame with his U2 bandmates in 2005.

Members of U2 in 1980, at the beginning of the band's pervasive influence on today's music. From left: the Edge, bassist Adam Clayton, singer Bono, and drummer Larry Mullen

THE EDGE'S AXES

Since the early 1980s, the Edge's signature ax has been a Gibson Explorer, actually a 1976 reissue of a much rarer model from the late 1950s. The Edge has openly praised its "distinctive" qualities, particularly its treble. With more than 200 guitars to his name, he is known for bringing somewhere around 45 with him while on tour, playing more than a dozen during a standard two-hour live concert.

"I'm interested in music. I'm a musician. I'm not a gunslinger. That's the difference between what I do and what a lot of guitar heroes do."

—THE EDGE, ON HIS LAID-BACK STYLE

PETER FRAMPTON

essential albums

WITH THE HERD
1967	*Nostalgia*
1972	*Paradise Lost*
2009	*Peter Frampton & The Herd*

WITH HUMBLE PIE
1969	*As Safe as Yesterday Is*
1969	*Town and Country*
1970	*Humble Pie*
1971	*Rock On*

SOLO
1972	*Wind of Change*
1973	*Frampton's Camel*
1974	*Frampton*
1974	*Somethin's Happening*
1976	*Frampton Comes Alive!*
1977	*I'm In You*
1989	*When All the Pieces Fit*
1992	*Shine On: A Collection*
1994	*Peter Frampton*
1995	*Frampton Comes Alive II*
1999	*Beat the Bootleggers: Coming Live*
1999	*Dreamtown*
2000	*Live in Detroit*
2001	*Anthology: The History of Peter Frampton*
2005	*Rock Masters*
2005	*Gold*
2006	*Fingerprints*
2007	*Breaking All The Rules*

Peter Frampton (born April 22, 1950, in Kent, England) is a British American guitarist who got his start with bands like the Herd and Humble Pie.

Classically trained on piano, Frampton first picked up a string instrument when he found his grandmother's ukulele. Alongside childhood friend David Bowie, Frampton partici-pated in a handful of school bands, but it was as a teenage singer that he first found the spotlight. Frampton helmed the Herd, a popular act that served as a precursor to the "boy bands" that emerged in the 1990s.

In 1969 Frampton joined Humble Pie and contributed to five of its albums. He left the band in 1971 to establish a solo career. Not successful initially, Frampton's fortunes suddenly—and dramatically—changed with the release of *Frampton Comes Alive!* in 1976, a live album that shot past a release from Fleetwood Mac to become the best-selling record of that year. To this day it remains one of the best-selling live albums of all time. Frampton gained a reputation for his huge, energetic arena appearances.

Frampton's career through the 1980s and 1990s cooled down, and though he has continued to record and tour, none of his albums have been as well received as his earlier work. An instrumental record released in 2007, *Fingerprints*, was awarded a Grammy, and plans are in the works for another release sometime in 2010.

HUMBLE PIE & THE TALK BOX

Considered one of the first supergroups of the 1970s, Humble Pie was the band guitarist Steve Marriott formed with Frampton, a friend from his youth, along with Greg Ridley and Jerry Shirley. During his time with the band Frampton got the chance to work with George Harrison on "All Things Must Pass" in 1970—where he discovered the talk box, an effect that would change the course of his sound.

The talk box utilizes a system of air tubes, amplifiers, and speakers to redirect an instrument's sound—usually a guitar—into the singer's mouth, allowing him to combine his own voice with the sound of the instrument, sending it back through a microphone for capture.

The talk box results in a unique distortion that seems to prove the existence of a "talking" instrument. Alvino Rey achieved a similar vocal effect for the first time with microphones in the late 1930s, but the technology wasn't refined until the 1940s. The Sonovox was a similar concept, using speakers to project sound away from the throat.

Both Doug Forbes and sound engineer Bob Heil deserve credit for the talk box as we know it today, but it's Heil's design that continues to be mass-produced by Dunlop. Frampton has jumped on the commercial bandwagon, too, with his own "Framptone" series of equipment that celebrates his affection for the device.

"To me [*Fingerprints*] was like a different career, the start of something new. And when I got the Grammy for it, to me, it's just like, 'Okay, we're on a different chapter now,' you know? It's another career. It's the credible musician Peter Frampton again. It just took thirty years to get rid of the stigma of *Frampton Comes Alive*. I'm not talking about the sales, I'm just talking about the reduced credibility as a guitar player."

—PETER FRAMPTON, 2008

Awards and Honors

2007 Grammy Award for Best Pop Instrumental, for *Fingerprints*

Peter Frampton, center, with his 1960s pop combo the Herd. The Herd also featured Andy Bown on keyboards, Gary Taylor on bass guitar, and Andrew Steele on drums.

JERRY GARCIA

Jerry Garcia (born August 1, 1942, in San Francisco, California; died August 9, 1995, in Forest Knolls, California) was the front man for the Grateful Dead, as well as an accomplished soloist and session musician. Born into a Spanish-American family that encouraged his creativity and musical talent from an early age, Garcia became an iconic musical figure and a symbol of the turbulent California culture of the 1960s and 1970s.

Garcia's late teens and early 20s were marked by tragedy. After surviving a disastrous car wreck that killed his 16-year-old friend, Garcia dedicated himself to becoming a skilled musician. Soon after meeting in 1962, Garcia and future Dead bassist Phil Lesh quickly achieved radio airplay with a few songs that they recorded themselves as an acoustic band. The Grateful Dead formed in 1965, beginning a nearly thirty-year period of recording and performing that would be famously dubbed the "Endless Tour."

As a guitarist, Garcia was influenced by his early exposure to blues, folk, and bluegrass. With the Dead, he developed a "psychedelic" improvisational style that was colored by his own experiments with such drugs as marijuana and LSD.

Garcia famously played a series of custom-built guitars, named Wolf, Tiger, Rosebud, and Lightning Bolt.

After years of declining health, largely due to his grueling professional schedule and a tumultuous relationship with chemical substances, Garcia died of a heart attack while checked into a rehab clinic in California.

"We were always motivated by the possibility that we could have fun, big fun. I was reacting in a way, to my bluegrass background, which was maybe a little overserious. I was up for the idea of breaking out."

—JERRY GARCIA, 1993

THE GRATEFUL DEAD

The Dead's thirty-year career is one of music's most celebrated. Regarded as originators of the jam band concept, the band members freely fused genres and influences, relying heavily on improvisation and the instinctual rapport that existed among one another. Early members of the band included rhythm guitarist Bob Weir, keyboardist Pigpen McKernan, and drummers Bill Kreutzmann and Mickey Hart. Over the years the constantly evolving Dead regularly lost and added new members.

The band first performed as the Warlocks, but legend says that Garcia stumbled upon the words grateful and dead together in the dictionary while in a haze of psychedelic drugs. The name stuck and, inspired by the success of bands like the Beatles, the Rolling Stones, and the Lovin' Spoonful, the loosely organized group began exploring a more ambitious sound, incorporating the electric guitar.

From the outset the Dead refused to nail down its set lists like other bands, enforcing its cred as an unpredictable, free-spirited live act. The listening public began taking notice after the one-two release of *Workingman's Dead* and *American Beauty* in 1970—and so did law enforcement. With the Dead's higher profile came increased scrutiny and legal action on drug charges, issues that would largely follow the band for the duration of its existence.

The Dead's founding members are as remembered for their unique personalities as they are for the specific talents that they contributed to the group's sound and success. After Garcia's passing, the surviving band members have, for the most part, stuck together, maintaining the Dead's legacy and famously dedicated fan base, serving as stewards of a vast catalog, and remaining politically vocal.

essential albums

WITH THE GRATEFUL DEAD
1967 *The Grateful Dead*
1968 *Anthem of the Sun*
1969 *Aoxomoxoa*
1969 *Live/Dead*
1970 *Workingman's Dead*
1970 *American Beauty*
1971 *Grateful Dead*
1972 *Europe '72*
1973 *History of the Grateful Dead, Volume 1*
1973 *Wake of the Flood*
1974 *Grateful Dead from the Mars Hotel*
1975 *Blues for Allah*
1976 *Steal Your Face*
1977 *Terrapin Station*
1978 *Shakedown Street*
1980 *Go to Heaven*
1981 *Reckoning*
1981 *Dead Set*
1987 *In the Dark*
1988 *Dylan and the Dead*
1989 *Built to Last*
1990 *Without a Net*
1991 *Infrared Roses*
1991 *The Very Best of the Grateful Dead*

WITH THE NEW RIDERS OF THE PURPLE SAGE
1971 *New Riders of the Purple Sage*
1986 *Before Time Began*
1986 *Vintage NRPS*

SOLO
1972 *Garcia*
1974 *Compliments*
1976 *Reflections*
1982 *Run for the Roses*

WITH MERL SAUNDERS
1972 *Heavy Turbulence*
1973 *Fire Up*
1973 *Live at the Keystone*
1988 *Keystone Encores, Volume 1*
1988 *Keystone Encores, Volume 2*

1988 *Live at the Keystone, Volume 1*
1988 *Live at the Keystone Volume 2*
1992 *Fire Up Plus*
2004 *Keystone Berkeley, September 1, 1974*
2005 *The Jerry Garcia Collection, Volume 1: Legion of Mary*
2006 *Well Matched: The Best of Merl Saunders & Jerry Garcia*

WITH OLD AND IN THE WAY
1975 *Old and In the Way*
1996 *That High Lonesome Sound*
1997 *Breakdown*
2008 *Live at the Boarding House*

WITH THE JERRY GARCIA BAND
1978 *Cats Under the Stars*
1991 *Jerry Garcia Band*
1997 *How Sweet It Is*
2001 *Don't Let Go*
2001 *Shining Star*
2004 *After Midnight: Kean College, 2/28/80*
2009 *The Jerry Garcia Collection, Volume 2: Let It Rock*

WITH JERRY GARCIA ACOUSTIC BAND
1988 *Almost Acoustic*

JERRY GARCIA AND DAVID GRISMAN
1991 *Garcia/Grisman*
1993 *Not for Kids Only*
1996 *Shady Grove*
1998 *So What*
2000 *The Pizza Tapes*
2001 *Grateful Dawg*
2004 *Been All Around This World*

Awards and Honors

1983 Ranked No. 13 on *Rolling Stone*'s list of the 100 Greatest Guitarists of All Time

HENRY GARZA

Henry Garza (born May 14, 1978, in San Angelo, Texas) is the guitarist for Los Lonely Boys, the Texas-based Latin rock group that shot to fame with its single, "Heaven," in 2004. Among the band's legions of fans is Willie Nelson, one of "outlaw" country's reigning icons.

Garza's father, Ringo Sr., was a successful conjunto musician with the Falcones in the 1970s and 1980s, which greatly influenced the young Garza. Garza also latched onto the music of Stevie Ray Vaughan and Jimi Hendrix in his youth, becoming a precocious songwriter at the very young age of 4.

Garza's signature tone is warm, fat—and loud. In interviews he has mentioned guitar technicians' attempts to lower his volume, but Garza refuses. He has spoken of his affection for El Musico, his beloved First Act custom model, and a Stratocaster Sunburst reissue. Garza has always placed an emphasis on the agility of his hands; his practice regimen involves heavy-gauge strings, ensuring that he has the strength during performances to produce the powerful sound for which he's known.

"When I play, it's like a big painting, and I have all these different colors to choose from. Like. I've got a little B.B. King color, a little Stevie Ray color, a little Jimi Hendrix, and a little Ritchie Valens, and when I mix them together, that's what makes me. I'm not afraid to say those guys are my influences and my teachers. I'm not trying to be those guys, but I definitely learn from them every time I hear their music."

—HENRY GARZA, 2006

Awards and Honors

2005 Grammy Award for Best Pop Performance by a Duo or Group with Vocal, for "Heaven," with Los Lonely Boys

STUDIO
2004 *Los Lonely Boys*
2006 *Sacred*
2008 *Forgiven*
2009 *1969*

LIVE
2005 *Live at the Fillmore*
2006 *Live at Blue Cat Blues*

LOS LONELY BOYS

Los Lonely Boys is a trio of brothers: the eldest is Henry on guitar, followed by Jojo on bass and Ringo on drums. Champions of a brand of music they call "Texican rock and roll," Los Lonely Boys weave together strands of rock, blues, country, and Tejano.

The Boys produced and distributed independently during the 1990s, and their major-label, self-titled debut came out on Epic in 2004. "Heaven" reached number one and made Los Lonely Boys one of the most popular American rock acts that year. In 2005 the band would team up with Carlos Santana for the recording of "All That I Am."

Sacred, the Boys' highly anticipated sophomore release, hit No. 1 on the U.S. rock charts in 2006. Two years later the band released *Forgiven*, its latest, slickly produced blues-based record.

Los Lonely Boys are active with Amnesty International, the major human rights group, especially through AI's Make Some Noise Project, which uses cover versions of John Lennon's catalog to promote various causes. The band covered Lennon's "Whatever Gets You Thru the Night" in 2007, which is part of *Instant Karma*, an album whose proceeds are directed at alleviating the conflicts in Darfur, Africa.

Los Lonely Boys are known for their relatively squeaky-clean image, passionate lyrics and imagery, and their mutual respect for each other, on and off the stage.

Henry Garza performs at the Austin City Limits Music Festival, 2006.

BILLY GIBBONS

"There was this tall, gorgeous creature across a wide boulevard—a four-lane road. As it began to rain, there was immediate concurrence on the part of all three of us: 'We've got to turn around and give her a ride. We can't let her get drenched.' We hadn't gone fifty feet, and, like vapor, she was gone. She used her own legs to get her out of the rain. 'She's got legs and knows how to use 'em,' was the thought that struck us. Doing the video a second time was a gift."

—Billy Gibbons,
on ZZ Top's hit song, "Legs"

Billy Gibbons (born December 16, 1949, in Houston, Texas) is the famously bearded lead guitarist for the American blues-rock band ZZ Top.

As a five-year old Gibbons attended a Mary Kaye Trio performance with his father, a piano player. The young Gibbons leapt on stage and proceeded to follow along with the beat, drumming on the set and the band's instruments. Gibbons stole the show, and he was hooked.

Gibbons came of age during rock's genesis on radio and television, witnessing Elvis's appearance on the *Ed Sullivan Show* and absorbing the work of Little Richard over the airwaves. With a starter Gibson guitar, Gibbons began imitating his idols and persuading his friends to play with him.

Gibbons got his professional start in the psychedelic music scene of 1960s Texas, opening for Jimi Hendrix with his band, the Moving Sidewalks. In 1969 Gibbons teamed up with Dusty Hill and Frank Beard to form ZZ Top, releasing the Texas boogie–tinged record *ZZ Top's First Album* two years later. After a hiatus and some contractual reshuffling, the band reunited—featuring the lengthy beards of Gibbons and Hill.

Eliminator, released in 1983, brought ZZ Top a worldwide profile, paving the way for a five-album contract with RCA a decade later. By now the band's iconography was complete. Its videos and performances traded on the same formula: three bearded "wild men," tricked-out guitars, and Gibbons's gloriously restored 1933 Ford three-door hot rod.

Gibbons remains active with the band he founded, and his appearances have extended to all corners of the music world, including gigs with Queens of the Stone Age, the Raconteurs, Hank Williams Jr., Jeff Beck, and B.B. King.

essential albums

WITH ZZ TOP

1970	First Album
1972	Rio Grande Mud
1973	Tres Hombres
1975	Fandango
1976	Tejas
1977	The Best of ZZ Top
1979	Deguello
1981	El Loco
1983	Eliminator
1985	Afterburner
1988	The ZZ Top Six Pack
1985	Afterburner
1990	Recycler
1994	Antenna
1996	Rhythmeen
1999	XXX
2003	Mescalero

Awards and Honors

2004   Inducted into the Rock and Roll Hall of Fame, with ZZ Top

Billy Gibbons, right, with bandmates Dusty Hill, left, and Frank Beard, center

Billy Gibbons, above, surrounded by replicas of his favorite guitar, known as "Pearly Gates." At right, one of the replica versions of Pearly Gates produced by Gibson Guitar

PEARLY GATES

Pearly Gates is Gibbons's favorite guitar—a 1959 Gibson Les Paul Standard that's been said to sing like angels. Crafted from maple with a mahogany neck, the original ax has been cloned and reissued by Gibson—right down to the very last scratch and imperfection. The limited-quantity guitar has met with significant controversy with fans stemming from its selling price—in excess of $20,000 for a specimen signed by Gibbons himself.

The heavenly moniker originally belonged to Gibbons's car, an old Packard that he borrowed from a girlfriend for a road trip to California. After she got the acting part she was pursuing, Gibbons cited divine inter-vention and named the clunker Pearly Gates. The girlfriend turned around and sold the car, but she was nice enough to send the proceeds to Gibbons. He immediately purchased the famed Les Paul Standard, and coopted the nickname as well.

DAVID GILMOUR

"It's hard for me to imagine why people would churn stuff out the way they do.... it isn't art that is driving them. It's their vanity. They can't bear the thought of being obsolete, when they quite plainly are.... The bug of success ... drives them, not art."

—DAVID GILMOUR, 2002

essential albums

WITH PINK FLOYD

1968	*A Saucerful of Secrets*
1969	*More*
1969	*Ummagumma*
1970	*Atom Heart Mother*
1971	*Meddle*
1972	*Obscured by Clouds*
1973	*The Dark Side of the Moon*
1975	*Wish You Were Here*
1977	*Animals*
1979	*The Wall*
1983	*The Final Cut*
1987	*A Momentary Lapse of Reason*
1988	*Delicate Sound of Thunder*
1994	*The Division Bell*
1995	*P·U·L·S·E*

SOLO

1978	*David Gilmour*
1984	*About Face*
2006	*On an Island*
2008	*Live in Gdansk*

David Gilmour (born March 6, 1946, in Cambridge, England) is a founding member of rock group Pink Floyd. His comfortable childhood and adolescence allowed him the luxury of picking up guitar, a hobby he shared with future bandmate Syd Barrett. After an unfocused and nearly disastrous turn traveling and playing around Europe with friends, Gilmour returned to England in 1967 and joined Pink Floyd at drummer Nick Mason's request.

Gilmour quickly cemented his role as the band's de facto leader; Barrett was unreliable and sometimes difficult to work with. The well-known albums *Dark Side of the Moon* and *Wish You Were Here* catapulted the group to fame, but Gilmour harbored doubts about how much respect the others had for his contributions. In 1978 he struck out on his own and recorded an eponymous solo album to showcase his guitar playing, but stuck with Pink Floyd as they recorded *The Wall*.

Another solo effort, *About Face*, propelled Gilmour even further from the band. Even amid its success, the mid-1980s marked a low point for Pink Floyd, which saw the lineup shuffle several times as Gilmour attempted to regain control and set the band's course back to a more musically driven style of recording.

A 2005 Live 8 concert featuring all of the original members brought in millions for charity. Gilmour has reflected on this performance as a final note in Pink Floyd's history, citing his preference for working alone.

GILMOUR THE SOLOIST

A handful of Gilmour's guitar solos on Pink Floyd recordings are considered some of the best of all time, namely his contributions on "Comfortably Numb," "Money," and "Time."

The signature solo in "Comfortably Numb" was actually conceived in fits and starts as Gilmour combined bits from disparate recording sessions in the studio. Starting with several individual solos, he painstakingly culled the best parts from each and wove them into the masterpiece we know today.

Gilmour has honed his famous bluesy sound principally on a 1969 Fender Stratocaster that's been extensively modified over time. Bits and pieces from other guitarists—and decades—have made their way into Gilmour's signature ax. The current neck is a 1957 maple V-shape reissue, and the strap once belonged to Jimi Hendrix.

Gilmour is noted for owning the first Stratocaster assigned a serial number—0001.

Gilmour's Fender Stratocaster made in 1954 with the serial number 0001, was the first of its kind ever made.

Awards and Honors

1994 Grammy Award for Best Rock Instrumental, for "Marooned," with Pink Floyd

2003 Appointed Commander of the British Empire (CBE)

David Gilmour onstage at Radio City Music Hall in New York, 2006

FLYING SOLO

The combination of long-brewing and frequent tensions within Pink Floyd, as well as his oft-acknowledged preference for working by himself, has driven Gilmour to establish himself as a recognized and successful solo artist. The only member of Pink Floyd to find success on his own, Gilmour has released four recordings under his name, all of them achieving a high level of popularity in Europe and the United States.

Gilmour has explored other instruments in his own recordings, namely the saxophone, which he highlights in 2006's *On an Island*. An ambitious work, Gilmour recruited a diverse stable of talent from around the world, including the Polish cinematic composer Zbigniew Preisner, whose arrangements and orchestrations frame the album and were performed live in 2006, resulting in the album *Live in Gdansk*.

Gilmour in concert in Munich, Germany, 20060

WARREN HAYNES

essential albums

WITH ALLMAN BROTHERS BAND

1990	*Seven Turns*
1991	*Shades of Two Worlds*
1992	*An Evening with the Allman Brothers Band: First Set*
1994	*Where It All Begins*
1995	*An Evening with the Allman Brothers Band: 2nd Set*
2003	*Hittin' the Note*
2004	*One Way Out*

WITH GOV'T MULE

1995	*Gov't Mule*
1998	*Dose*
2000	*Life Before Insanity*
2001	*The Deep End, Volume 1*
2002	*The Deep End, Volume 2*
2004	*Deja Voodoo*
2006	*High & Mighty*
2007	*Mighty High*
2008	*Holy Haunted House*
2009	*By a Thread*

SOLO

1993	*Tales Of Ordinary Madness*
2004	*Lucky*

Warren Haynes (born April 6, 1960, in Asheville, North Carolina) is a guitarist known for his close ties to the Allman Brothers Band, the Grateful Dead, the Dave Matthews Band, and Gov't Mule.

Haynes got his first lucky break performing in small clubs near his childhood home in Asheville, North Carolina. David Allan Coe was on the hunt for a new guitarist for his band, and Haynes's gigs had been attracting some attention. When offered the job, Haynes accepted immediately—and kicked off a long period of worldwide touring and recording with Coe's band, allowing him the chance to meet Gregg Allman.

In 1984 Haynes left Coe's band and started the Rich Hippies in Nashville, a project that only lasted a year. He moved on to the Nighthawks, during which time he wrote a song for Garth Brooks that hit No. 1 in the United States.

Three years later his old bandmates from the Coe days came knocking—Dickey Betts was in need of a backup vocalist for his new album and eventually talked Haynes into playing guitar as well. They released *Pattern Disruptive* as the Dickey Betts Band in 1988. On Betts's recommendation, Haynes joined a reunited Allman Brothers Band the following year, kicking off a string of successful album releases as well as a near-constant touring presence as a featured member of the group.

Haynes is a frequent solo performer, citing a wide variety of influences, including Eric Clapton, Jimi Hendrix, and Johnny Winter. Haynes relies primarily on Gibson Les Paul guitars.

"The whole jam band scene is an open-minded scene and hopefully it continues to grow and grow and become even more open-minded. It should contain reggae music and jazz, bluegrass and rock and roll and soul music and contain all genres of music. . . . I'm a big fan of songwriting and regardless of a band's ability or desire to improvise really doesn't matter. There have to be songs that maintain your attention and prove some sort of timelessness."

—WARREN HAYNES, 2007

GOV'T MULE

Most recently Haynes has focused his efforts on Gov't Mule, the band he started with Matt Abts and Allen Woody. The group quickly became known for its liberal policies regarding the recording and unofficial distribution of its material. Gov't Mule celebrates a vibrant live aesthetic, and the band recorded three albums before Woody died in 2000. With a new lineup, the band has continued to release live recordings and concert DVDs, frequently enlisting the help of special guests to perform with it. The group has drawn comparisons to the Grateful Dead for its generous, rambling live shows full of audience participation—and indeed, Haynes frequently jams with former Dead members, including Phil Lesh. The band's latest album debuted in 2009, and shows are lined up into 2010.

Warren Haynes, left, performing a free concert with Gov't Mule, alongside drummer Matt Abts, center, and bassist Allen Woody, right

THE CHRISTMAS JAM & OTHER CHARITY

Haynes is noted for his charity work and philanthropy, especially in his hometown of Asheville—his fond tradition, the annual Christmas Jam, began in 1989 as a casual reunion of best friends, but it's since grown to a massive extravaganza that tends to sell out within hours of tickets going on sale. Originally held at a small club in Asheville, Haynes has expanded to the Asheville Civic Center to accommodate the legions of fans—and musicians—that want to take part. Habitat for Humanity is the primary beneficiary, having long been one of Haynes's pet causes.

Awards and Honors

1995	Grammy Award for Best Rock Instrumental Performance, for "Jessica," with Allman Brothers Band

JIMI HENDRIX

Jimi Hendrix (born November 27, 1942, in Seattle, Washington; died September 18, 1970, in London, England) was a feverishly innovative guitarist, known for his experimental, unmistakable sound and his tragically short career. Considered a genius and one of the best guitarists of all time, his mark on modern music is incalculable.

As a child in an unstable household, Hendrix (born Johnny Allen Hendrix) spent his early years shuffling between the United States and Vancouver, Canada, where his grandmother lived. His shyness led him to practice the guitar nonstop, first with a used model he acquired at 15, and then with a Supro Ozark he purchased with his father's assistance. Inspired by Chuck Berry and Elvis Presley and the records of B.B. King and Muddy Waters, Hendrix dropped out of high school to hone his wild playing skills in several bands.

After a lackluster stint in the U.S. Army, Hendrix moved to the southern United States and embedded himself in the influential Chitlin' Circuit, a breeding ground and network of concert venues that showcased black performers and R&B and blues-based music.

The year 1964 saw a move to New York City's Harlem for Hendrix, where he gained exposure at the Apollo Theater and landed a recording deal with the Isley Brothers. Hendrix spent the next few years bouncing from gig to gig, contributing to some early recordings that would only gain attention after his ascent to fame.

A series of serendipitous meetings beginning in 1966 led Hendrix to London. There he changed the spelling of his first name and formed the Jimi Hendrix Experience with bassist Noel Redding and drummer Mitch Mitchell, following the "power trio" model set by Cream. Hendrix also jammed with Eric Clapton and Pete Townshend, cementing his extreme popularity in Europe. Recording contracts and records followed, with the first album *Are You Experienced* (1967) nearly overtaking the Beatles' *Sgt. Pepper's Lonely Hearts Club Band*'s No. 1 chart position.

American success would follow after Hendrix met Frank Zappa in the summer of 1967. Fascinated by Zappa's new wah-wah peddle, Hendrix quickly incorporated it into his repertoire and pushed its possibilities to the limit.

The Jimi Hendrix Experience would record two more albums and continue to expand its presence worldwide, giving Hendrix the opportunity to indulge his eccentric perfectionism, as well as explore the boundaries of his art. The Experience disbanded in 1969, playing a dramatic last concert to a rioting crowd in Denver.

After the Experience, Hendrix played with a hired group he dubbed Gypsy Sun and Rainbows. Together they played Woodstock and made a number of highly visible TV appearances. Hendrix also released a live record, *Band of Gypsys*.

In the midst of a grueling tour, Hendrix was found dead in his basement suite at a London hotel in September 1970.

essential albums

WITH THE JIMI HENDRIX EXPERIENCE
1967	*Are You Experienced*
1967	*Axis: Bold as Love*
1968	*Electric Ladyland*

LIVE
1970	*Band of Gypsys*
1970	*The Jimi Hendrix Experience/ Otis Redding at Monterey*

POSTHUMOUS RELEASES
1971	*The Cry of Love*
1971	*Rainbow Bridge*
1972	*War Heroes*
1974	*Loose Ends*

Left and above: Hendrix performing at the Newport Jazz Festival, 1969

Hendrix performs with the Experience in Amsterdam, 1973.

THE HENDRIX STYLE

Hendrix is as famous for the way he played guitar as he is for the wondrous sounds he produced. A southpaw, Hendrix innovated by restringing his right-handed axes and playing them upside down, putting a particular color on the licks and giving him a new level of physical control over the instrument. Using mainly a series of Fender Stratocasters, one of which sold for more than $150,000 in 2006, he originated or perfected a number of techniques that are taken for granted today.

Hendrix had a voracious appetite for new music technology, electronics, and effects. After the introduction of the wah-wah pedal, Hendrix snapped one up and made it an iconic part of his sound.

Breaking new ground in the studio as well, Hendrix experimented with new ways of recording, laying down tracks, and mixing, often turning normally frowned-upon components like dissonance and feedback on their ears and making them integral to the track.

The 1960s aesthetic drove Hendrix's fashion and lifestyle choices (including the use and abuse of drugs). The quintessential hippie, Hendrix still influences today's musicians. His flamboyant stagecraft matched his big hair and elaborate wardrobe, heavy with jewelry, pendants, and bandanas.

Hendrix set at least three guitars alight onstage. This Fender Strat, with burns still visible along the neck and pickguard, survived its onstage burning at the London Astoria in 1967.

"I want to get up in the morning and just roll over in my bed into an indoor swimming pool and then swim to the breakfast table, come up for air and get maybe a drink of orange juice or something like that. Then just flop over from the chair into the swimming pool, swim into the bathroom and go on and shave and whatever."

—JIMI HENDRIX,
ON COMFORTABLE LIVING, 1970

Hendrix in 1968 with his Experience bandmates, Mitch Mitchell, left, and Noel Redding, right

Hendrix at Woodstock, 1969

Awards and Honors

1992	Inducted into the Rock and Roll Hall of Fame
1992	Grammy Award for Lifetime Achievement
1994	Received star on Hollywood Walk of Fame
2003	Ranked No. 1 on *Rolling Stone*'s list of 100 Greatest Guitarists of All Time
2005	Inducted into the United Kingdom's Music Hall of Fame

JOAN JETT

Joan Jett (born Joan Marie Larkin on September 22, 1958) is the Philadelphia-born and Los Angeles–bred rocker who helms Joan Jett and the Blackhearts.

Jett's experience growing up all over the United States gave a unique color to the music she'd later pursue and create. After finishing high school in Maryland, Jett moved with her family to Southern California, where she fell in with her idol and mentor, Suzi Quatro, a prototypical female rocker.

Jett spent the second half of the 1970s with the Runaways, a band she formed with front woman Cherie Currie. Always more successful abroad than in its homeland, the Runaways cut five albums and opened for acts including Cheap Trick and Van Halen, but broke up in 1979.

Jett quickly began plotting a solo career. During a stint in England, she hooked up with Sex Pistols members Paul Cook and Steve Jones. Together the three recorded a cover of the Arrows' "I Love Rock and Roll," a song that would later become Jett's trademark.

Back in the States, Jett met Kenny Laguna, a musician and producer who would be indispensable in the recording of her solo album. Unable to find studio backers, Jett and Laguna formed Blackheart Records and put the album out themselves.

Jett, above, performs at the Bumbershoot festival in Seattle, Washington, 1994.

Opposite page: Jett at the Tropicana Motel in 1977

Joan Jett and the Blackhearts evolved out of the partnership between Jett and Laguna. Jett decided to shake up the formula from the Runaways days and recruited a band from Los Angeles, talking the members into moving to New York. By 1982 the band was hot in the United States and abroad. "I Love Rock and Roll" was at the top of the charts, and Joan Jett and the Blackhearts was selling out major concerts with Aerosmith, the Police, and Queen.

Building on her success in the music arena, Jett has gone on to become a successful actress, having appeared on film and television, as well as on Broadway. Credited with paving the way for the Riot Grrrl movement and reinvigorated punk scenes that flourished in the 1990s, Jett continues to perform and tour with the Blackhearts and is set to release an album of greatest hits in 2010.

Awards and Honors

2003 Named No. 87 on Rolling Stone's 100 Greatest Guitarists of All Time list

Jett is one of only two women on *Rolling Stone*'s list of top guitarists. At right, Jett performs during a 2008 tour, wearing her signature black leather vest and pants with leather and metal choker necklaces.

essential albums

WITH THE RUNAWAYS
- 1976 *The Runaways*
- 1977 *Queens of Noise*
- 1977 *Live in Japan*
- 1977 *Waitin' for the Night*
- 1977 *And Now . . . The Runaways*

SOLO
- 1980 *Joan Jett*

WITH JOAN JETT AND THE BLACKHEARTS
- 1981 *Bad Reputation*
- 1981 *I Love Rock 'n Roll*
- 1983 *Album*
- 1984 *Glorious Results of a Misspent Youth*
- 1986 *Good Music*
- 1987 *The Big Easy*
- 1988 *Up Your Alley*
- 1990 *The Hit List*
- 1991 *Notorious*
- 1994 *Pure and Simple*
- 2004 *Naked*
- 2006 *Sinner*

"It changed the level that we did everything at. It was definitely a mindfuck. I wouldn't change it for anything. The experience was incredible. A lot of it was really intense, and scary, and weird, and nasty, and people treat you funny. You become a product, which is very strange. I went from being so low in the gutters to being so up there, going to number one and being able to turn around and say, 'Ha ha.' I mean, I didn't want to do that too much, and I didn't. But I felt it. You don't want to laugh too much, because you know it could all be over in a second."

—JOAN JETT, ON THE SUCCESS OF "I LOVE ROCK 'N' ROLL"

Jett, left, performs with the Blackhearts at the Bumbershoot festival, and, above, she rocks out at the Beale Street Music Festival in Memphis, 2008.

Opposite page: Jett, during her Runaways days sits backstage with Debbie Harry of Blondie at a Blondie concert, 1977.

THE RUNAWAYS

The Runaways broke ground in the 1970s with their all-female take on punk. Originally a duo consisting of the young Jett and percussionist Sandy West, the Runaways enlisted the assistance of producer Kim Fowley to expand the group to five members. The expanded band rapidly made a name for itself in Los Angeles. Even though the youngest member of the band was just 16, the Runaways scored a recording contract in 1976 and dispatched with their self-titled debut. The girls gained outsize attention for their carefully crafted looks—each member drew on the inspiration of both male and female rock stars; in Jett's case, she seemed to channel Keith Richards and later mentor Suzi Quatro.

By 1977 the Runaways had another album under their belts, a world tour in progress, and close ties to the major punk groups on both coasts of the United States—not to mention the United Kingdom. The Runaways soon joined their New York–based counterparts, rooted to that city's famed CBGB music club on the Lower East Side, on the short list of definitive punk rock acts. Perhaps nowhere else on the globe was the band more popular than in Japan, where they travelled in 1977 for a series of hysterically received appearances. The calamitous—and some say, unexpected—popularity abroad led to a few

lineup changes in the band; both lead singer Cherie Currie and bass player Jackie Fox decamped, opening a clear path for Jett's ascent to the role of front woman.

A fourth album would be released in 1977 and the Runaways toured with their East Coast contemporaries, the Ramones, but the end was near. Producer Kim Fowley has been accused of driving wedges between the band's members, ultimately leading to their breakup. *And Now . . . The Runaways* came out in 1978; it would prove to be the band's last record.

Jett's fans at the 2010 Sundance Film Festival eagerly anticipated the premiere of a partially fictionalized portrayal of the Runaways's rise to fame and the band's ultimate demise, produced by Joan Jett. Set for wider release, *The Runaways* features Kristen Stewart (of *Twilight* fame) as Jett, with Dakota Fanning and Alia Shawkat from TV's *Arrested Development*.

The project's successful completion represents the second major attempt to immortalize the Runaway's exploits in film. Jett worked closely on a movie called *We're All Crazy Now* at the end of the band's career, but the movie was canceled halfway through shooting. After Jett became a star in her own right, producers recycled the footage into 1984's *duBEAT-e-o*, a zany film within a film that features a sound track by punk rock band Social Distortion.

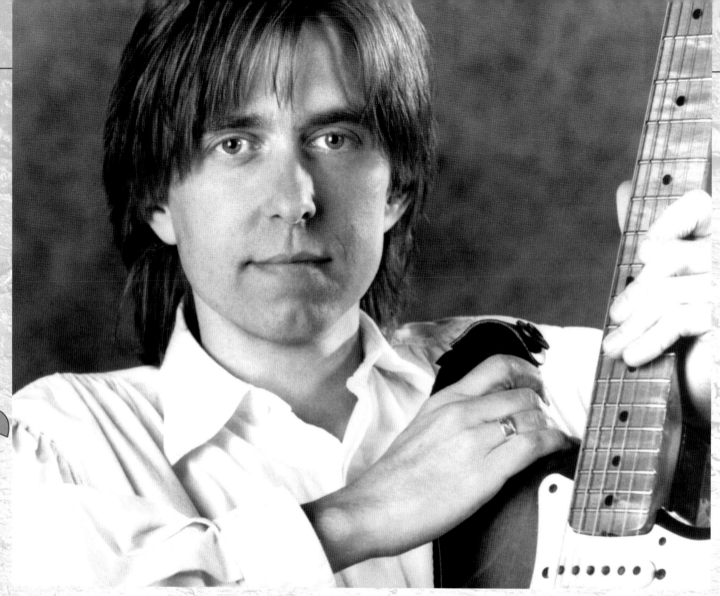

ERIC JOHNSON

Eric Johnson (born August 17, 1954, in Austin, Texas) is a primarily instrumental guitarist best known for melding a dizzying variety of styles, including country and western and jazz, as well as his notorious perfectionism in the studio.

Johnson came of age in a musical family: his three sisters practiced piano, and Johnson's father encouraged him to pick up guitar when he was 11. Just four years later, Johnson was playing guitar as a member of a psychedelic rock group called Mariani. A demo cut by the band remains a hard-to-find treasure for music fanatics.

Johnson was a member of the Electromagnets during his college years and formed the Eric Johnson Group, which recorded its first album in 1978. It would take a long twenty years for the album to see the light of day after several issues stemming from contracts and management conspired to hold it up.

During that twenty-year period, Johnson built his credentials as a talented session guitarist. Among the stars he worked with was Christopher Cross, who was instrumental in helping Johnson secure a contract with Warner Bros. The resulting album, 1986's Grammy-nominated *Tones*, brought him rapturous attention from the professional music community, but the consuming public was less enthusiastic.

Discarded by Warner Bros., Johnson found a home at a smaller label and released *Ah Via Musicom* in 1990, which was much more successful, garnering accolades for Johnson's peerless sound and uncompromising production values. "Cliffs of Dover" was a major hit and became Johnson's calling card—it even makes an appearance in the video game Guitar Hero III.

Since this commercial pinnacle, Johnson has found himself at odds with traditional labels, forced back into the realm of the unsigned once again after his *Musicom* follow-up fizzled, wracked by delays and Johnson's own second-guessing. Still respected to the utmost by his peers like Eric Clapton and Joe Satriani, Johnson has continued to tour and release new material, including an Internet album in 2002, and several recordings of live performances accompanied by DVDs.

Eric Johnson in 1997

JOHNSON'S EQUIPMENT

Reluctant to show allegiance to any specific brand or model of guitar, Johnson is known for his extensive instrument collection and complex arsenal of effects pedals. A distinctive aspect of Johnson's setup is his use of three amps—giving him the utmost control over the tones he produces. In recent years Johnson has begun experimenting with acoustic guitar and digital methods of recording, both sure to profoundly affect upcoming releases.

With Fender, Johnson crafted the Stratocaster Rosewood guitar in 2009, made of alder with a maple neck and available in four finishes. Johnson has also lent his name and expertise to the design of other axes and equipment from C. F. Martin, DiMarzio, GHS, and Fulton-Webb.

essential albums

1986	*Tones*
1990	*Ah Via Musicom*
1996	*Venus Isle*
2002	*Souvenir*
2005	*Bloom*
2005	*Live from Austin, TX*

Awards and Honors

1992   Grammy Award for Best Rock Instrumental Performance, for "Cliffs of Dover"

Johnson performs at a benefit concert to aid the victims of Hurricane Katrina, 2005.

"I think maybe the most important thing is to play what really gives you joy on the guitar, and couple that with pushing yourself. You have to be discriminate, and you have to push yourself, I think, and that's not always going to feel comfortable. In fact, most of the time it'll be uncomfortable. But it's a sweet kind of pain, and I think you have to make peace with that sweet pain, and realize that's actually sweeter than it is painful."

—ERIC JOHNSON, 2008

JORMA KAUKONEN

essential albums

WITH JEFFERSON AIRPLANE
1967	*Surrealistic Pillow*
1967	*After Bathing at Baxter's*
1968	*Crown of Creation*
1969	*Bless Its Pointed Little Head*
1969	*Volunteers*
1971	*Bark*

WITH HOT TUNA
1970	*Hot Tuna*
1971	*First Pull Up, Then Pull Down*
1972	*Burgers*
1973	*The Phosphorescent Rat*
1975	*Yellow Fever*
1976	*Hoppkorv*
1978	*Double Dose*
1984	*Splashdown*
1990	*Pair a Dice Found*

SOLO
| 1974 | *Quah* |

Jorma Kaukonen (born December 23, 1940, in Washington, D.C.) is one of the original members of Jefferson Airplane. He is known as a master of the finger-style technique and favors Gibson guitars.

As a teenager Kaukonen committed himself to the blues and scoffed at rock and roll, but in college his perspective shifted. Immersed in the coffee shop and club culture of 1960s San Francisco, Kaukonen got a small gig playing with the then unknown Janis Joplin. Kaukonen attended a band rehearsal at the behest of friend and future bandmate Paul Kantner, and the collection of pedals, effects, and equipment the rock band had at its disposal blew him away.

Kaukonen agreed to join up with the fledgling band, and he quickly brought his electric guitar skills up to speed. His acoustic mastery, too, featured heavily in Jefferson Airplane's releases, contributing to a catalog that would span a wide range of styles and techniques.

Kaukonen's improvisational instincts led to the creation of Hot Tuna in 1969, a side project that made the same transition from an acoustic to electric sound. The band also served as a vehicle for Kaukonen to build on his songwriting, a talent that was left largely unexplored with Jefferson Airplane.

Jefferson Airplane broke up in 1972, which led to the establishment of Kaukonen's solo career in the mid-1970s. Hot Tuna's disintegration (in 1978) wasn't far behind, and Kaukonen spent the period touring and working on his second solo album, *Jorma*.

A notable misstep occurred in 1980 with the founding of Vital Parts, another side project. The band's debut album, *Barbeque King*, was packaged with a new stage persona for Kaukonen—consisting of wildly colored hair and conspicuous tattoos. Fans from his earlier days largely revolted, and the album was a flop.

By 1988 Hot Tuna was back together again, and a Jefferson Airplane reunion followed the next year.

Kaukonen's recent career is rounded out by his frequent performances and collaborations with other artists, notably former members of the Grateful Dead, including Tom Constanten and Phil Lesh. He continues to participate in Hot Tuna, and his last solo album debuted in 2009.

1979	*Jorma*
1981	*Barbeque King*
1985	*Magic*
1994	*Embryonic Journey*
1995	*Magic Two*
2002	*Blue Country Heart*
2007	*Stars in My Crown*
2009	*River of Time*

Awards and Honors

1996	Inducted into the Rock and Roll Hall of Fame, with Jefferson Airplane
2003	Ranked number 54 on *Rolling Stone*'s list of the 100 Greatest Guitarists of All Time

Jorma Kaukonen in 1969

FUR PEACE RANCH

Kaukonen's Fur Peace Ranch, a 120-acre camp and retreat for guitarists and others musicians of all skill levels, is situated in the fringes of the Appalachian mountain range in southern Ohio. Kaukonen started the ranch with his wife, Vanessa, in 1989, and he oversees a staff that provides lodging and instruction for guitarists in a drug-free and distraction-free, all-inclusive setting.

Many of Kaukonen's fellow musicians—and best friends— have spent time at the ranch, regularly teaching lessons and appearing with students at the ranch's performance hall, along with Kaukonen himself. The Fur Peace recordings are regularly broadcast on local radio.

JEFFERSON AIRPLANE

A seminal psychedelic rock band, Jefferson Airplane was one of the first groups to achieve a high level of success based on an alternative take on the prevailing rock and roll sound of the time. Reaching its peak in the 1960s, the band was highly visible from 1967 to 1969, playing in every single one of the decade's trio of legendary music festivals: Monterey, Woodstock, and Altamont.

The band's releases were often the target of censorship by nervous record executives. Its first album, *Jefferson Airplane Takes Off*, contained subtle lyrical nods to sex and drugs that were scrubbed clean from later pressings of the record. The rare original issues are difficult to find today, and existing specimens have been known to fetch thousands of dollars.

Surrealistic Pillow, released in 1967, was the album that brought Jefferson Airplane worldwide attention. With heavy input from Jerry Garcia, the album propelled the band to perform at that year's Monterey International Pop Festival, where it gained even more exposure and would be forever associated with San Francisco's Summer of Love.

By 1972 the band had weathered several storms, and a San Francisco show that autumn would prove to be its last until its 1989 reunion.

Jefferson Airplane, about 1969, clockwise from top left: Marty Balin, Jack Casady, Jorma Kaukonen, Paul Kantner, Grace Slick, and Spencer Dryden

MARK KNOPFLER

Mark Knopfler (born August 12, 1949, in Glasgow, Scotland) is best known as the founder and head of the best-selling UK band Dire Straits.

Knopfler fiddled with a cheap guitar as a teen and listened to the popular acts of the day like B.B. King, Django Reinhardt, and Elvis Presley, but he initially focused his studies on English and journalism. He actually worked as a reporter for a short time, but eventually started moonlighting as a musician while he was finishing his academic career.

After moving to London, Knopfler joined a band called Brewers Droop, and it was his experience coaxing sound out of a forlorn guitar that convinced him he was on the right path.

In 1977 Dire Straits cut its first album, which was self-titled. The first single the band released slowly gained traction in Europe, catalyzing sales of its album, and by the time of its second record two years later, the band was a hit.

Dire Straits became more and more "Mark's band" over the course of its later releases, with its music taking a deeper, more complicated turn. The band would replace several members during the 1980s, and Knopfler began branching out in other directions, beginning his first of several film scores, including music for *The Princess Bride*.

In 1985 the band released its biggest album, *Brothers in Arms*. After a stunningly successful world tour in support of the record, the band decided to treat the pinnacle as an opportunity to take time off. Knopfler continued with his film work, and Dire Straits continued to give charity performances—finally releasing a follow-up album in 1991 coupled with a tour, the stress of which led to the band's demise in 1995.

Knopfler's solo career is alive and well; *Get Lucky* dropped in 2009 and Knopfler continues to tour in support of the record.

"Nothing comes of nothing. You have to put yourself in the driver's seat. Chet Atkins said, 'Learn to fall asleep playing.' I started doing that as soon as I started to play—to the detriment of other activities. I didn't feel as I if had any choice in the matter. I still feel that way."

—MARK KNOPFLER, 2007

essential albums

WITH DIRE STRAITS

1978	*Dire Straits*
1979	*Communique*
1980	*Making Movies*
1982	*Love Over Gold*
1983	*Twisting by the Pool*
1984	*Alchemy: Dire Straits Live*
1985	*Brothers in Arms*
1988	*Money for Nothing*
1991	*On Every Street*

SOLO

1996	*Golden Heart*
2000	*Sailing to Philadelphia*
2002	*The Ragpicker's Dream*
2004	*Shangri-La*
2005	*One Take Radio Sessions*
2005	*The Trawlerman's Song*
2007	*Kill to Get Crimson*
2009	*Get Lucky*

WITH OTHER ARTISTS

1990	*Neck and Neck* (with Chet Atkins)
1989	*The Booze Brothers* (with Brewers Droop)
2006	*All the Roadrunning* (with Emmylou Harris)

Awards and Honors

1986	Grammy Award for Best Rock Performance by a Duo or Group with Vocal, for "Money for Nothing," with Dire Straits
1986	Grammy Award for Best Country Instrumental Performance, for *Cosmic Square Dance*, with Chet Atkins
1991	Grammy Award for Best Country Vocal Collaboration, for *Poor Boy Blues*, with Chet Atkins
1999	Appointed Officer of the Order of the British Empire (OBE)
2001	Three paleontologists identify a new dinosaur from bones found in Madagascar and name it *Masiakasaurus knopfleri* in honor of Knopfler, whose music they were listening to when they made the discovery.
2003	Ranked No. 27 on *Rolling Stone*'s list of the 100 Greatest Guitarists of All Time

Mark Knopfler performs live at Wembley Arena in London, 2006 .

KNOPFLER'S COUNTRY INSTINCT

From unlikely Scottish and British roots, Knopfler has explored country music via his band the Notting Hillbillies, a group he founded in 1988. The band released only one album, but it would remain an active force through most of the 1990s.

Knopfler has continued to indulge his country focus through several collaborations. Knopfler's résumé includes a 1990 Chet Atkins album, *Neck and Neck*. In the 1990s he would work with John Anderson, Mary Chapin Carpenter, and Kris Kristofferson. *Real Live Roadrunning* is his most recent country-inspired project; he shares credit for the well-received album with Emmylou Harris.

Right: Knopfler in concert in Portugal, 2008

Opposite page: Knopfler in 1989. The next year he would tour with the Notting Hillbillies, whose sole album is *Missing . . . Presumed Having a Good Time*.

LENNY KRAVITZ

"Putting a track together is like sculpture, or like landscaping, like, 'Where can I sprinkle the guitar?' 'Where will this ringing chord bring out a feeling?' The great records of the sixties are far more subtle—even if it was hard music—and expressive, than much of the stuff that's out there today. The key for a guitar player is to listen, think and ask yourself, 'How can I complement this track, and not just take it over?'"

—LENNY KRAVITZ, 2008

Lenny Kravitz (born May 26, 1964, in New York, New York) is a singer/songwriter and multi-instrumentalist who has reinterpreted the notion of "rock star" for a new generation of musicians and fans.

Kravitz was born into an accomplished family: his father was a news producer and jazz enthusiast, and his mother starred on TV's *The Jeffersons*. His colorful childhood spanned Manhattan's Upper East Side to Brooklyn's Bedford-Stuyvesant, the home of his grandmother, where he began to learn drums and guitar. His parents' connections provided him access to actors and musicians at the top of their game; Duke Ellington, a friend of his father's, performed "Happy Birthday" for Kravitz's 5th birthday.

After the family relocated to Los Angeles, Kravitz immersed himself in his high school music scene. He started as a choir singer, picked up bass and piano, and by the time of his graduation was certain he wanted to be a musician. Channeling his idols David Bowie and Prince, Kravitz dubbed himself Romeo Blue, a nickname that would stick until his self-titled debut album hit the stores. Kravitz parlayed his college fund into studio time, cutting a demo and rousing the attention of multiple record labels.

His eclectic debut, *Let Love Rule*, was received warmly in the United States but even more enthusiastically in Europe. In 1990 Kravitz entered into a high-profile collaboration with Madonna, penning her hit "Justify My Love" and stoking rumors of a possible affair.

Kravitz spent the 1990s releasing several albums and building on his credits as a songwriter and producer, working with the likes of Mick Jagger, Steven Tyler, and Stevie Wonder.

In 1998 Kravitz's stock rose further with the Grammy-winning hit "Fly Away," paving the way for a series of hit albums, covers, and collaborations with even more stars. Kravitz's career is vibrant as ever today—he's broken into acting with an appearance in 2009's acclaimed *Precious*, and a new album is slated for 2010.

essential albums

1989	*Let Love Rule*
1991	*Mama Said*
1993	*Are You Gonna Go My Way*
1995	*Circus*
1998	*[5]*
2001	*Lenny*
2004	*Baptism*
2008	*It Is Time for a Love Revolution*
2010	*Negrophilia*

Awards and Honors

1998	Grammy Award for Best Male Rock Vocal Performance, for "Fly Away"
1999	Grammy Award for Best Male Rock Vocal Performance, for "American Woman"
2000	Grammy Award for Best Male Rock Vocal Performance, for "Again"
2001	Grammy Award for Best Male Rock Vocal Performance, for "Dig In"

Kravitz live at the Carling Brixton Academy in London, during the *Let Love Rule* 2009 tour

KRAVITZ'S STYLE

Kravitz's sound is a radio-friendly but unpredictable hybrid of the funk styles to which he was first attracted and the harder rock of Aerosmith, Kiss, and Led Zeppelin. Kravitz's talent as a multi-instrumentalist was first harnessed on *Let Love Rule*; on the suggestion of his audio engineer, he decided to forgo the whole band and instead played all of the parts himself. Kravitz is also noted for the importance that he places on rhythm guitar and soulful, repetitive "grooves," a habit he attributes to his early love of funk and soul—and his own perceived shortcomings as a showy, speedy lead guitarist. Kravitz has stated, "I approach every instrument as a percussion instrument."

Not satisfied to just shred, sing, and leave the studio, Kravitz takes a primary role in the production process as well, ensuring that all of the elements of a successful recording are in balance before the track is laid down. Suspicious of using too many effects and studio tricks that tend to obscure his sound, Kravitz prefers to record in a cleaner, simpler fashion. His preference for a simple amp setup with minimal effects and processing has been looked upon as quaint or "retro," but Kravitz insists that it's all in the name of character and quality.

Kravitz in concert, 2004

ROBBY KRIEGER

essential albums

essential albums

WITH THE DOORS

1967	*The Doors*
1967	*Strange Days*
1968	*Waiting for the Sun*
1969	*The Soft Parade*
1970	*Morrison Hotel*
1971	*L.A. Woman*
1971	*Other Voices*
1972	*Full Circle*
1978	*An American Prayer*

SOLO

1977	*Robby Krieger & Friends*
1983	*Versions*
1985	*Robby Krieger*
1989	*Door Jams*
1989	*No Habla*
1990	*Eric Burdon & Robby Krieger*
2000	*Cinematix*

Awards and Honors

1993	Inducted into the Rock and Roll Hall of Fame, with the Doors
2007	Grammy Award for Lifetime Achievement, with the Doors
2003	Ranked No. 91 on *Rolling Stone*'s list of the 100 Greatest Guitarists of All Time

Robby Krieger (born January 8, 1946, in Los Angeles, California) is best remembered for his work as guitarist and songwriter with the Doors.

Krieger grew up among a diverse set of musical interests—his parents were classical music fans, but it wasn't until high school that he took an earnest interest in the guitar. He first latched onto a borrowed flamenco guitar, teaching himself to play.

Krieger's early output was influenced by Eastern sounds, especially the music of India, with which he had developed a fascination and began to study in college at UCLA. After meeting drummer John Densmore and the rest of the future Doors members through a meditation workshop, Krieger took every opportunity to introduce this style at early Doors rehearsals.

The band released *The Doors* in 1967—to overwhelming response. Krieger wrote the band's smash hit "Light My Fire."

Krieger's career post-Doors took him into new territory. Branching out, he established a group called the Butts Band with former Doors drummer Densmore, and he recorded as the Robby Krieger Band though the 1980s.

Most recently Krieger has delved into exclusively instrumental works, releasing *Cinematix* in 2000. He also attempted a Doors revival in 2002, but when other former members objected, Krieger changed the revival band's name to Riders of the Storm, after the Doors song of that name.

THE DOORS

The Doors are among the most dynamic and memorable American bands to come out of the 1960s, immortalized for its thrilling live shows and high-minded lyrical aesthetic.

The band as it's known today got its start in 1966 as the house band at the famed Whiskey a Go Go venue in Los Angeles. The Doors found a label almost immediately, despite front man Jim Morrison's eccentric, drug-fueled performances. The band released its legendary first album in 1967, based on the live set that it had perfected as a club act. The Krieger-penned track "Light My Fire" was its first huge hit, reaching all the way to No. 1 in the United States.

The Doors became a household name via a string of visible—and sometimes controversial—television appearances on *The Ed Sullivan Show* and *The Jonathan Winters Show*. *Strange Days* was also released in 1967, but this follow-up LP failed to excite to the same extent as the band's debut effort. Morrison's behavior was growing more erratic—performances around the country were often marred by Morrison's brushes with law enforcement—and fans were growing frustrated with his petulant and inconsistent stage presence.

A third and fourth LP came in rapid succession. *The Soft Parade* was more of a pop-flavored effort that found success, despite internal tensions stemming from Morrison's behavior. *Morrison Hotel*, released in 1970, represented a homecoming for the Doors, putting them back in the good graces of fans and the music press. Morrison's worst breakdown yet wasn't far ahead; an incident in December of that year forced the band to stop performing live.

After the release of the acclaimed *L.A. Woman* in 1971, Morrison quit the Doors and moved to Paris, where he ultimately died. The Doors soldiered on, with other members filling in for Morrison's vocals, but broke up soon thereafter. Several albums were released after Morrison's death, containing material he recorded while he was still alive, and the band's legacy survives through a substantial catalog of rare recordings, in addition to its officially released work.

Members of the band have been extremely protective of the band's most famous songs; lucrative licensing offers have been made, but so far, refused.

"Before [Jimi Hendrix], rock and roll guitar to me was more of a means than an end. . . . I didn't really consider rock and roll guitar as being that big of a deal until he came out. Before that playing guitar for me was more of a way to meet girls and stuff."

—ROBBY KRIEGER, 2009

The Doors—one of the most controversial acts of the late 1960s. From left: Jim Morrison, John Densmore, Ray Manzarek, and Robby Krieger

BRIAN MAY

essential albums

WITH QUEEN

1973	*Queen*
1974	*Queen II*
1974	*Sheer Heart Attack*
1975	*A Night at the Opera*
1976	*A Day at the Races*
1977	*News of the World*
1978	*Jazz*
1980	*The Game*
1982	*Hot Space*
1984	*The Works*
1986	*A Kind of Magic*
1989	*The Miracle*
1991	*Innuendo*
1995	*Made in Heaven*

SOLO

1983	*Star Fleet Project*
1992	*Back to the Light*
1998	*Another World*

Brian May (born July 19, 1947, in London, England) served as lead guitarist and vocalist for Queen. In addition to his musical accomplishments, he is a recognized astrophysicist, having earned a PhD in 2007.

May started exploring music in grammar school, forming a band with his good friend Tim Staffell and naming it *Nineteen Eighty-Four*, after the George Orwell novel.

Queen came together after vocalist Freddie Mercury came on board; the band released its self-titled debut in 1973 to limited but effusive praise. *Queen II*, released in 1973, showcases May's instrumental virtuosity as well as the band's most complex, ethereal work, hinting at the massive success that was just around the corner.

In Queen's recordings and his solo work, May has explored every style and technique of guitar playing known, including slide guitar, sweep picking, and tapping. Onstage May has been known to utilize tape-delay effects and complex arrangements of harmony and melody.

MAY AS ASTROPHYSICIST

As a student, May excelled in science and math from an early age. He earned a bachelor's degree with honors in physics and mathematics from Imperial College London and proceeded to enter the PhD track, concentrating on the physics of reflected light and interplanetary dust in space, balancing his commitment to Queen at the same time. As the band demanded more from May, he abandoned his studies, but not before publishing two academic papers based on his research.

Decades later, May successfully completed his PhD and published his thesis, titled "A Survey of Radial Velocities in the Zodiacal Dust Cloud" in 2007.

May remains active in the academic world: he currently serves as chancellor of Liverpool John Moores University.

"I think the most important thing must be to have a feel for what you're aiming for, and not to lose sight of the end product and get absorbed in things that don't make any difference. In other words, you need a feel for the sort of music it's going to be playing. But then, you need a bit of every sort of skill. For instance, it doesn't have to be finished that well in order to perform its function, but you want it to be."

—BRIAN MAY, ON THE CRAFT OF GUITAR BUILDING, 1973

RED SPECIAL

Brian May cobbled together Red Special, one of the most famous guitars of all time, from a random assortment of spare parts when he was only 16. Composed of scrap wood from an old fireplace and pieces of old bicycles and motorcycles, the guitar is renowned for its ability to produce strange and unique sounds. It remains May's favorite instrument and is the one he most often uses.

Around the same time, May intended to design another guitar, but he was so enchanted with Red Special that his plans fell by the wayside. Andrew Guyton, a respected guitar craftsman, got hold of the plans in 2005 and actually built the guitar to May's specifications. May dubbed the instrument the Spade, and has remained protective of it, thus far neither performing nor recording with it.

May has been known to play with coins, not the usual pick or plectrum, because it affords him more control.

Brian May in 1979, during his days with Queen

GARY MOORE

"[Albert King] said, "Gary, play every other lick." That's such a profound thing. . . . But he was absolutely right. If you leave that space, if you've got a good tone and you play expressively, and you can make people feel from your guitar, they won't be able to wait for the next note. It creates that tension if you've got a great sound and great feel. I grew up listening to Peter Green, and he was amazing when he would leave that space. You would just go, 'Come on and play the next note, man!' It just sounds so amazing just when you play one note with great tone and feel."

—GARY MOORE, 2007

A difficult-to-peg guitar virtuoso, Gary Moore (born April 4, 1952, in Belfast, Ireland) is known for his extensive resume and as a protégé of Fleetwood Mac's skilled axman Peter Green.

Growing up in Ireland, Moore was inspired early on by the likes of the Beatles, Elvis Presley, and Jimi Hendrix. Moore began honing his sound as a member of Skid Row in 1969, and though the band would only issue two albums with Moore, it was here that he met singer Phil Lynott, with whom he would collaborate frequently until Lynott's death in 1986.

Grinding Stone, released in 1973 by the Gary Moore Band, was Moore's first solo offering, which initially failed to excite many fans. Moore also began his association with Thin Lizzy ("The Boys Are Back in Town") during this time, initiating an on-again-off-again relationship that would fluctuate throughout the 1970s. In those years Moore found time for other projects as well, offering himself up as a session guitarist and

carving out memorable appearances on several albums by bands like Eddie Howell and Colosseum II.

"Parisienne Walkways," released in 1979, featured the voice of Phil Lynott and was Moore's first true hit. Another effort with Thin Lizzy, *Black Rose*, would also prove to be a success in the UK.

Moore put out a series of albums in the 1980s, even experimenting with an uncharacteristic metal sound. The 1990s began on a high note for Moore; his *Still Got the Blues* would bring him popular attention and acclaim for one of the first times in his career. *Blues for Greeny*, Moore's tribute album of Peter Green covers, was released in 1995.

Moore courted controversy in 1997 when he released *Dark Days in Paradise*, a dance-infused record that broke away from his chiefly blues-based sound. He soon returned to form, however, in the early 2000s, issuing a stream of albums that confirmed his guitar mastery—and maverick musicianship.

essential albums

SOLO

1978	*Grinding Stone*
1978	*Back on the Streets*
1982	*Corridors of Power*
1983	*Dirty Fingers*
1983	*Victims of the Future*
1984	*We Want Moore!*
1985	*Run for Cover*
1987	*Wild Frontier*
1989	*After the War*
1990	*Still Got the Blues*
1992	*After Hours*
1993	*Blues Alive*
1994	*BBM: Around the Next Dream*
1995	*Blues for Greeny*
1999	*A Different Beat*
2001	*Back to the Blues*
2002	*Scars*
2003	*Live at the Monsters of Rock*
2004	*Eagle Rock*
2007	*Close as You Get*
2008	*Bad for You Baby*

Gary Moore onstage in London, England, 2007

BLUES FOR GREENY

One of the most famous transactions in rock and roll history took place between Moore and Peter Green. Amid his exit from Fleetwood Mac and subsequent breakdown, Green sold his 1959 Gibson Les Paul to Moore, sensing it would be in good hands. The ax is known for its "nasal" quality, the result of a neck inexpertly rewired with Fender wire by an inexperienced technician. Moore lovingly protected the guitar, using it frequently on several albums.

Green's interest in Moore dates back to the early days of Skid Row, when the young band served as opening act to Fleetwood Mac. Green was quite impressed with the band and talked his recording company into signing them as well.

Moore's association with Gibson continues today; in 2008 the company issued the Gary Moore Les Paul BFG, a simple but powerful model that sports a vintage look.

Moore performing with Thin Lizzy in London, 1978

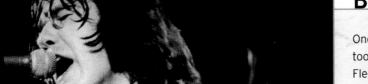

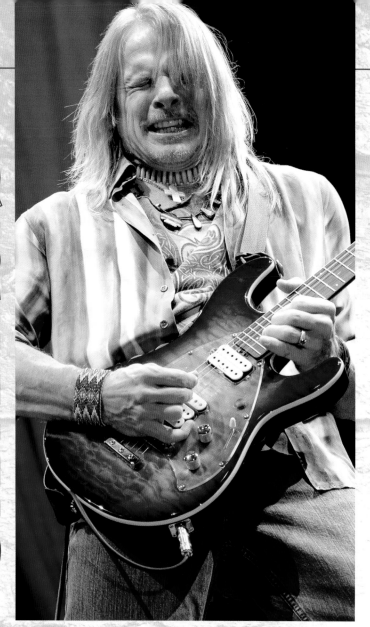

STEVE MORSE

essential albums

WITH THE DIXIE DREGS

1977	*Free Fall*
1977	*The Great Spectacular*
1978	*What If*
1979	*Night of the Living Dregs*
1980	*Dregs of the Earth*
1981	*Unsung Heroes*
1982	*Industry Standard*
1988	*Off the Record*
1989	*Divided We Stand*
1992	*Bring 'Em Back Alive*
1994	*Full Circle*
2000	*California Screamin'*

WITH THE STEVE MORSE BAND AND SOLO

1984	*The Introduction*
1985	*Stand Up*
1989	*High Tension Wires*
1991	*Southern Steel*
1992	*Coast*
1995	*Structural Damage*
2000	*Major Impacts*
2002	*Split Decision*
2005	*Prime Cuts*
2009	*Outstanding in Their Field*

Steve Morse (born July 28, 1954, in Hamilton, Ohio) is a founding member of the Dixie Dregs, a former member of Kansas, and the lead guitarist in Deep Purple.

Morse's musical beginnings took off in tandem with his brother Dave's. Together Steve and Dave played in a handful of bands in Michigan and Georgia. Dixie Grit, focused on covering Cream and Led Zeppelin songs, formed in the late 1960s, but the project was short-lived, eventually morphing into the Dixie Dregs while Morse was still in high school.

As a student in the University of Miami's top music program, Morse explored his skills as a composer, and with many of his Dregs bandmates continued recording and put together a demo in 1975.

By 1976 a reconfigured Dixie Dregs was signed to Capricorn Records, the home of the Allman Brothers Band. Perfecting a Southern rock and folk sound, the band released several albums in the late 1970s, but none of them translated into an explosive hit. The Dixie Dregs switched labels and, in 1980, released *Dregs of the Earth*, a Morse-helmed, jazz-influenced record. Under pressure from its label, the band became simply the Dregs and added vocals over the instrumental work in an effort to appeal to a wider audience. Morse's playing was widely lauded, but the band struggled against the commercial pressures that they were subject to and broke up in 1983.

In 1984 Moore recruited a bassist and drummer and began recording and touring as the Steve Morse Band, an endeavor that produced two albums: 1985's *Stand Up* featured Peter Frampton and Eric Johnson.

The year 1986 marked Morse's debut with Kansas, and his work appears on two of the band's albums. Deep Purple also recruited Morse in 1993 to replace Ritchie Blackmore.

Living Loud is Morse's 2003 side project, and he continues to record as a solo artist.

WITH KANSAS

1986   *Power*
1988   *In the Spirit of Things*

WITH DEEP PURPLE

1996   *Purpendicular*
1998   *Abandon*
1999   *Live at the Royal Albert Hall*
2001   *Live at the Rotterdam Ahoy*
2001   *The Soundboard Series*
2003   *Bananas*
2005   *Rapture of the Deep*
2007   *They All Came Down to Montreux*

WITH LIVING LOUD

2003   *Living Loud*

THE MORSE EFFECT

Steve Morse is the quintessential guitarist's guitarist, perennially faring very well in readers' polls by several prominent magazines (*Guitar Player*, for example). He is known for his chameleonlike talent in multiple styles of playing, as well as his technical prowess as an arranger and composer, bringing a level of complexity and sophistication to his instrumental work that is seldom seen in guitar-based music.

Morse has endorsed a Music Man namesake model, based on the guitar he built himself during college from Fender and Gibson parts, constantly tweaking it in his early days to get the right sound and feel. In the 1980s Morse collaborated on the commercial model of the famous instrument, and it's now a keystone of Music Man's lineup.

DEEP PURPLE

With Morse's arrival in 1993, some sense of stability was restored to one of the world's greatest hard rock bands. By 1996 Deep Purple was recording and touring again with a vengeance, releasing *Purpendicular* and *Abandon* in quick succession. In 2000 the band released *Live at Albert Hall*, a unique hybrid of recorded live material and solo hits from the band's members. The bulk of the performance consisted of the "Concerto for Group and Orchestra," a massive work Deep Purple staged in the late 1960s, the score for which was lost and recreated thirty years later for this event.

Founding member Jon Lord decamped in 2002; Ian Paice is the only original member remaining. On the heels of several recent releases, the band continues to tour and sell out around the world. Deep Purple is known for its massive live show, often running neck and neck in terms of ticket sales with bands like the Rolling Stones—a tradition that has continued in earnest during Morse's tenure.

Roger Glover and Steve Morse of Deep Purple jam onstage in Toronto, 2005.

RICK NIELSEN

R ick Nielsen (born December 22, 1946, in Rockford, Illinois) is the lead guitarist and chief songwriter for hard-edged power pop band Cheap Trick.

Nielsen spent the early 1970s with a few bands, none of which found much success. Sick Man of Europe eventually became Cheap Trick after a European tour in 1973, coming to dominate the prevailing power pop scene in the United States. Cheap Trick began backing bigger bands like Kansas, Queen, and Santana, eventually being chosen to tour with Kiss on their 1977 tour.

Immensely popular in the United States, the band did well in Japan as well, visiting that country for the first time in 1978. The Japanese tour resulted in the hit album *Live at Budokan*, a record that was initially available in the United States only as an import. When it finally dropped in the United States in 1979, it hit No. 4 on the charts.

Nielsen is known for his distinctly campy—almost comically so—stage wardrobe, consisting of bow ties, caps, and checkered patterns, as well as his massive stable of dazzling, customized guitars, including a handful of behemoths with five necks.

essential albums

WITH CHEAP TRICK

1977	*Cheap Trick*
1977	*In Color*
1978	*Heaven Tonight*
1979	*Dream Police*
1980	*Found All the Parts* (EP)
1980	*All Shook Up*
1982	*One on One*
1983	*Next Position Please*
1985	*Standing on the Edge*
1986	*The Doctor*
1988	*Lap of Luxury*
1990	*Busted*
1994	*Woke Up With A Monster*
1997	*Cheap Trick*
2003	*Special One*
2006	*Rockford*
2009	*The Latest*

"I've said it plenty of times before but I think the song dictates what you need. You can put the kitchen sink on something if you really want to but if the song wants it, the song deserves it. Or if the song deserves nothing, give it nothing. If one guitar sounds great, why have twelve?"

—RICK NIELSEN, 2009

CHEAP TRICK & BUDOKAN

Comparisons to the Beatles are sometimes made, if not for the sonic similarities, then definitely for the reputation Cheap Trick has enjoyed abroad, especially in Japan, where they were famously greeted in 1978.

The band's formation can be traced to the early 1960s. Rick Nielsen was a Midwestern boy with an interest in music and collecting guitars, and the bands he led cycled through several iterations before arriving at the lineup that would be dubbed Cheap Trick.

It wasn't until its smash success in Japan that fans in the United States began taking notice. The bands's first records failed to move many copies, but the Japanese-only Budokan ("I Want You to Want Me") became an overnight legend, and fans succeeded in pushing the label to release it stateside.

Dream Police, released in 1979, was received with less fervor, but it was notable for showcasing a harder-edged sound that the band would adapt to sold-out arena and stadium shows through the 1980s.

All Shook Up played on Cheap Trick's associations with the Beatles; legendary Beatles producer, George Martin, worked on the album, and the band would go on to collaborate with John Lennon and Yoko Ono, covering a Beatles tune for their 1980 EP *Found All the Parts*.

The rest of the 1980s saw tensions within the band reach a head; not one, but two bassists were replaced. Cheap Trick also struggled with creative expansion, all the while trying to maintain the appeal of its earlier sound. Several of the band's singles gained exposure on popular film sound tracks, but for the most part, the band's releases fizzled.

Members of Cheap Trick pose for a publicity shot at the height of their Budokan popularity in the late 1970s to early 1980s. From left: Robin Zander (lead vocals, rhythm guitar), Rick Nielsen (lead guitar, backing vocals), Bun E. Carlos (drums, percussion), and Tom Petersson (electric bass, backing vocals).

Lap of Luxury turned things around in 1988, generating a string of hits that were more in line with popular late-1980s style music. The ensuing decade was full of ups and downs. Cheap Trick switched labels several times and released a backlog of older hits and live material in an attempt to capitalize on its famous live shows and win over a new audience.

Most recently the band has focused on releasing its own music, a combination of new songs and rerecorded classics. Notable recent projects include its 2008 release of a collector's edition tribute to the thirtieth anniversary of its appearance at Budokan, as well as a live reinterpretation of the Beatles' classic *Sgt. Pepper's Lonely Hearts Club Band*.

JIMMY PAGE

"My vocation is more in composition really than anything else—building up harmonies using the guitar, orchestrating the guitar like an army, a guitar army."

—JIMMY PAGE

Jimmy Page (born January 9, 1944, in Heston, Middlesex, England) is one of the forefathers of heavy metal, having gotten his start with the Yardbirds and finding fame as a member of Led Zeppelin.

The young Jimmy Page literally discovered a guitar that its previous owner had abandoned in the house his family moved into in the mid-1950s. He was playing proficiently by the age of 13, mainly self-taught.

During a scattered period of gigging and busking, Page came down with serious illness and was forced to take a break from the road. He enrolled in art school as a painter until he regained his energy and strength. Still, even at school, Page would jam with other musicians—including Jeff Beck and Eric Clapton—at London's Marquee Club. It was at the Marquee that he got his first offer to play studio work.

Page developed a reputation as a reliable workhorse session musician in the 1960s, kept on retainer by a large stable of popular acts, including Donovan, the Kinks, the Rolling Stones, and the Who.

Page succeeded Jeff Beck as lead guitarist of the Yardbirds in 1966, but internal tensions drove him to set off on his own the following year. With singer Robert Plant, drummer John Bonham, and bassist John Paul Jones, Page formed Led Zeppelin and released *Led Zeppelin* in 1969. The record, showcasing Page's daring and skill as a soloist, was an instant success and brought the new band a lengthy residency on the charts, as well as an extensive tour on two continents.

The immediate follow-up, *Led Zeppelin II*, was another success, as were *Led Zeppelin III* and *Led Zeppelin IV*, released in 1971. The fourth album brought "Stairway to Heaven" to the world, the ubiquitous track that has served as a touchstone song—and a punch line, at times—ever since.

The late 1970s saw the band meet with a number of obstacles that led to its breakup in 1980. Ever since, Page has taken the reins of several film sound track projects and collaborated with former bandmate Plant. The most recent Zeppelin reunion took place in 2007 in London, featuring Jason Bonham, the late John Bonham's son, on percussion.

Awards and Honors

1992 Inducted into the Rock and Roll Hall of Fame, with the Yardbirds

1995 Inducted into the Rock and Roll Hall of Fame, with Led Zeppelin

2003 Ranked No. 9 on *Rolling Stone*'s list of the 100 Greatest Guitarists of All Time

Right: Page leaves his handprints to inaugurate London's "Walk of Fame" at Piccadilly Circus in London, 2004.

Below: Page in concert, 1973

essential albums

LED ZEPPELIN

1969	*Led Zeppelin*
1969	*Led Zeppelin II*
1970	*Led Zeppelin III*
1971	*Led Zeppelin IV*
1973	*Houses of the Holy*
1975	*Physical Graffiti*
1976	*Presence*
1979	*In Through the Out Door*
1982	*Coda*

LIVE

1976	*The Song Remains the Same*
1997	*BBC Sessions*
2003	*How the West Was Won*

SOLO

1988	*Outrider*

PAGE THE HOMEBODY

Success in the entertainment world always guarantees access to the most lavish dwellings available, but Page is a real estate enthusiast with a unique appreciation for unusual and historic structures. He has owned several well-known English properties, each with a story all its own.

In 1972 Page purchased the William Burges–designed Tower House in London, a gothic-style stone edifice with a graceful turret. The Tower House remains his primary residence.

For 24 years Page owned the Mill House in Windsor, famous as John Bonham's place of death.

Page once owned the Boleskine House, well-known for its mystical associations and as the former residence of occultist Aleister Crowley. The house also appeared in Led Zeppelin's film *The Song Remains the Same*.

Left: Page, 1980

Below: Page at the Mojo Awards ceremony in London to collect the Best Live Act Award for Led Zeppelin, 2007

"I think . . . the quality of musicianship of the band has given it the longevity. I thought the music would endure, I didn't think I would. I always thought I'd be dead by 30 then dead by 40 and on and on. Now I'm 55 so I didn't even die at 50."
—JIMMY PAGE

PAGE'S SKILL

Page is noted as an enterprising guitarist as well as an innovative studio technician and producer. Not afraid to take chances with new or unusual equipment, Page has played guitar with a cello bow and wielded a formidable Gibson double-necked ax.

During his tenure with Led Zeppelin, Page was responsible for expanding the band's sound by bucking conventional studio wisdom and returning to a 1950s-based style of ambient recording, which hinged on the placement of many different microphones at various distances from the instruments within the recording space. Page also claims to have originated and perfected the use of reverb, or backwards playback.

Page is an insatiable collector of guitars, reckoning to own more than 1,500 assorted axes.

Above: Led Zeppelin in 1970, from left, Jimmy Page, Robert Plant, and John Bonham

Right: From left, Robert Plant, Jimmy Page, John Bonham, and John Paul Jones of Led Zeppelin, 1969

JOE PERRY

essential albums

WITH AEROSMITH
1973   *Aerosmith*
1974   *Get Your Wings*
1975   *Toys in the Attic*
1976   *Rocks*
1977   *Draw the Line*
1979   *Night in the Ruts*
1985   *Done with Mirrors*
1987   *Permanent Vacation*
1989   *Pump*
1993   *Get a Grip*
1997   *Nine Lives*
2001   *Just Push Play*
2004   *Honkin' on Bobo*

THE JOE PERRY PROJECT
1980   *Let the Music Do the Talking*
1981   *I've Got the Rock 'n' Rolls Again*
1983   *Once a Rocker, Always a Rocker*
1999   *The Music Still Does the Talking: The Best of the Joe Perry Project*
2009   *Have Guitar, Will Travel*

SOLO
2005   *Joe Perry*

Joe Perry (born September 10, 1950, in Lawrence, Massachusetts) is the lead guitarist of Aerosmith, the best-selling American hard rock band of all time.

Perry grew up in a middle-class Portuguese-Italian-American family and attended boarding school in Vermont. Inspired by the Rolling Stones, Perry formed the Jam Band with childhood friend Tom Hamilton, who would help him form Aerosmith in 1970, along with Steven Tyler. Aerosmith's first records met with success, and the band quickly gained a following composed mostly of males—known collectively as the "Blue Army" because of their penchant for head-to-toe denim. Perry and Tyler earned monikers of their own—the "Toxic Twins"—owing to their onstage antics and legendary backstage partying and drug use. By 1979 the fast lane had taken its toll on Aerosmith, and tensions within the group led to its demise, sending Perry off in his own direction.

Perry immediately put together the Joe Perry Project and released *Let the Music Do the Talking* in 1980, an album that mined some unproduced Aerosmith material to which Perry had claim. Though album sales were respectable, the Project was renowned mainly for its energetic concerts. Later albums failed to gain much traction, and Perry agreed to an Aerosmith reunion in 1984.

The year 1998 was a banner one for Aerosmith, its major comeback hinging on the hit single "I Don't Want to Miss a Thing" and an extensive tour.

Still active with Aerosmith, Perry has released two solo albums and a record with a revived Joe Perry Project in 2009.

PERRY & HIS SOUND

Perry has long been associated with the Gibson Les Paul. Gibson first honored him in the 1990s with a signature Joe Perry model in a slick black finish, which was updated in 2004. The new model is emblazoned with Perry's infamous "boneyard" logo and finished with a wild tiger-stripe pattern.

One of Perry's signatures is his unique technique on bass guitar, which he plays like a normal axe, bringing an edgy, growling sound to the forefront of many of his recordings.

Perry has voiced a diverse set of influences, including the early work of Fleetwood Mac, Jeff Beck, Jimi Hendrix, and Queen.

Perry's distinct riffs, rooted in the blues, are part of rock and roll history. He has called his work on *Let the Music Do the Talking* his favorite.

Awards and Honors

2001 Inducted into the Rock and Roll Hall of Fame, with Aerosmith

2003 Ranked No. 48 on *Rolling Stone*'s list of the 100 Greatest Guitarists of All Time

Joe Perry still gives his all when performing live onstage.

AEROSMITH

The quintessential American rock band, Aerosmith's Boston-flavored formula of blues, rock, and heavy metal has translated into major success—the band has moved nearly 67 million albums in the United States and more than 150 million worldwide. The band's story is pure rock and roll: meteoric rise to the top, drug-fueled infighting and breakup, followed by an even more glorious (and lucrative) reunion.

With the 1975 release *Toys in the Attic*, Aerosmith came out from under the shadow of such influences as Led Zeppelin and the Rolling Stones to prove that the band had a point of view and wasn't just a group of mimicking poseurs. *Rocks*, released in 1976, sold well and was equally acclaimed, but the next few albums met with lukewarm receptions.

The band experienced a nadir with the departure of Perry and rhythm guitarist Brad Whitford, but the entire band reunited in 1984 for an epic reunion tour. Its members still struggling with drugs, Aerosmith again found its footing in the late 1980s, recording a series of hits—"Dude (Looks Like a Lady)" and "Janie's Got a Gun"— and winning its first Grammy. By 1990 the members of Aerosmith were American darlings once again, appearing in the famous "Wayne's World" sketch on the comedy show *Saturday Night Live*.

The next decade was good to Aerosmith, allowing it several opportunities to record hit singles for films (*Armageddon,*

Charlie's Angels), play the Super Bowl (2001), and continue to tour. *Honkin' on Bobo*, the band's fourteenth proper album, which is composed primarily of covers, was released in 2004 and represented a return to a more unplugged, blues-based sound. A fifteenth album is anticipated, but on hold due to recent complications stemming from Steven Tyler's continuing prescription drug problems.

Brad Whitford, Steven Tyler, and Joe Perry of Aerosmith performing at the National Football League kickoff in Washington, D.C., 2003

JOHN PETRUCCI

"I mean, obviously, you have to be in top shape. The way that we look at it, and the way it feels, is that every time we perform a concert there's an element that's almost like a gymnastics event. You have to put all of your focus and concentration into getting all of these different routines as perfect as you can. So it takes a lot of preparation and a lot of constant maintenance of your chops and everything. You can't just have a couple of beers and not practice and then go onstage."

—JOHN PETRUCCI, ON PLAYING LIVE, 2008

John Petrucci (born July 12, 1967, in Long Island, New York) provides his services as guitarist to progressive metal group Dream Theater.

Hooked on guitar since age 12, Petrucci developed a rigorous regimen of practice that has served as his musical foundation ever since. Though he attended the elite Berklee College of Music, Petrucci is mainly self-taught on guitar. He formed Dream Theater with a crew of high school and college friends. After a few lineup changes, the band finally found success in 1992 with *Images and Words*, even managing to secure airplay for its single "Pull Me Under" on MTV and radio.

The band's success led to worldwide acclaim for Petrucci's stylings, immediately recognized as some of the most technically proficient metal guitar playing ever.

A 2001 appearance on Joe Satriani and Steve Vai's G3 tour exposed Petrucci to an even larger base of potential fans and led to his first solo release, *Suspended Animation*. Petrucci has been a fixture on the G3 circuit ever since. Petrucci is also behind Liquid Tension Experiment, a side project he helms with several of his Dream Theater bandmates.

Petrucci swears by Music Man guitars, and he developed a signature model that bears his name with the company.

essential albums

WITH DREAM THEATER

1989	*When Dream and Day Unite*
1992	*Images and Words*
1994	*Awake*
1997	*Falling Into Infinity*
1999	*Metropolis, Pt. 2*
1999	*Scenes From a Memory*
2002	*Six Degrees of Inner Turbulence*
2003	*Train of Thought*
2005	*Octavarium*
2007	*Systematic Chaos*
2008	*Chaos in Motion 2007–2008*
2009	*Black Clouds & Silver Linings*

SOLO

2000	*An Evening with John Petrucci and Jordan Rudess*
2005	*Suspended Animation*

DREAM THEATER

With the exception of 1992's attention-grabbing "Pull Me Under," Dream Theater has largely remained in the American music underground. Respected for its technical prowess and dedication to craft, the band's members are frequently recognized for their talents across the board.

Several of Dream Theater's albums have done well on the U.S. charts, perhaps not finding the success of larger metal-based acts that have enjoyed the benefit of endless exposure on MTV and FM radio. *Black Clouds & Silver Linings*, released in 2009, debuted at No. 6 and No. 1 in the United States and Europe respectively, representing a career best for the band.

The band in its early incarnations struggled through financial difficulties and internal creative differences. With the hiring of Canadian singer James LaBrie and the successful recording of new material that would become *Images and Words*, the band trod onto solid ground, launching an extensive Dream Theater tour that spanned the United States, Europe, and Japan.

Awake in 1994 would mark a darker turn for the band, coinciding with the departure and eventual replacement of its keyboardist. A few years of work led to 1997's *Falling Into Infinity*, a confused endeavor that seemed to represent the band's "mainstream" effort. Morale within Dream Theater was stretched by this time, and the members talked—though not publicly—of breaking up.

The 1999 album *Metropolis Pt. 2* and accompanying world tour was a second chance for the band. The album didn't experience blockbuster sales, but its music was heralded as some of the band's best work. Wresting more creative control from its label, the band fulfilled a long-standing wish and released a double album in 2002, *Six Degrees of Inner Turbulence*.

The band's recent releases and tours have succeeded in expanding its reach to a larger, more diverse audience while maintaining its spirit of musical risk-taking and exploration. Notable projects have included *Greatest Hit (. . . and 21 Other Pretty Cool Songs)*, a jab at their one-time MTV glory, as well as smash shows at such esteemed venues as New York City's Radio City Music Hall. The band still commands as much awe as ever for its unpredictable yet meticulous live shows—out of respect for its repeat-attending fans, every set list is unique to that performance.

Dream Theater performs live on the main stage as part of the Download Festival 2009 at Castle Donnington, Derbyshire, England. At right is John Petrucci on guitar; at left is John Myung on bass.

EXPERT & TEACHER

Citing David Gilmour, James Hetfield, and Steve Morse among his largest influences, Petrucci is known for practicing a speedy, two-handed approach to picking. His formal music education has allowed him to excel as a teacher, too: he appears on an instructional guitar video called *Rock Discipline*, and his columns have been printed in *Guitar World* magazine.

With the Ernie Ball/Music Man company, Petrucci has been known to run instructional clinics and master classes for aspiring and accomplished musicians.

KEITH RICHARDS

"It's those nights you forget, but you know what happened because there are fifteen other people telling you that you were hanging naked upside down from the chandelier. The other best bit is the morning after, when you wake up and realize you've had a great time. I mean drugs have got really nothing to do with life. Drugs are there if you want them, and it's not a big fucking deal."

—KEITH RICHARDS, 2007

Keith Richards (born December 18, 1943, in Kent, England) is the rhythm guitarist and a songwriter in the Rolling Stones. Regularly showered in superlatives and ranked near the top of every list concerning rock and roll, Richards is one of music's most iconic characters.

Richards grew up in a musically supportive family; his grandfather was a big band jazz musician, and his mother purchased him his first guitar. As a student Richards was involved in the school choir, at one point performing for Queen Elizabeth II.

Richards transferred to art school in 1959, fully throwing himself into studying the guitar and meeting several characters along the way, one of whom would turn out to be Mick Jagger, his future Stones bandmate. The two immediately

bonded over their shared worship of American blues heroes like Chuck Berry and Muddy Waters, and they formed the Rolling Stones in 1962.

Richards has gained immortality in part for his full embrace of the rock star persona. As famous for his music as he is for his penchant for drugs, drinking, destructive—and sometimes downright strange—behavior, Richards's numerous skirmishes with the law are part of rock lore. Richards has been caught with cannabis and heroin on multiple occasions—but he's also known for his gentler, more academic pursuits and his extensive personal library. A consummate team player, Richards has taken few ventures into the realm of solo recording and performing, preferring instead to stick to his role as axman for one of the world's most important bands.

essential albums

WITH THE ROLLING STONES

1964	*England's Newest Hit Makers*
1964	*12 x 5*
1965	*The Rolling Stones, Now!*
1965	*December's Children (And Everybody's)*
1965	*Out of Our Heads*
1966	*Aftermath*
1966	*High Tide and Green Grass*
1967	*Their Satanic Majesties Request*
1967	*Flowers*
1967	*Between the Buttons*
1968	*Beggars Banquet*
1969	*Through the Past Darkly*
1969	*Let It Bleed*
1970	*Get Yer Ya-Ya's Out!*
1971	*Sticky Fingers*
1971	*Hot Rocks 1964–1971*
1972	*Exile On Main St.*
1973	*Goats Head Soup*
1974	*It's Only Rock 'n' Roll*
1975	*Made in the Shade*
1975	*Metamorphosis*

1976	*Black and Blue*
1977	*Love You Live*
1978	*Some Girls*
1980	*Emotional Rescue*
1981	*Sucking in the Seventies*
1981	*Tattoo You*
1983	*Undercover*
1984	*Rewind (1971–1984)*
1986	*Dirty Work*
1989	*Steel Wheels*
1994	*Voodoo Lounge*
1997	*Bridges to Babylon*
1998	*No Security*
2000	*Flashpoint*
2005	*A Bigger Bang*
2008	*Shine A Light*
2009	*Stripped*
2009	*Live Licks*

SOLO

1988	*Talk is Cheap*
1991	*Main Offender*

Awards and Honors

1989	Inducted into the Rock and Roll Hall of Fame, with the Rolling Stones
2003	Ranked No. 10 on *Rolling Stone*'s list of the 100 Greatest Guitarists of All Time

Right: Keith Richards onstage with the Stones in Rio de Janeiro, Brazil, during the Voodoo Lounge World Tour, 1995

Left: Richards in the early 1960s

THE ROLLING STONES

The Stones were part of the "British Invasion" of the United States in the 1960s, but their sound has established the band as a riskier, edgier alternative to the equally popular Beatles. The band has also demonstrated some amazing longevity, continuing to record and tour today.

Richards is often hard to divorce from front man Mick Jagger, the flamboyant, indestructible Stones lead singer; together, the pair has provided a face for the band—and for rock and roll—for nearly fifty years.

Drawing inspiration from Muddy Waters, the fledgling band minted itself the Rolling Stones in 1962 and set to the business of securing gigs at clubs and pubs in London. After quickly convincing a label to sign them, the Stones released several singles and covers that became hits, finding success across the pond in the United States with a Buddy Holly cover in 1964. With success growing by the day on both sides of the Atlantic, the Stones dropped "(I Can't Get No) Satisfaction," permanently establishing its members as rock and roll gods and commercial darlings.

The late 1960s were the beginnings of an experimental period for the Stones—not only musically, but with drugs. Albums like *Between the Buttons* and *Their Satanic Majesties Request* served up challenges to releases by the Beatles and other popular acts, and the Stones grew quite comfortable indulging in the dangerous, fast-track lifestyle to which they had gained access.

By 1969 the band had returned to a rawer, more rock-based style with some blues and country thrown in for good measure. *Beggars Banquet* was seen as a return to form, and it would be the last album recorded with the participation of guitarist Brian Jones; he died that year. A disastrous performance at Altamont led to the death of a fan, convincing the Stones to retreat from the public eye and focus on its upcoming material.

The 1970s brought more turmoil: Jagger grappled with his worldwide mega-celebrity, Richards tangled with substances, and Mick Taylor left the band, to be replaced by Ron Wood. Critically and musically, the band was up and down, contributing a handful of records and even taking a tentative dip into disco and punk (1978's *Some Girls*).

Since the 1980s members of the band have increasingly gone in their own directions; a rift between Richards and Jagger festered, but was eventually mended. A revitalized Stones resumed recording and touring in the late 1980s, and in the last decade have overseen several hit albums and a number of blockbuster tours around the world.

The Stones show no sign of slowing down—persistent rumors of continued tours refuse to be quieted.

The original members of the Stones pose for a publicity shot, about 1965. From left: Brian Jones, Keith Richards, Mick Jagger, Charlie Watts, Bill Wyman

Richards in 1966

"I SNORTED MY FATHER"

Without a doubt one of the most memorable—and strangest—Richards tale is his alleged treatment of his late father's ashes. During his life the two never enjoyed a perfect relationship; after Richards joined the Stones he didn't speak to his father for nearly twenty years.

In a 2007 interview with *NME* magazine, Richards explained that after accidentally spilling some of his father's ashes, he didn't want to brush them into the trash bin—so he snorted them like cocaine. A bit of explosive media coverage resulted from the confession, with Richards's flack attempting to frame the admission as a joke—but in a later interview, Richards assured everyone that he really did it, and "My dad wouldn't have cared."

"You've got the sun, you've got the moon, and you've got the Rolling Stones."

—KEITH RICHARDS, 2009

RICHARDS'S SIGNATURE STYLE

For all his headline-grabbing antics and excess, Richards has established himself as a relatively humble, straight-forward guitarist, always deferring and paying homage to the bluesmen who weaned him. He has always practiced a "weaving" technique along with the Stones's frequently changing lead guitarists.

In line with his back-to-basics cred, Richards's true passion lies with the acoustic guitar, and his playing can be heard on many classic Stones recordings, sometimes with subtle distortions. Richards is also recognized for his uncanny ability to "tame" guitars; regardless of the manufacturer or model, "Give me five minutes and I'll make 'em all sound the same."

A choirboy in his youth, Richards has made good use of his vocal talents with the Stones; he frequently shares lead singing duties with Mick Jagger.

Richards performs a solo during a Stones concert in Gothenburg, Sweden, 2007.

FRANCIS ROSSI

essential albums

WITH STATUS QUO

1977	*Live!*
1984	*Live At The N.E.C.*
1968	*Picturesque Matchstickable Messages*
1969	*Spare Parts*
1970	*Ma Kelly's Greasy Spoon*
1971	*Dog of Two Head*
1972	*Piledriver*
1973	*Hello!*
1974	*Quo*
1975	*On the Level*
1976	*Blue for You*
1977	*Rockin' All Over the World*
1978	*If You Can't Stand the Heat*
1979	*Whatever You Want*
1980	*Just Supposin'*
1981	*Never Too Late*
1982	*1+9+8+2*
1983	*Back to Back*
1986	*In the Army Now*
1988	*Ain't Complaining*
1989	*Perfect Remedy*
1991	*Rock 'Til You Drop*
1994	*Thirsty Work*
1996	*Don't Stop*
1999	*Under the Influence*
2000	*Famous in the Last Century*
2002	*Heavy Traffic*

Francis Rossi (born May 29, 1949, in London, England) is a founding member of British rock and boogie act Status Quo, known for his distinctive vocal style and role as lead guitarist with the group. Rossi has been a near-constant presence with the group, which enjoys status as a near-institution, largely in the UK.

Apart from his lengthy tenure with Quo, Rossi has contributed to a multitude of notable groups and projects. He covered the Beatles' "Getting Better" for the film *All This and World War II* in 1976, backed by the London Symphony Orchestra.

During Status Quo's 1980s hiatus, Rossi branched out on his own and found some success on the UK charts with collaborator and songwriting partner Bernie Frost. The partnership resulted in two singles and an album that has never actually been released. The pair would also work on concept album *Ships in the Night* with a handful of other artists.

In 1996 Rossi's solo career took a major step forward with the release of *King of the Doghouse*; he plans to follow up in 2010 with a second album.

Rossi favors a green original 1957 Telecaster that has been in his possession since 1968.

2003 *Riffs*
2005 *The Party Ain't Over Yet*
2007 *In Search of the Fourth Chord*

SOLO
1985 "Modern Romance
       (I Want to Fall in Love Again)" (Single)
1985 "Jealousy" (Single)
1996 *King of the Doghouse*

Awards and Honors

2010 Appointed Officer
       of the Order of
       the British Empire
       (OBE)

Rossi performing with Status
Quo at Wembley Arena, 2009

STATUS QUO

Status Quo resulted from the rubble and evolution of several bands Rossi started in his schooldays with friends Alan Lancaster and Rick Parfitt—by 1966 their efforts had paid off in a recording contract. Billing themselves as the Spectres, their first singles failed to gain much of a foothold.

It wasn't until 1967 that the guys decided to call themselves Status Quo, and with the name change came a shift in musical direction—Rossi and his bandmates had come to fully embrace the sound and aesthetic of psychedelia. The following year the band had hits with "Pictures of Matchstick Men" and "Ice in the Sun."

With sophomore album *Spare Parts*, the band faced an identity crisis when its psychedelic sound failed to make it a household name. In a major about-face, the band adopted a radically different sonic direction, taking a cue from other popular acts and going rock and roll. With the release of *Piledriver* in 1972, the band brandished a harder sound and started dressing in faded jeans.

The formula worked: the Quo would spend much of the 1970s at the top of the charts, mounting a regular series of raucous, well-attended performances. *Rockin' All Over the World*, released in 1977, was another highlight—but the band would soon hit a few bumps in the road. The mid-1980s saw the departure of John Coghlan, and the band also ran into trouble with Lancaster. Unhappy with his lot within the group, he relocated to Australia and attempted to prevent the remaining members from performing as Status Quo. The parties reached a settlement, and *In the Army Now* was released in 1986, faring quite well.

Through the last two decades, Status Quo's output has slowed but the band has regularly performed. *In Search of the Fourth Chord* was released in 2007, and a new studio album is in the works. The band has traditionally done very well in the UK, where it remains especially popular.

Status Quo on stage at the Colston Hall in Bristol, 2005. From left: Rick Parfitt, Francis Rossi, John "Rhino" Edwards, and Andrew Bown

RITCHIE SAMBORA

"You know, the great part about this band—and I think one of the reasons that people still come to see us—is because of the camaraderie of what we have together, you know? . . . Certainly, we survived all this—you know, shit, this hair-band criticism stuff—by just going out there and working hard and making good music and staying together. And I think . . . people want to see people stay together. . . . I mean, we still like each other. It's pretty unbelievable after twenty-two years."

—RICHIE SAMBORA, ON BON JOVI'S LONGEVITY, 2005

essential albums

WITH BON JOVI

1984	*Bon Jovi*
1985	*7800° Fahrenheit*
1986	*Slippery When Wet*
1988	*New Jersey*
1992	*Keep the Faith*
1995	*These Days*
2000	*Crush*
2002	*Bounce*
2005	*Have a Nice Day*
2007	*Lost Highway*
2009	*The Circle*

SOLO

1991	*Stranger in This Town*
1998	*Undiscovered Soul*

Richie Sambora (born July 11, 1959, in Perth Amboy, New Jersey) is the guitarist and contributing songwriter to American hair metal band Bon Jovi.

Sambora got into music as a child after Jimi Hendrix's passing, learning respect along the way for such legends as Jeff Beck, Jimmy Page, and Joe Perry. An early fascination with both classical music and Spanish guitar gave way to classic blues and rock; all of these influences have colored Sambora's output since. Before Jon Bon Jovi tapped him to take over Dave Sabo's spot in his band, Sambora had tried out for gigs with Kiss and Poison.

In the 1990s Sambora returned to his roots and went solo, releasing *Stranger in This Town*, a low-key affair that featured Eric Clapton. In 1998 he followed up with *Undiscovered Soul*, a record he paired with a global tour.

BON JOVI

Young musician Jon Bon Jovi was still struggling to find an outlet for his New York area–based band when he recruited Sambora in 1983 to play guitar. The band released its eponymous debut in 1984 after signing with Mercury Records, and the single "Runaway" became a success. The band began touring extensively in the mid-1980s, opening for acts like Kiss, the Scorpions, and ZZ Top.

Slippery When Wet, the band's third record, became a career-defining hit in 1986, spawning several No. 1 singles and rendering the band a household name with the help of heavy rotation on MTV. It did just as well with follow-up LP *New Jersey*, continuing to tour around the globe and boasting record-breaking ticket sales.

By the end of the 1980s, after a lengthy period of non-stop touring and success, the band members retreated to focus on their personal lives and solo efforts. A few years lapsed before 1992's *Keep the Faith*, considered to be the band's "growing up" album. More hits resulted, leading up to 1994's *Greatest Hits*.

Bon Jovi entered the mid-1990s with a new bassist, continuing to add layers of nuance and maturity to its sound. After *These Days*, the band took another break until it reunited in 2000 to release *Crush*, which earned several Grammy nominations.

In the last decade Bon Jovi has continued a string of blockbuster tours, breaking new ground in the studio as well as with a live album (released in 2001) and two successful country crossover efforts (*Have a Nice Day* in 2005 and *Lost Highway* in 2007). *The Circle*, released in 2009, promises an epic tour in 2010 that will take the band to thirty countries around the world.

SAMBORA'S GUITARS

A noted multi-instrumentalist, Sambora has lent his name and input to several custom axes over the years. Stemming from his preferences for Kramers in the 1980s, the company producer the Richie Sambora model from 1987 to 1989; the current incarnation is produced by MusicYo.

In 1991 Sambora worked with Fender to design a custom Strat in versions for both the U.S. and Japanese markets. Several modified models have followed, and Sambora continues a close association with the guitar company, with his collection containing more than forty Stratocasters.

Sambora has also worked with other guitar companies, such as ESP, Martin, Ovation, and Taylor, all of which have issued signature namesake models or custom jobs—in the case of Ovation, the company manufactured his double-neck acoustic-electric model.

Sambora onstage with Bon Jovi, 2006. From left: David Bryan, Sambora, Jon Bon Jovi, and Tico Torres

CARLOS SANTANA

Carlos Santana (born July 20, 1947, in Jalisco, Mexico) is a guitarist and solo musician best known for several iterations of his eponymous act and, in recent years, his popular collaborations with other pop and rock vocalists and musicians.

A pioneer in the genres of jazz fusion and salsa, Santana came to prominence in the late 1960s with a sound that combined the melody and spirit of traditional blues with the exotic (for the time) tones of Latin music.

Born to a musical family, Santana spent his early years in Mexico but eventually moved to San Francisco, where he finished high school in 1965. Santana demonstrated talent at both the guitar and violin by the age of eight and closely followed his idols, namely B.B. King, often attending live performances in Northern California.

Santana's first band found early success in the Bohemian milieu of late-1960s San Francisco, solidifying its early success with a highly visible performance at Woodstock in 1969.

After a period of relatively poor album sales and low visibility in the 1980s and early 1990s, Santana staged a dramatic comeback in the last decade with two highly successful albums, *Supernatural* and *Shaman*, featuring crossover collaborations with several popular vocalists, including Rob Thomas, Michelle Branch, Chad Kroeger, and Alex Band. These collaborations received extensive radio airplay and netted Santana a number of Grammy Awards.

"I have the courage to say I transcended and graduated being American or Mexican or all that kind of stuff. I have no allegiance or alliance to any flag or country. That to me is like Starbucks or Pepsi-Cola. It's just a business. It doesn't mean anything to me. My only alliance is to the heart of humanity, like Desmond Tutu, like the Dhali Lama, like Nobel Peace Prize women. You know, there comes a point where all that dying means is I graduated from being the little Mexican or the little American, into the universal concept of I'm not a drop of water anymore, I am part of the ocean. And if you can claim that, with humility, then you're able to create miracles."

—CARLOS SANTANA, 2006

From the beginning of his career, guitar virtuoso Carlos Santana has forged a unique sound that melds strains of rock, blues, jazz and Latin music.

SANTANA'S SPIRITUALITY

Evident in his catalog and playing style—and as a principle function of his formative years in the culture of 1960s San Francisco—Carlos Santana has explored various spiritual movements and themes in his life and music. Santana met fellow guitarist John McLaughlin in 1972, then involved with a fusion band called the Mahavishnu Orchestra. McLaughlin led Santana to study meditation with Sri Chinmoy, a spiritual guru.

Santana's spiritual explorations resulted in the formation of a new band, culling members from McLaughlin's group and featuring new members as well. The collaboration produced two albums, which received a lukewarm reception from Santana's label, CBS Records, due to the material's unwieldy scope and less-than-concrete themes.

By the early 1980s Santana's growing success pitted him against his mentor, Sri Chinmoy, who sought to impose restrictions on Santana's schedule and future decisions. In 1982 Santana, along with his wife, Deborah, broke their ties with Chinmoy, clearing the way for a period of freedom and further commercial success.

Santana rocking the house in Melbourne, Australia, 2003

"My job in this life is to give people spiritual ecstasy through music. In my concerts people cry, laugh, dance. If they climaxed spiritually, I did my job. I did it decently and honestly."

—Carlos Santana

essential albums

WITH SANTANA

1969	Santana
1970	Abraxas
1971	Santana III
1972	Caravanserai
1973	Welcome
1974	Lotus
1974	Borboletta
1976	Amigos
1977	Festival
1977	Moonflower
1978	Inner Secrets
1979	Marathon
1981	Zebop!
1982	Shango
1985	Beyond Appearances
1987	Freedom
1988	Viva Santana!
1990	Spirits Dancing in the Flesh
1992	Milagro
1993	Sacred Fire: Live in South America
1997	Live at the Fillmore '68
1999	Supernatural
2002	The Essential Santana
2002	Shaman
2005	All That I Am
2009	The Woodstock Experience

Santana has been making his magical music for more than forty years.

SANTANA'S AXES

Throughout his career, Santana has utilized an astonishing variety of instruments by various makers, in recent years becoming a champion and endorser of Paul Reed Smith guitars. Several models have been created to Santana's exact specifications, many incorporating his preference for a fretboard and neck made from solid Brazilian rosewood, responsible for Santana's instantly recognizable clear, ringing tone.

Awards and Honors

1988	Grammy Award for Best Rock Instrumental Performance (Orchestra, Group or Soloist), for "Blues For Salvador"
1999	Grammy Award for Record of the Year, for "Smooth," featuring Rob Thomas
1999	Grammy Award for Album of the Year, for *Supernatural*
1999	Grammy Award for Best Pop Performance by a Duo or Group with Vocal, for "Maria Maria"
1999	Grammy Award for Best Pop Collaboration with Vocals, for "Smooth" featuring Rob Thomas
1999	Grammy Award for Best Pop Instrumental Performance, for "El Farol"
1999	Grammy Award for Best Rock Performance by a Duo or Group with Vocal, for "Put Your Lights On," featuring Everlast
1999	Grammy Award for Best Rock Instrumental Performance, for "The Calling," featuring Eric Clapton
1999	Grammy Award for Best Rock Album, for *Supernatural*
2002	Grammy Award for Best Pop Collaboration with Vocals, for "The Game of Love," with Michelle Branch
2003	Ranked No. 15 on *Rolling Stone*'s list of the 100 Greatest Guitarist of All Time

Santana at the Cow Palace, a longtime venue for San Francisco concerts, on New Year's Eve, 1976. Santana began play professionally in the Bay Area in the 1960s.

PETE TOWNSHEND

Pete Townshend (born May 19, 1945, in London, England) is legendary for his tenure as guitarist and songwriter with the Who, one of the most important British bands of the last fifty years.

Townshend is just one of many musicians who benefited from the historic cross-pollination that was occurring between American and British bands during the mid-twentieth century. His saxophonist father and singer mother encouraged his interest in American rock, and his grandmother provided him with his first guitar, a modest Spanish model, when Townshend was 12.

By 1964 the nucleus of the Who had formed; a few false starts and experiments with other names led to a lineup that consisted of Townshend, front man Roger Daltrey, bassist John Entwistle, and drummer Keith Moon. The band's early appearances gave Townshend the chance to chisel his stage persona, incorporating wild, often violent dramatics, including his now-famous windmill guitar attack and frequent smashing of guitars.

Townshend's contributions to the Who's DNA are not limited to his playing on stage or in the studio; he is a songwriter of admirable skill, and the band has recorded more than 100 of his compositions. Townshend is also a pioneer in the rock opera genre—the revered *Tommy* is a prime example of his musical and narrative vision.

Technically, Townshend has shown himself to be an adept and enthusiastic explorer and risk-taker. Musicians commonly credit him with bringing both the synthesizer and feedback to the forefront of rock and roll—such respected players as Jeff Beck and Jimmy Page have publicly cited Townshend for doing so.

Outside his work with the Who, Townshend can lay claim to a notable solo career, as well as several expansive concept albums and rock operas. Townshend is also an accomplished writer and something of a cultural critic, having contributed to publications like *Rolling Stone*, acquiring a reputation for his articulate, lengthy interviews.

essential albums

WITH THE WHO

1965	*The Who Sings My Generation*
1966	*My Generation*
1966	*A Quick One*
1967	*The Who Sell Out*
1968	*Magic Bus—The Who On Tour*
1969	*Tommy*
1970	*Live At Leeds*
1971	*Meaty Beaty Big and Bouncy*
1971	*Who's Next*
1973	*Quadrophenia*
1974	*Odds And Sods*
1975	*The Who by Numbers*
1978	*Who Are You*
1979	*The Kids Are Alright*
1981	*Hooligans*
1981	*Face Dances*
1982	*Who's Last*
1982	*It's Hard*
1985	*Who's Missing*
1987	*Two's Missing*
1988	*Who's Better, Who's Best*
1993	*Talkin' 'Bout Their Generation*
1994	*30 Years of Maximum R&B*
1996	*Live at the Isle of Wight Festival 1970*
2000	*BBC Sessions*
2002	*The Ultimate Collection*
2003	*Live at the Royal Albert Hall*
2004	*Then and Now*
2006	*Endless Wire*
2009	*Greatest Hits*

SOLO

1972	*Who Came First*
1977	*Rough Mix*
1980	*Empty Glass*
1982	*All The Best Cowboys Have Chinese Eyes*
1983	*Scoop*
1985	*White City*
1986	*Deep End Live!*
1987	*Another Scoop*

1989	*The Iron Man: The Musical by Pete Townshend*
1993	*Psychoderelict*
1996	*The Best of Pete Townshend: Coolwalk-ingsmoothtalkingstraightsmokingfirestoking*
2000	*Lifehouse Elements*
2001	*The Oceanic Concerts*
2001	*Scoop 3*
2002	*Scooped*
2004	*Magic Bus—Live From Chicago*
2005	*Gold*

Awards and Honors

1983	BRIT Awards Life Achievement Award
1993	Tony Award Best Original Score for *The Who's Tommy*
1993	Grammy Award for Best Musical Show Album, for *The Who's Tommy*
2003	Ranked No. 50 on *Rolling Stone*'s list of the 100 Greatest Guitarists of All Time
2008	Kennedy Center Honors

Pete Townshend in 1989

THE WHO

The Who has stood the test of time to go down as one of history's most explosive and well-loved bands. After coming together in 1964, the band quickly built a following due to the strength of numerous, memorable singles and a jarring, guitar-smashing stage act. Only founding members Townshend and Daltrey are still alive and serve as the bearers of the band's legacy, which has left its mark on every genre from Britpop to punk to the concept album.

The band found early success with catchy singles, including "I Can't Explain" and "My Generation." Townshend's creative ambitions would take the band far beyond the realm of radio-friendly hits—with his leadership, the band entered a period of producing rock operas and concept albums, including *A Quick One* and *The Who Sell Out*.

As the Who's star rose, the band made a high-profile appearance at Central Park in New York City in 1968 with the Rolling Stones, and the notion of Townshend's role as a musical visionary was starting to gain popularity in the music press. *Tommy*, the rock opera the band had been laboring on, was finally unveiled to the public in 1969, at Woodstock, and its status as one of the world's best bands was secure.

Homer Simpson makes an appearance with the Who, complete with onstage acrobatics à la Townshend. From left: Townshend, Simpson, Entwistle, and Daltrey

The 1970s kicked off with the release of *Live at Leeds* and *Who's Next*, two of the band's most inspired albums. The latter marked the beginning of Townshend's love affair with the synthesizer, considered pioneering for the time.

In 1975 the film version of *Tommy* debuted, with Roger Daltrey in the title role. The film and Townshend's score went to rack up several Academy Award nominations. The decade came to a close on high and low notes—1978's release *Who Are You* was the band's best-performing effort to date, but drummer Keith Moon died not long after the record's release.

By the 1980s the stresses of fame were evident in the Who's remaining members. After albums in 1981 and 1982, the band members agreed to cut back on touring and instead focus on studio work, largely because of Townshend's struggles with drugs and alcohol. Townshend actually left the band in 1983, choosing to focus on his own ambitious solo work.

Through the rest of the 1980s and 1990s, members of the band staged various reunions but never officially reconstituted as the Who, even as fellow musicians, institutions, and the press were unanimously immortalizing the band as one of the world's greatest.

In 1999 the band made its first official, intact appearance since 1985 in Las Vegas. Well-received, the show inspired the Who to continue touring for several years in the United States and Europe, soldiering on even after bassist John Entwistle's death in 2002.

Endless Wire was released in 2006, the band's first record of new material in almost 30 years. The band has continued to tour in support of the album and its greatest hits.

The Who, 1979. From left: Roger Daltrey, John Entwistle, Keith Moon, and Townshend

FATHER OF THE ROCK OPERA

With 1969's *Tommy*, Townshend and the Who fused their music with a novel narrative and thematic structure that would prove to be one of the finest examples of the rock opera. Unapologetic in its reliance on characters and a narrative throughline, *Tommy* paved the way for copycats and similar works by the Kinks, Andrew Lloyd Webber, David Bowie, and Pink Floyd. Many of these projects have translated successfully into film or theater projects.

Right: In a scene from the 1975 version of *Tommy*, Eric Clapton, center, plays the role of the Preacher. At left (with cane) is Roger Daltrey as Tommy Walker. To Clapton's left is John Entwistle and to his right is Pete Townshend.

Below: Townshend readies himself to destroy something other than a guitar.

"No, it doesn't get to be a drag to talk about it. Sometimes it gets a drag to do it. I can explain it, I can justify it, and I can enhance it, and I can do a lot of things, dramatize it and literalize it. Basically it's a gesture which happens on the spur of the moment. I think, with guitar smashing, just like performance itself, it's a performance, it's an act, it's an instant and it really is meaningless."

—PETE TOWNSHEND,
ON GUITAR DESTRUCTION, 1968

ROBIN TROWER

"Too many young players today are basing what they're doing on somebody else. I've always said when anybody asked me what I would say to young guitar players starting out, I always say, 'Well, what worked for me, and I was very lucky in having a sense of this, not to copy anybody else's playing, not to sit down and work out other people's riffs and licks or whatever they're doing.' Obviously, you've got be influenced by people you really love, music, you know, you can't avoid that. What you need to do is sit down and find stuff of your own. You can't expect to find stuff on your own when you've just started."

—ROBIN TROWER, 2008

Robin Trower (born March 9, 1945, in London, England) is a guitarist associated with a handful of acts, most notably Procol Harum.

Trower's first endeavor of note was the Paramounts, a short-lived band he started in 1962. He briefly moved on to another group, the Jam, before settling in with Procol Harum. Trower appeared on five of the band's studio albums, but he eventually left for greener pastures.

In 1973, confident in his abilities and ready to flesh out his own style, he created the Robin Trower Band, a partnership that resulted in the well-received *Bridge of Sighs*, a 1974 release that paid sonic homage to Jimi Hendrix. *Long Misty Days* and *In City Dreams* followed, and while both were hits, neither matched up to his initial breakthrough.

In 1981 Trower partnered with Jack Bruce (formerly of Cream) to release two albums, but the union was temporary.

Trower's recent projects have seen him team up with past bandmates and collaborators, including members of Procol Harum as well as the earlier members of his eponymous band. Trower continues to tour and release music as the Robin Trower Band.

Trower usually sports a custom Fender Stratocaster, tuned one step below standard turning for his live appearances.

essential albums

WITH PROCOL HARUM

1967	*Procol Harum*
1968	*Shine on Brightly*
1969	*A Salty Dog*
1970	*Home*
1971	*Broken Barricades*
1991	*The Prodigal Stranger*
1995	*The Long Goodbye*

WITH THE ROBIN TROWER BAND

1973	*Twice Removed from Yesterday*
1974	*Bridge of Sighs*
1975	*For Earth Below*
1976	*Long Misty Days*
1977	*In City Dreams*
1978	*Caravan to Midnight*
1980	*Victims of the Fury*
1983	*Back It Up*
1985	*Beyond the Mist*

1987	*Passion*
1988	*Take What You Need*
1990	*In the Line of Fire*
1997	*Someday Blues*
2000	*Go My Way*
2004	*Living Out of Time*
2005	*Another Days Blues*
2009	*What Lies Beneath*

WITH BRYAN FERRY

1993	*Taxi*
2000	*Mamouna*
2007	*Dylanesque*

WITH JACK BRUCE

1981	*B.L.T.*
1982	*Truce*
2007	*Seven Moons*

PROCOL HARUM

Trower's old friend Gary Brooker from the Paramounts started the band Procol Harum in 1967. The unusual name, immortalized as the namesake for an asteroid, is said to be either a bastardization of a Latin phrase—or the name of someone's cat.

Before Trower came on board, the band scored big with "A Whiter Shade of Pale," a hit on both sides of the Atlantic. Trower joined up to record "Hornburg" and appears on the band's first five LPs. *Procol Harum* and *A Salty Dog*, two of the group's first official releases, fared respectably but failed to incite the excitement that revolved around the mammoth single "A Whiter Shade of Pale."

Trower advanced a blues-based sound with the band that often—but not always—complemented founder Brooker's more mainstream rock and roll intentions. The band's fifth album, *Broken Barricades*, marked Trower's last—he decamped in the early 1970s.

The band weathered a sea of ups and downs during the 1970s and 1980s, stabilizing a bit for a 1991 reunion and subsequent release of *The Prodigal Stranger*. Trower went his separate way again soon after, but Brooker—since 1995, the only original member—continues to helm the band.

The members of Procol Harum in 1967, from left: Dave Knights, Mathew Celestial-Smith, Robin Trower, Barrie James Wilson, and Gary Brooker

DEREK TRUCKS

"A lot of people that could go either way, they're kind of on the fence, if they hear enough pop music, that is what they're going to be listening to. I think it really destroys music in general because there is much less of a market for musicians that are really trying to do something. . . . I think it is very dangerous and very detrimental, the lack of musicianship out there and the lack of musical intelligence. I think once music and art goes in society, I don't think the rest is too much far behind."

—DEREK TRUCKS

Derek Trucks (born June 8, 1979, in Jacksonville, Florida) is a slide guitarist most frequently associated with the Allman Brothers Band. Trucks gained attention for his talent at an extremely young age—he managed to strike up a friendship with blues great Buddy Guy, and members of the Allman Brothers Band took him under their collective wing before anointing him a full-time member in 1999.

Trucks grew up on TABB's music, and his connections run deep—his uncle is a drummer and continues to perform with the band today. In TABB, Trucks has developed a partnership with Warren Haynes, the senior guitarist.

In 2006 Trucks got the chance to meet his idol, Eric Clapton, when he was recruited to assist with the recording of *The Road*

to Escondido, a collaboration that led to the Derek Trucks Band being selected to open for Clapton and Johnny Winter at a Chicago-area performance in 2007. Trucks and Clapton turned out to be ideal partners, and Trucks continued on the worldwide tour as a featured guest.

TABB staged an epic two-week performance in 2009 for their fortieth anniversary, which featured Trucks performing alongside legends like Trey Anastasio, Eric Clapton, Phil Lesh, and Johnny Winter.

Trucks's family life is deeply connected to his work as a musician. He is married to singer Susan Tadeschi, and the pair frequently perform and tour together as Soul Stew Revival, often with their young children in tow.

essential albums

WITH DEREK TRUCKS BAND

2009	*Already Free*
2006	*Songlines*
2003	*Soul Serenade*
2002	*Joyful Noise*
1998	*Out of the Madness*
1997	*The Derek Trucks Band*

WITH THE ALLMAN BROTHERS BAND

2000	*Peakin' at the Beacon*
2003	*Hittin' the Note*
2004	*One Way Out*

TRUCKS'S PRECOCIOUS TECHNIQUE

Trucks has prodigiously embraced all forms of music, but it is the blues and Southern rock he heard as a child that form the bedrock of his sound. Technically, Trucks is linked to the Sacred Steel movement, drawing inspiration from Duane Allman and Elmore James, both accomplished slide players. Eastern influences can also be detected in Trucks's playing with his namesake band, the result of his studying the sarod (similar to the sitar, but with a richer sound) and the music of Nusrat Fateh Ali Khan.

Trucks's tone is the toast of the guitar world, with accomplished players like John Mayer lauding its soulful sound. A Gibson player, Trucks seldom resorts to complex effects, instead relying on a straight, simple guitar-to-amp setup.

Awards and Honors

2003	Ranked No. 81 on *Rolling Stone*'s list of the 100 Greatest Guitarists of All Time
2010	Grammy Award for Best Contemporary Blues Album, for *Already Free*, with the Derek Trucks Band

Trucks, onstage with his resonator guitar, 2007

THE DEREK TRUCKS BAND

In 1994, already touring with TABB, Trucks established the Derek Trucks Band, a six-member project that remains intact today. The band has acquired a reputation as Trucks's more experimental outlet, with many of the members coming from diverse, global musical backgrounds and representing several generations. The band places a high value on improvisation and eclecticism—flute and a variety of African drums figure heavily across the band's eight official releases. Their ninth album, composed of live tracks, debuted in 2010.

Trucks playing with a slide on his Gibson SG

STEVE VAI

"We all have the ability to be inspired. It is just a matter of letting down certain defenses and letting inspiration come in and then acting upon it with courage. I think for people, who are like geniuses, it is always there. But when it comes to people like me, I kind of have to wait for the gods of inspiration to sprinkle some fairy dust on me or something. But once it's there, it is quite liberating."

—STEVE VAI, 2007

Steve Vai (born June 6, 1960, in Carle Place, New York) is a maverick guitarist with ties to Frank Zappa and is a founding member and regular player with the G3 tour. Since 1999, Vai has also helmed Favored Nations Records.

Vai is the one-time protégé and partner of Joe Satriani, with whom he leads the G3 tour. In 1979, after graduating from the Berklee College of Music, Vai won the attention of Frank Zappa and entered into a partnership as Zappa's transcriptionist and, later, as member of Zappa's band. Zappa came to rely on Vai to play some of his most technically challenging passages. Vai loved showing off his sight-reading skills—he was able to instantly play sheet music that he had never seen before.

In 1982 Vai went solo, releasing *Flex-Able*. The 1980s also saw Vai team up with the likes of David Lee Roth of Van Halen and the Sex Pistols' John Lydon, moves that would bring Vai much recognition.

Vai has continued work with his band through the 1990s and 2000s, also electing to focus on his unique compositions, often melding rock instruments and influences with classical structures. Vai enjoys a close relationship with Ibanez, having contributed to the research and design of several models, including a unique seven-string guitar.

Steve Vai on his signature Ibanez. His ax skills led Frank Zappa to use Vai as "stunt" guitarist, playing some of the trickier riffs on Zappa's recordings.

VAI THE VIRTUOSO

Vai is the rare rock and roller who also has music theory under his belt. His interest in classical arrangements and compositions has led to a number of collaborations around the world. In 2002 Vai performed in Japan with the Tokyo Metropolitan Symphony Orchestra in a massive concerto for electric guitar and orchestra by Ichiro Nodaira called "Fire Strings." The Metropole Orchestra in the Netherlands recognized Vai's brilliance in 2004, when they incorporated several of his works into a concert titled The Aching Hunger. Vai continued to compose in 2005, performing the Blossom Suite in Paris, a piece he wrote for classical and electric guitar.

More recently, Vai has appeared with the Hollywood Bowl Orchestra in Los Angeles during a concert series devoted to video game tunes. *Sound Theories*, Vai's latest classically influenced work, was released in 2007. The record features live material from his sessions with the Metropole Orchestra, and its track "The Attitude Song" was nominated for a Grammy in 2008.

essential albums

SOLO

1984	*Flex-Able*
1984	*Flex-Able Leftovers*
1990	*Passion and Warfare*
1993	*Sex & Religion*
1995	*Alien Love Secrets*
1996	*Fire Garden*
1999	*The Ultra Zone*
2000	*The 7th Song*
2001	*Alive in an Ultra World*
2002	*The Elusive Light and Sound, Volume 1*
2003	*The Infinite Steve Vai: An Anthology*
2004	*Live In London*
2005	*Real Illusions: Reflections*
2007	*Sound Theories*
2009	*Where the Wild Things Are*

Awards and Honors

1994	Grammy Award for Best Rock Instrumental Performance, for "Sofa"
2008	Grammy Award for Best Rock Instrumental Performance, for "Peaches En Regalia"

Vai onstage at G3 in Milan, Italy, 2005

EDDIE VAN HALEN

"I was 7 years old when we came to America with my mom, my dad, my brother, with fifty bucks and a piano. Who ever would have thought I would be a guitar god, you know? If I'm a guitar god, then my son would be Jesus, right? That means on the next tour, he'd have to walk on water."

—EDDIE VAN HALEN, 2009

essential albums

WITH VAN HALEN

1978	Van Halen
1979	Van Halen II
1980	Women and Children First
1981	Fair Warning
1982	Diver Down
1984	1984
1986	5150
1988	OU812
1991	For Unlawful Carnal Knowledge
1995	Balance
1998	Van Halen III

Eddie Van Halen (born January 26, 1955, in Nijmegen, Netherlands) is a Dutch–American musician who founded the hard rock group Van Halen.

Eddie's father, a musician, moved the family to Pasadena, California, when Eddie was 7. Along with his brother Alex, Eddie took up the piano and drums—but quickly grew frustrated and turned his attention to the guitar instead. Enthralled by Eric Clapton's guitar solos in his work with Cream, Van Halen devoted himself to getting drunk in his bedroom and practicing into the early hours of the morning.

Eddie and Alex formed Van Halen in 1972 with David Lee Roth, playing covers before venturing into original material. A few years later Gene Simmons caught a Van Halen show in Los Angeles and encouraged the band to record a demo, even offering his financial assistance. A studio contract followed,

and the band produced six albums in a short span of time. In 1984 the single "Jump" hit the No. 1 spot on the U.S. charts; even so, Eddie had reservations about the band's future—largely instilled by friction between him and Roth.

Roth exited the band in 1985, and was replaced by Sammy Hagar, who brought with him a new sound and new opportunities for Eddie to broaden his style.

Since the mid-1990s, Van Halen has been without a permanent lead singer; Gary Cherone took a stab at the gig after Hagar's departure, and both Hagar and Roth have returned to contribute to greatest hits albums and a 2007–2008 reunion tour, respectively. In 2006, Eddie Van Halen's son, Wolfgang, joined the lineup on bass.

In 2009, after his divorce from actress Valerie Bertinelli, Van Halen married for the second time and now keeps a low profile.

EDDIE'S STYLE

Eddie Van Halen is known for his extremely varied, technical, self-taught style that relies heavily on a technique known as "tapping", in which both hands remain on the fretboard. His solo in "Eruption" is often considered one of the best in rock.

Tapping has a history in American music that's difficult to trace. Jazz guitarists in the 1950s and 1960s pioneered the technique, which made its way into mainstream rock and roll via any number of musicians, who were beginning to experiment with the technique and adapt it to a wide variety of sounds and styles. Van Halen has mentioned Jimmy Page as a possible inspiration behind his technique, which he didn't employ widely until the late 1970s.

Van Halen has described his sound as "brown"—a tone that is, at the same time, the result of his unique technical setup and something deeply personal.

Known for breaking established conventions and musically experimenting to a high degree, Van Halen regularly employs distorted chords that are rare in rock, and he demonstrates a flair for manipulating dynamics and volume, which results in a sound that mimics other instruments, including the organ and piano.

A Peavey Wolfgang Special: Eddie van Halen signature model

Awards and Honors

1992 Grammy Award for Best Hard Rock Performance, for *For Unlawful Carnal Knowledge*, with Van Halen

2003 Ranked No. 70 on *Rolling Stone*'s list of the 100 Greatest Guitarists of All Time

Eddie Van Halen at the Emmy Awards, 1993

EDDIE'S EQUIPMENT

The famous striped red, white, and black "Frankenstrat" pattern appears on many of his guitars, inspired by the original art he applied to the guitar he assembled himself from both Fender and Gibson parts. The Frankenstrat design lives on in a series of commercial replicas manufactured by Fender. Van Halen has also helped design the Peavey Wolfgang series, named in honor of his son.

Eddie Van Halen is something of an inventor—he holds U.S. Patent 4656917 for a "Musical Instrument Support"— a panel that attaches to a guitar and swings down to rest against the player's torso. The device orients the instrument perpendicular to the guitarist's body, enabling him to tap with ease and leaves him "free to explore the musical instrument as never before."

Eddie Van Halen shredding his guitar while playing with Van Halen, 1977

JACK WHITE

"When it all comes down to it, what I really want is folk music to still be around. It's a shame because the culture worldwide is becoming so affluent and so computerized, that all of that's really gonna go away . . . But that's all everyone talks about—why MTV's not good, why radio's not good. And the answer is really because whatever you want to call it—blues, country, folk—isn't around any more. That's why everyone's so mad, and I'm tired of it being my job to bring it back."

—JACK WHITE, 2004

Jack White (born John Anthony Gillis on July 9, 1975, in Detroit, Michigan) is one half of blues and rock group the White Stripes, the band he formed with his then wife, Meg, in 1996. Recognized for his talent as a back-to-basics rock and blues virtuoso, White is also a founding member of two supergroups, the Raconteurs and the Dead Weather, and is something of a film actor, having taken on small but memorable roles in a number of respected films.

Originally drawn to percussion at an early age, White gradually learned guitar as a child and teenager in a large family, playing in a number of local Detroit bands. Looking for something more, White found the ideal partner in Meg, an inexperienced drummer with a startling, raw attack. They joined forces as the White Stripes and advanced a confident, straightforward blues sound that immediately had the ear of critics and fans.

Though the Whites divorced in 2000, the band is still intact; a highly anticipated new album is rumored to have a 2010 release date. White married British model Karen Elson in 2005.

essential albums

WHITE STRIPES
1999	*The White Stripes*
2000	*De Stijl*
2001	*White Blood Cells*
2003	*Elephant*
2005	*Get Behind Me Satan*
2007	*Icky Thump*

WITH THE RACONTEURS
2006	*Broken Boy Soldiers*
2008	*Consolers of the Lonely*

WITH THE DEAD WEATHER
2009	*Horehound*

Awards and Honors

2003   Ranked No. 17 on *Rolling Stone*'s list of the 100 Greatest Guitarists of All Time

WHITE'S SIDE PROJECTS

White is the mastermind between two closely related super-groups, the Raconteurs and the Dead Weather. Formed in 2005 and 2009, both bands explore similar sounds with the benefit of four members versus the Stripes' two.

With the Raconteurs, success was immediate and the quartet secured a gig opening for Bob Dylan and a steady tour itinerary through 2008. The band's last album, *Consolers of the Lonely*, was Grammy-nominated.

White's own record label is responsible for producing the Dead Weather, still basking in the glow of its mid-2009 album which debuted near the top of the charts in the United States and the United Kingdom. Another record is said to be on the way, likely to be released in 2010.

Jack and Meg White of the White Stripes at the O2 Wireless Festival in London, 2007

WHITE'S SETUP

White's once famously simple setup as front man for the White Stripes has evolved as he has pursued new sounds and styles with his other groups. White still relies on his pair of two signature red and white 1965 Airline axes, originally cheap hobby models available to the public through mail-order. His rig is fleshed out with an array of effects pedals and other equipment, which he meticulously paints red or, when he appears with the Raconteurs, copper.

White is a capable multi-instrumentalist, proficient on drums, piano, keyboard, and mandolin. He has been known to dabble across the range of available instruments during recording sessions, making it difficult to ascertain for certain his exact contribution or playing on a record.

White, right, with Brendan Benson, performing with the Raconteurs

NEIL YOUNG

CRAZY HORSE

For his second solo album in 1969, Young recruited a backup band—guitarist Danny Wilson, bassist Billy Taylor, and drummer Ralph Molina, all formerly of the Rockets. They took the name Crazy Horse after the famous Sioux chief. In May 1969 the group released *Everybody Knows This Is Nowhere*, a showcase for Young's iconic guitar solos, which contained three monster songs, "Cinnamon Girl," "Cowgirl in the Sand," and "Down by the River." The album was recorded in just two weeks, and Young supposedly wrote all three songs on the same day while in bed suffering from a 103-degree fever.

Neil Young (born November 12, 1945, in Toronto, Ontario) is a musician and singer/songwriter known for his guitar expertise and for incorporating his political and personal beliefs into his music.

As a teen Young was influenced by rock and roll, doo-wop, R&B, country music, rockabilly, and especially by Elvis Presley. Although a childhood bout of polio left him with a slight weakness on his left side, that didn't prevent him from learning to play the guitar and forming two high school bands, the Jades and the Squires.

Young left Canada in 1966, lured by the protean music scene of Southern California, and formed the folk-rock band Buffalo Springfield with Steven Stills, Richie Furay, Dewey Martin, and fellow Canadian Bruce Palmer. The band's commentary on youthful protest, "For What It's Worth," became an enduring radio standard.

After internal conflicts split the band, Young turned to solo touring and recording, creating some of his most memorable songs, before joining the supergroup Crosby, Stills and Nash. Young's politics came to the forefront in their single, "Ohio,"

a musical eulogy to the Kent State students killed by the National Guard during a campus protest. The band's 1970 cover of Joni Mitchell's song "Woodstock"—from the album *Déjà Vu*—became the anthem of an entire generation.

The year 1970 also saw the release of Young's third solo effort, the breakthrough album *After the Gold Rush*, which addressed the drug culture, the environment, relationships, and racism. With the subsequent success of *Harvest*, *Rust Never Sleeps*, and later *Freedom*, *Harvest Moon*, and *Sleeps with Angels*, Young's status as a music legend was assured. His signature use of heavy feedback and electronic distortion was often cited as a major influence by grunge rockers.

In 1985 Young organized Farm Aid to benefit America's beleaguered farmers, and the decade ended on a high note for Young, with a single from the album *Freedom*, "Rockin' in the Free World," rising to No. 2 on the U.S. charts. The 1990s saw a return to his folk-rock roots with the release of the album *Harvest Moon*, which features vocals by Linda Ronstadt and James Taylor.

The new millennia brought with it a return to overt political and social themes, such as the single "Let It Roll," a tribute to the victims of the 9/11 terrorist attacks. *Living with the War*, released in 2006, was a wholesale condemnation of the war in Iraq, and even featured "Let's Impeach the President"—aimed at then commander in chief George W. Bush.

Under the name Bernard Shakey, Young has also directed five films, plus home video and DVD releases.

essential albums

Neil Young in concert at the Hammersmith Apollo, London, 2008

WITH BUFFALO SPRINGFIELD

1966 *Buffalo Springfield*
1967 *Buffalo Springfield Again*

SOLO ALBUMS

1968 *Neil Young*
1970 *After the Gold Rush*
1972 *Harvest*
1973 *Time Fades Away*
1974 *On the Beach*
1977 *American Stars 'N Bars*
1978 *Comes a Time*
1980 *Hawks and Doves*
1982 *Trans*
1985 *Old Ways*
1986 *Landing on Water*
1989 *Freedom*
1992 *Harvest Moon*
1995 *Mirror Ball* (featuring Pearl Jam)
2000 *Silver and Gold*
2005 *Prairie Wind*
2006 *Living with War*
2009 *Fork in the Road*

WITH CRAZY HORSE

1969 *Everybody Knows This Is Nowhere*
1975 *Zuma*
1979 *Rust Never Sleeps*
1981 *Re-ac-tor*
1990 *Ragged Glory*
1994 *Sleeps with Angels*
1996 *Broken Arrow*
2003 *Greendale*

WITH CROSBY, STILL, NASH AND YOUNG

1970 *Déjà vu*
1971 *Four Way Street*
1974 *So Far*
1988 *American Dream*
1999 *Looking Forward*

WITH THE STILLS-YOUNG BAND

1976 *Long May You Run*

"There's an edge to real rock 'n' roll. It's all that matters."

—NEIL YOUNG

Awards and Honors

1982 Inducted into the Canadian Music Hall of Fame
1994 Juno Award for Album of the Year, for *Harvest Moon*
1995 Inducted into the Rock and Roll Hall of Fame
1997 Inducted into the Rock and Roll Hall of Fame, with Buffalo Springfield
2001 Spirit of Liberty Award, People for the American Way
2003 Ranked No. 83 on *Rolling Stone*'s list of the 100 Greatest Guitarists of All Time
2007 A new species of trapdoor spider named *Myrmekiaphila neilyoungi*
2010 Person of the Year, Musicares

Young in Florence, Italy, 2008

POP MUSIC

Considered by some to be rock's younger, gentler sibling, "pop" handily describes the ubiquitous genre that is lighter, more accessible, and—of course—popular. The first pop acts took the best parts of rock and roll in the 1950s and 1960s, repackaging it all into easily digestible "singles," and traveled around the globe to wherever the fans were.

In the final decades of the twentieth century, pop became a force all its own with scores of young, savvy artists and practitioners harnessing the powers of the Internet and its promise of instant, constant exposure to recruit unheard-of quantities of fans—if only for a brief fifteen minutes. The pioneers of the genre have maintained their territory and relevance, standing as some of the highest-earning entertainers in the world.

SHERYL CROW

"[The Internet] hasn't really changed the way I write. Although I do love the idea that the worse things get, the more I feel like being an anarchist. . . . I love the idea that technology is changing things in a way that . . . well, in a climate where everything is about commerce in entertainment, it's creating a new way to get music heard. I think the days of trying to get music bought are probably behind us. I love the idea that there are so many ways to get the music out there."

—SHERYL CROW, 2008

Sheryl Crow (born February 11, 1962, in Kennett, Missouri) is a popular musician and activist known for her frequent collaborations with some of the music business's top figures.

Music has always been in Crow's blood. The daughter of a trumpet player and piano teacher, Crow actively participated in her high school and college music scenes. Her professional career began with a stint as an elementary school music teacher in Missouri, during which time she would pursue club gigs and commercial work in her off hours.

Crow scored a break when she was asked to tour with Michael Jackson in 1987. She spent two years on the road, and with the help of Phil Collins's producer, started piecing together a debut album. It wasn't until 1992, however, that Crow would release *Tuesday Night Music Club* with a roster of friends that made up her band. A huge hit, the album brought Crow three Grammys and instant fame.

Crow carved out her place as a premiere female singer and songwriter in the 1990s with *Sheryl Crow*, generating an uninterrupted string of hits and even greater accolades. *The Globe Sessions* was Crow's third album, containing "My Favorite Mistake," a single allegedly inspired by her stillborn relationship with Eric Clapton—a claim Crow has downplayed in interviews.

In the 2000s Crow launched a series of partnerships with such artists as Kid Rock, John Mayer, Stevie Nicks, Michelle Branch, Sting, and Johnny Cash, while compiling material for three new records as well as a greatest hits album. The mainstream press and celebrity gossip machine has frequently dissected the singer's personal life; Crow has been linked to elite athlete Lance Armstrong.

In 1999 Gibson honored Crow with a signature model, based on her prized 1962 Gibson Country Western acoustic and incorporating elements of the company's Hummingbird.

EARLY TRAGEDIES

Like many artists in a cannibalistic industry, Crow has had to fight against a tide of negative, often unfounded, accusations related to the ownership and origin of her own work. As a struggling singer and songwriter in 1990s Los Angeles, Crow counted herself among the members of a songwriting collective that would form the basis for her *Tuesday Night Music Club* debut. After a late night television performance of "Leaving Las Vegas" on David Letterman's show, Crow vaguely took credit for writing the song, when in fact friend David Baerwald was behind it. The resulting schism ended their relationship, and he tragically committed suicide soon after. Another member of the collective, former boyfriend Kevin Gilbert, died accidentally in 1996.

Left with little choice, Crow eschewed the remaining members of the group that helped her find fame and brought in her own producing team for her eponymous sophomore record. With a focus on Crow's own songwriting and compositions for guitar, *Sheryl Crow* was the unmistakable product of its namesake.

Awards and Honors

1993	Grammy Award for Best New Artist
1995	Grammy Award for Best Female Pop Vocal Performance, for "All I Wanna Do"
1995	Grammy Award for Record of the Year, for "All I Wanna Do"
1997	Grammy Award for Best Rock Album, for *Sheryl Crow*
1997	Grammy Award for Best Female Rock Vocal Performance, for "If It Makes You Happy"
1999	Grammy Award for Best Rock Album, for *The Globe Sessions*
2000	Grammy Award for Best Female Rock Vocal Performance, for "Sweet Child O' Mine"
2001	Grammy Award for Best Female Rock Vocal Performance, for "There Goes the Neighborhood"
2003	Grammy Award for Best Female Rock Vocal Performance, for "Steve McQueen"

Crow performing in London, 2008

essential albums

STUDIO

1993	*Tuesday Night Music Club*
1996	*Sheryl Crow*
1999	*The Globe Sessions*
2002	*C'mon C'mon*
2005	*Wildflower*
2008	*Detours*

LIVE

1999	*Sheryl Crow & Friends: Live From Central Park*
2008	*Wildflower Tour: Live in New York*

Crow performing at the 2008 Parkpop Festival in the Hague, Netherlands

DAVE DAVIES

"Good rock music always tends to be around."

—DAVE DAVIES

essential albums

WITH THE KINKS

1964	*The Kinks*
1965	*Kinda Kinks*
1965	*The Kink Kontroversy*
1966	*Face to Face*
1967	*Something Else by The Kinks*
1968	*The Kinks Are the Village Green Preservation Society*
1969	*Arthur (Or the Decline and Fall of the British Empire)*
1970	*Lola versus Powerman and the Moneygoround, Part One*
1971	*Muswell Hillbillies*
1972	*Everybody's in Show-Biz*
1973	*Preservation Act 1*
1974	*Preservation Act 2*
1975	*Soap Opera*
1976	*Schoolboys in Disgrace*
1977	*Sleepwalker*
1978	*Misfits*
1979	*Low Budget*
1981	*Give the People What They Want*
1983	*State of Confusion*
1984	*Word of Mouth*
1986	*Think Visual*
1989	*UK Jive*
1993	*Phobia*

SOLO

1980	*AFL1-3603*
1981	*Glamour*
1983	*Chosen People*
1998	*Purusha and the Spiritual Planet*
1999	*Fortis Green*
2001	*Fragile*
2002	*Bug*
2007	*Fractured Mindz*

Dave Davies (born February 3, 1947, in London, England) is a founding member of the Kinks. The youngest of eight children, Davies grew up being exposed to a wide variety of music, all of which would influence his later work with his band.

The Kinks, formed in 1963, composed of Davies' brother, Ray, and Peter Quaife, Dave's childhood friend. The band shot to fame a year later with the single "You Really Got Me," distinctive for its distorted riff, which resulted from Davies' deliberate butchering of the speaker cone inside his amplifier.

The band continued to record and tour through the 1960s, even as tensions within the band occasionally erupted, resulting in several violent onstage fights. Dave Davies' famously testy relationships with both his brother and bandmate Mick Avory would simmer for decades, finally resulting in Avory's departure from the band in 1985.

DAVIES AS SOLO ARTIST

At various times during the Kinks' up-and-down career, Davies set out on his own with several solo projects. His 1967 "Death of a Clown" single was credited with his name only, despite the fact that the song involved all the members of the Kinks. Davies was quickly offered a solo contract by his record company, but after the following two singles failed to gain traction, hesitant music execs pulled the plug on what would have been Davies' first solo album.

As a stand-alone act, Davies' momentum significantly slowed in the 1970s. His bandmates publicly noted Davies' preference for engineering and producing records at the Kinks' own Konk studio in London.

Davies returned to the studio in 1980 and that year released an album he called *AFL1-3603*, taking its name from the work's serial number. Notable for showcasing Davies' playing every instrument himself, *AFL1-3603* commenced an extended period of solo work marked by much new material, which Davies continues today.

Awards and Honors

1990 Inducted into the Rock and Roll Hall of Fame, with the Kinks

2003 Ranked No. 88 on *Rolling Stone*'s list of the 100 Greatest Guitarists of All Time

2004 Appointed Commander of the Order of the British Empire (CBE)

2005 Inducted into the UK Music Hall of Fame, with the Kinks

Dave Davies, right front, with the Kinks in 1965. From left, Pete Quaife, Ray Davies, and Mick Avory

THE FLYING V

Davies is credited with bringing the Gibson Flying V back into style in the mid-1960s. After baggage handlers lost his favored custom-built Guild in 1965, Davies purchased a dusty, forlorn Flying V in an American guitar shop for about $60. This particular guitar has since won a following that includes the likes of Jimi Hendrix, Albert King, and Lonnie Mack, becoming a favorite of the heavy metal virtuosos who would follow in Davies' footsteps.

The Kinks onstage in 1969, from left, Ray Davies, Pete Quaife, and Dave Davies

RAY DAVIES

"Those three chords were part of my life—
G, F, B♭—yeah, it is, it is, and I can't help
noticing it. But there have been other things
nearly as close to it which people haven't
noticed, other things we have done."

—RAY DAVIES, 2009

Awards and Honors

1990	Inducted into the Rock and Roll Hall of Fame, with the Kinks
2004	Appointed Commander of the Order of the British Empire (CBE)
2005	Inducted into the UK Music Hall of Fame, with the Kinks
2006	Icon Award, BMI

Ray Davies (born June 21, 1944, in London, England) is known for his role as the front man and—along with his younger brother, Dave—guitarist in the Kinks, the indelible British rock band. Later on in his career, Davies assumed the role of successful singer-songwriter. In most music circles, Ray is given the lion's share of credit for creating the Kinks' sound and driving the band's considerable output.

When the Kinks came together in the early 1960s, Davies was enrolled in a London art school. He has helmed the band since the beginning, serving as its main songwriter and most public face from the band's 1964 inception. Along with its contemporaries, the Beatles, the Kinks led the first wave of the British Invasion, demonstrating remarkable staying power—and keeping its fans captivated with the often-public rivalry that existed between the Davies brothers.

Davies has championed various modes and styles throughout his career. The earliest Kinks work consisted mainly of straightforward pop and rock firecrackers, although his later

solo output took a turn for the mature and lyrically complex. He can take credit as a musical theater composer as well—three of his shows have been produced.

Davies released his first solo album, *Return to Waterloo*, in 1985. More than a decade would pass before the next, 1998's *The Storyteller*. Since 2006 Davies has followed up three times, most recently with *The Kinks Choral Collection* in 2009, a novel vocal treatment of many Davies-penned songs originally laid down by the Kinks.

An author and filmmaker as well, Davies published both a somewhat fictionalized memoir and a collection of short fiction in the 1990s. His first film project was tied to *Return to Waterloo*; he directed the film of the same name, which effectively served as an extended music video for the album.

Although brother Dave Davies is more recognized for his guitar playing, it is Ray's vision that provided the conduit for the entire group's success and its role as champions of British culture and values.

THE KINKS

The Kinks' long reign has its roots in skiffle and rock and roll—the kinds of music its members grew up listening to. The band's 1964 record deal with Pye allowed it to record a handful of singles, two of which, "You Really Got Me" and "All Day and All of the Night" were universal hits. After demonstrating its earning potential to its label, the Kinks released a self-titled LP, ushering in a demand for its energetic live performances—but not in the United States, where music industry officials deemed the band's stage act too violent.

As the band's popularity continued to mount, Davies shifted the Kinks in a new stylistic direction, beginning with *The Kink Controversy* in 1965. Its work began to take on a richer, more observational quality, driven by Davies' song-writing. *Face to Face* continued the trend, and the touching single "Waterloo Sunset," released in 1967, is a highlight of the Kinks catalog. After 1967's *Something Else by the Kinks*, the band's sales slowed, and it took a break from the road to concentrate on studio work. The result: *The Kinks are the Village Green Preservation Society*, a heralded concept album that represented a band pushing ever further beyond its boundaries.

In 1971 the Kinks aligned with RCA, winning a huge contract that dictated a future five albums. The band set to work immediately, with *Muswell Hillbillies* the first project. Trouble set in soon, with Davies collapsing during a performance in 1973. The band's releases during this decade were generally overwrought and received poorly, but the Kinks pulled out of the dive with 1977's *Sleepwalker*. Around this time other bands started paying the Kinks homage as a living legend, with acts like the Jam and the Pretenders covering its hits.

Going into the 1980s the band was in top form, racking up brisk album sales—at least in the United States, where its fan base had shifted—and selling out arenas. Things soon turned, though, as multiple members jumped ship. After signing to MCA in 1986, only to be dropped a few years later, the Kinks did some soul searching. Its early 1990s output via Columbia was largely dead on arrival, so by 1996 the band broke up. Both Davies brothers have hinted at a possible reunion, but other former Kinks have expressed little enthusiasm for the endeavor.

essential albums

WITH THE KINKS

1964	*The Kinks*
1965	*Kinda Kinks*
1965	*The Kink Kontroversy*
1966	*Face to Face*
1967	*Something Else by The Kinks*
1968	*The Kinks Are the Village Green Preservation Society*
1969	*Arthur (Or the Decline and Fall of the British Empire)*
1970	*Lola versus Powerman and the Moneygoround, Part One*
1971	*Muswell Hillbillies*
1972	*Everybody's in Show-Biz*
1973	*Preservation Act 1*
1974	*Preservation Act 2*
1975	*Soap Opera*
1976	*Schoolboys in Disgrace*
1977	*Sleepwalker*
1978	*Misfits*
1979	*Low Budget*
1981	*Give the People What They Want*
1983	*State of Confusion*
1984	*Word of Mouth*
1986	*Think Visual*
1989	*UK Jive*
1993	*Phobia*

SOLO

1985	*Return to Waterloo*
1998	*The Storyteller*
2006	*Other People's Lives*
2007	*Working Man's Café*

Davies in Vancouver, British Columbia, in 2006, during the tour to support *Other People's Lives.* His latest project is a choral album recorded with the Crouch End Festival Chorus. An extended version, called *The Kinks Choral Collection,* includes a charity Christmas single "Postcard from London," featuring Davies' duet with his famous ex, Chrissie Hynde.

JOHN FOGERTY

John Fogerty (born May 28, 1945, in Berkeley, California) is a guitarist connected with American hit-making band Creedence Clearwater Revival. Fogerty is also noted for his solo career that has its roots in country music.

With his older brother, Tom, John formed a blues out-fit called the Golliwogs, and the band succeeded in getting limited airplay on local radio stations in Northern California. Under John's direction, the band rebranded itself as Creedence Clearwater Revival and released a self-titled album in 1968, which contained the hit "Suzie Q."

Fogerty's solo career kicked off with *The Blue Ridge Rangers*, an album of covers that enjoyed some success in the early 1970s. Fogerty's second album, self titled, produced the song "Rockin' All Over the World," which was given a high-profile treatment by British boogie rock band Status Quo in 1977.

Asylum Records actually cancelled an album slated for 1976, *Hoodoo*, due to underwhelming buzz and the disappoint-ing flop of a single released ahead of the LP's official debut.

In 1985 Fogerty came back with *Centerfield*, a well-received album with Fogerty as the sole player on all tracks. *Eye of the Zombie* was his next effort, a release that didn't track, perhaps owing to its perceived darker tone.

"Even though I have often recorded alone, I still feel the best music is made by musicians playing off each other. "

—JOHN FOGERTY, 2007

Through the late 1980s and 1990s, after the death of brother Tom, Fogerty began slowly reincorporating old Creedence Clearwater Revival material into his live performances.

After a ten-year hiatus from recording, Fogerty offered up the Grammy-winning *Blue Moon Swamp* in 1997. In 2004 Fogerty returned with a series of albums incorporating old Creedence mainstays with new tunes. Lately Fogerty has enjoyed the attention of several large, sold-out performances around the world and has dusted off his Blue Ridge Rangers concern to release another album of covers, *The Blue Ridge Rangers Rides Again* in 2009.

Fogerty has spoken in glowing terms about Rickenbacker guitars and Gibson Les Pauls and maintains an impressively diverse arsenal of axes and amps.

essential albums

WITH CREEDENCE CLEARWATER REVIVAL

1968	*Creedence Clearwater Revival*
1969	*Bayou Country*
1969	*Green River*
1969	*Willy and the Poor Boys*
1970	*Cosmo's Factory*
1970	*Pendulum*
1972	*Mardi Gras*

SOLO

1973	*The Blue Ridge Rangers*
1985	*Centerfield*
1986	*Eye of the Zombie*
1997	*Blue Moon Swamp*
1998	*Premonition*
2004	*Deja Vu All Over Again*
2006	*The Long Road Home: In Concert*
2007	*Revival*
2009	*The Blue Ridge Rangers Rides Again*

CREEDENCE CLEARWATER REVIVAL

The Bay Area band first came to prominence with their bluesy sound, a marked contrast to the more popular psychedelic rock that prevailed in the region at the time. After "Suzie Q," the band quickly took to recording its second album, 1969's *Bayou Country*. The release resonated, hitting No. 7 on the U.S. charts and including the hit "Proud Mary," a song that has been covered memorably by Ike and Tina Turner, among countless others.

Creedence actually appeared at Woodstock, but an anxious John Fogerty put the surviving recordings under lock and key for years, feeling the set didn't represent the band at its best. The incident marked the beginning of tensions between Fogerty and the rest of the band. The band finished out the 1960s, though, at the top of critics' and the public's lists.

By 1971, after the success of *Cosmo's Factory*, Tom had developed doubts about the band's direction and John's pervasive influence; Tom departed that year. The band would record six albums in total, but the remaining members quibbled about responsibilities and credit. After the release of *Mardi Gras* in 1972, Creedence Clearwater Revival dissolved.

Awards and Honors

1993	Inducted into the Rock and Roll Hall of Fame, with Creedence Clearwater Revival
1997	Grammy Award for Best Rock Album, for *Blue Moon Swamp*

John Fogerty live at the Blue Balls Festival in Lucerne, Switzerland, 2009

GEORGE HARRISON

"I think people who can truly live a life in music are telling the world, 'You can have my love, you can have my smiles. Forget the bad parts, you don't need them. Just take the music, the goodness, because it's the very best, and it's the part I give.'"

—GEORGE HARRISON, 1995

HARRISON'S STYLE

Harrison's evolution as a guitarist is closely linked to the Beatles' transition from giddy 1960s pop sensation to peerless cultural and musical juggernaut.

Even in his latest days, Harrison referred to himself as simply "an old skiffle man," calling back to one of his earliest inspirations, Lonnie Donegan, the reigning British king of the improvisational style, which has its roots in African-American informal blues and jazz.

Stylistically, Harrison's handling of the guitar was innovative but stable and rarely flashy; he took his cues from the guitar pioneers of the 1950s and 1960s. He experimented with a wide variety of axes, including a number of Gretsch models in the early days and a specially modified Rickenbacker that quickly grabbed attention for its unmistakable jangly sound. Harrison is also revered for his slide guitar work and his mastery of the sitar.

Left: A Gretsch Country Gentleman guitar, the model Harrison launched to prominence when he played one during the Beatles' historic appearance on the *Ed Sullivan Show* in 1963

Opposite Page: From left, Ringo Starr, John Lennon, Paul McCartney, and George Harrison during their *Sgt. Pepper* days

George Harrison (born February 25, 1943, in Liverpool, England; died November 29, 2001, in Los Angeles, California) was lead guitarist for the Beatles. He was responsible for the band's shift from its Merseybeat roots to an exploration and embrace of Eastern spirituality and sounds and continued to perform, write, and produce after the Beatles' breakup in 1970 until his death from lung cancer in 2001.

Harrison first hooked up with schoolmate Paul McCartney, who introduced him to the members of the Quarrymen, a precursor to the Beatles. After working at clubs in Liverpool and Hamburg, Germany, the band would break out as the Beatles. By 1963 it seemed as if the whole world was in the grip of Beatlemania. As the youngest member of the "Fab Four," Harrison occupied a niche as the protected "baby" of the group, and because of his low-key demeanor he gained a reputation as the "quiet Beatle."

After meeting Indian musician Ravi Shankar in 1965, Harrison developed a deep interest in the music of the sitar, which features famously in *Sgt. Pepper's Lonely Hearts Club Band* (1967), one the group's finest album, as well as one of the most important records of all time.

essential albums

WITH THE BEATLES

1963	*Please Please Me*
1963	*With The Beatles*
1964	*Introducing . . . The Beatles*
1964	*Meet The Beatles!*
1964	*Twist and Shout*
1964	*The Beatles' Second Album*
1964	*The Beatles' Long Tall Sally*
1964	*A Hard Day's Night*
1964	*Something New*
1964	*Beatles for Sale*
1965	*Beatles '65*
1965	*Beatles VI*
1965	*Help!*
1965	*Rubber Soul*
1966	*Yesterday and Today*
1966	*Revolver*
1967	*Sgt. Pepper's Lonely Hearts Club Band*
1968	*The Beatles*
1969	*Yellow Submarine*
1969	*Abbey Road*
1970	*Let It Be*

SKIFFLE ROOTS

The most critically acclaimed and commercially successful rock band ever, the Beatles grew out of John Lennon's Liverpudlian skiffle band, the Quarrymen. Skiffle has ties to the jazz, blues, roots, and country music of the American South in first half of the twentieth century. This form of music, which relies mainly on improvised instruments, such as washboards, jugs, tea chest basses, cigar-box fiddles, musical saws, and comb-and-paper kazoos backed up by acoustic guitars and banjos, had real appeal to working-class Brits in the 1950s, who had little money to invest in costly instruments and equipment. Harrison joined the Quarrymen when he was just 15, after Paul McCartney persuaded a reluctant Lennon to accept the talented youngster.

"I think we must have been pretty tough, because I've heard of people cracking up and having nervous breakdowns with not even a fraction of what we went through."

—GEORGE HARRISON, 1995

essential albums

SOLO

1968	*Wonderwall Music*
1969	*Electronic Sound*
1970	*All Things Must Pass*
1971	*The Concert for Bangladesh*
1973	*Living in the Material World*
1974	*Dark Horse*
1975	*Extra Texture (Read All About It)*
1976	*Thirty Three & 1/3*
1979	*George Harrison*
1981	*Somewhere in England*
1982	*Gone Troppo*
1987	*Cloud Nine*
1992	*Live in Japan*
2002	*Brainwashed*

WITH THE TRAVELING WILBURYS

1988	*Traveling Wilburys, Volume 1*
1990	*Traveling Wilburys, Volume 3*

During his Beatles days, Harrison, shown at right in 1974, worked with many types of guitars, including the twelve-string, the sitar, and the slide. He played the sitar on the haunting "Norwegian Wood" during the *Rubber Soul* sessions. After the band broke up he often joined in other artists' sessions, for instance, playing slide guitar on Bob Dylan's "If Not for You" in 1970. The next year, Dylan made a rare live appearance at Harrison's Concert for Bangladesh, along with Eric Clapton, Leon Russell, Badfinger, Billy Preston, and Harrison's former bandmate Ringo Starr.

SOLO CAREER

Harrison, though close to the other Beatles, had always occupied his own orbit. His initial attempts at projecting a singular voice came across in a handful of songs he wrote for the band. Only a small number of them were actually recorded and awarded a place on an album; more often than not, the band vetoed his material. When the band broke up in 1970, Harrison was well prepared to make his own way, having already crafted two mostly instrumental solo albums, *Wonderwall Music* and *Electronic Sound*.

All Things Must Pass, Harrison's first true solo effort, was released in 1970 as a three-album set to much critical praise. His subsequent albums generated less critical attention but still found commercial success. Post-Beatles, Harrison also devoted significant time to producing concerts and other albums, often collaborating with his former bandmates.

"It's being here now that's important. There's no past and there's no future. Time is a very misleading thing. All there is ever, is the now. We can gain experience from the past, but we can't relive it; and we can hope for the future, but we don't know if there is one."

—GEORGE HARRISON

TRAVELING WILBURYS

Great ideas are often born at meals shared between friends. But when the friends are Roy Orbison, George Harrison, and Jeff Lynne, the great idea turned into an amazing reality. Although the original plan was for the three to record just a B-side for Harrison's single release "This Is Love," the song—"Handle with Care"—sounded too fine to be relegated to a B-side.

The "Handle with Care" recording session also included Bob Dylan and Tom Petty, and the participants had so much fun that they decided to work as a band. In ten days, the supergroup, calling itself the Traveling Wilburys, had laid down a full album's worth of work. Warner Bros. and Wilbury Records released *Traveling Wilburys, Volume 1* in fall 1988, with the band members credited under various Wilbury pseudonyms: Harrison as "Nelson Wilbury," Lynne as "Otis Wilbury," Orbison as "Lefty Wilbury," Petty as "Charlie T. Wilbury Jr.," and Dylan as "Lucky Wilbury." It was an immediate hit, selling 2 million copies within six months, and going on to grab a Grammy for Best Rock Performance by a Duo or Group with Vocal.

Orbison died later that year, but the other four went ahead with recording a second collection, *Traveling Wilburys, Volume 3*, using new Wilbury pseudonyms—Spike, (Harrison), Boo (Dylan), Muddy (Petty), and Clayton (Lynne)—and dedicating the LP to "Lefty Wilbury."

Awards and Honors

1964	Grammy Award for Best Performance by a Vocal Group, for *A Hard Day's Night*, with the Beatles
1964	Grammy Award for Best New Artist of 1964, for *A Hard Day's Night*, with The Beatles
1965	Appointed Member of the Order of the British Empire (MBE), with the Beatles
1967	Grammy Award for Best Contemporary Album, for *Sgt. Pepper's Lonely Hearts Club Band*, with the Beatles
1967	Grammy Award for Album of the Year, for *Sgt. Pepper's Lonely Hearts Club Band*, with the Beatles
1970	Grammy Award for Best Original Score Written for a Motion Picture or a Television Special, for *Let It Be*, with the Beatles
1970	Academy Award for Best Original Score, for *Let It Be*, with the Beatles
1972	Grammy Award for Album of the Year, for *The Concert for Bangladesh*, with Ravi Shankar, Bob Dylan, Leon Russell, Ringo Starr, Billy Preston, Eric Clapton, and Klaus Voormann
1988	Inducted into the Rock and Roll Hall of Fame, with the Beatles
1989	Grammy Award for Best Rock Performance by a Duo or Group with Vocal, for *Traveling Wilburys, Volume 1*, with the Traveling Wilburys
1996	Grammy Award for Best Music Video, Long Form, for *The Beatles Anthology*, with the Beatles
1996	Grammy Award for Best Music Video, Short Form, for "Free as a Bird," with the Beatles
1996	Grammy Award for Best Pop Performance by a Duo or Group with Vocal, for "Free as a Bird," with the Beatles
2003	Grammy Award for Best Pop Instrumental Performance, for "Marwa Blues"
2003	Ranked No. 21 on *Rolling Stone*'s list of the 100 Greatest Guitarists of All Time
2004	Inducted into the Rock and Roll Hall of Fame
2008	Grammy Award for Best Compilation Sound track Album for Motion Picture, Television or Other Visual Media, for *Love*, with the Beatles

From left, Paul McCartney, George Harrison, Ringo Starr, and John Lennon in a scene from the Academy Award–nominated *A Hard Day's Night*. This groundbreaking mock documentary about a few days in the life of the Beatles won critical acclaim at its release and later earned a spot on *Time*'s list of the 100 greatest films. The film's sound track snagged two Grammys—the first of many awards for the Fab Four.

JOHN MAYER

John Mayer (born October 16, 1977, in Bridgeport, Connecticut) is a singer-songwriter whose catalog of music has made a marked shift from pop to, more recently, blues-inspired sounds. Mayer remains an imposing figure in popular music and celebrity circles.

Mayer was a music student in middle school, starting on clarinet and eventually migrating to the guitar. Finding himself hooked on the blues, he traded in the guitar his father had rented for him to acquire a Stevie Ray Vaughan signature Stratocaster. While still in high school Mayer started taking his guitar to play gigs in small local venues and test his mettle as a songwriter and performer.

After a brief stint at Boston's Berklee College of Music, Mayer packed up and migrated south to Atlanta, Georgia, immersing himself in the music scene and charting a course as a singer-songwriter. After recording the independent EP *Inside Wants Out*, Mayer set out on a tour of the South, which brought him to the attention of launch label Aware Records.

Mayer's 2001 debut, *Room for Squares*, was initially given life as an online download, but after parent label Columbia snapped it up, expanded its track listing, and offered it for wide release, Mayer became an overnight sensation. Several singles won significant exposure on U.S. radio, and critics noted Mayer's skill as a guitarist and lyricist.

Two years later Mayer followed up with *Heavier Things*, a Grammy-winning collection of songs that explored similar territory as his debut.

"Have you ever heard me play guitar? I'm really fucking good. You know what I'm bad at? Answering questions about public health care. This is not in my wheelhouse. Do you have any questions about music?"

—JOHN MAYER, 2009

essential albums

STUDIO ALBUMS

2001	*Room for Squares*
2003	*Any Given Thursday*
2003	*Heavier Things*
2006	*Continuum*
2009	*Battle Studies*

LIVE ALBUMS

2004	*As/Is*
2005	*Try! John Mayer Trio Live In Concert*
2008	*Where The Light Is: John Mayer Live In Los Angeles*

TAKING ON THE BLUES

In the time leading up to his third album, *Continuum*, Mayer announced an active shift in his direction and sound as a musician, dedicating himself to becoming more of a blues guitarist and less a singer-songwriter trading in "acoustic sensitivity."

Mayer began working with greats like B.B. King, Buddy Guy, Eric Clapton, and Herbie Hancock, recording and touring in an effort to perfect his sound and style. In the tradition of countless bluesmen before him, Mayer established the John Mayer Trio in 2005.

Mayer's new focus resulted in the release of 2006's *Continuum*, a decidedly blues-influenced effort that attracted multiple Grammy nominations as well as accolades from major publications, including *Rolling Stone*, for Mayer's obvious expertise as a new guitar standard-bearer.

Mayer's fourth release, *Battle Studies*, came out in 2009 to mixed reviews but enthusiastic sales.

Awards and Honors

2002	Grammy Award for Best Male Pop Vocal Performance, for "Your Body is a Wonderland"
2004	Grammy Award for Best Male Pop Vocal Performance, for "Daughters"
2004	Grammy Award for Song of the Year, for "Daughters"
2006	Grammy Award for Best Pop Vocal Album, for *Continuum*
2006	Grammy Award for Best Male Pop Vocal Performance, for "Waiting on the World to Change"
2008	Grammy Award for Best Solo Rock Vocal Performance, for "Gravity"
2008	Grammy Award for Best Male Pop Vocal Performance, for "Say"

Mayer performs at London's Royal Albert Hall, 2007.

CELEBRITY

Mayer has gained significant press for his unique role as both music figure and willing celebrity at large. Romantically linked to a number of women in many cases more famous than himself, Mayer has proven adept at staying in the public eye while retaining tight control over his message and persona. Omnipresent via his Web site, his Twitter feed, and his frequent appearances on television and as a writer and columnist, especially for *Esquire*, Mayer has seemingly avoided the negative gossip and backlash often endured by his peers, opting to diffuse controversy with his sense of oddball humor or, in the case of his breakup with Jennifer Aniston, frank and candid honesty.

On occasion Mayer has come to the public defense of troubled and embattled public figures such as Britney Spears and Jessica Simpson.

John Mayer, a frequent red carpet walker, arrives at a benefit for the VH1 Save the Music Foundation in New York City, 2007.

LIZ PHAIR

"[*Guyville* evokes] a period when I was on the edge. . . . What I had been raised to do I was certainly not doing. I was scamming my way through life, not really working. And I think I had some self-destructive tendencies. But it was also wild and fun. I was probably my coolest back then, and I've seriously fallen off the cool radar now. But at the same time I'm a lot more secure. . . . There's something grounded about getting older. You get older and you have to deal with yourself. Going back and listening to those songs is kind of titillating for me because listening to the person I was makes me feel a little sexier, a little cooler, a little more dangerous, a little Angelina Jolie, which I don't mind so much right now."

—LIZ PHAIR, 2008

L iz Phair (born April 17, 1967, in New Haven, Connecticut) is known for her exemplary take on the role of singer/songwriter as well as her groundbreaking 1993 debut, *Exile in Guyville*.

Phair was adopted and grew up in the tony Chicago outpost of Winnetka, Illinois. As an art student at Oberlin College, Phair indulged her burgeoning interest in music, too, spending her immediate post-college years in the hipper parts of San Francisco and Chicago, penning and recording songs as Girly Sound. Hungry for more exposure, Phair sent her demos to Matador Records, where they met with immediate praise. An advance and studio time followed, resulting in *Exile in Guyville*.

In the aftermath of *Guyville*, Phair found herself a player on the national scene—but not quite a blockbuster seller. Her follow-up, *Whip-Smart*, was considered a more MTV-ready concoction, but sales were lower than expected. The same fate befell *whitechocolatespaceegg*, Phair's rumination on her new role as a wife and mother.

Phair's eponymous fourth album stoked a firestorm when it hit the airwaves in 2003. After multiple delays in writing and production, the resulting collection of songs earned Phair accusations of "selling out" and pandering to the lowest, most commercial denominator. Several singles from the record brought Phair the greatest exposure of her career, but her oldest fans felt something like betrayal.

Somebody's Miracle, released in 2005, reined in the saccharine production heard on *Liz Phair* but fell far short of matching the excitement of her debut.

essential albums

STUDIO
1993	*Exile in Guyville*
1994	*Whip-Smart*
1998	*whitechocolatespaceegg*
2003	*Liz Phair*
2005	*Somebody's Miracle*

Left: Phair at a film preview in Hollywood, 2004

Below: Phair performs at the South by Southwest music festival in Austin, 2003.

EXILE IN GUYVILLE

Phair's sprawling, gutsy debut has become an icon of the 1990s indie scene, a frequent fixture on critics' best-of lists from the decade. Acclaimed for its frank songwriting, complex point of view, and Phair's no-nonsense vocals, the album stands as Phair's best work by far. *Rolling Stone* has called it "virtually perfect."

Obvious singles "Never Said" and "Fuck and Run" enjoyed some mainstream success, and the entire album is allegedly structured as a response to *Exile on Main Street*, one of the Rolling Stones' finest albums.

In 2008 Phair reissued the album to mark the occasion of its fifteenth anniversary; the new release included a trio of new songs, and was available as an electronic download for the first time. A companion DVD, *Guyville Redux*, was also made available, chronicling the album's genesis in 1990s Wicker Park, Chicago, and containing interviews with many of the album's key personnel—including Phair's ex-boyfriend Nash Kato, allegedly the record's chief inspiration.

PRINCE

Prince (born Prince Rogers Nelson on June 7, 1958, in Minneapolis, Minnesota) is a prolific pop star whose releases have topped the charts for more than two decades. Known for his eccentric appearance and his temporary adoption of a sole graphic symbol in place of his name, Prince's career thus far has been an unqualified success.

Raised by working musicians, Prince started lending his talents on piano and guitar to various bands during high school. Influenced by popular funk and rock and roll bands like Sly and the Family Stone; Earth, Wind and Fire; and Jimi Hendrix, Prince cut a demo when he was just 17. He parlayed his talent into a record contract and debuted *For You* in 1978.

Prince's first singles were hits, leading to immediate TV appearances and, in 1980, a tour with Rick James. After releasing *Controversy* the following year, Prince made his first appearance as musical guest on *Saturday Night Live*. The 1982 LP *1999* made Prince a household name, and his videos became MTV mainstays, virtually assuring his role as a major music player throughout the 1980s.

Now billing himself as Prince and the Revolution, Prince released *Purple Rain* in 1984. One of the artist's best-selling works, the album was released with the hit film of the same name. Near the end of the 1980s, Prince made a concerted expansion into the world of film, directing Kristen Scott Thomas in *Under the Cherry Moon*. With *Sign o' the Times*, Prince stirred up even more critical praise in 1987.

In 1993 Prince infamously adopted the Love Symbol, an unpronounceable combination of the symbols for male and female, in place of his name; the move inspired scores of late-night punch lines but ultimately had little effect on Prince's popularity. Through the 1990s, the "Artist Formerly Known as Prince" let loose with a mind-boggling amount of material, both new and unreleased. Reviews and sales were mixed, and some in the music press suggested Prince was simply trying to get out from under his corporate recording contract.

The artist reclaimed his name in 2000, putting out a series of jazz-infused albums, leading up to *Musicology* in 2004. The release and its companion tour was a hit, helping Prince rake in nearly $60 million that year alone. Most recently the artist has made a number of epic appearances on television and the concert circuit, playing to 140 million viewers around the world during 2007's Super Bowl and selling out premiere venues around the world. *LotusFlow3r* dropped in 2009, heavily featuring Prince's guitar playing.

essential albums

Prince, shown above in 1981, has an extensive collection of unique, often colorful, axes. His Yellow Cloud guitar, shown at left, now resides in the Smithsonian.

WITH PRINCE AND THE REVOLUTION
- 1985 *Around the World in a Day*
- 1984 *Purple Rain* (sound track)

SOLO
- 1978 *For You*
- 1979 *Prince*
- 1980 *Dirty Mind*
- 1981 *Controversy*
- 1987 *Sign 'o' the Times*
- 1988 *Lovesexy*
- 1991 *Diamonds and Pearls*
- 1992 *Love Symbol*
- 1994 *Come*
- 1994 *The Black Album*
- 1995 *The Gold Experience*
- 1996 *Chaos and Disorder*
- 1996 *Emancipation*
- 1999 *Rave Un2 the Joy Fantastic*
- 2001 *The Rainbow Children*
- 2004 *Musicology*
- 2007 *Planet Earth*
- 2009 *LotusFlow3R*
- 1982 *1999*
- 2006 *3121r*

"I was brought up in a black-and-white world . . . night and day, rich and poor. I listened to all kinds of music . . . and when I was younger, I always said that one day I would play all kinds of music and not be judged for the color of my skin but the quality of my work, and hopefully I will continue."

—PRINCE, 1986

ICONOGRAPHY

Prince is known for his larger-than-life attitude and persona, manifested especially in his flamboyant wardrobe—both on and off the stage—and his collection of surreal guitars. Among them are Yellow Cloud, a custom job originally crafted by an independent Minnesota luthier, and the Symbol Guitar, an intricate replica of Prince's Love Symbol, built by a German craftsman. Yellow Cloud is, of course, an electrifying shade of yellow, and the Symbol Guitar is finished in a dreamlike gold tone. Replicas of both are frequently sold at auction and are available through various channels; they tend to fetch several thousand dollars each.

Prince's other singular contribution, though less tangible, is the "Minneapolis sound," a novel fusion of funk, rock, and R&B that Prince largely brought to brief prominence with his first releases in the late 1970s. Other pop musicians like Sheila E. and Sheena Easton were disciples of the Minneapolis sound at the earliest points in their careers. The artist's output has branched out far beyond these beginnings, but the sound holds its own as a defining aspect of that decade's popular repertoire.

TODD RUNDGREN

Todd Rundgren (born June 22, 1948, in Upper Darby, Pennsylvania) is an American rock musician known for the solo career he crafted beginning in the early 1970s, as well as his daring forays into digital media and unorthodox music production and distribution techniques.

Rundgren's origins are tied to the bands Woody's Truck Stop and the Nazz in the late 1960s; he stayed with the latter for three years before it dissolved. The group had some success with its singles in Canada, but the Nazz lacked the momentum to establish a truly successful presence.

Rundgren's 1970 project, Runt, largely served as a vehicle for his expanding solo ambitions. "We Gotta Get You a Woman" was the first of a few minor hits credited to Runt, but by 1972, Rundgren was recording and releasing albums as a solo artist. *Something/Anything?* debuted to acclaim, praised for its energetic deployment of early pop, rock, and soul styles. It produced his first true pop hits; "I Saw the Light" and "Hello, It's Me," the latter reaching No. 5 on the U.S. charts.

By the mid-1970s, Rundgren's progressive influences were coming through, evident on a trio of albums released between 1973 and 1975. Rundgren experimented with an eclectic canvas of sounds, incorporating Eastern and orchestral influences. At about this time he formed backup band Utopia.

Rundgren's releases through the remainder of the 1970s and 1980s embraced new wave, pop, soul, and vocal sampling techniques. "Bang the Drum All Day," one of Rundgren's best-known singles, was recorded during this period, though it garnered little attention at the time of its release.

"When [*A Wizard, A True Star*] first came out it was roundly considered an overt act of career suicide. . . . In its own way, it's as different still as it was then. . . . The idea that a musical fragment is as valid outside of a conventional setting as it would be within. When it came out, singles were very important and they still are; a song that is essentially three to four minutes long has a certain form to it. But if that's all that music was, it wouldn't be a very interesting format to work in and I suppose anything that's a testament to other ways of approaching music plays part in what keeps the form vital, what keeps it from becoming stagnant."

—TODD RUNDGREN, 2009

essential albums

SOLO

1971	*Runt: The Ballad of Todd Rundgren*
1972	*Something/Anything?*
1973	*A Wizard, a True Star*
1974	*Todd*
1975	*Initiation*
1976	*Faithful*
1978	*Hermit of Mink Hollow*
1978	*Back to the Bars*
1981	*Healing*
1983	*The Ever Popular Tortured Artist Effect*
1985	*A Cappella*
1989	*Nearly Human*
1991	*2nd Wind*
1993	*No World Order*
1995	*The Individualist*
1995	*With a Twist*
1998	*Up Against It*
1998	*Free Soul*
1998	*Somewhere-Anywhere*
2000	*One Long Year*
2001	*Reconstructed*
2004	*Liars*
2008	*Arena*

WITH UTOPIA

1974	*Todd Rundgren's Utopia*
1977	*Ra*
1977	*Oops! Wrong Planet*
1980	*Adventures in Utopia*
1980	*Deface the Music*
1982	*Swing to the Right*
1982	*Utopia*
1984	*Oblivion*
1985	*P.O.V.*

TR-i & THE NEW FRONTIER

Rundgren commenced a project entitled TR-i, standing for Todd Rundgren Interactive, in 1993. This experimental venture was part marketing ploy with Philips Electronics, part opportunity for Rundgren to delve into the world of dance, hip-hop, and multimedia. Breaking the conventions of the album, Rundgren released a collection of extremely short cuts on *No World Order* that gave the listener complete control over the sequence in which they were played. *The Individualist* was similar, but in this effort Rundgren paired the audio with video content.

Rundgren's embrace—in the face of his industry's collective suspicion—of electronic distribution and the possibilities of the Internet have set him apart. Since the beginnings of MTV, Rundgren has been on the forefront; his video for "Time Heals" was among the first the music network played. He is also a founder of now-defunct Patronet, an early electronic music subscription service. Rundgren continues this do-it-yourself tradition via his Web site, offering his newest music for direct download to paying fans, charting a course for such ubiquitous services as MySpace and iTunes.

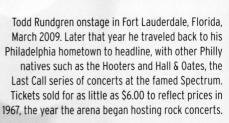

Todd Rundgren onstage in Fort Lauderdale, Florida, March 2009. Later that year he traveled back to his Philadelphia hometown to headline, with other Philly natives such as the Hooters and Hall & Oates, the Last Call series of concerts at the famed Spectrum. Tickets sold for as little as $6.00 to reflect prices in 1967, the year the arena began hosting rock concerts.

STEPHEN STILLS

Awards and Honors

1969   Grammy Award for Best New Artist of the Year, with Crosby, Stills and Nash

1997   Inducted into the Rock and Roll Hall of Fame, with Buffalo Springfield

1997   Inducted into the Rock and Roll Hall of Fame, with Crosby, Stills and Nash

2003   Ranked No. 28 on *Rolling Stone*'s list of the 100 Greatest Guitarists of All Time

"Yeah, I'm a much better blues player than anybody knows, but being in the kind of group I'm in, we were always trying to make popular records."

—STEPHEN STILLS, 1975

Stephen Stills (born January 3, 1945, in Dallas, Texas) has worked with folk group Buffalo Springfield and has long been the "Stills" in Crosby, Stills and Nash.

Stills's childhood as a military brat, growing up in several locations in the U.S. South and Latin America, exposed him to a diverse musical palette. After dropping out of college, Stills's music career took root in New York City in the early 1960s, where he was part of a singing group and later, a short-lived folk group. This association led Stills to meet Neil Young, his future on-again-off-again bandmate.

Buffalo Springfield formed in Los Angeles in 1966, composed of Stills, Young, and Richie Furay. The band only released three albums, and had some success with a single, "For What It's Worth," but Stills and Young would use their time with the band to hone their respective talents.

Apart from Crosby, Stills and Nash, Stills has enjoyed an illustrious solo career. His self-titled debut in 1970 featured Eric Clapton, Ringo Starr, and Jimi Hendrix and spawned the hit single "Love the One You're With" A side project launched in 1972, Manassas, resulted in a highly respected double LP.

Starting in the early 1990s Stills took a long hiatus from solo work before rebooting with the release of *Man Alive!* in 2005.

Stills onstage at Madison Square Garden's Woodstock '79 event, commemorating the first Woodstock Festival of August 1969. As a new act CS&N had performed its second live gig at the first Woodstock. The band later recorded the Joni Mitchell song memorializing this generation-defining celebration of hippiedom.

essential albums

WITH BUFFALO SPRINGFIELD

1966	*Buffalo Springfield*
1967	*Buffalo Springfield Again*
1968	*Last Time Around*

WITH CROSBY, STILLS, NASH & YOUNG

1969	*Crosby, Stills & Nash*
1970	*Déjà Vu*
1971	*Four Way Street*
1974	*So Far*
1977	*CSN*
1982	*Daylight Again*
1988	*American Dream*
1990	*Live It Up*
1994	*After The Storm*
1999	*Looking Forward*

COMPILATIONS

1970	*Stephen Stills*
1971	*Stephen Stills 2*
1972	*Manassas*
1973	*Down The Road*
1975	*Stills*
1976	*Illegal Stills*
1976	*Long May You Run*
1978	*Thoroughfare Gap*
1984	*Right By You*
1991	*Stills Alone*
2005	*Man Alive!*
2007	*Just Roll Tape*
2009	*Pieces*

Above, Crosby Stills and Nash singing, circa 1969. From left, David Crosby, Stephen Stills, and Graham Nash. The trio's lyrical, soaring vocal harmonies made the group unique during hard rock's coming-of-age years.

CROSBY, STILLS & NASH (YOUNG, TOO)

CS&N is David Crosby, Stephen Stills, and Graham Nash—and, occasionally through the supergroup's history, Neil Young. Upon the band's formation, all the members were coming off acrimoniously aborted projects. In naming the new group after themselves, they meant to provide insurance against future rifts or dissolutions—an all or nothing approach.

The band's self-titled first album came out in 1969 and was a smash success. Multi-instrumentalist Stills, already overworked, realized that they would need to recruit a full band in order to fulfill the demands of reproducing their music live on the road. Neil Young, already familiar to Crosby and Stills, came on board as keyboardist, with Greg Reeves on bass. After a memorable gig at Woodstock, the expanded group recorded *Déjà Vu*, basking in its success—but not for long. Reeves soon departed, and the band fell apart in 1970.

The band's members spent the early 1970s recording and touring as solo entities, finally agreeing to a reunion tour with a refreshed rhythm section. The new configuration generated material for a slew of albums that saw release through the rest of the 1970s.

Long-brewing tensions erupted between all members of the foursome, with each musician playing another's anger off the others. Contractual obligations seemed to be the only thing holding the group together until the release of *CSN* in 1977, the first album sans Young.

The 1980s and 1990s consisted of similar patterns, with Crosby's and Stills's legal woes and substance problems preventing a true breakthrough. Young's involvement waxed and waned in the coming years, but as of 2009, he maintains ties with the group. Fans cherish the band for its political relevance and stylistic flexibility over its lifespan.

NEAL SCHON

"It's not the money. It's not the fame. I've had both of those. It's just plain-out fun. I'm looking for fun. I'm growing up with my kids. They teach you how to stay young, if you stay in tune with them. I'm looking to keep the music young. I want it to be fun. I want it to be painless. I want it to be creative. In order to do that, I think you have to put everything else aside."

—NEAL SCHON

Above: Journey live in Minneapolis, Minnesota, in 2008. From left, Ross Valory, Jonathan Cain, Arnel Pineda, Neal Schon, and Deen Castronovo.

Opposite page: Schon shows what he can still do when he takes center stage during the Download Festival 2009 at Castle Donnington, Derbyshire, England.

Neal Schon (born February 27, 1954, in Oklahoma City, Oklahoma) is Journey's lead guitarist and the sole member to appear on every one of the band's albums.

Growing up on his parents' blues and jazz recordings, Schon settled with his family in San Francisco, giving him access to an artistic culture that would inspire his music career. By the age of 17, Schon had already quit high school with his musician father's permission and roused the attention of Eric Clapton and Carlos Santana, the latter with whom he would work on 1971's *Santana III*.

Schon's presence in Journey has provided the band with an anchor through multiple lineup changes. In the meantime, he has nurtured his own solo career, which spans six albums, as well as musical collaborations and side projects including Bad English, Hardline, Jan Hammer, and Soul SirkUS.

JOURNEY

One of the premiere arena rock bands and American exports of the 1970s and 1980s, Journey has been a best-selling act since its formation in 1973. To date, "Don't Stop Believin'" is the most-downloaded track in the iTunes Store catalog.

Journey established itself in the mid-1970s as a primarily instrumental group, and it wasn't until 1977 that the group recruited singer Steve Perry. It released the smash *Infinity* the following year and two more albums in the next two, leading to the acquisition of keyboard virtuoso Jonathan Cain. Cain's work would contribute to the even bigger blockbuster *Escape*. The band had reached the top by this time, but the rest of the 1980s wouldn't proceed so smoothly.

Journey broke up after the replacement of two key members and a final album, *Raised on the Radio*, in 1986. In the interim Journey's label released a greatest hits compilation, which still continues to move hundreds of thousands of copies every year.

At Perry's behest, the band regrouped in 1995 for *Trial by Fire* and enjoyed several hits, as well as a Grammy nomination. It would be Perry's last Journey album; he departed in the wake of an injury.

New singer Steve Augeri took Perry's place for the next two albums, to be relieved by relative unknown Arnel Pineda in 2007, based on a YouTube audition. Pineda made his debut on *Revelation*, Journey's latest effort.

essential albums

WITH JOURNEY

1975	*Journey*
1976	*Look into the Future*
1977	*Next*
1978	*Infinity*
1979	*Evolution*
1980	*Departure*
1981	*Escape*
1983	*Frontiers*
1986	*Raised on Radio*
1996	*Trial by Fire*
2001	*Arriva*
2005	*Generations I*
2008	*Revelation*

WITH SCHON AND HAMMER

1981	*Untold Passion*
1982	*Here to Stay*

WITH SOUL SIRKUS

2005	*World Play*

SOLO

1989	*Late Nite*
1995	*Beyond the Thunder*
1997	*Electric World*
1998	*Piranha Blues*
2001	*Voice*
2005	*I on U*

SCHON'S SETUP

Schon has been renowned for his slick, melodic playing since he was a teenager. Inspired by classic blues and soul sounds, his preference is for memorable, anthemic licks with minimal fuss or pretension. Schon started out on a Stella acoustic but soon graduated to a Gibson ES-335, a pioneering hybrid acoustic/electric guitar. Schon continues to hold Gibsons in high esteem, working with them in 2005 to produce an extremely limited-edition Les Paul.

FOLK AND COUNTRY

These genres have attracted some of music's most singular, iconoclastic, and intriguing personalities. The idioms place an emphasis on substance over style, providing a fertile breeding ground for a distinguished stable of prophetic voices and vital entertainers. Built on timeless oral and musical traditions that have been imported and modified in countless ways, the contemporary forms of folk and country are sonically and thematically diverse.

Owing a debt to the first rock and rollers, as well as the traveling poets and minstrels of older times, today's stars have little in common with the lone storyteller with a guitar. Country, especially, has experienced a resurgence—its contemporary acts enjoy a large and devoted following, primarily in the United States.

JOHNNY CASH

"You build on failure. You use it as a stepping-stone. Close the door on the past. You don't try to forget the mistakes, but you don't dwell on it. You don't let it have any of your energy, or any of your time, or any of your space."

—JOHNNY CASH, 1993

Johnny Cash (born February 26, 1932, in Kingsland, Arkansas; died September 12, 2003, in Nashville, Tennessee) was a uniquely American singer-songwriter with his roots firmly planted in the styles of country, rockabilly, and rock and roll. His lengthy career, complex persona on and off the stage, and contributions to the American canon of rock and roll make him a continued object of acclaim and curiosity.

Cash was one of seven children in a rural family whose fortunes had been affected by the Great Depression. Cash's mother encouraged his early interest in singing and gospel music, supporting his decision to start practicing guitar. After exiting the U.S. Air Force and marrying first wife, Vivian Liberto, Cash moved to Memphis in 1954, first pursuing a career as a radio personality.

After his initial gospel stylings failed to interest potential record producers, Cash recorded two country singles in 1955, followed by "I Walk the Line," a No. 1 hit that appealed to fans of both country and pop. A successful recording artist almost overnight, Cash left Sun Records (also the first home of Elvis Presley) and signed with major player Columbia.

Cash quickly established himself as a hit maker—and an unapologetic consumer of drugs and alcohol. As his behavior and heavy touring schedule strained his marriage to Liberto, Cash was growing closer to singer June Carter, a member of the musical Carter Family that had spent time touring with Cash; Cash and Carter married in 1968. As Cash's substance problems alienated him from the music establishment, Carter was one of his few supporters, encouraging him to embrace his faith as a path to sobriety.

Cash claims, in a legendary account, to have give up illegal substances in 1968 after suffering a near overdose and coming close to ending his life in a Tennessee cave. That year resulted in his hit album *Johnny Cash at Folsom Prison*, which generated several crossover hits.

Cash leveraged his newly cleaned-up image to great effect, securing a role as a television host in 1969 in which he had the opportunity to trot out a wide range of performers who were, more often than not, personal friends, including Neil Young, Eric Clapton, and Bob Dylan.

By the 1970s Cash was an established public figure. Though his musical output failed to match his earlier career efforts, regard for Cash was higher than ever, stemming from his best-selling 1975 autobiography and his iconic manifestation of the lone "man in black."

Cash established the Highwaymen, featuring Waylon Jennings, Kris Kristofferson, and Willie Nelson, in the 1980s, a successful touring and recording enterprise that produced two records. After a period of reduced output and chilly relations with his record label, Cash unexpectedly reinvigorated his career in the 1990s with the Grammy-winning *American Recordings*, the sparse 1994 effort that featured mostly covers. Cash took advantage of the refocused spotlight to release his second autobiography in 1997.

At the end of the 1990s Cash's health took a turn for the worse, only exacerbated by the death of his beloved wife in 2003. His last public performance was in the summer of that year, and Cash passed away in September.

Johnny Cash plays at Folsom Prison as June Carter watches.

Awards and Honors

1967	Grammy Award for Best Country & Western Performance Duet, Trio or Group, for "Jackson," with June Carter
1968	Grammy Award for Best Country Vocal Performance, for "Folsom Prison Blues"
1969	Grammy Award for Best Country Vocal Performance, for "A Boy Named Sue"
1970	Grammy Award for Best Country Vocal Performance by a Duo or Group, for "If I Were a Carpenter," with June Carter
1986	Grammy Award for Best Spoken Word or Non-Musical Recording, for Interviews *From the Class of '55 Recording Sessions*, with Carl Perkins, Chips Moman, Jerry Lee Lewis, Rick Nelson, Roy Orbison, and Sam Phillips
1991	Grammy Legend Award
1992	Inducted into the Rock and Roll Hall of Fame
1994	Grammy Award for Best Contemporary Folk Album, for *American Recordings*
1996	Awarded Kennedy Center Honors
1997	Grammy Award for Best Country Album, for *Unchained*
1998	Grammy Hall of Fame Award, for "I Walk the Line"
1999	Grammy Award for Lifetime Achievement
1999	Grammy Hall of Fame Award, for "Ring of Fire"
2000	Grammy Award for Best Male Country Vocal Performance, for "Solitary Man"
2001	Grammy Hall of Fame Award, for "Folsom Prison Blues"
2002	Grammy Award for Best Male Country Vocal Performance, for "Give My Love To Rose"
2003	Grammy Award for Best Short Form Music Video, for "Hurt," with Mark Romanek and Aris McGarry
2004	Grammy Hall of Fame Award, for *Johnny Cash at San Quentin*

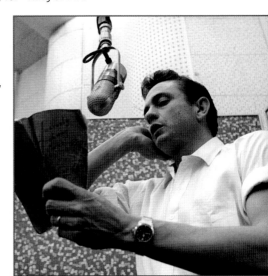

Cash in the studio

Johnny Cash on VH1's *Storytellers* in 1998

CASH'S LEGACY

An iconoclast, a lifetime outsider, and a stubborn supporter of the causes he most respected, Cash defied attempts by the recording industry to be placed into a box; his influence and legacy is apparent in the wide swath of current popular and independent music icons that continue to pay homage to him.

Known as a champion of the underdog, both in the music industry and society in general—Cash is a known advocate for prisoners' rights—Cash nurtured a gruff yet concerned persona, never positioning himself simply as a country singer or popular, commercial entertainer. His storied, affectionate relationship with June Carter also won him admirers—their marriage largely inspired *Walk the Line*, the 2005 biopic starring Joaquin Phoenix as Cash and Reese Witherspoon as Carter.

Late in his career, Cash won over a new generation of fans via collaborations with U2, Tom Petty and the Heartbreakers, and several memorable stints in popular television and culture. More or less a country artist in his early days, Cash came to embrace many styles and genres as his profile rose and his base of fans expanded and shifted. Many of his singles at the height of his output charted well outside the confines of country's usual territory.

Ax maker Martin has honored Cash, most recently, with an all-black D-35 acoustic guitar, harkening back to the thumping, rhythmic playing Cash pioneered in his early work.

Cash takes a break while recording in the studio.

essential albums

STUDIO

1957	*Johnny Cash with His Hot and Blue Guitar*
1958	*Sings the Songs That Made Him Famous*
1959	*Hymns by Johnny Cash*
1959	*Songs of Our Soil*
1959	*The Fabulous Johnny Cash*
1960	*Ride This Train*
1961	*Now Here's Johnny Cash*
1962	*All Aboard the Blue Train*
1962	*The Sound of Johnny Cash*
1963	*Blood, Sweat, and Tears*
1964	*Bitter Tears: Ballads of the American Indian*
1964	*I Walk the Line*
1965	*Orange Blossom Special*
1966	*Everybody Loves a Nut*
1966	*Happiness Is You*
1967	*Carryin' On with Johnny Cash and June Carter*
1968	*From Sea to Shining Sea*
1968	*Heart of Cash*
1969	*Get Rhythm*
1970	*Hello, I'm Johnny Cash*
1970	*Johnny Cash: The Legend*
1970	*Showtime*
1970	*Sunday Down South*
1970	*The Rough Cut King of Country Music*
1970	*The Singing Storyteller*
1971	*Johnny Cash: The Man, His World, His Music*
1971	*Man in Black*
1972	*A Thing Called Love*
1972	*International Superstar*
1973	*Any Old Wind That Blows*
1974	*Junkie and the Juicehead Minus Me*
1974	*Ragged Old Flag*
1975	*John R. Cash*
1975	*Look at Them Beans*
1976	*One Piece at a Time*
1977	*The Last Gunfighter Ballad*
1977	*The Rambler*
1978	*Gone Girl*
1978	*I Would Like to See You Again*
1979	*Silver*
1980	*Rockabilly Blues*
1981	*The Baron*

1982	*The Adventures of Johnny Cash*
1983	*Johnny*
1985	*Rainbow*
1987	*Johnny Cash Is Coming to Town*
1988	*Water from the Wells of Home*
1990	*Boom Chicka Boom*
1991	*The Mystery of Life*
1994	*American Recording*
1994	*Wanted Man*
1996	*Unchained*
2000	*American III: Solitary Man*
2002	*American IV: The Man Comes Around*
2002	*The Essential johnny Cash*
2003	*Unearthed*
2006	*American V: A Hundred Highways*
2010	*American VI: Ain't No Grave*

LIVE

1968	*At Folsom Prison*
1969	*At San Quentin*
1970	*The Johnny Cash Show*
1973	*På Österåker*
1975	*Strawberry Cake*
1983	*Koncert V Praze*

Jazz trumpeter Louis Armstrong, left, appearing on the *Johnny Cash Show* in 1970. Cash and Satchmo teamed up for a duet of "Blue Yodel No. 9."

BOB DYLAN

"Back then I guess most of my influences could be thought of as eccentric. Mass media had no overwhelming reach so I was drawn to the traveling performers passing through. The sideshow performers . . . I learned about dignity from them. Freedom too. Civil rights, human rights. How to stay within yourself."

—BOB DYLAN, 2009

Bob Dylan (born May 24, 1941, in Duluth, Minnesota) is an American singer-songwriter who, more than anyone, became the sonic manifestation of the turbulent 1960s. Since then, his poetic, observational style has searched out new ground and embraced an array of musical genres. His signature track, "Like a Rolling Stone"—also referred to as the "poor boy's lament"—is one of the most celebrated songs in the history of rock and roll.

Dylan's role as outsider stems from his middle-class Jewish upbringing in the upper Midwest. Entranced by the music he heard on the radio, he embraced everything from American Southern jazz to the budding genre of rock and roll. Although he held rockers like Little Richard and Buddy Holly in high esteem, Dylan began exploring folk music as a university student in the late 1950s. Drawn to its gravity and uncon-cern with frills, Dylan became active in the local scene and dropped his birth name, Robert Zimmerman.

In 1961 Dylan's idol Woody Guthrie was dying—which prompted Dylan's move to New York City. After a few public performances, critics started to notice Dylan's stage pres-ence and harmonica playing, leading up to a contract with Columbia at the end of that year. On his eponymous debut, Dylan mostly concentrated on safe interpretations of his favor-ite folk and blues standards. The general public showed little interest, but Dylan found a backer in Johnny Cash.

Dylan put more original material forward with *The Freewheelin' Bob Dylan* in 1963. Drawing on topical social and political events of the day, Dylan's songs contained a fair amount of folksy humor too—making fans out of the Beatles. Joan Baez, the popular folkstress, took an interest as well, inviting Dylan to perform with her and famously covering a number of his songs.

Dylan spent most of the 1960s adjusting to his newfound fame, confusing and sometimes rankling a bemused public with his eccentric stage persona and ever-changing musical style. By 1965 Dylan had come to fully embrace the electric guitar, which features prominently in *Highway 61 Revisited*, without a doubt Dylan's magnum opus.

Dylan's output slowed after a motorcycle accident in 1966; he didn't tour again until 1974. Dylan's releases during that decade and the 1980s veered wildly between songwriting and production extremes—Dylan also fervently embraced Christianity, a theme he would regularly expound upon dur-ing performances and in several records. A number of releases flopped, but Dylan regained his balance in the 1990s, concen-trating on simpler blues and folk sounds and releasing new material on *Time Out of Mind* in 1997.

In the last decade Dylan has put forth the beginnings of his autobiography and added to his impressive canon of record-ings. *With Modern Times* in 2006, Dylan had his first No. 1 release in thirty years—the album was showered in Grammy awards and glowing press.

essential albums

STUDIO

1962	*Bob Dylan*
1963	*The Freewheelin' Bob Dylan*
1964	*Another Side of Bob Dylan*
1964	*The Times They Are a-Changin'*
1965	*Bringing It All Back Home*
1965	*Highway 61 Revisited*
1966	*Blonde on Blonde*
1967	*Bob Dylan's Greatest Hits*
1967	*John Wesley Harding*
1969	*Nashville Skyline*
1970	*New Morning*
1970	*Self Portrait*
1973	*Dylan*
1973	*Pat Garrett & Billy The Kid*
1974	*Before The Flood*
1974	*Planet Waves*
1975	*Blood on the Tracks*
1975	*The Basement Tapes*
1976	*Desire*
1978	*Hard Rain*
1978	*Street Legal*
1979	*Slow Train Coming*
1980	*Saved*
1981	*Shot of Love*
1983	*Infidels*
1985	*Biograph*
1985	*Empire Burlesque*
1986	*Knocked Out Loaded*
1988	*Down in the Groove*
1988	*Dylan and the Dead*
1989	*Oh Mercy*
1990	*Under the Red Sky*
1991	*The Bootleg Series, Volumes 1–3*
1992	*Good as I Been to You*
1993	*World Gone Wrong*
1994	*Bob Dylan's Greatest Hits, Volume 3*
1997	*Time Out of Mind*
2001	*Love and Theft*
2005	*No Direction Home*
2006	*Modern Times*
2007	*Dylan*
2008	*Tell Tale Signs*
2009	*Together Through Life*

DYLAN'S SIGNIFICANCE

Never just a musician, Bob Dylan's influence has bled into every aspect of popular culture and public discourse. Immortalized for his musical scope and vision, as well as his off-beat, enigmatic public face, innumerable musicians and many major publications consider Dylan to be a living American treasure—certainly one of the most important voices in music over the last century.

A master at crystallizing complex, literate principles in the form of the popular song, Dylan has always innovated lyrically. Drawing comparisons to some of the greatest writers and artists in recorded history, Dylan's body of work is the subject of passionate and growing academic and literary study, encompassing everything from his early folk songs to his electric-guitar-accompanied 1960s work and more recent explorations of disparate genres.

Awards and Honors

1979	Grammy Award for Best Album of the Year, for *The Concert for Bangladesh*, with Billy Preston, Bob Dylan, Eric Clapton, George Harrison, Klaus Voormann, Leon Russell, Ravi Shankar, and Ringo Starr
1979	Grammy Award for Best Rock Vocal Performance, Male, for "Gotta Serve Somebody," with Billy Preston, Bob Dylan, Eric Clapton, George Harrison, Klaus Voormann, Leon Russell, Ravi Shankar, and Ringo Starr
1988	Inducted into the Rock and Roll Hall of Fame
1989	Grammy Award for Best Rock Performance by a Duo or Group With Vocal, for *The Traveling Wilburys, Volume One*, with the Traveling Wilburys
1991	Grammy Award for Lifetime Achievement
1994	Grammy Award for Best Traditional Folk Album, for *World Gone Wrong*
1997	Grammy Award for Album Of The Year, for *Time Out Of Mind*
1997	Grammy Award for Best Contemporary Folk Album, for *Time Out of Mind*
1997	Grammy Award for Best Male Rock Vocal Performance, for "Cold Irons Bound"
2000	Academy Award for Best Original Song, for "Things Have Changed," from Wonder Boys
2001	Grammy Award for Best Contemporary Folk Album, for *Love and Theft*
2006	Grammy Award for Best Contemporary Folk/Americana Album, for *Modern Times*
2006	Grammy Award for Best Solo Rock Vocal Performance, for "Someday Baby"

DON FELDER

"I just told the truth as I saw it, as I remembered it. You can't stop someone from telling the truth. I tried to be as honest and truthful not only about myself but about everyone who was there. Like any story or divorce, there's his side, her side, and the truth. This is as close to the truth as I could get without pulling any punches, especially about myself. It's me, with all my ugliness, my warts, everything. My sins and evils, so everyone could see it. That's the truth. I didn't try to paint [the Eagles] in some ugly and bitter way and make myself out to be the shining star. That's just crap."

—DON FELDER

Don Felder (born September 21, 1947, in Gainesville, Florida) is usually noted for his twenty-seven-year stint as lead guitarist for the Eagles.

After witnessing Elvis's game-changing performances on television, Felder took to the guitar, at one point teaming up with Stephen Stills when they were both teenagers. While at Gainesville High School, he met future bandmate Bernie Leadon. After finishing high school, Felder went north, first to New York and then Boston, where he met the rest of the Eagles. After moving to the West Coast in 1972, Felder stayed in touch with members of the band, occasionally collaborating and eventually joining as guitarist after playing slide guitar their song "Good Day in Hell."

Felder is responsible for the music—and famed guitar solo—of "Hotel California," the Eagles' biggest hit by far and an iconic track in the rock and roll canon.

Felder used the band's 1980 breakup as an opportunity to plant his solo career. Only one true record resulted, 1983's *Airborne*, but Felder soldiered on as a session contributor and a television host and musician. Most recently Felder is an author, having written a 2008 tell-all recounting his time with the Eagles, his ejection, and the ensuing legal battle.

THE EAGLES

The Eagles were already an established, successful enterprise when Felder was invited into the fold in 1974, largely to assist in the band's desired transition from a folksy country sound to louder, harder mainstream rockers. Felder first appeared on *On the Border*, but before long, it became apparent he had boarded a sinking ship. Egos and allegiances within the band were already inflamed, and the band's increasing exposure and success was taking a toll.

One Of These Nights was an objective hit, only to be outdone by *Their Greatest Hits* in 1976, one of the best-selling American albums of all time. Later that year the band would release *Hotel California*, their most important work and best-selling studio record.

Whether everyone in the band knew it or not, the Eagles were nearing the end of its union. In the aftermath of the release of *The Long Run* in 1977, tensions between Glenn Frey and Felder reached a head; they spent a significant amount of time bickering on stage during a tour in 1980. The Eagles squeezed out one more album, *Eagles Live*, composed of cuts from it live act, before dissolving.

The 1974–75 Eagles lineup. From left: Bernie Leadon, Glenn Frey, Don Henley, Randy Meisner, and Don Felder. On the first album that Felder appeared on, 1974's *On the Border*, Felder only contributed to two tracks: he plays slide on "Good Day in Hell" and performed a guitar duet with Glenn Frey on "Already Gone."

essential albums

WITH THE EAGLES
1974	*On the Border*
1975	*One of These Nights*
1976	*Hotel California*
1979	*The Long Run*
1980	*Eagles Live*
1994	*Hell Freezes Over*

SOLO
1983	*Airborne*

Awards and Honors

1975	Grammy Award for Best Pop Vocal Performance by a Duo, Group or Chorus, for "Lyin' Eyes," with the Eagles"
1977	Grammy Award for Record of the Year, for "Hotel California, with the Eagles"
1977	Grammy Award for Best Arrangement for Voices, for "New Kid In Town," with the Eagles
1979	Grammy Award for Best Rock Vocal Performance by a Duo or Group, for "Heartache Tonight," with the Eagles

VINCE GILL

"I had so many songs written and I always do. I always write a lot of songs and I feel like sometimes there's some really fine songs that just get shoved in a desk drawer and never come out again. That's kind of disheartening after a lot of years, so I just went for it and it was unique and it was curious and people really seemed to enjoy it, and all in one fell swoop they saw the diversity that I love in my music and what I like and what I've learned, a great experience."

—VINCE GILL, 2010

Vince Gill (born April 12, 1957, in Norman, Oklahoma) is a popular country and rock and roll artist who rose to fame as a member of Pure Prairie League and, in the 1980s, as a singer and solo artist in his own right. With his integrity—and fan base—intact, he currently reigns as one of the winningest and most bankable contemporary country stars.

Gill's early music interests revolved around the sounds of bluegrass, including the banjo and harmonica, which his mother played. Gill gained a reputation as a talented and charismatic multi-instrumentalist stemming from his work with several bands in high school. After high school, he moved to Los Angeles to stake out a music career.

The country-rock band Pure Prairie League awarded Gill the spot as its lead singer in 1979, leading to a successful trio of albums and the 1980 hit "Let Me Love You Tonight."

Gill set off for Nashville in 1983, after signing a solo recording deal. His singles received moderate attention and airplay, but it was his album *The Things That Matter*, featuring Roseanne Cash, that put Gill at the top of the country-rock scene.

In 1989, Gill built on his success with *When I Call Your Name*, paving the way for a solid decade of hit albums, top-charting singles, and multiple Grammy nominations. As his profile rose, Gill stole the attention of Dire Straits front man Mark Knopfler, who asked him to join the band; Gill declined.

Gill is a champion of the Fender Telecaster, citing its simplicity and its place as the favorite ax of so many of his idols as major selling points.

GILL'S RECENT SUCCESSES

Since 1990 Gill has enjoyed the status of a bona-fide star with near universal appeal across multiple musical genres. His 1992 album *I Still Believe in You* generated his first single to hit No. 1 on the U.S. charts, and a later release, *When Love Finds You*, sold well despite its pop leanings.

Gill challenged himself with a string of more ambitious and complex releases in the mid-1990s, calling back musically to his bluegrass beginnings but debuting some of his most nuanced, introspective lyrics yet. Every one of Gill's albums since 1989 has reached the top five on the U.S. country charts, and he can count Reba McEntire, Amy Grant, Barbra Streisand, Sheryl Crow, Bonnie Raitt, and Dolly Parton among his collaborative and duet partners.

essential albums

STUDIO

1984	*Turn Me Loose*
1985	*The Things That Matter*
1987	*The Way Back Home*
1989	*When I Call Your Name*
1991	*Pocket Full of Gold*
1992	*I Still Believe in You*
1994	*When Love Finds You*
1996	*High Lonesome Sound*
1998	*The Key*
2000	*Let's Make Sure We Kiss Goodbye*
2003	*Next Big Thing*
2006	*These Days*

Awards and Honors

1990	Grammy Award for Best Country Vocal Performance, Male, for "When I Call Your Name"
1991	Grammy Award for Best Country Vocal Collaboration, for "Restless," with Ricky Skaggs and Steve Wariner
1992	Grammy Award for Best Country Song, "I Still Believe in You," with John Jarvis
1992	Grammy Award for Best Country Vocal Performance, Male, for "I Still Believe In You"
1993	Grammy Award for Best Country Instrumental Performance, for "Red Wing," with Asleep at the Wheel
1995	Grammy Award for Best Male Country Vocal Performance, for "When Love Finds You"
1995	Grammy Award for Best Country Song, for "Go Rest High on that Mountain"
1996	Grammy Award for Best Country Collaboration With Vocals, for "High Lonesome Sounds," with Alison Krauss and Union Station
1996	Grammy Award for Best Male Country Vocal Performance, for "World's Apart"
1997	Grammy Award for Best Male Country Vocal Performance, for "Pretty Little Adriana"
1998	Grammy Award for Best Country Instrumental Performance, for "A Soldier's Joy," with Randy Scruggs
1998	Grammy Award for Best Male Country Vocal Performance, for "If You Ever Have Forever In Mind"
1999	Grammy Award for Best Country Instrumental Performance, for "Bob's Breakdown," with Asleep at the Wheel
2001	Grammy Award for Best Country Instrumental Performance, for "Foggy Mountain Breakdown," with Albert Lee, Earl Scruggs, Gary Scruggs, Glen Duncan, Jerry Douglas, Leon Russell, Marty Stuart, Paul Shaffer, Randy Scruggs, and Steve Martin
2003	Grammy Award for Best Male Country Vocal Performance, for "The Next Big Thing"
2006	Grammy Award for Best Male Country Vocal Performance, for "The Reason Why"
2007	Grammy Award for Best Country Album, for *These Days*
2008	Grammy Award for Best Country Instrumental Performance, for "Cluster Pluck," with Albert Lee, Brad Paisley, Brent Mason, James Burton, John Jorgenson, Redd Volkaert, and Steve Wariner

Gill onstage at the 2007 Crossroads Guitar Festival at Toyota Park in Bridgeview, Illinois

BERT JANSCH

"There's one thing we never talk about, music. We don't. We never talk music to each other. You understand? It's like, we talk about what we're going to do next. Where we're going, what bars we're going to visit, whether we can have a game of golf at all, or who won the football game. We never talk about music, never. You talk about everything else, but never music. The only time we ever talk about music is to say, 'Let's have a rehearsal,' and that's it, we get together and play. If anything comes out there you go. Other than that you don't talk, you know? 'Cause you don't need to. And we find it hard to talk to anyone else about music cause we just don't."

—BERT JANSCH, 1970

Bert Jansch (born November 3, 1943, in Glasgow, Scotland) is a folk singer-songwriter respected especially for his handling of the acoustic guitar.

Jansch had a meager beginning as an artist, immersing himself in the 1960s British folk scene. He aligned himself with the reigning generation of folk acts, spending a few years as a traveling musician with a hand-to-mouth existence.

After settling in London, Jansch quickly found success after submitting a scrappy demo tape to Transatlantic Records, resulting in his self-titled debut in 1965. Capitalizing on the warm reception his music received, as well as welcome—if inaccurate—comparisons to popular American Bob Dylan, Jansch released a series of two albums, firmly establishing himself as a culturally and politically relevant acoustic master and songwriter. Jansch became the toast of the London scene, settling into an informal residency.

In 1967, he teamed up with songwriter/guitarist John Renbourn to form the band Pentangle. After some commercial success as a jazz-influenced folk group, Pentangle dissolved in 1973.

After a detour from the music business, Jansch returned to the scene in 1977 and set up shop with a band called Conundrum, opening a chapter of collaborating and recording that would culminate with a Pentangle reunion in 1980. Jansch's health hit a roadblock owing to his alcohol abuse, but he sobered up in 1987 and forged ahead with a renewed sense of creativity.

Since the 1990s and beyond, Jansch has continued to perform gigs large and small, considered his bread and butter, in the Great Britain and abroad. Most recently he has released a 2006 album, *The Black Swan*, and worked with contemporary British band Babyshambles on stage and in the studio.

Awards and Honors

2001 Lifetime Achievement Award, BBC Radio 2, with Pentangle

PENTANGLE & HIATUS

Pentangle grew out of Jansch's collaboration with John Renbourn, a fellow British folkie. The pair decided to expand their sound and recruited a full band, including singer Jacqui McShee, drummer Terry Cox, and double bassist Danny Thompson. Bringing together an impressive array of influences and sounds, from jazz to liturgical music to contemporary folk and rock, the band's first public appearance in 1967 was a smash.

In 1968 the band got serious about recording and touring, booking progressively larger venues and signing up with Jansch's original solo label, Transatlantic. Pentangle released two albums that year, following up with *Basket of Light* in 1969, its bestselling work. Just a year later, though, Pentangle's star fell after the release of *Cruel Sister*, a record full of traditional folk songs. On the outs with its record label, the band eked out two more albums, but Jansch would call it quits in 1973 and assume a self-imposed exile on a Welsh farm, effectively ending the band.

A decade later the core of the band got back together, sans a few founding members. Three albums resulted from the reunion. McShee took the reigns from Jansch after his second departure, and the band has reappeared in various configurations in recent years, nursed by significant nostalgia and fans' respect for their singular style of music.

essential albums

SOLO

1965	*It Don't Bother Me*
1965	*Bert Jansch*
1967	*Nicola*
1969	*Birthday Blues*
1971	*Rosemary Lane*
1973	*Moonshine*
1975	*Santa Barbara Honeymoon*
1979	*Avocet*
1980	*Thirteen Down*
1982	*Heartbreak*
1985	*After the Long Night/Playing the Game*
1990	*The Ornament Tree*
1990	*Sketches*
1992	*After the Dance*
1993	*Charlie Girl*
1995	*When the Circus Comes to Town*
1995	*Chasers*
1997	*Heavy Machinery*
1998	*Blackwater Side*
1998	*Toy Balloon*
2000	*Crimson Moon*
2002	*Edge of a Dream*
2004	*The River Sessions*
2007	*Fresh as a Sweet Sunday Morning*
2008	*Three Chord Trick*

WITH PENTANGLE

1968	*The Pentangle*
1968	*Sweet Child*
1969	*Basket of Light*
1970	*Cruel Sister*
1971	*Reflection*
1972	*Solomon's Seal*
1985	*Open the Door*
1986	*In the Round*
1989	*So Early in the Spring*
1991	*Think of Tomorrow*
1993	*One More Road*
1995	*Live 1994*

Bert Jansch performs at the Bumbershoot music and arts festival in Seattle, 2007.

JONI MITCHELL

Joni Mitchell (born November 7, 1943, in Fort McLeod, Alberta) is a Canadian singer-songwriter and guitarist noted for her complex, unorthodox tunings and chords. A self-professed "ham," Mitchell, born Roberta Joan Anderson, discovered singing at the age of 9 while in a hospital recovering from polio. Teaching herself guitar and ukulele as a teenager, Mitchell left college after a year and moved to Toronto in 1964 to sing and perform full time. After a move to New York City and a brief period of exposure and success in the East Coast folk club and coffeehouse scene, Mitchell eventually migrated to Los Angeles, where she recorded and released her self-titled, debut solo album in 1968.

Mitchell's playing style is the product of her acoustic beginnings as well as her love for other sounds and rhythms, largely informed by classical, jazz, and percussion. Her personal, emotional lyrics and ability to consistently reinvent herself—most recently, as a visual artist—have influenced her peers as well as a new, diverse generation of performers.

Awards and Honors

1969	Grammy Award for Best Folk Performance, for "Clouds"
1974	Grammy Award for Best Arrangement Accompanying Vocalists, for "Down To You"
1995	Grammy Award for Best Pop Album, for *Turbulent Indigo*
1997	Inducted into the Rock and Roll Hall of Fame
2000	Grammy Award for Best Traditional Pop Vocal Album, for *Both Sides Now*
2002	Grammy Award for Lifetime Achievement
2003	Ranked No. 72 on *Rolling Stone*'s list of the 100 Greatest Guitarists of All Time
2007	Grammy Award for Best Pop Instrumental Performance, for "One Week Last Summer"

essential albums

STUDIO

1968	*Song to a Seagull*
1969	*Clouds*
1970	*Ladies of the Canyon*
1971	*Blue*
1972	*For the Roses*
1974	*Court and Spark*
1974	*Miles of Aisles*
1975	*The Hissing of Summer Lawns*
1976	*Hejira*
1977	*Don Juan's Reckless Daughter*
1979	*Mingus*
1980	*Shadows and Light*
1982	*Wild Things Run Fast*
1985	*Dog Eat Dog*
1988	*Chalk Mark in a Rain Storm*
1991	*Night Ride Home*
1994	*Turbulent Indigo*
1998	*Taming the Tiger*
2000	*Both Sides Now*
2002	*Travelogue*
2007	*Shine*

MITCHELL'S CAREER

Following her debut, Mitchell released a string of increasingly well-received records, topping out with 1971's *Blue*, her most iconic work. Considered a gold standard by which future singer-songwriters have come to be judged, the album continues to draw accolades for its poetic lyrics.

Mitchell married critical praise with commercial success as the 1970s rolled on, scoring another hit with 1974's *Court and Spark*. Later releases would look to jazz and global percussion for inspiration, further distinguishing Mitchell's catalog. Her infatuation with jazz is perhaps best exemplified in the double release *Don Juan's Reckless Daughter*, featuring Larry Carlton, Wayne Shorter, and Chaka Khan. The LP grabbed the attention of jazzman Charles Mingus, with whom Mitchell worked on an album as lyricist.

Through the 1980s Mitchell experimented with electronic production techniques and synthesizers before coming back to her acoustic home ground with *Night Ride Home* and *Turbulent Indigo* in 1991 and 1994.

After releasing her unique take on a greatest hits collection, 1996's *Hits and Misses*—containing favorite tracks that failed to chart—Mitchell has made a concerted career shift. She announced her "retirement" in 2002, which has been interpreted by the press as her official divorce from the corporate recording industry. Nevertheless, *Shine* was revealed in 2007 via the Starbucks Hear Music label.

Mitchell is a noted visual artist; her recent endeavors have coalesced around this aspect of her life at her homes in Los Angeles and British Columbia, and her painting and photography have been exhibited, but not offered for sale.

"The more I can surprise myself, the more I'll stay in this business, and the twiddling of the notes is one way to keep the pilgrimage going. You're constantly pulling the rug out from under yourself, so you don't get a chance to settle into any kind of formula."

—JONI MITCHELL, ON OPEN TUNING, 1996

Joni Mitchell in concert, 1998

BRAD PAISLEY

"We knew we wanted to talk about technology and how the world is changing. It's the hardest thing in the world to take the emotions I've had in the last six months and put them in a song, [including] having two boys now and thinking about them. That whole first verse just so resonates with the world I grew up in and the world they're going to grow up in. They're two different places. I was thinking back to the world my grandfather grew up in. In spite of some of the worst times economically that we've ever had, there's a feeling of hope and a feeling of pride."

—BRAD PAISLEY, ON WRITING "WELCOME TO THE FUTURE," 2009

Brad Paisley (born October 28, 1972, in Glen Dale, West Virginia) is a contemporary singer-songwriter working in the country and Southern rock vein. Paisley's records have performed consistently well on the U.S. country charts.

Paisley has been penning songs from the age of 12. With the support of his church and local community, Paisley frequently had access to a captive audience on which to test his compositions and developing skills as a guitarist. As a teenager Paisley was a featured performer on popular country music radio program *WWVA Jamboree*.

After graduating as an ASCAP (the American Society of Composers, Authors, and Publishers) scholarship student at Belmont University, Paisley got work at Arista Nashville as a songwriter, making the connections that would clear the way for his major-label debut, *Who Needs Pictures*, in 1999. Appearances at the Grand Ole Opry as well as on a cable

television special exposed Paisley to a vast, diverse audience. Music institutions took notice and, before long, Paisley was the recipient of his first CMA and Grammy awards.

Almost overnight, Paisley found himself in the good graces of some of country's biggest names; he has appeared or toured with Reba McEntire, Alan Jackson, Taylor Swift, Carrie Underwood, Vince Gill, and B.B. King—not to mention his usual backing band, the Drama Kings.

Commercially it seems Paisley is incapable of taking a misstep; each release has been received by fans more rapturously than the last, and he has broken several country chart records. In his brief yet potent career, Paisley has performed at the White House and served as host of the CMA awards.

Recently Paisley has branched out into the realm of Hollywood; he is set to produce and provide music for a new series, *Nashville*, on cable television in 2010.

essential albums

STUDIO

1999	*Who Needs Pictures*
2001	*Part II*
2003	*Mud on the Tires*
2005	*Time Well Wasted*
2007	*5th Gear*
2008	*Play*
2009	*American Saturday Night*

Awards and Honors

2007   Grammy Award for Best Country Instrumental Performance, for "Throttleneck"

2008   Grammy Award for Best Country Instrumental Performance, for "Cluster Pluck," with James Burton, Vince Gill, John Jorgenson, Albert Lee, Brent Mason, Redd Volkaert, and Steve Wariner

2008   Grammy Award for Best Male Country Vocal Performance, for "Letter to Me"

Paisley performing in Pelham, Alabama, during the Bonfires and Amplifiers Tour in 2007

PAISLEY & CROOK

Paisley supports Crook Custom Guitars, an independent luthier that specializes in made-to-order instruments, including baritone guitars—one area of Paisley's expertise. Founded by Bill Crook, the company provides full-service design and repair options, and Crook's axes are known for their unique, wild finishes as well as a level of customization not usually offered by larger companies.

Paisley poses with his wife, actress Kimberly Williams-Paisley, at the 2005 Country Music Awards in New York City.

BONNIE RAITT

Bonnie Raitt, (born November 8, 1949, in Burbank, California) is a Harvard-educated singer-songwriter and guitarist who came to prominence in the 1970s with a series of blues-tinged radio-friendly hits.

Raitt's parents were both involved in the musical world—her father was Broadway actor John Raitt—and they encouraged her to pursue her interest in guitar playing at home. She started on a Stella guitar as an 8-year old and fully dedicated herself to playing at summer camp in the Adirondacks.

As a politically inclined college student at Harvard's Radcliffe College, Raitt befriended Cambridge blues producer Dick Waterman, falling in with his circle and eventually cutting her studies short to devote herself full time to playing in Boston-area venues.

Raitt was soon a fixture on the Boston and New York scenes, and she issued her major label debut, *Bonnie Raitt*, in 1971. Her efforts through the 1970s were critically lauded, but none of them generated significant sales. Slowly moving out of her blues and folk roots, Raitt scored big with *Sweet Forgiveness* in 1977.

Raitt spent the 1980s struggling to define her audience and sound, switching record labels in the process. Finally finding solid ground after a long period of professional uncertainty and personal struggles with drugs and alcohol, 1989's *Nick of Time* was a definitive comeback effort for Raitt. The singer found herself at the height of popularity, raking in Grammy awards and dollars, a trend that would carry her through the 1990s.

Luck of the Draw and *Longing in Their Hearts* were both solid chart successes; her several efforts between 1998 and 2006 have fared less well, but Raitt continues to perform for adoring crowds, especially at politically and socially progressive events.

"I think speaking about how you're treated and what you're longing for, that's what songs have been about, whether they're Celtic or African or Gypsy music. The form and the specific words may change, but anger, jealousy, hurt, and loss are all there. . . . But that whole argument about 'How can a white girl sing the blues? How can you have validity?' Well, I have yet to meet somebody who doesn't have real pain. And as you get older, those things become richer because experience brings depth. I prefer people in their older, more seasoned form, but I also think it's thrilling to hear Alanis Morissette and Liz Phair. Those are two of my favorite artists right now. It'll be great to hear what Liz Phair is singing about when she's 75."

—BONNIE RAITT, 1995

Raitt is still touring, most recently with Taj Mahal during their 2009 tour.

essential albums

STUDIO ALBUMS

1971	*Bonnie Raitt*
1972	*Give it Up*
1974	*Streetlights*
1975	*Home Plate*
1977	*Sweet Forgiveness*
1979	*The Glow*
1982	*Green Light*
1986	*Nine Lives*
1989	*Nick of Time*
1991	*Luck of the Draw*
1994	*Longing in Their Hearts*
1995	*Road Tested*
1998	*Fundamental*
2002	*Takin' My Time*
2002	*Silver Lining*
2005	*Souls Alike*
2006	*Bonnie Raitt and Friends*

RAITT'S ACTIVISM

The musician's list of pet causes is nearly as long as her résumé as singer, guitarist, and entertainer. The engaging, progressive scene drew her to college in Cambridge, Massachusetts in the 1960s, and her activism kicked off on a national level the following decade, starting with her work on the environment's behalf. She is a founder of M.U.S.E., or Musicians United for Safe Energy, a staunchly antinuclear energy and war coalition.

Raitt has dedicated herself to uniquely American causes as well. In addition to voicing her concern for Native American rights and performing in support of various local and national candidates for office, she backs the Rhythm & Blues Foundation, an advocacy group that serves to protect the interests of many of the blues and R&B heroes she befriended early in her career and has idolized all her life.

Awards and Honors

1989	Grammy Award for Album of the Year, for *Nick Of Time*
1989	Grammy Award for Best Pop Vocal Performance, Female, for "Nick of Time"
1989	Grammy Award for Best Rock Vocal Performance, Female, for "Nick of Time"
1989	Grammy Award for Best Traditional Blues Recording, for "I'm in the Mood," with John Lee Hooker
1991	Grammy Award for Best Pop Vocal Performance, Female, for "Something To Talk About"
1991	Grammy Award for Best Rock Performance by a Duo or Group with Vocal, for "Good Man, Good Woman," with Delbert McClinton
1994	Grammy Award for Best Pop Album, for *Longing in Their Hearts*
1996	Grammy Award for Best Rock Instrumental Performance, for "SRV Shuffle," with Art Neville, B.B. King, Dr. John, Buddy Guy, Eric Clapton, Jimmie Vaughan, and Robert Cray
2000	Inducted into the Rock and Roll Hall of Fame.

Raitt performing at the Berkeley Community Theater in the late 1970s

RICHARD THOMPSON

essential albums

WITH FAIRPORT CONVENTION

1968	*Fairport Convention*
1969	*Unhalfbricking*
1969	*Liege & Lief*
1970	*Full House*
1971	*Angel Delight*

WITH LINDA THOMPSON

1974	*I Want To See The Bright Lights Tonight*
1975	*Hokey Pokey*
1975	*Pour Down Like Silver*
1978	*First Light*
1979	*Sunnyvista*
1982	*Shoot Out The Lights*

SOLO

1972	*Henry the Human Fly*
1981	*Strict Tempo!*
1983	*Hand of Kindness*
1984	*Small Town Romance*
1985	*Across a Crowded Room*
1986	*Daring Adventures*
1988	*Amnesia*
1991	*Rumor & Sigh*
1992	*Sweet Talker*
1993	*Watching the Dark*
1994	*Mirror Blue*
1996	*You? Me? Us?*
1997	*Industry*
1999	*Mock Tudor*
2003	*The Old Kit Bag*
2005	*Front Parlour Ballads*
2005	*Grizzly Man*
2007	*Sweet Warrior*

Richard Thompson (born April 3, 1949, in London, England) is a respected songwriter and guitarist who has penned tunes for a legion of musicians, including David Gilmour, Bonnie Raitt, and Elvis Costello.

Thompson's father and several other family members were amateur and professional musicians, and Thompson grew up listening to everything from jazz standards to the new sounds of rock and roll that were taking hold in America and Europe.

Thompson's first significant exposure came as an 18-year-old via Fairport Convention, the band with which he would sign his first recording contract. It was Thompson's formidable guitar playing and growing songwriting ability that brought the group rapid acclaim, as it quickly moved out of playing covers to breathing life into Thompson's own compositions.

Following his ambition and instinct, Thompson abandoned the band that he started in 1972 and set off on his own as a solo artist. He met singer Linda Peters, who appears on his debut. Thompson and Peters soon married and, after the chilly reception of *Henry the Human Fly*, began recording as a duo. After three albums that failed to generate much buzz, Richard and Linda Thompson committed themselves full time to their expanding exploration of Islam.

The year 1977 saw the Thompsons' return to the music scene, but it wasn't until 1982's *Shoot Out the Lights*—the last collaboration with soon-to-be ex-wife, Linda—that the guitarist would enjoy any significant critical or commercial success.

In the 1980s Thompson fleshed out a bigger, more accessible sound, nurturing a lucrative relationship with PolyGram records and relocating permanently to the United States. Thompson earned a Grammy nomination in 1991 for *Rumor and Sigh* but would endure label troubles, eventually electing to produce and distribute his own music beginning in 2003.

"In writing songs, you ought to pull things into a sharper focus, so you draw characters who are larger than life, and you write about experiences that perhaps most people don't have from day to day. . . . People want to hear about the extremes of human nature. They want things that are larger than their own lives, and more romantic, and not necessarily of their own experiences. People want to hear stories that are a bit more of an escape, and I want to write stories that are a bit more of an escape. To write about my own life seems mundane. To twist the stories of your own life or to write fiction without any real intention other than to entertain yourself seems far more interesting."

—RICHARD THOMPSON, 2001

A SIZEABLE CAREER

Thompson has covered considerable ground as a session player and contributor to other musicians' work. Much of his work outside his solo career has gone in more experimental or challenging directions, frequently bridging traditional and contemporary compositions with counterintuitive instrumentations; for example, the electronic interpretation of English standards on *Morris On* in the early 1970s.

Thompson maintains his ties to Fairport Convention, serving as a regular guest at the band's Cropredy Festival every year.

Awards and Honors

2004 Ranked No. 19 on *Rolling Stone*'s list of the 100 Greatest Guitarists of All Time
2006 BBC Lifetime Achievement Award

Thompson performing in Prospect Park at a Celebrate Brooklyn! festival in 2007. The festival brings an array of artists to New York every year.

THOMPSON'S DUAL TALENTS

Thompson is noted for his level of comfort with both acoustic and electric playing; luthier Danny Ferrington has constructed a number of both types for him. Otherwise Thompson is a known Stratocaster aficionado and prefers Lowdens for his acoustic needs. The company issued a model under his name in 2007.

One of many skilled guitarists to use the technique, Thompson sometimes employs a double-picking method by playing low notes with a plectrum and the higher range with his free bare fingers.

Thompson has demonstrated his stature as a music historian and scholar, too—he is behind a project called *1,000 Years of Popular Music*, inspired by *Playboy*'s solicitation of the music industry to draft a list of the top songs from the last 1,000 years. In performances, Thompson has embraced everything from medieval and Victorian music to the more recent work of infamous pop sensation Britney Spears, accompanied by only his guitar, a piano, and percussion.

HARD ROCK AND METAL

Hard rock and heavy metal have given the world some of its most flamboyant performers and simply unforgettable— even downright despicable—moments on stage. Tending to interpret the trinity of "sex, drugs, and rock and roll" as birthright and business plan, the hard rockers and metal gods of the 1960s onward studiously devoured the blues and rock greats of the time—and went on to laugh in their faces, sometimes all the way to the grave.

Wielding the guitar as instrument as well as weapon and placing an emphasis on speed and sonic acrobatics, these axmen have never been afraid to break the rules—but they've contributed more than their fair share of groundbreaking techniques to the modern guitarist's bag of tricks.

NUNO BETTENCOURT

Nuno Bettencourt (born September 20, 1966, in Azores, Portugal) is a guitarist and solo artist, associated with metal group Extreme, whose influence is rooted in a counterintuitive stable of pop and rock and roll greats, including Brian May, Jimmy Page, and Eddie Van Halen.

Bettencourt's parents moved him and his brothers from the Azores to the outskirts of Boston when he was small. Following in his older brother's footsteps, Bettencourt took an interest in the drums and, later, the guitar, finding himself more interested in teaching himself how to play than going to school. Without finishing high school, Bettencourt threw himself into music full time, finding commercial success in the mid-1980s.

After Bettencourt had made a name for himself, Chicago-based Washburn Guitars approached him about lending his name to a signature series, a line that has expanded significantly since its 1990 debut. The Nuno Bettencourt N4 is unique for its unusually generous cutaway, and the model has proven to be a major factor in the guitarist's funky, rhythmic sound.

BETTENCOURT'S PROJECTS

During Extreme's late-1990s hiatus, Bettencourt took the opportunity to establish several other projects, principally a solo career which has so far produced one album, 1997's *Schizophonic*. Bettencourt can also take credit for helming Mourning Widows and, after that band's dissolution in 2001, DramaGods (originally known as Population 1). The latter outfit has appeared on Craig Ferguson's *Late Late Show* and, without the support of a formal recording contract, has been releasing its work via iTunes and other online avenues.

Bettencourt has worked as a supporting artist with members of Jane's Addiction, illusionist Criss Angel, Dweezil Zappa, Steve Perry of Journey, Rihanna, and Baby Animals, his wife's band.

Opposite: Bettencourt promoting Extreme's 1995 album, *Waiting for the Punchline*

EXTREME

Extreme formed out of the rubble of three other Boston-area bands, Bettencourt's Sinful, bass player Pat Badger's group In the Pink, and Gary Cherone and Paul Geary's the Dream. After the four musicians met in 1985, they commenced songwriting, and by 1988 their new band was signed to A&M Records. Extreme's debut, though a modest seller, earned its place in 1980s pop culture; one of its cuts was featured in the film *Bill & Ted's Excellent Adventure*.

The foursome followed up in 1990 with *Pornograffitti*, an extravagant effort that spawned two hit singles in the United States. Enjoying increasing exposure, the band made a very visible appearance at the Freddie Mercury Tribute Concert for AIDS Awareness in 1992, leading up to its third album, *III Sides to Every Story*. Struggling to find new listeners, the band dropped one more album before calling it quits in 1996.

Extreme's members occupied themselves with solo projects and, in singer Cherone's case, a collaboration with Van Halen. Almost a decade passed before the band would decide to reunite. In 2004 the band members made a stop in the Azores, Bettencourt's birthplace, before announcing a string of Extreme dates in the northeastern United States, and by 2008 they were prepared to take to the road worldwide in support of their latest album, *Saudades de Rock*.

essential albums

1989	*Extreme*
1990	*Pornograffitti*
1992	*III Sides to Every Story*
1995	*Waiting for the Punchline*
2008	*Saudades de Rock*

"*Saudades* is a Portuguese word which comes from my background but it's not necessarily there because of that. I wanted to signify our time away and kind of how much we've been longing and missing the rock and roll that we do. In Portuguese you say that to things that you lost and something that went away and you aren't sure that you'll have ever again. Or you can say it about a person near to you. We also felt the same thing from the fans too, that they were kind of missing the band. I think this was the appropriate title for how we were feeling."

—NUNO BETTENCOURT, 2008

RITCHIE BLACKMORE

"That's the bottom line with us: we are musical nomads, because no one else is doing what we're doing. If other musicians do the old music, they tend to do it in a very traditional form, exactly how it was written. We like to mess with it a bit, which I think is how the minstrels back in those days would have done it. Oftentimes, the minstrels in those days could not read music, so they would improvise on a theme that they'd heard in the other village, which would result in interpretive changes in the music."

—RITCHIE BLACKMORE, 2009

Ritchie Blackmore (born April 14, 1945, in Weston-super-Mare, England) is the formidable guitarist known for founding Deep Purple, Rainbow, and Blackmore's Night. With an outsize reputation for eccentricity and stubbornness, Blackmore is one of rock and roll's institutions.

Blackmore's parents, though supportive of his musical talent, were strict, insisting that he learn proper classical guitar technique, a system that Blackmore has called "nonsense." As a young guitarist in the 1960s, Blackmore lined up gigs, did session work, and met the associates and fellow musicians who would help him found Deep Purple and produce the band's debut.

Blackmore has achieved status as a premiere axman of uncommon precision; his classically influenced riffs and solos, via his favored Fender Stratocaster, are highly respected. Blackmore is known for his discerning instrumental needs—many of his guitars feature a "scalloped" fretboard, where the wood is painstakingly grooved out and smoothed to allow for freer and more accurate playing.

Blackmore's Night is Blackmore's Renaissance-inspired band that he formed in 1997 with his wife, Candice Night. An occasionally kitschy vanity project, the band is especially popular in the Renaissance fair and festival circuit. With seven albums under its belt, Blackmore's Night makes a point of regularly performing at European castles and other historic sites with an authentic arsenal of period instruments that includes the domra, cornamuse, and rauschpfeife.

Deep Purple's 1968 dandily dressed lineup: top row from left: Nick Simper, Rod Evans, and Ritchie Blackmore. Seated: Ian Paice and Jon Lord

essential albums

WITH DEEP PURPLE

1968	*Shades of Deep Purple*
1968	*The Book of Taliesyn*
1969	*Deep Purple*
1970	*Deep Purple in Rock*
1971	*Fireball*
1972	*Machine Head*
1973	*Who Do We Think We Are*
1974	*Burn*
1984	*Perfect Strangers*
1987	*The House of Blue Light*
1993	*The Battle Rages On*

WITH RAINBOW

1975	*Ritchie Blackmore's Rainbow*
1976	*Rising*
1978	*Long Live Rock 'n' Roll*
1979	*Down to Earth*
1981	*Difficult to Cure*
1982	*Straight Between the Eyes*
1983	*Bent out of Shape*
1995	*Stranger in Us All*

WITH BLACKMORE'S NIGHT

1997	*Shadow of the Moon*
1999	*Under a Violet Moon*
2001	*Fires at Midnight*
2001	*Minstrels and Ballads*
2002	*Past Times with Good Company*
2003	*Ghost of a Rose*
2006	*The Village Lanterne*
2006	*Winter Carols*
2008	*Secret Voyage*

Awards and Honors

| 2003 | Ranked No. 55 on *Rolling Stone*'s list of the 100 Greatest Guitarists of All Time |

Ritchie Blackmore with Blackmore's Night at the House of Blues, Chicago, 2009

EARLY CAREER & REUNIONS

Deep Purple's beginnings can be traced to a hard rock band called Roundabout, founded by Blackmore and Wayne Blade in 1968. After releasing three preliminary albums and shuffling its roster around, the band committed to a harder-edged rock sound and produced *In Rock*, grabbing attention with a unique blend of vocals, organ, and Blackmore's peerless guitar licks.

After a run of four albums, culminating with 1973's *Who Do We Think We Are*, Deep Purple replaced its bassist and singer, resulting in the record *Bum*, a funk-influenced release. Blackmore's dissatisfaction with the band's direction had begun to grow, and after memorably—and publicly—trashing its next release, *Stormbringer,* he quit and formed Rainbow.

Ritchie Blackmore's Rainbow was released in 1975, representing a recommitment to the harder, baroque sound Blackmore preferred. Seemingly impossible to satisfy, Blackmore recruited an entirely new roster for *Rainbow Rising*, Rainbow's 1976 release. For the rest of the 1970s, Blackmore continued to shuffle his lineup with each Rainbow record, even calling in former Deep Purple bandmates to assist in the recording process, which led to the thawing of relations and Blackmore's eventual return to Deep Purple in 1984.

Deep Purple enjoyed a successful tour that year, but in the next few years subsequent releases garnered less-than-stellar sales numbers. Tensions between Blackmore and singer Ian Gillan led to Gillan's firing in 1989, but it soon became apparent that Gillan was critical to the band's survival. He returned to the fold in 1993, only to see Blackmore make his final exit later that year.

With Blackmore replacement Steve Morse, Deep Purple has enjoyed yet another lease on life. Meanwhile, Blackmore took another stab at resurrecting Rainbow, resulting in one final album, before he committed himself full time to Blackmore's Night.

JERRY CANTRELL

"I think we worked really hard and we faced a lot and I think the reason we're doing it is extremely genuine and I'm just really proud of all of us for taking on that sort of a challenge and coming through it the way that we have, and the only way to do that is to really depend on each other and communicate and to make sure that it's right with everybody as far as to keep taking that next step. . . . Things just kept building without a plan. So to be here today is just as much a surprise for us as anybody else, and it's all good."

—JERRY CANTRELL, ON THE RELEASE OF *BLACK GIVES WAY TO BLUE*, 2009

Jerry Cantrell (born March 18, 1966, in Tacoma, Washington) came to prominence on the 1990s grunge scene with Alice in Chains as its guitarist and occasional vocalist. In addition to overseeing a solo career, Cantrell has remained linked to Alice in Chains, which has enjoyed a recent renaissance despite the death of lead singer and song-writer Layne Staley in 2002.

As a high school student Cantrell was active in the arts and began playing the guitar. The Seattle-based band Cantrell formed in the mid-1980s, called Diamond Lie, eventually mor-phed into Alice in Chains, commencing a fifteen-year run that would, unfortunately, end in tragedy.

Cantrell is a two-time solo artist, albeit a reluctant one—he has made frequent comments in interviews that he prefers the culture and routine of life in a band. Indeed, working alone proved to be a challenge; he recruited several former Chains members to help him record 1998's *Boggy Depot*. The follow-up, 2002's *Degradation Trip*, is the result of a lengthy period of isolation and songwriting, Cantrell has stated. Dedicated to the memory of Staley, the record received a significant amount of attention. One of its tracks was chosen to appear on the soundtrack to the film *Spider-Man*, and Cantrell exposed himself to a larger audience via an extensive tour in support of the album.

Cantrell's sound is unique for its blues and country under-tones and unorthodox time signatures. He maintains a close relationship with the G&L guitar company, which recently debuted the Cantrell Rampage signature model.

ALICE IN CHAINS

Alice in Chains bridged the gap between metal and grunge in the 1990s, rendering themselves icons in the process. Its sound was dark but driving and musically sophisticated enough to keep critics happy, for the most part.

The band began as a predominantly metal outfit in 1987 and within two years, it was signed. The LP *Facelift* debuted in 1990, hitting a popular sweet spot and earning the band opening slots with bands like Van Halen and Poison.

With the rise of Nirvana, Alice in Chains adjusted its presentation and released *Dirt*, its lauded sophomore record. The band was a sensation by this point, but word of Staley's drug addiction had begun to seep out and only added to the band's morose reputation.

In lieu of another immediate, full release, the band cut a few successful EPs in the early 1990s before releasing *Alice in Chains* in 1995. Fans and the press noted the band's seeming unwillingness to tour, sparking allegations that drug use was tearing the band apart. With the exception of an appearance on MTV and a companion live album in 1996, Alice in Chains had all but ceased to exist. Its nervous label put out an elaborate compilation in 1999, and things continued to get worse—Staley would die in 2002.

Following a hiatus, Cantrell recruited singer William DuVall to join the reconstituted band, resulting in *Black Gives Way to Blue*, released in 2009.

Jerry Cantrell, left, with Alice in Chains vocalist William Duvall, right, in the studio

essential albums

WITH ALICE IN CHAINS

1990	*We Die Young*
1990	*Facelift*
1992	*Sap*
1992	*Dirt*
1994	*Jar of Flies*
1995	*Alice in Chains*
1996	*Unplugged*
1999	*Nothing Safe: Best of the Box*
1999	*Music Bank*
2000	*Live*
2009	*Black Gives Way to Blue*

SOLO

1998	*Boggy Depot April*
2002	*Degradation Trip*
2002	*Degradation Trip, Volumes 1 & 2*

Cantrell performing at Scala in London, England, 2009

PHIL COLLEN

"Records are less important now. I mean, for an artist you still need to do that, make a record, but from a business point of view you really end up not having an album to promote at all as opposed to having it the other way around, the way it used to be like. It is very hard to get stuff out there on a major level today but on a grassroots level, it's very different as you can get stuff out there on the Internet. . . . And because of that, it creates a lot of artists who are not afraid at doing their own thing, and are not being told what to do by some A&R guy. So they're following their own noses and being very natural about it. . . . And I think music is very, if not more, important in people's lives than it used to be too."

—PHIL COLLEN, 2008

Phil Collen (born December 8, 1957, in London, England) took over the role of lead guitarist from Pete Willis in Def Leppard in 1982. Collen has also released his own solo material and has worked as a music producer.

A self-taught player, Collen got his hands on his first guitar, a Gibson SG, as a teenager. Collen's first taste of renown came as a member of Girl, his first serious band, and his tenure with the group resulted in the well-received albums *Sheer Greed* and *Wasted Youth*.

With Collen's heightened profile came greater attention. Def Leppard, already an established act, had a guitarist in Pete Willis—but asked Collen to come aboard anyway. Collen declined, sticking with Girl until Willis's departure—finally taking the band up on its invitation and joining forces with Steve Clark, Leppard's other axman.

Technologically, Collen is a pioneer, having had an eye for ergonomics since the late 1980s. He partnered with Jackson Guitars to design a groundbreaking wrap-around-the-body ax in 1989. Although the wraparound project wasn't a complete success—Collen himself found the prototype hard to play—the resulting model still stands as a milestone in guitar design, if only for its looks.

DEF LEPPARD

Heavy metal god since 1977, Def Leppard didn't ask Collen to join up until it was in the middle of recording *Pyromania*, its third long player. Popular success wasn't far ahead, with MTV putting the "Photograph" video on constant rotation. With only Michael Jackson's juggernaut *Thriller* competing for the peak position on the charts, Def Leppard was assuredly at the top of its game, especially in the United States.

By 1984 the band had established Dublin as its home base and dealt with some significant personnel changes—producer Mutt Lange temporarily jumped ship, and at the end of the year percussionist Rick Allen was severely injured in a car wreck. Even after the amputation of his arm, Allen adapted his playing and was able to successfully contribute to the band's 1987 album *Hysteria*. Def Leppard finally achieved the popularity in the UK it had so desired, and "Pour Some Sugar On Me" became a smash hit on both sides of the pond.

Hysteria proved to be a font of white-hot hits, generating seven in total—a record in several categories. Leppard swept the Heavy Metal categories at the American Music Awards in 1989, the inaugural year for trophies in that genre.

The 1990s opened with a rocky start—Clark was in and out of alcoholic rehab and abusing drugs; he died at the beginning of 1991. Collen, though esteemed for his precise, masterful playing, found himself in over his head when tasked with reproducing Clark's much looser style of playing on *Adrenalize*, the band's 1992 effort. The album succeeded

Collen at the Hammersmith Apollo in London, England, 2006

as expected, but the band's fortunes would wane as the musically spastic 1990s droned on.

Def Leppard went alternative in 1996 with *Slang*, a critically praised album that was less well received by Leppard's old-guard fans. Watching its shine fade with the surging popularity of a new style of music, Leppard released several live albums and a few new studio efforts, embracing sounds from pop and country. Sales have been mixed, but Def Leppard's frequent tours are regular blockbusters.

essential albums

1979	*The Def Leppard* (EP)
1980	*On Through the Night*
1981	*High 'n' Dry*
1983	*Pyromania*
1987	*Hysteria*
1988	*Historia*
1992	*Adrenalize*
1993	*Visualize*
1993	*Retro Active*
1996	*Slang*
1999	*Euphoria*
2006	*Yeah*
2008	*Songs from the Sparkle Lounge*

BEYOND LEPPARD

In the early 1990s Collen expanded his resume with several producing credits, first working with Australian group BB Steal in the studio. Already in high demand as a dynamic collaborator—he worked under an alias on Donny Osmond's album *Eyes Don't Lie*—Collen went on to assist old friends Sheer Greed with their 1993 record *Sublime to the Ridiculous*.

Other projects include Cybernauts, Collens's David Bowie tribute band that he formed in conjunction with Leppard front man Joe Elliott. Additionally Man-Raze is Collens's latter-day supergroup, pulling together former Girl Simon Laffy and Paul Cook of the Sex Pistols. *Surreal*, Man-Raze's first LP, debuted in 2008.

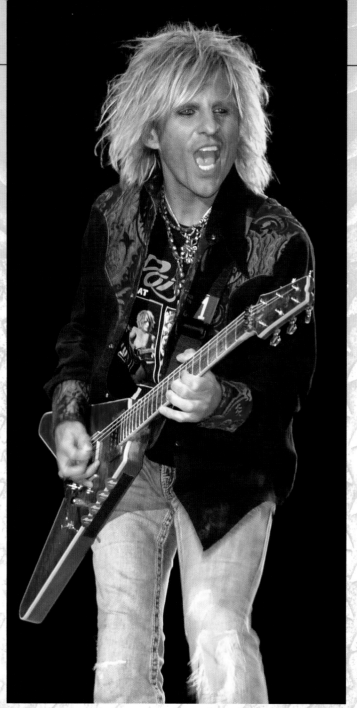

C. C. DEVILLE

"Sometimes when you're given a soapbox at an early age, you abuse that privilege by default, simply because you're ignorant. You have a finite amount of time when people listen, and if you make it at an early age, sometimes you waste that, because you're new and you don't have much to say, and you don't think much. So, sometimes I've had not just the pleasure, but I've had the anxiety of listening to myself when I was much younger and sometimes, you know, I was living in the minute. But, I try to be a bit more responsible for how I am now. Which might actually make me for a duller person."

—C. C. DEVILLE, 2007

The sometimes-actor at the forefront of glam metal group Poison, C. C. DeVille (born May 14, 1962, in Brooklyn, New York) is most often recognized for his stint as the band's lead guitarist.

Influenced by early Beatlemania, DeVille's first guitar was a cheap Japanese Telecaster knockoff. He soon set to emulating the sounds of the original rock and roll pantheon, including the Rolling Stones, and later acts like Aerosmith and Kiss.

DeVille's interest in glam found fertile soil in late-1970s New York City, where he was attending New York University. He then started his first band and took his first steps as a songwriter. By 1981 DeVille had dropped out of college and packed up for Los Angeles, where he fleshed out his résumé with gigs in a number of bands. At a ballsy audition for new band Poison he ignored the passage the band wanted him to play and instead presented his own noodling, DeVille won over the group—except front man Bret Michaels. Ironically, the impromptu riff would make its way into one of the band's first hits, "Talk Dirty to Me." Poison's 1986 debut was a winner, and the band was off to quite a start.

DeVille and Michaels didn't get along from the outset, but by 1991 their sometimes physical fighting—and DeVille's reckless substance abuse—resulted in DeVille's exit from Poison.

POISON

After the success of its debut, *Look What the Cat Dragged In*, the band quickly set its sights on a follow-up. That record turned out to be *Open Up and Say . . . Ahh!* Generating Poison mainstay "Every Rose Has Its Thorn," the album helped cement the band's cred as one of the most bankable acts of the 1980s, as well as one of the most controversial—*Open Up*'s album cover was just the first of Poison's offerings to be censored at the demand of jittery record officials and merchants.

Poison and its members took a permanent, though taxing, position in the fast lane of the late 1980s and early 1990s. Drugs and alcohol were in unlimited supply, and no one enjoyed them more than DeVille. The band continued to release and tour despite DeVille's tense departure.

Poison hobbled through the 1990s, chewing up guitarists and spitting them out, until DeVille returned to the fold in 1999, commencing a new period of sell-out concert appearances and a slew of new albums, DVDs, and compilations, including the recent remastered re-release of some of Poison's early, most popular works.

Both Michaels and DeVille have established themselves as reality TV stars: Michaels in *Rock of Love* and DeVille in *The Surreal Life*.

Above: Poison performing at the Moondance Jam, Walker, Minnesota, 2008

Below left: DeVille at the Virgin Megastore in Los Angeles, California, making an appearance for the Rock and Roll Fashion Show, 2006

essential albums

WITH POISON

1986	*Look What the Cat Dragged In*
1988	*Open Up and Say . . . Ahh!*
1990	*Flesh & Blood*
1991	*Swallow This Live!*
1993	*Native Tongue*
2000	*Crack a Smile . . . and More!*
2000	*Power to the People*
2002	*Hollyweird*
2003	*Best of Ballads & Blues*
2007	*Poison'd!*

WITH BRETT MICHAELS

1998	*A Letter from Death Row*
2003	*Songs of Life*

WITH SAMANTHA 7

2000	*Samantha 7*

ACE FREHLEY

"All guitar players influence other guitar players whether they want to admit it or not, even if it's subconsciously. Even if you hear something, you may not remember it, but your subconscious does. But it's all good, you know. Just the fact that Eddie [Van Halen] may not have remembered me influencing him in any way shape or form, who knows, you know? Eddie's a great guitar player in his own right, and he doesn't need me as an influence to stand on his own."

—ACE FREHLEY

Frehley donning the "Spaceman" suit with Kiss, circa 1979

Ace Frehley (born April 27, 1951, in the Bronx, New York) is one of the founding members of metal band Kiss. After leaving the band in 1982 but rejoining in 1996 for a reunion tour, Frehley has since put himself forward as a solo artist.

As a 22-year old, Frehley auditioned in New York in front of Paul Stanley, Gene Simmons, and Peter Criss, who were looking for a lead guitarist. Three weeks later Frehley got the gig and Kiss was born. Immediately they agreed to boldly paint their faces for live performances, with Frehley taking on the persona of the "Spaceman." This gimmick would become Kiss's signature.

A champion of the Gibson Les Paul, Frehley also handled a stable of converted Cara models that could actually output smoke during his solos. He often accompanied his wild performance style with the band with on-stage rockets and pyrotechnics that he controlled himself.

KISS

The act known as Kiss came out of an early band called Wicked Lester, a hard rock outfit that contained Gene Simmons and Paul Stanley. The group made its first appearance in New York City in 1973 and was an instant sensation, owing to its members' elaborately theatrical stage setup, which, even in the early days, threatened to overshadow the band's music. Word of mouth provided the band with momentum for its eponymous 1974 debut, which gained a fair amount of attention and airplay.

It wasn't until a later release, 1975's *Alive!*, however, that the band truly achieved superstar status. By 1977 Kiss's influence had bled into comic books, toys, games, and television, reaching a saturation point a year later, culminating in solo releases by every member of the band. Kiss's commercially successful sound, hitting a sweet spot between hard rock and heavy metal, drew comparisons to Black Sabbath.

The early 1980s represented something of a decline for the band. Much of its troubles stemmed from management troubles and lineup changes, Frehley's departure in particular. His replacement, Vinnie Vincent, failed to sit well with the group, leading to further tensions. Vincent was eventually ejected from Kiss in 1984, for resaons still unexplained.

A reconfigured—and unmasked—Kiss did well for the duration of the 1980s, producing a steady lineup of albums while marking a subtle transition of leadership and power from Simmons to Paul Stanley. Drummer Eric Carr would pass away in 1991, necessitating the recruitment of yet another new member.

A resurgence in popularity and a wave of Kiss nostalgia peaked with the original band's 1996 Grammy reunion. Kiss remained sporadically active in the 2000s, coming together in various configurations for events and performances around the world. *Sonic Boom* was released in 2009 to the surprise and delight of fans. Simmons and Stanley billed it as a return to the band's late-1970s sound.

essential albums

WITH KISS

1974	*Kiss*
1974	*Hotter Than Hell*
1975	*Dressed to Kill*
1975	*Alive!*
1976	*Destroyer*
1976	*Rock and Roll Over*
1977	*Love Gun*
1977	*Alive II*
1978	*Double Platinum*
1979	*Dynasty*
1980	*Unmasked*
1981	*The Elder*
1982	*Creatures of the Night*
1996	*Kiss Unplugged*
1996	*You Wanted the Best, You Got the Best!!*
1998	*Psycho Circus*

WITH FREHLEY'S COMET

1978	*Ace Frehley*
1987	*Frehley's Comet*
1988	*Second Sighting*
1989	*Trouble Walkin'*
2009	*Anomaly*

Kiss during the 1970s, composed of Gene Simmons, Ace Frehley, Peter Criss, and Paul Stanley. The band's extravagant makeup, costumes, and stage antics have entered the annals of rock lore and are often parodied in other pop culture venues.

MARTY FRIEDMAN

"Especially at the time, there was really nobody and probably even now, nobody who could touch what we were doing as far as guitar intensity and melody. . . . Sometimes we were over the top and kind of overplaying and there were a hell of a lot of guitar solos, but I'm still proud of it. I have to agree that we were definitely pioneers when it comes to making intense music out of a guitar."

—MARTY FRIEDMAN, ON HIS BAND CACOPHONY, 2007

essential albums

WITH CACOPHANY
1987   *Speed Metal Symphony*
1988   *Go Off!*

SOLO
1988   *Dragon's Kiss*
1992   *Scenes*
1995   *Introduction*
1996   *True Obsessions*
2002   *Music for Speeding*
2006   *Loudspeaker*
2006   *Kick Ass Rock*
2008   *Future Addict*
2009   *Tokyo Jukebox*

WITH MEGADETH
1990   *Rust in Peace*
1992   *Countdown to Extinction*
1994   *Youthanasia*
1997   *Cryptic Writings*
1999   *Risk*

Marty Friedman (born December 8, 1962, in Laurel, Maryland) played guitar in Megadeth for ten years. More recently, the Japanese expatriate has established a second career as a television host and eclectic solo artist in his adopted home country.

Friedman's style blends Eastern and Western sounds and his complex, athletic solos are known for their improvised, hard-to-mimic sound. His family moved from the U.S. East Coast to Hawaii when Friedman was in his teens. There he began playing guitar in a number of bands, the most significant one being Cacophony, a band that gained a following with its dueling guitar sound.

Ever perfecting his own signature style, Friedman put out a solo album in 1988, which would come to serve as his calling card. Before joining established group Megadeth, Cacophony would produce one more album, *Go Off!*, in 1989.

During his time with Megadeth Friedman was usually seen playing Jackson guitars; at various points in his career he has worked out signature deals with Ibanez and Paul Reed Smith.

MEGADETH

Led by Dave Mustaine, members of the established thrash band Megadeth were exhausted after a lengthy search for their next guitarist when they finally chose Friedman in 1990. *Rust in Peace*, considered by many to be the band's masterpiece, followed soon thereafter. Many attributed the band's resurgence to a newly instituted sobriety policy that allowed the band members to work more efficiently than ever before, and their work resulted in several Grammy nominations.

Released in 1992, *Countdown to Extinction* achieved even greater commercial success than Megadeth's previous effort.

The band continued its streak as a Grammy darling, though substances troubles would return to haunt it. In 1993 the band made a very rare joint appearance with Metallica; the two groups were locked in a contentious rivalry. Through the mid-1990s, Megadeth pushed for a cleaner, more mainstream sound and was one of the first bands to promote an album, 1994's *Youthanasia*, via the blossoming World Wide Web.

Megadeth closed out the 1990s with even more radio-friendly fare, misfiring to a gross extent with 1999's dance and pop-infused (and more than aptly named) album *Risk*. Friedman left the band at the end of 1999, ending a residency that lasted nearly a decade.

Unable to right the listing vessel that the band had become, Mustaine dismantled Megadeth in 2002 after he suffered an especially debilitating arm injury. Its label issued an elaborate comeback album in 2004, and since then, a continually reshuffling Megadeth lineup has toured and released studio albums, most recently in 2009. All the while, Mustaine has remained at the helm of the band he created.

FRIEDMAN THE EXPAT

Fluent in the Japanese language, Friedman enjoys the status of true guitar hero and national treasure in Japan, where he has resided since 2003. For several years Friedman starred on *Hebimeta-san* ("Mr. Heavy Metal"). He next appeared on his own program, *Rock Fujiyama*, which lasted just under a year from 2006 to 2007.

In addition to performing and touring with some of Japan's favorite musicians, Friedman serves as something like a cultural ambassador and intermediary. He has contributed articles and columns to multiple Japanese newspapers and music publications, and on *Jukebox English*, another TV show, Friedman translated English language lyrics into Japanese for curious music fans.

With Shinichiro Suzuki, Friedman started Lovefixer in 2008, a J-rock band. He has also lent his talents to the work of Nana Kitade, Nami Tamaki, Takeomi Matsuura, and Nanase Aikawa. *Tokyo Jukebox* is Friedman's latest release, a 2009 album consisting almost entirely of J-pop tunes.

Friedman performing at the Gods of Metal festival, Monza, Italy, 2009

JANICK GERS

J anick Gers (born January 27, 1957, in Hartlepool, England) forms one-third of Iron Maiden's guitar trio, occasionally serving as a songwriter as well.

The son of a former Polish naval officer, Gers played in a number of bands, including White Spirit, Gillan (with Deep Purple's Ian Gillan), and Gogmagog—where he would meet Clive Burr and Paul Di'Anno, formerly of Iron Maiden.

Gers is the champion of a jarring style and ragged, distorted tone that is manifested through his preference for sharp, staccato notes. Known to count Jeff Beck and Ritchie Blackmore among his influences, Gers is something of a ham during performances, frequently thrashing and throwing his guitar—usually a Fender Stratocaster—around the stage.

"That is what playing live is about to me, taking chances. Sometimes you come up with egg all over your face and I love that! That is rock and roll. For too long now it has become very cabaret and everything is worked out and that is not what it was meant to be. It was meant to be a medium where you took chances, and I think that disappeared out of rock music for a while. I like bands when I go and see them, and I know that it is not choreographed and he took a chance, and there is something there."

—JANICK GERS, 1999

Gers at the Field of Rock festival in the Netherlands, 2007

IRON MAIDEN

Gers joined Iron Maiden during a particular tumultuous time in the band's history; the group had been around for a decade and had seen its fair share of members come and go. Adrian Smith had just abandoned his post as guitarist, following the release of his solo album in 1989. Gers first appeared in 1990's *No Prayer for the Dying*, an album that would do particularly well in the UK. Gers would contribute as songwriter on the next release, *Fear of the Dark*, in 1992. The band visited Latin America for the first time on tour, and singer Bruce Dickinson would leave the following year.

Following a long period of regrouping, Iron Maiden released *The X Factor* in 1995, featuring new vocalist Blaze Bayley. The album fared poorly, but nevertheless, the band pushed ahead with plans to tour, touching down in Israel and South Africa for the first time. *Virtual XI* was another flop, leading to Bayley's departure in 1999.

Effective immediately, the remaining members of the band announced Dickinson and Smith were coming back for a reunion tour, featuring three Iron Maiden guitarists for the first time, a move that would dramatically reverse the band's fortunes. *Ed Hunter*, an album of greatest hits was followed by *Brave New World* in 2000, the first studio album from the reconstituted Iron Maiden.

The band enjoyed a resurgence in the 2000s, unleashing a series of literary-minded records and mounting several massive tours, including a thirtieth-anniversary extravaganza, accompanied by a DVD release, in 2005. The band has continued visiting new parts of the world and has also starred in a documentary film, released in 2009. Its 2010 album is sure to reinforce Iron Maiden's position on the short list of the world's best heavy metal acts.

essential albums

WITH WHITE SPIRIT
1980   *White Spirit*

WITH GILLAN
1981   *Double Trouble*
1982   *Magic*

WITH FISH
1990   *Vigil in a Wilderness of Mirrors*

WITH IRON MAIDEN
1990   *No Prayer for the Dying*
1992   *Fear of the Dark*
1993   *Real Live One*
1993   *A Real Dead One*
1995   *The X Factor*
1998   *Virtual XI*
2000   *Brave New World*
2002   *Rock in Rio*
2003   *Dance of Death*
2005   *Death on the Road*
2006   *A Matter of Life and Death*
2009   *Flight 666*

WITH IAN GILLAN
2006   *Gillan's Inn*

Dave Murray, left, and Gers, right, onstage with Iron Maiden in Bucharest, Romania, 2008

KIRK HAMMETT

Honors and Awards

1989   Grammy Award for Best Metal Performance,
        for "One," with Metallica

1990   Grammy Award for Best Metal Performance,
        for "Stone Cold Crazy," with Metallica

1991   Grammy Award for Best Metal Performance, for
        Metallica, with Metallica

1998   Grammy Award for Best Metal Performance,
        for "Better Than You," with Metallica

1999   Grammy Award for Best Hard Rock Performance,
        for "Whiskey in the Jar," with Metallica

2000   Grammy Award for Best Rock Instrumental
        Performance, for "The Call of Ktulu," with Metallica
        and Michael Kamen

2003   Grammy Award
        for Best Metal
        Performance,
        for "St. Anger,"
        with Metallica

2003   Ranked No. 11
        on *Rolling Stone*'s
        list of the 100
        Greatest Guitarists
        of All Time

2008   Grammy Award
        for Best Metal
        Performance, for
        "My Apocalypse,"
        with Metallica

2009   Inducted into the
        Rock and Roll Hall
        of Fame

Kirk Hammett performing with
Metallica in Glasgow, Scotland, 2004

Kirk Hammett (born November 18, 1962, in San
Francisco, California) has played lead guitar in
Metallica since Dave Mustaine's departure in 1983.
Active in thrash metal since his teens, Hammett is considered
one of the contemporary stars of the genre.

Hammett got hooked on rock and roll listening to his older
brother's Jimi Hendrix, Led Zeppelin, and—especially—UFO
recordings. His first guitar was a feeble mail-order model
from Montgomery Ward, but Hammett soon graduated to a
Stratocaster, followed by a Gibson Flying V. Teaching himself to reproduce Hendrix's work on "Purple Haze" riff by riff,
Hammett grew to idolize UFO guitarist Michael Schenker,
fascinated by his precise, almost classical handling of scales
and rhythm.

In the early 1980s Hammett founded thrash group Exodus
and got the chance to open for a very loosely formed Metallica
on several occasions. In 1983 Hammett was invited to the East
Coast to try out for the band; he left for New York for the first
time and scored the gig.

Hammett is known for his slavish devotion to practice and
structured musical education; he has studied under master Joe
Satriani, and took several high-level music classes at the City
College of San Francisco in the 1990s. Hammett is said to play
or practice all but four days in any given year.

Outside of Metallica, Hammett has appeared or recorded
with Carlos Santana, Orbital, My Morning Jacket, and
Septic Death.

essential albums

STUDIO

1983	*Kill 'Em All*
1984	*Ride the Lightning*
1986	*Master of Puppets*
1988	*. . . And Justice for All*
1991	*Metallica*
1996	*Load*
1997	*ReLoad*
1998	*Garage, Inc.*
2003	*St. Anger*
2008	*Death Magnetic*

LIVE

| 1993 | *Live Shit: Binge & Purge* |
| 1999 | *S&M* |

"Some other artists, say, that paint or create sculptures or do something, their ultimate thing is that they finally finished their sculpture and they go put it into a room, you know, and people come by and look at it. I guess that's the ultimate for them, but for us, you know, we create a song that is in us, and it moves with us. And we play it, and people take it with them. And it creates certain feelings. It's something that they get to do, too. You know, they get to sing it and, you know, this is . . . I can't think of anything better to do in life."

—KIRK HAMMETT

GUITARS AND TECHNIQUE

Hammett aims for a clean tone with just the right amount of distortion. In the tradition of Jimi Hendrix, Hammett shares a fascination with the whammy bar and wah-wah pedal; the tool is a near-constant in his solos with Metallica and was given renewed prominence in the band's latest, 2008's *Death Magnetic*. Hammett has praised its role in creating an "unpredictable" sound and notes that it should always be used with a purpose. Dunlop manufactures the KH95 wah-wah pedal, designed with heavy input from Hammett.

Hammett endorses ESP guitars. ESP released the extravagant KH-20 limited-edition guitar in 2007, based upon an earlier signature model. Retailing for just shy of $10,000, fewer than fifty of these axes were made.

Hammett built an early reputation for forceful but controlled playing—to this day, he wraps his right hand to protect his old wounds as he picks and mutes the strings. In recent years with Metallica, the self-professed flashy-playing Hammett has embraced a relatively more mellow style in contrast with his earlier, more frantic and menacing work. Hammett's extensive arsenal of effects and other equipment adds up to what has been dubbed the "Frankenstein" approach, allowing for endless experimentation and flexibility in his sound.

Hammett, left, and Lars Ulrich of Metallica, in the 2004 documentary *Some Kind of Monster*. The film, named after the song from the album *St. Anger*, won an Independent Spirit Award for Best Documentary Feature and focused on the band members' relationship during their creative process.

JAMES HETFIELD

"I definitely don't want to tell people how to live. We've said since day one, 'Think for yourself.' If someone's dumb enough to just follow somebody else, that's their own fault. When you're a role model, you have a responsibility and you lose your creative juices. You worry about what other people think of you. Why worry about what people think? You have to be true to yourself, write what you feel. When people see that you're full of shit, then it's over. We can't fool our fans very much."

—JAMES HETFIELD, 1993

essential albums

STUDIO

1983	*Kill 'Em All*
1984	*Ride the Lightning*
1986	*Master of Puppets*
1988	*. . . And Justice for All*
1991	*Metallica*
1996	*Load*
1997	*ReLoad*
1998	*Garage, Inc.*
2003	*St. Anger*
2008	*Death Magnetic*

LIVE

1993	*Live Shit: Binge & Purge*
1999	*S&M*

James Hetfield (born August 3, 1963, in Downey, California) is a founding member of Metallica, one of the world's genre-defining heavy metal acts. Steward of the band's famously hard sound and unapologetic commercial appeal, Hetfield is also noted for his reluctant quasiconservative beliefs.

Coming of age in a vaguely musical Christian Scientist family, Hetfield first learned to play the piano at the age of 9. A few years later he took an interest in guitar, absorbing the music of Aerosmith and branching out into the catalogs of everyone from Jimi Hendrix to ZZ Top.

In concert with Lars Ulrich, a new friend and colleague Hetfield found through a newspaper ad, he would launch Metallica in San Francisco in 1983. Very briefly, the initial lineup also contained Dave Mustaine, who would famously go on to start up rival band Megadeth.

Hetfield has primarily served the band as lead singer, songwriter, and rhythm guitarist, but he has been known to jump in and solo, as well as flesh out melodies for vocals and guitar. Rock and roll has not always been kind to the guitarist: he has suffered numerous grotesque accidents, almost all while performing on stage or rehearsing, and alcoholism has taken its toll on his health.

Though he frequently plays Gibson axes, Hetfield and the ESP Guitar Company enjoy a cozy relationship; the company has produced six models marketed under Hetfield's name.

METALLICA

For almost three decades, the band Metallica has been at the forefront of the particularly aggressive brand of heavy metal known as thrash. With sales matched by few other groups, the band is considered one of the "big four" players in this particular genre.

On the strength of a few early cobbled-together demos and independently released albums, Metallica had made a name for itself from Los Angeles to San Francisco. After replacing Mustaine with guitarist Kirk Hammett, the band traveled back east to quickly record its label debut in 1983, *Kill 'Em All*.

As the increasingly popular band forged a reputation on the road, it looked to its next album, 1986's *Master of Puppets*, which it would ride to worldwide recognition and brisk sales. By now the band was touring with names like Ozzy Osbourne and Bon Jovi. A grisly tour bus accident in Sweden that year resulted in the death of bass player Cliff Burton. Jason Newsted signed on as his replacement, and the band wasted no time throwing him into the recording of material for a new EP.

The year 1988 finally saw the release of . . . *And Justice For All*. The album received attention from the Grammy establishment for the first time, but Metallica lost to English rock band Jethro Tull in a highly publicized upset.

Metallica opened up the 1990s at the top of their game, with the hit video "One" on MTV—and a blockbuster album, that year's *Metallica*. The disc's rapturous reception compelled the band to tour into 1994, making the band members global superstars.

Load, released in 1996, was another giant success, and Metallica would gain notoriety in 2000 when it threw itself into the roiling maelstrom of electronic file sharing. After discovering the leak of a new single available on Napster, one of the more popular file-sharing services, Metallica sued the company—and a handful of universities, including Yale and the University of Southern California, effectively leading to the dismantlement of Napster as it existed in 2002. Hetfield, Ulrich, and other members of the band remain vocal opponents of file-sharing and piracy to this day.

The band struggled to maintain its internal harmony and live up to the often lofty expectations of fans through the 2000s. Recent albums and DVDs have met with mixed reviews, but the band still commands impressive audiences and has toured with the Rolling Stones.

A shot of Hetfield performing in the 2004 documentary *Some Kind of Monster*. The film about Metallica features both concert performances and band rehearsals.

Awards and Honors

1989 Grammy Award for Best Metal Performance, for "One," with Metallica

1990 Grammy Award for Best Metal Performance, for "Stone Cold Crazy," with Metallica

1991 Grammy Award for Best Metal Performance, for *Metallica*, with Metallica

1998 Grammy Award for Best Metal Performance, for "Better Than You," with Metallica

1999 Grammy Award for Best Hard Rock Performance, for "Whiskey in the Jar," with Metallica

2000 Grammy Award for Best Rock Instrumental Performance, for "The Call of Ktulu," with Metallica and Michael Kamen

2003 Grammy Award for Best Metal Performance, for "St. Anger," with Metallica

2008 Grammy Award for Best Metal Performance, for "My Apocalypse," with Metallica

2009 Inducted into the Rock and Roll Hall of Fame

Hetfield at the 02 Arena in London, 2008

TONY IOMMI

essential albums

WITH BLACK SABBATH
1970	*Black Sabbath*
1970	*Paranoid*
1971	*Master of Reality*
1972	*Black Sabbath, Volume 4*
1973	*Sabbath Bloody Sabbath*
1975	*Sabotage*
1976	*Technical Ecstasy*
1978	*Never Say Die!*
1980	*Heaven and Hell*
1981	*Mob Rules*
1982	*Live Evil*
1983	*Born Again*
1986	*Seventh Star*
1987	*The Eternal Idol*
1989	*Headless Cross*
1990	*Tyr*
1992	*Dehumanizer*
1994	*Cross Purposes*
1995	*Forbidden*
2002	*Past Lives*

SOLO
| 2000 | *Iommi* |

WITH HEAVEN AND HELL
| 2009 | *The Devil You Know* |

Tony Iommi (born February 19, 1948, in Birmingham, England) is noted for his founding and permanent role with heavy metal rocker Black Sabbath. Iommi is peerless within the heavy metal establishment; *Guitar World* ranked him No. 1 on its list of all-time metal guitarists in 2004. He is frequently referenced for his pioneering, riff-heavy sound.

Iommi's success is all the more impressive in light of an early injury he sustained to his right hand. After nearly giving up music forever, he pushed himself to work around his limitation, modifying his guitars with banjo strings and fashioning his own finger protection to enforce his weak hand.

A young Iommi spent the late 1960s gigging and touring throughout Europe with a series of bands. Iommi and a collective of fellow musicians formed Earth in 1968, a precursor to Black Sabbath, the band that would occupy the bulk of Iommi's time and energy for more than thirty years.

In the last decade Iommi has stepped out as a solo artist, releasing *Iommi* in 2000, which featured contributions from Billy Corgan, Dave Grohl, and Ozzy Osbourne. He followed up in 2004 with the release of a set of songs actually recorded in 1996, *The DEP Sessions*, and *Fused* in 2005.

A side project/supergroup Iommi formed with current and former members of Black Sabbath goes by the moniker "Heaven and Hell," partly stemming from Iommi's previously contended use of the Black Sabbath name. Heaven and Hell released an album titled *The Devil You Know* in 2009.

BLACK SABBATH

Black Sabbath established itself in the 1970s as a powerhouse of heavy metal and one of the genre's standard-bearers. One of the first bands to consistently tune its guitars lower than usual—partially due to Iommi's injury—the band is also known for its extensive stable of members over the years.

After ditching the name Earth to avoid confusion with another band, Black Sabbath steered its sound away from blues and took a much darker direction. Its eponymous debut album of 1970 was a sales success, but it offered few hints of the band's future sonic potential.

By the middle of 1971, Black Sabbath had already released album number three—and was recklessly bingeing on drugs and self-destruction. The band scored an elusive critical hit with 1973's *Sabbath Bloody Sabbath*, written and rehearsed in a British castle dungeon. With the album's success came a wider audience, and the band took to an ambitious tour in 1974 with some of the era's biggest names in popular music.

In the late 1970s the band tinkered with its sound, all the while attempting to hold onto its commanding commercial appeal. Mired in drug addiction and alcoholism, the members of the band struggled to release much inspired material, and the other members kicked out Osbourne in 1979.

Ronnie James Dio joined up, pushing Black Sabbath's sound in a different direction. *Heaven and Hell*, released in 1980, restored the band's fortunes, but Dio would depart just two years later. By 1984 the revolving door of talent had taken its toll, and Iommi, the sole surviving member of the original lineup, took more interest in producing the band's material himself.

After a string of largely ignored releases in the late 1980s, the band brought Dio and Geezer Butler back into the fold, albeit temporarily. *Dehumanizer*, released in 1992, was a success, and yet another lineup would come together to record 1995's *Forbidden*, officially the last Black Sabbath studio album released.

The band tread on uncertain footing until 1997, when Iommi reunited again with Butler and Osbourne, initiating a sort of coda for the band during which it won its first Grammy for "Iron Man," off the successful live album *Reunion*. Attitudes have shifted more recently; in 2002 Osbourne became a reality television star with an MTV show featuring his entire family, and he has challenged the remaining members of Black Sabbath to the rights of that name.

"How the writing is, is we agree we all have to like it. We have to feel it. You don't think, 'Oh, are people going to like this?' You don't really think like that because you have to write how you feel and you have to like it. You have to do it from your feelings. If I started writing for other people, I'd probably be doing pop stuff. Years ago, people'd say, 'You shouldn't be playing this stuff, you should be playing more commercial stuff.' If I listened to them, God knows what I'd be playing. I have my own mind of what I want it to sound like."

—TONY IOMMI, 2009

Awards and Honors

1999   Grammy Award for Best Metal Performance, for "Iron Man" with Black Sabbath

2003   Ranked No. 86 on *Rolling Stone*'s list of 100 Greatest Guitarists of All Time

2006   Inducted into the Rock and Roll Hall of Fame, with Black Sabbath

Black Sabbath in the Great Britain, 1983. Clockwise from top: Geezer Butler, Ian Gillan, Tommy Iommi, Bev Bevan

runk sluts

KERRY KING

"Slayer has always been really streetwise. We've never tried to be anything we weren't. Like for example, I don't believe in God or the devil but I do put religion on trial because that is who I am and so that translates into the music. If people get that and they like us they will cling onto us. A Slayer record or a Slayer show to me is almost like a guarantee, you know that if you like Slayer, then you're going to dig it all. And we've always come through and done it."

—KERRY KING, 2007

essential albums

STUDIO	
1983	*Show No Mercy*
1985	*Hell Awaits*
1986	*Reign in Blood*
1988	*South of Heaven*
1990	*Seasons in the Abyss*
1994	*Divine Intervention*
1996	*Undisputed Attitude*
1998	*Diabolus in Musica*
2001	*God Hates Us All*
2006	*Christ Illusion*
2009	*World Painted Blood*

LIVE	
1984	*Live Undead*
1991	*Decade of Aggression*

Heavily tattooed heavy metal rhythm guitarist Kerry King (born June 3, 1964, in Los Angeles, California) is most often cited as a founding member of Slayer, one of thrash metal's "big four."

King attended high school in Canada, but found his way back to the States to immerse himself in music on a full-time basis. Known for his extreme appearance, even by metal standards, and his outspoken, combative personality, King has come to verbal blows on several occasions with Megadeth's Dave Mustaine, drummers Joe Nunez, Adrian Erlandsson, and Raymond Herrera, the band Machine Head, and even thrash's premiere producer, Rick Rubin.

King plays B.C. Rich guitars almost exclusively, and fans revere him for his stormy, chaotic playing and his way with evocative, twisted lyrics.

SLAYER

King set to forming Slayer after his return to Southern California upon earning his high school diploma. Originally a cover band focusing on material by Iron Maiden and Judas Priest, opening act Slayer was spotted by a producer at a Bitch concert, leading to a bare-bones studio contract, which the band members were forced to bankroll themselves.

Show No Mercy dropped in 1983, and the band earned the opportunity to mount a limited worldwide tour. Slayer's friction with Megadeth developed at this time, fueled by King's brief experience playing alongside Mustaine as a member of his band. Mustaine invited King to join, but King snubbed him by returning to Slayer permanently, commencing the pair's war of words.

With sophomore release *Hell Awaits*, Slayer began moving in the direction of a snappier, more mainstream sound, a trend amplified when the band signed to major label Def Jam in 1986. *Reign in Blood*, the band's thematically controversial third album, did well despite limited support from its nervous corporate label.

Slayer's subsequent releases through the mid-1990s did well, with each release recruiting new legions of listeners and fans, despite several lineup changes. By 1994 the band had joined forces on tour with several other top metal acts, including Ozzy Osbourne. As the band's profile reached its pinnacle, Slayer's dark themes brought accusations from the public of subliminal messages embedded in its music, even claiming that the messages drove a young girl to her death in 1996; sympathetic judges tended to rule on the band's side.

The band's releases up until 2006's *Christ Illusion* failed to generate significant buzz; the band actually found much success playing old material from their *Reign in Blood* album on tour in 1993. *Christ Illusion* put Slayer back at the top of the charts, a position it hadn't truly enjoyed since *Divine Intervention*. The band was the toast of that year, winning a Grammy and traveling to play for U.S. troops stationed in Germany. The year 2007 kicked off with an appearance on Jimmy Kimmel's late night television program, and much of the remaining year was spent touring. *World Painted Blood*, the last Slayer album, came out in 2009.

Awards and Honors

2006 Grammy Award for Best Metal Performance, for "Eyes of the Insane," with Slayer

2007 Grammy Award for Best Metal Performance for "Final Six," with Slayer

Above: Kerry King performing with Slayer in Belo Horizonte, Brazil, 2006

Left: King at the Tuska festival, Helsinki, Finland, 2008

ALEX LIFESON

"I have so many guitars and they all feel different to me, and they all respond differently. I use them like tools. For different things, one guitar will be better suited than another, whether it's for performance or for the sound. And amps, I think you could have a wall of amps and get a good sound out of any one of them. I don't know how much emphasis I'd put on the technical end of it, to be honest with you. I'm pretty confident that you could give me any amp and any guitar, and I'll get the kind of sound that I'm searching for."

—ALEX LIFESON, 2009

Alex Lifeson (born August 27, 1953, in Fernie, British Columbia) is an original member and guitarist of the Canadian band Rush. A versatile multi-instrumentalist, Lifeson, whose real name is Aleksandar Živojinovi, is the son of Serbian immigrants.

Lifeson was first exposed to music playing the viola as a child, but by the time he was 12, he had moved onto the guitar, first taking an interest in a family member's flamenco model. He took lessons from a friend during high school, putting down the roots that would become Rush in 1968.

Lifeson is an elastic guitarist whose sound draws from the classical and flamenco styles he first heard while learning to play, and he frequently employs more technically demanding techniques that he has largely taught himself. Lifeson's output is the result of a heavy array of effects and technology that he puts to good use in the studio and on stage.

By 1973 Rush had a record deal, and its first move as a signed band would be to release to a much wider audience the self-titled set of songs it had already compiled.

Lifeson playing with Rush in Charlotte, North Carolina, 2008

THE RUSH YEARS

Toronto-based Rush, formed in 1968, has been a three-piece band for most of its existence. Highly regarded for its progressive metal sound and sophisticated lyrics and musicality, the band has always been popular in Canada, but took some time to gain a foothold outside of North America.

Once Lifeson nailed down the lineup, the band started performing in and around Toronto in 1971, independently releasing an eponymous album in 1974. The new band's songs caught on in the United States as well, and soon Rush had major-label backing.

With a new drummer, the band launched its first visit to the United States that summer, soon releasing 1975's *Fly by Night*

and *Caress of Steel*. Not finding the success it desired, Rush fared better with *2112*, the first album to truly win over fans and critics.

Following that achievement, Rush entered a progressive era in the late 1970s, attempting to capture a more interesting, ambitious sound. The band shook up its formula again as the 1980s dawned, incorporating heavy synthesizers and reggae styles into 1980's *Permanent Waves*. A commercial success, the record helped Rush make significant headway into the U.S. market, generating a handful of hits for the band that continue to be heard today.

Moving Pictures, released in 1981, was even more successful, giving the band its best returns yet. With *Signals* the following year, Rush embraced the popular trend of the time and brought an electronic sound front and center. The band spent the duration of the 1980s in this vein, also releasing several live albums and compilations during this period.

Up through 1997, the band slowly brought its trademark guitar sound back into focus, while subtly incorporating elements of funk and jazz. After an extended hiatus, drummer Neil Peart returned to the band to release *Vapor Trails* in 2002.

Since its reformation, Rush has toured in honor of its thirtieth anniversary as a band, releasing several live albums, DVDs, and a studio album titled *Snakes & Arrows* in 2007.

essential albums

STUDIO

1974	*Rush*
1975	*Fly by Night*
1976	*2112*
1977	*A Farewell to Kings*
1978	*Hemispheres*
1980	*Permanent Waves*
1981	*Moving Pictures*
1982	*Signals*
1984	*Grace Under Pressure*
1985	*Power Windows*
1987	*Hold Your Fire*
1989	*Presto*
1991	*Roll the Bones*
1993	*Counterparts*
1996	*Test for Echo*
2002	*Vapor Trails*
2007	*Snakes & Arrows*

LIVE

1976	*All the World's a Stage*
1981	*Exit . . . Stage Left*
1989	*A Show of Hands*
1998	*Different Stages*
2003	*Rush in Rio*
2006	*Grace Under Pressure Tour*
2008	*Snakes & Arrows Live*

Lifeson, left, and bandmate Geddy Lee, right, play off each other onstage at Rush's thirtieth-anniversary concert at Wembley Arena in London, England, 2004

YNGWIE MALMSTEEN

"[The guitar] is still a developing instrument. There is no wrong or right way of doing it. Whatever's the best way for you. However, what I think is the most important thing to learn about any instrument, is the basics of music. Learn your ABCs before you write a Hemingway novel, you know? Don't skip any of that stuff. You learn your modes, your scales, your fucking relative keys, and you know all that shit. That stuff is key."

—YNGWIE MALMSTEEN, 2005

Yngwie Malmsteen (born June 30, 1963, in Stockholm, Sweden) is a technically ferocious solo guitarist who came to the forefront of the 1980s metal scene. Known as the master of shredding, or speedy playing, Malmsteen's reputation in Europe and Asia precedes him despite—or perhaps due to—his flamboyant, bad-boy persona.

Malmsteen's influences early on were diverse; he counts Jimi Hendrix, Deep Purple, and classical violin player Niccolò Paganini among his first idols. By the age of 20 his talents had impressed record scout and producer Mike Varney, who invited Malmsteen to the United States to explore his talent, where he quickly teamed up with a number of heavy metal bands, including Alcatraz and Steeler.

Malmsteen's work with Alcatraz led to his 1984 solo debut *Rising Force*, marking his emancipation from the band. The album brought Malmsteen immediate critical attention and scored him his first Grammy nomination. Encouraged by the warm reception, Malmsteen formed a band, named it after

his first album, and went on to release three additional studio albums through the end of the decade, including the 1988 career highlight *Odyssey*, and a live collection in 1989.

By now a respected master worldwide—if not in the United States—Malmsteen followed up with a solid stream of releases in the early 1990s. Even while combating occasional charges of resting on his laurels or failing to innovate, Malmsteen forged ahead, despite his label's waning interest.

Renegotiating a contract with longtime home Pony Canyon Records, Malmsteen unveiled *Concerto Suite for Electric Guitar and Orchestra*, his favorite and most ambitious work to date, a lush, orchestral release with healthy doses of his signature electric guitar.

In the 2000s Malmsteen has nurtured his career with an appearance on Joe Satriani's prestigious G3 guitar tour in 2003 and a collaboration with Ozzy Osbourne—not to mention a score of releases containing new and classic work as recently as 2009.

essential albums

WITH STEELER

1983   *Steeler*

WITH ALCATRAZ

1984   *No Parole from Rock 'N' Roll*

1984   *Live Sentence*

SOLO

1984   *Rising Force*

1985   *Marching Out*

1986   *Trilogy*

1988   *Odyssey*

1990   *Eclipse*

1991   *The Yngwie Malmsteen Collection*

1992   *Fire and Ice*

1994   *The Seventh Sign*

1994   *Power and Glory*

1994   *I Can't Wait*

1995   *Magnum Opus*

1996   *Inspiration*

1997   *Facing the Animal*

1998   *Concerto Suite for Electric Guitar and Orchestra in E flat minor, Opus 1*

1999   *Alchemy*

2000   *War to End All Wars*

2002   *Attack!!*

2002   *The Genesis*

2005   *Unleash the Fury*

2008   *Perpetual Flame*

2009   *Angels of Love*

2009   *Genesis*

2009   *High Impact*

Although he was often viewed as a rebel in high school, avoiding homework and riding a motorcycle, Yngwie Malmsteen spent countless hours practicing the guitar, transforming himself into a master of the neoclassical metal style.

MALMSTEEN, VIRTUOSO

Malmsteen's technical prowess is nearly unmatched. Taking his cues from the sometimes-obscure classical music of composers like Bach and Beethoven that he enjoyed in his youth, he regularly employs unusual arpeggios and scales in his playing, in sharp contrast to the frequently blues-infused style championed by many of his peers. Malmsteen's heavy, gothic style fell out of favor near the end of the 1980s but has since enjoyed a resurgence, especially outside of the United States.

Fender chose Malmsteen as one of the first artists ever, along with Eric Clapton and Jeff Beck, to have a signature series Stratocaster issued in his honor in 1988.

Malsmteen's talent was obvious at a young age. By 21 he had already released his first solo album, *Rising Force*.

MICK MARS

"I would say that when you start any kind of career, anything, and music sounds very glamorous and in a way it kind of is, but my point is that whatever it is you choose to do make damn sure that it's what you want to do with the rest of your life. It may sound in a way kind of stupid and in a way make sense. . . . When you choose your career you gotta really make sure you want to do that because people do tend to hate their job. Regardless of what it is you do it becomes work. . . . Sometimes I hate the music business too, but it's what I chose to do and it's all I want to do."

—MICK MARS, 2006

M ick Mars (born May 4, 1951, in Terre Haute, Indiana) is the accomplished yet subdued lead axman for Mötley Crüe. The source of most of Mötley Crüe's best-loved riffs, Mars is one of heavy metal's most grizzled and treasured figures.

The young Mars devoured the recordings of the Beatles, Paul Butterfield, and Jeff Beck. As a California teenager freshly uprooted from his Midwest childhood, Mars explored his identity through stints in several local bands, including Vendetta and White Horse but largely drifted through his early to mid-20s, unsure of the direction his career would take.

In 1981 Mars put out a newspaper want ad in search of potential bandmates and was invited to audition for Tommy Lee and Nikki Sixx. After convincing them of his guitar talent and aggressive attitude, the trio formed a new band, naming it Mötley Crüe on Mars's suggestion. Older than the other members, Mars has grown into the role of mysterious elder statesman, speaking little during interviews and maintaining an aloof, remote persona.

Mars stands out as a talented slide and pedal steel guitar player in a sea of hard rock shredders and is equally comfortable playing lead and rhythm.

essential albums

STUDIO

1981	*Too Fast for Love*
1983	*Shout at the Devil*
1985	*Theatre of Pain*
1987	*Girls, Girls, Girls*
1989	*Dr. Feelgood*
1994	*Mötley Crüe*
1997	*Generation Swine*
2000	*New Tattoo*
2008	*Saints of Los Angeles*

LIVE

1999	*Live: Entertainment or Death*
2006	*Carnival of Sins Live*

MÖTLEY CRÜE

Often dismissed as mere "hair metal," Mötley Crüe's contributions to the music of the 1980s isn't so easily summed up. With the addition of Mars and vocalist Vince Neil in 1981, the band's lineup was complete, and the crew quickly developed a reputation for its over-the-top live show.

By the end of 1981 the band released *Too Fast for Love*, a modest but solid-selling debut. On a Canadian tour, the band teased the music press and titillated fans with its antics, working up appetite for similar displays in the United States.

Soon the band had major-label backing and an overhauled, re-released version of its debut to show off. *Shout at the Devil* dropped in 1983, followed by *Theatre of Pain* in 1986, both hit records whose frequent exposure on radio and MTV aided their popularity.

Mötley Crüe finished out the decade of decadence amidst a flurry of celebrity romances, hit albums and tours, and dangerous brushes with drugs. *Dr. Feelgood* hit No. 1 on the charts after its release in 1989, going down in the books as the band's best-performing album.

Above: Mötley Crüe dressed to impress and sporting the hair that gave a subgenre its name. From left to right: Nikki Sixx, Mick Mars, Vince Neil, and Tommy Lee

Left: Mick Mars at the Mötley Crüe comeback tour in London, England, 2005

Sensing changes in the music industry, the band renegotiated its lucrative contract with Elektra and set to introducing a typically 1990s grunge sound into its newest material. The new albums' lackluster performance, coupled with Neil's departure and Lee's domestic troubles and subsequent exit from the band, added up to a rocky decade for the group.

Mötley Crüe opened the 2000s as fractured as ever, and new drummer Randy Castillo would sadly pass away in 2002. Lee was still estranged from the group, and the other remaining members seemed incapable of doing anything to restore the band's former sheen.

Despite Mars's less-than-stellar health, 2005 saw the reunion of Mötley Crüe's original lineup as well as a commemorative greatest hits release and a new live album. *Saints of Los Angeles*, revealed in 2008, is the band's latest studio release, and it commenced the now-annual record-breaking Crüe Fest tour and festival that year as well.

DAVE MURRAY

Dave Murray (born December 23, 1956, in Edmonton, London, England) is one of the most senior members of Iron Maiden. With Steve Harris, the famously easygoing Murray holds the distinction of playing on every Iron Maiden album ever released.

As a child Murray indulged an active interest in sports, but his focus shifted during his teens after he heard Jimi Hendrix for the first time. Dabbling in early bands like Stone Free and Urchin, Murray's dedication to practicing guitar took flight, leading to the formation of Iron Maiden with some childhood friends in 1976.

Murray is most often associated with the Fender Stratocaster, and the Fender company issued a Dave Murray signature 1957 reissue model in 2009, finished in sophisticated black and white. His smooth playing style is recognized for being self-assured yet reserved, always complementing but never drowning out the efforts of Maiden's two other axmen.

essential albums

STUDIO
1980	*Iron Maiden*
1981	*Killers*
1982	*The Number of the Beast*
1983	*Piece of Mind*
1984	*Powerslave*
1986	*Somewhere in Time*
1988	*Seventh Son of a Seventh Son*
1990	*No Prayer for the Dying*
1992	*Fear of the Dark*
1995	*The X Factor*
1998	*Virtual XI*
2000	*Brave New World*
2003	*Dance of Death*
2006	*A Matter of Life and Death*

LIVE
1985	*Live After Death*
1993	*A Real Live One*
1993	*A Real Dead One*
1993	*Live at Donington*
2002	*Rock in Rio*
2005	*Death on the Road*
2009	*Flight 666*

"We basically try to first play around with the chords and try and make it all blend together. When it comes to stuff like working out guitar harmonies, someone will naturally go to a part on the neck that they're comfortable with. So basically we just sit down and work out those little details in the recording studio just so we kind of know that we are all on the same page. But it is a real easy and natural effort between the three of us. We don't spend hours and hours analyzing it all. It just tends to flow naturally, which is the beauty of it really. Because sometimes it just sounds like one big guitar and at other times, you can hear the three individual players coming through."

—DAVE MURRAY, 2007

Iron Maiden in the 1980s. Top row from left: Dave Murray, Adrian Smith, and Bruce Dickinson. Seated in front: Nicko McBrain and Steve Harris

MURRAY'S IRON MAIDEN

Murray predates fellow Maiden guitarist Janick Gers by about fifteen years. Taking a cue from the Alexandre Dumas novel *The Man in the Iron Mask*, founder Harris chose the name "Iron Maiden" and proceeded to perfect the group's lineup and colorful live act.

By the time Maiden recruited singer Paul Anno, it was finally ready to record. A 1978 demo sold well, and after the few additions and subtractions from the roster, Iron Maiden signed up with EMI in 1979 and produced its self-titled debut the following year. Kiss and Judas Priest tapped the young band to open for them that year, and Adrian Smith came aboard to assist Murray by the end of 1980. After *Killers* came out in 1981, Maiden found a new singer in Bruce Dickinson.

The band's third studio effort, *The Number of the Beast*, was its biggest hit to date, going all the way to No. 1 in its home country. Iron Maiden occupied itself during the 1980s with several jaunts around the world, as well as defending itself against conservative accusations of indecency related to objectionable lyrics. Later in the 1980s the band toyed with the notion of a concept album not once but twice, adding keyboards and synthesizers into the mix, as was in vogue at the time. *Seventh Son of a Seventh Son*, released in 1988, was another hit in the UK. The band finished out the decade by releasing a massive compilation, spanning ten discs, of their work to date in 1990 and soon welcomed Janick Gers into the fold as the newest Iron Maiden guitarist.

VERNON REID

"Complicated is wonderful, because we have these clever brains and we work out puzzles and secret passages and pathways, vexation pathways, and that's great, but I'm attracted to simple melodies, funky rhythms, groovy things. In a way the first thing that got me into jazz was when a teacher played Coltrane's version of "My Favorite Things" and I just was just like 'Wow.' I was blown away by that."

—VERNON REID

Vernon Reid (born August 22, 1958, in London, England), heralded for his eclecticism, founded funk metal group Living Colour in 1983. A British citizen by way of the Caribbean, Reid actually grew up in New York City.

After his family settled in Brooklyn, Reid began studying the jazz music to which he had easy access and started playing guitar. His first serious gig in 1980 was working alongside Ronald Shannon Jackson in his Decoding Society ensemble; Reid's talent would take root in the group and factor heavily into six of its releases.

After the breakup of Living Colour in 1995, Reid released the solo album *Mistaken Identity* the following year. Reid also aligned himself with DJ Logic to form Yohimbe Brothers, an experimental duo that produced an album and tour in 2002 and *The Tao of Yo* in 2004.

In addition to his noted collaboration with James "Blood" Ulmer, Reid helped form the Free Form Funky Freqs, a collective that debuted its *Urban Mythology: Volume 1* in 2008. He has also appeared or worked with the Roots, Mariah Carey, and blues great B.B. King.

Recognized as a speedy, convention-defying soloist, Reid has endorsed both Hamer and Parker guitars.

LIVING COLOUR

A fusion band in every sense of the word, Living Colour owes its genesis to the conflux of funk, heavy metal, and hard rock long endorsed by its founder.

Rooted in the fledgling, progressive Black Rock Coalition, Living Colour was the name of more than one of Reid's early projects. With a heavy early emphasis on jazz sounds, the band's slant was decidedly political. Once Reid had a lineup he could rely on, the band set its sights on CBGB, the iconic New York punk club that has nurtured an unparalleled number of famed acts. Supported by Mick Jagger, *Vivid* was the band's 1988 debut, spawning the Grammy-winning hit "Cult of Personality" and popular single "Type."

After touring with Guns N' Roses and the Rolling Stones, Living Colour returned to the studio to create *Time's Up*, its 1990 sophomore effort. The ambitious album incorporated elements of electronica, funk, and thrash, earning the band another Grammy for Best Hard Rock Album.

Stain debuted in 1993 to diminished enthusiasm, perhaps due to the departure and replacement of bassist Muzz Skillings. After releasing *Pride*, a hits compilation, the members of the band went their separate ways.

Living Colour would reunite in 2000 at the renowned CBGB, leading up to a new album called *Collideøscope* and *Live from CBGB*, containing material from the most recent club performance. In recent years the band has mounted a European tour and released a number of compilations and DVDs. *The Chair in the Doorway*, Living Colour's latest studio album, debuted at No. 161 in 2009.

essential albums

WITH LIVING COLOUR (STUDIO)

1988	*Vivid*
1993	*Stain*
2003	*Collideøscope*
2009	*The Chair in the Doorway*

WITH LIVING COLOUR (LIVE)

1994	*Dread*
2005	*Live from CBGB's*
2009	*The Paris Concert*

SOLO

1996	*Mistaken Identity*
2004	*Known Unknown*
2006	*Other True Self*

Awards and Honors

1989	Grammy Award for Best Hard Rock Performance, for "Cult of Personality," with Living Colour
1990	Grammy Award for Best Hard Rock Performance, for "Time's Up," with Living Colour
2003	Ranked No. 66 on *Rolling Stone*'s list of the 100 Greatest Guitarists of All Time.

Reid playing with Living Colour at Sala Heineken in Madrid, Spain, 2008

JOE SATRIANI

essential albums

SOLO

1986	*Not of This Earth*
1987	*Surfing with the Alien*
1988	*Dreaming #11*
1989	*Flying in a Blue Dream*
1992	*The Extremist*
1995	*Joe Satriani*
1998	*Crystal Planet*
2000	*Engines of Creation*
2002	*Strange Beautiful Music*
2003	*The Satch Tapes*
2004	*Is There Love in Space?*
2006	*Super Colossal*
2008	*Professor Satchafunkilus and the Musterion of Rock*

LIVE

1993	*Time Machine*
2006	*Satriani Live!*

WITH G3

1997	*G3 Live*

Joe Satriani (born July 15, 1956, in Westbury, New York) is an instrumental guitarist and teacher known for his singular level of mastery and as a founder of the prestigious G3 tour.

Satriani's first salient influence was Hendrix, who inspired a teenaged Satriani to pick up a guitar. Initially a teacher—perhaps most famously as Steve Vai's—Satriani moved to the West Coast and committed himself to music on a full-time basis. Satriani released an eponymous EP in 1984, gigged with an assortment of other musicians, and continued to teach, all while watching former protégé Vai pass him by. The good vibes between the pair paid off, though; it was likely that Vai's very public praise led to brisk sales for *Not of This Earth* and *Surfing with the Alien* in 1987, Satriani's first major breakthrough work.

By the end of the 1980s the guitar world had effectively crowned Satriani king. *Flying in a Blue Dream* only cemented his reputation and showed off his vocal skills as well. A newly celebrated Satriani continued recording in the 1990s and took a temporary spot in the lineup of legendary rockers Deep Purple, turning down a very serious offer to join the band permanently.

In 1996 Satriani teamed up with old friend Vai to launch G3, the world's premiere showcase and annual tour for a trio of guitarists. Along with its founders, John Petrucci and Eric Johnson are regular participants.

At the end of the 1990s Satriani dipped into the electronica genre with *Engines of Creation*, a Grammy-nominated collection. Like many of his contemporaries, as well as legacy acts, Satriani has not shied away from releasing considerable live material and concert footage on DVD. *Professor Satchafunkilus and the Musterion of Rock*, Satriani's latest, high-concept effort, debuted in 2008.

Chickenfoot is Satriani's side project in conjunction with Michael Anthony, Sammy Hagar, and Chad Smith. A self-titled debut was unveiled in 2009.

"There's not really a lot of room for instrumental guitar music. I know everybody knows that. So I tend to tell people that all the obvious stuff still counts. You have to know what you're doing, so that means notes, chords, and scales. You have to have a great sense of rhythm and a good sense of pitch and intonation. You have to know how to play with people, and you have to know how to play for people. Then there are the two conflicting pieces of advice, which are, learn to sound like other people so you can get work, but develop a totally original sound at the same time so that if luck shines your way and you get that one moment to show people what you're all about, then you've got something to show them. That's important."

—JOE SATRIANI, 2006

Satriani live at the Fillmore Miami Beach/Jackie Gleason Theater, 2008

HIS TECHNIQUE AND SOUND

Satriani's skill is, by any estimation, untouchable. His gifted grasp of music theory and precise control of the instrument itself inform his playing. Never content to settle into one style of playing or sound, Satriani has consistently challenged himself—and his fans.

Satriani—affectionately known by his disciples as "Satch"—can shred with the best of them, but there remains an underlying delicacy and precision to even his most blazing passages. Satriani has been known to employ harmonics, tapping, and volume swells in his playing to dramatic effect, principally on Ibanez guitars. Ibanez established its JS signature series in 1988, and Satriani endorses Peavey equipment as well.

Literary and science fiction references abound in Satch's work—take *Surfing with the Alien* or *Is There Love in Space?*, for example. Such preoccupation with the boundaries of the universe—or lack thereof—seem appropriate given Satriani's cred as a virtuoso seemingly from another planet.

Satch performing in Mumbai, India

SLASH

"As long as I've known Axl, we've had so many differences that have been like the end of the line as far as we were concerned. I think that happens with most singers and guitar players, or whatever that cliché is. It might look a little intense on the outside, seeing all this shit that we're going through, but it makes for a tension that's—in a morbid kind of way—really conducive to the music we collaborate on. But as far as Axl goes, he is the best singer-lyricist around."

—SLASH, 1991

Slash (born Saul Hudson July 23, 1965, in Stoke-on-Trent, England) is a solo guitarist immortalized for his decade-long stint with Guns N' Roses. Most recently Slash is a solo artist, with a new album waiting in the wings for a 2010 release—featuring every original member of Guns N' Roses save for Axl Rose.

The son of an artistically inclined father and mother, Slash's family moved him to Los Angeles when he was 11. He earned his nickname early on owing to his frenetic pace and personality, and with childhood friend Steven Adler—a future member of Guns N' Roses—Slash took up the guitar, dropping out of school to hone his skills.

A student of Aerosmith, Cream, Led Zeppelin, and Motörhead, Slash started his first band in 1983 with Adler, calling the group Road Crew. While playing gigs around town Slash and his bandmates encountered a group billing itself as Hollywood Rose. The bands joined forces, and the merger would result in Guns N' Roses.

Snakepit was Slash's short-lived side project post-GN'R. Enjoying the solid reputation that he established as a member of GN'R, he found himself a popular session player. He even joined Michael Jackson to record *Dangerous* in 1990 and accompanied Jackson on the album's tour. Slash and Jackson would frequently work together throughout the remainder of the decade.

The rest of Slash's resume is equally impressive: he has worked with Quentin Tarantino and the Yardbirds. Established in 1998, Velvet Revolver is Slash's side supergroup; like Snakepit, Velvet Revolver has welcomed several refugees of Guns N' Roses. Currently the band is taking a break, but the Internet has been host to murmurs that the group is ready to dust itself off and reenter the studio.

Slash is known for his affectionate treatment of one of his favorite guitars, a 1959 Gibson Les Paul replica that he put to heavy use on *Appetite for Destruction*. His fondness for Gibsons had led to a flourishing and extensive line of signature models with the company.

SLASH THE SHREDDER

Alongside bandmate Stradlin, Slash relished his role as the even wilder child in what the press was calling the "world's most dangerous band." By 1991 the band had reached the top, with that year's *Use Your Illusion II* debuting at No. 1 on the Billboard 200. Along with a massive twenty-eight-month-long tour, the albums were backed up by heavy MTV airplay, including the video for "November Rain," which became one of the most requested videos ever. After Stradlin left the band during the tour, Slash had to adjust to sharing the stage with newcomers Gilby Clark and Matt Sorum. After the tour the new Guns N' Roses released *The Spaghetti Incident?* composed entirely of cover songs. This was Slash's last album with the band—leading to a toxic feud between Rose and Slash that has yet to be settled amicably.

Like many of his contemporaries, Slash's playing is infused with the blues. Known for keeping a rigorous practice schedule–and for being extremely punctual in general—Slash's indelible solos are often ranked as some of the best in rock and roll.

essential albums

WITH GUNS N' ROSES

1987	*Appetite for Destruction*
1988	*G N' R Lies*
1991	*Use Your Illusion I*
1991	*Use Your Illusion II*
1993	*"The Spaghetti Incident?"*

WITH SLASH'S SNAKEPIT

1995	*Ain't Life Grand*
2000	*It's Five O'Clock Somewhere*

WITH VELVET REVOLVER

2004	*Contraband*
2007	*Libertad*

Awards and Honors

2004   Grammy Award for Best Hard Rock Performance, for "Slither," with Velvet Revolver

Guns N' Roses in the mid-1980s. From left: Izzy Stradlin, Duff McKagan, Axl Rose, Slash, and Steve Adler

Slash performing with Velvet Revolver in London, 2007

ADRIAN SMITH

essential albums

WITH URCHIN

| 1977 | *Black Leather Fantasy* |
| 1977 | *She's A Roller* |

WITH IRON MAIDEN

1981	*Killers*
1982	*The Number of the Beast*
1983	*Piece of Mind*
1984	*Powerslave*
1985	*Live After Death*
1986	*Somewhere in Time*
1988	*Seventh Son of a Seventh Son*
2000	*Brave New World*
2002	*Rock in Rio*
2002	*Beast Over Hammersmith*
2003	*Dance of Death*
2005	*Death on the Road*
2006	*A Matter of Life and Death*
2009	*Flight 666*

WITH ASAP

| 1989 | *Silver and Gold* |

WITH PSYCHO MOTEL

| 1996 | *State of Mind* |
| 1997 | *Welcome to the World* |

WITH BRUCE DICKINSON

| 1997 | *Accident of Birth* |
| 1998 | *The Chemical Wedding* |

Adrian Smith (born February 27, 1957, in East London, England) rounds out the three-pronged guitar enterprise of Iron Maiden. Smith is respected by bandmates for his mellow attitude and lackadaisical playing style.

Inspired by the classic hard rock of Deep Purple and Jimi Hendrix, Smith, along with schoolmate Dave Murray formed the band Urchin. Indeed, it was Murray who sold Smith his first guitar, although Smith rejected several overtures to come aboard the band Murray had joined in 1976—Steve Harris's Iron Maiden. Smith finally joined Iron Maiden in 1980.

In the years following Iron Maiden, Smith fashioned himself as the Adrian Smith And Project (ASAP), releasing a 1989 record called *Silver and Gold*. Some members of Iron Maiden felt bitter about this project—Smith had released it before he'd officially broken off from the group.

Through the 1990s Smith kicked off such projects as *Instant Clarity* with Michael Kiske and alternative effort Psycho Motel. Psycho Motel released two albums between 1996 and 1997. Smith has also collaborated on Bruce Dickinson's own solo releases.

Smith has been associated with many guitars, but most frequently it's his Jackson Dinky signature model and his beloved Gibson Les Paul Goldtop, one of his oldest—and best—axes that take center stage.

"Metal has changed beyond recognition. . . . For many the guitar is an instrument of pure aggression rather than melody. There's a place for aggression but melody should contrast it. Like I said, you'll remember the quiet."

—ADRIAN SMITH, 2009

Iron Maiden publicity photo. From left: Adrian Smith, Bruce Dickinson, Steve Harris, Dave Murray, and Nicko McBrain

SMITH'S ROLE

Though Smith met fellow Maiden Dave Murray in his youth, it wasn't until 1980 that he joined the band, replacing Dennis Stratton and famously beating Phil Collen to the punch. Smith and Murray took the idea of a twin guitar attack to new levels through the 1980s, beginning on the 1981 release *Killers*.

On 1982's controversial record *The Number of the Beast*, Smith's skill as songwriter is not to be overlooked; he is credited as author on "Two Minutes to Midnight," "Can I Play With Madness," and "Wasted Years," among other hit Iron Maiden tunes. Often working in tandem with new singer Bruce Dickinson, who entered the picture for *Beast*, Smith's compositions were built around his rapid, meticulously structured solos—unmistakably rock and roll, but with one foot firmly rooted in the blues.

With *No Prayer for the Dying*, released in 1990, Smith realized his role in the band was changing. That year Smith decamped, only to return in 1999 when Maiden staged a tour and set to work on several new studio albums.

Smith plays alongside bandmate Janick Gers at an Iron Maiden concert at Cotroceni Stadium in Bucharest, Romania, 2008

GLENN TIPTON

"I love music, but I don't eat breathe and live it. I like to enjoy it when I'm ready to write and ready to pick the guitar up and I get hungry to pick the guitar up. That's when I'm excited and that's when I produce a lot and that's when I think a lot. So, I'm a bit of a strange guitar player really."

—GLENN TIPTON, 2006

essential albums

WITH JUDAS PRIEST (STUDIO)
1974	*Rocka Rolla*
1976	*Sad Wings of Destiny*
1977	*Sin after Sin*
1977	*Stained Class*
1978	*Hell Bent for Leather/Killing Machine*
1980	*British Steel*
1981	*Point of Entry*
1982	*Screaming for Vengeance*
1984	*Defenders of the Faith*
1986	*Turbo*
1988	*Ram It Down*
1990	*Painkiller*
1997	*Jugulator*
2001	*Demolition*
2005	*Angel of Retribution*
2008	*Nostradamus*

WITH JUDAS PRIEST (LIVE)
1979	*Unleashed in the East*
1987	*Priest . . . Live!*
1998	*'98 Live Meltdown*
2003	*Live in London*
2009	*A Touch of Evil: Live*

SOLO
1997	*Baptizm of Fire*
2006	*Edge of the World*

Glenn Tipton (born October 25, 1947, in West Midlands, England) is principally known as one half of the guitar duo in Judas Priest. As a child he took piano lessons from his mother, but it wasn't until he was 21 that he picked up the guitar.

Judas Priest had already formed when Tipton came aboard as the second guitarist in 1974. He quickly contributed to playing and songwriting. In 1979, after a few preliminary albums, Priest released the live album *Unleashed in the East*, the first record to bring the band mainstream success. Future releases garnered much popular success but mixed critical reviews, with some critics calling into question the band's production techniques and tendency to release similar-sounding material.

With K. K. Downing, Tipton fashioned a sound and a style without parallel, going on to define the metal genre from the mid-1970s. Tipton and his bandmates, especially front man Rob Halford, are remembered for their extreme style on stage, too—usually incorporating leather, running motorcycles, and other extreme theatrics.

TIPTON'S STYLE

Tipton has developed a straightforward but electrifying style, alongside fellow Priest guitarist K. K. Downing. His approach has increased in complexity over the years, incorporating tapping and sweep picking into his notably melodic sound.

Tipton's best known guitar is his Hamer Phantom GT, which he adopted in 1984. A model based on this ax went into mass production for consumers in the mid-1980s.

Tipton has stated in interviews that he believes in the most simple guitar and amp setup possible to avoid problems and increase reliability.

Tipton playing at a Judas Priest concert in Bucharest, Romania, 2008

Awards and Honors

2010   Grammy Award for Best Metal Performance, for "Dissident Aggressor," with Judas Priest

SUBLIMINAL LYRICS

This hard-edged band's effect on young and impressionable listeners was called into question in 1990 after two young men in Reno, Nevada, shot themselves at a playground after listening to Judas Priest—and one of them succeeded in his suicide attempt. The parents of the men claimed that a "subliminal message" in "Better by You, Better Than Me" instructed them to "do it" and harm themselves. The lawsuit was dismissed after a month-long trial, with the band maintaining that there was no hidden message in the music, much less one that would encourage fans to end their lives before buying more Judas Priest records.

Judas Priest in the band's earlier days

ANGUS YOUNG

"We started life as a band. AC/DC was a band first and foremost. We never looked at ourselves as individual pieces. That has always been the way we have looked at it. I have never said AC/DC is one guitar solo and here is your drum solo. AC/DC is a combination of five guys who all play with the same intent in mind. We go out there to play a bit of rock and roll. We aren't five individual guys displaying their technique."

—ANGUS YOUNG, 2008

Angus Young (born March 31, 1955, in Glascow, Scotland) is best known as a founding member of AC/DC. After moving to Australia with his family in 1960, Angus picked up the banjo as a hobby, soon taking up the guitar. His first instrument was a decrepit Gibson SG with a warped, crooked neck—and he continues to endorse the same instrument today, having overseen the creation of his own signature model by the company.

In 1973 Angus formed AC/DC with his older brother, Malcolm. By 1979 the band, already subject to a revolving lineup of members, found success with their album *Highway to Hell*. The year 1980 brought the death of lead singer Bon Scott and also the band's best-selling album, *Back In Black*, second only to Michael Jackson's *Thriller* in terms of total albums sold worldwide.

Known for his schoolboy uniform, a look he adopted at the height of the glam rock scene and has maintained to this day, Young has built a reputation as an accomplished blues guitarist, citing masters like Chuck Berry, B.B. King, and Buddy Guy as influences. His style firmly relies on the power chord, occasionally leading to charges of lazy or repetitive playing, but Young consistently surprises during performances with unexpected passages of improvisation or phrases inspired by the blues and folk music that nurtured his musical development.

essential albums

STUDIO

1976	*High Voltage*
1976	*Dirty Deeds Done Dirt Cheap*
1977	*Let There Be Rock*
1978	*Powerage*
1979	*Highway to Hell*
1980	*Back in Black*
1981	*For Those About to Rock*
1983	*Flick of the Switch*
1985	*Fly on the Wall*
1986	*Who Made Who*
1988	*Blow Up Your Video*
1990	*The Razors Edge*
1995	*Ballbreaker*
2000	*Stiff Upper Lip*
2008	*Black Ice*

LIVE

1978	*If You Want Blood You've Got It*
1992	*Live*
1997	*Live from the Atlantic Studios*

AC/DC

AC/DC's lineup—and image—was completed with the addition of singer Bon Scott, a former chauffeur and Australian army reject who lent the group a palpable edge. Before *Highway*, the band released a number of albums, but they spent much of the 1970s perfecting their wickedly energetic live performances.

After Scott's alcohol-related death and some soul-searching, AC/DC regrouped, recruiting Brian Johnson and recording *Back in Black*, a true blockbuster.

The 1980s heralded a period of upheaval for the band; AC/DC band members cast off their producer and chose to release their follow-up effort, 1983's *Flick of the Switch*, on their own. Internal tensions resulted in the firing of percussionist Phil Rudd.

After a brief period of commercial cooling off, AC/DC struck again with *Blow Up Your Video* in 1988. The successful album swept the band into the 1990s with renewed popularity, backed up by a series of well-attended tours and the return of Rudd in 1994.

Young on guitar, right, with singer Brian Johnson, performing with AC/DC, 2000

In the last decade the band has found itself once again surprisingly relevant, with a new record deal and several expansive boxed sets and DVD collections under its belt. *Black Ice*, AC/DC's 2008 album, has been a boon for the band—and its record label—selling widely and contributing to AC/DC's $105 million haul in 2009.

The band's legacy as the world's premiere, universally popular hard rock band is difficult to contest. Singles like "You Shook Me All Night Long" are perennially popular, and the band has spawned legions of tribute groups and enjoys an always-enthusiastic fan base.

Awards and Honors

2003 Inducted into the Rock and Roll Hall of Fame, with AC/DC

2003 Ranked No. 96 on *Rolling Stone*'s list of the 100 Greatest Guitarists of All Time

2010 Grammy Award for Best Hard Rock Performance, for "War Machine," with AC/DC

Angus Young live with AC/DC in St. Paul, Minnesota, 2008

ALTERNATIVE, INDIE, AND PUNK

Navigating the constantly shifting lines between personal integrity, commercial success, social action, and musical innovation, alternative, indie, and punk artists frequently find themselves subject to criticism wholly unrelated to their handling of the guitar. The punk aesthetic originated as an ideological response to the prevailing establishment of the 1960s and 1970s; the movement's far-reaching music would be its longest-lasting legacy.

Early practitioners like the Ramones and the Clash would prove themselves open to later innovation, paving the way for later do-it-yourselfers (and adept entrepreneurs) like Ani DiFranco. The alternative and grunge acts of the 1990s found unexpected, unbelievable commercial success—certainly signaling a mainstream acceptance of values once relegated to the cultural fringe.

MATTHEW BELLAMY

"I think sometimes [a record label's] approach can damage an artist; I think sometimes it's best to allow them to develop without too much pressure, especially in the early years. Some bands get so much put on their shoulders straight away, that it can sometimes turn them off or completely distract them away from what they're supposed to be doing, which is just making good music and being a good live act."

—MATTHEW BELLAMY, 2009

Matthew Bellamy (born June 9, 1978, in Cambridge, England) is the front man and lead guitarist for British rock outfit Muse. The band is largely his vision; Bellamy contributes to most songwriting and serves as the often-photographed public face for the group.

Bellamy's father was a rhythm guitarist of note as a member of the Tornadoes, one of the first British bands to find a large American audience. Initially drawn to the piano, Bellamy gravitated toward guitar after his parents split up.

Popular with audiences in England and around the world as well, Bellamy is regularly ranked as one of the favorite guitarists of the contemporary generation and is a regular fixture in publications like *NME, Q, Cosmopolitan, Total Guitar,* and *Kerrang!* He has already staked out a place alongside the greats with his energetic riffs.

Bellamy is known for his onstage antics—especially the destruction of his axes. He actually holds a record for doing so, with the current count verified by the *Guinness Book of World Records.* In conjunction with luthier Hugh Manson, Bellamy has designed a sizeable number of custom guitars, many of which he uses as his primary instruments.

Bellamy is a commanding singer, too. His elastic voice is capable of spanning the gulf between a low, gravely rumble and higher registers, inching into falsetto.

Matthew Bellamy playing with Muse, 2001

essential albums

STUDIO

1999	*Showbiz*
2001	*Origin of Symmetry*
2003	*Absolution*
2006	*Black Holes and Revelations*
2009	*The Resistance*

LIVE

2008	*HAARP*

Right: Bellamy playing during Muse's 2009 tour for *The Resistance*. The album, which ranked No. 3 in the United States upon its release, was the first to be produced by the band.

Below: Bellamy in concert with Muse in 2001

MUSE

Bellamy formed the band Muse in Devon, England, with a coterie of friends in 1994. Muse released a string of EPs in quick succession, leading to a record deal and the band's first trip to the United States. *Showbiz*, Muse's debut album, came to light in 1999, and the band followed that release with *The Origin of Symmetry*.

Muse finally won victory on the U.S. charts with *Absolution*, opening the way for an American tour, including an appearance at California's prestigious Coachella festival.

Coming off a successful tour and enjoying increased levels of exposure, the band offered up *Black Holes and Revelations* in 2006. Another winner, the album won Muse several major European music awards.

By 2007 the band was performing with bands like Daft Punk, Rage Against the Machine, Queens of the Stone Age, and Linkin Park. *The Resistance* came out in 2009; a self-produced affair, it reached the No. 3 position on U.S. charts. At the beginning of 2010 the band found itself in the midst of a massive tour with dates scheduled well into that year.

The band has distinguished itself thanks to elaborate, technologically flavored live performances and a sound that combines electronica with harder, more classic rock styles.

PETER BUCK

Peter Buck (born December 6, 1956, in Berkeley, California) is a guitarist and one of the original members of R.E.M., the seminal alternative rock group of the 1980s and 1990s.

Buck spent his college years in and around Atlanta, Georgia, where he casually met singer Michael Stipe. In 1980 Buck and Stipe joined with bassist Mike Mills and drummer Bill Berry to form R.E.M.

Buck maintains a vibrant working life in several locations across the United States. He currently claims membership in a number of various side projects and supergroups and is a noted curator of records, maintaining a massive personal collection, numbering more than 25,000.

A proponent of Rickenbacker guitars and open tuning, Buck's stylings have been praised by Bono of U2, among others, as a crucial part of R.E.M.'s daring, textured sound. Recent R.E.M. releases have delved more into electronics and synthesizers, occasionally displacing Buck's contributions.

Buck's playing is frequently cited as one of the band's most intriguing attributes. His folk-based style, rife with arpeggios, shies away from lengthy guitar solos, instead playing into the larger texture or idea at the center of the song. Buck is known for pushing the band's musical boundaries, but, especially in the early days of the original lineup, Buck has stated that he often deferred to Stipe and the more musically opinionated Mike Mills and Bill Berry regarding ultimate artistic decisions.

essential albums

WITH R.E.M.

1983	*Murmur*
1984	*Reckoning*
1985	*Fables of the Reconstruction*
1986	*Life's Rich Pageant*
1987	*Dead Letter Office*
1987	*Document*
1988	*Eponymous*
1988	*Green*
1991	*Out of Time*
1992	*Automatic For The People*
1993	*Man on the Moon*
1994	*Monster*
1994	*Shiny Chatty People*
1996	*New Adventures in Hi-Fi*
1998	*Up*
1999	*Star Profiles*
2001	*Reveal*
2004	*Around the Sun*
2007	*R.E.M. Live*
2008	*Accelerate*
2009	*Live at the Olympia*

WITH THE MINUS 5

1995	*Old Liquidator*
1997	*The Lonesome Death of Buck McCoy*
2001	*Let the War Against Music Begin*
2003	*Down with Wilco*
2004	*At the Organ*
2004	*In Rock*

WITH TUATARA

1996	*Breaking the Ethers*
1998	*Trading with the Enemy*
2001	*Cinemathique*
2003	*The Loading Program*
2007	*East of the Sun*
2007	*West of the Moon*

Opposite: R.E.M. in 1994. From left: Mike Mills, Bill Berry, Michael Stipe, and Buck

R.E.M.

R.E.M. almost single-handedly ushered in a new sound for the 1980s, providing a link between the waning days of punk and the less substantial alternative bands of the late 1980s and 1990s. Its topical, evocative style was popular from the release of the *Chronic Town* EP in 1982. A fixture for much of the decade on campus radio in the United States, R.E.M. still lacked the major recognition it was searching for. It wasn't until 1987's *Document* and the single "The One I Love" that R.E.M. could truly claim to be a major musical force.

After following up with *Green* in 1988, the band disappeared for a time, and it wouldn't resurface until 1991 when it released *Out of Time*. Easily one of its most popular records, largely due to game-shifting tune "Losing My Religion," the band put out its definitive work *Automatic for the People* just one year later. A broad, folk-inspired masterpiece, the album contains "Everybody Hurts," one of the band's most recognized contributions.

With new material, R.E.M. set out for a major tour in the mid-1990s. In line with its then exalted status within the music establishment, R.E.M.'s 1996 contract renegotiation netted its band members nearly $100 million, one of the most lucrative deals in music history. From that point, critics would acclaim future R.E.M. releases, but none its later efforts succeeded in eclipsing or matching the performance of its earlier work. In 1997 Bill Berry announced his retirement, rendering the band a trio whose work has continued with the release of a studio album as recently as 2008.

Despite its profile, the band's reputation for integrity and independence is still intact. All members of the band have vocalized their support for an array of progressive social causes and have participated in performances for charity on multiple occasions.

Awards and Honors

1991	Grammy Award for Best Alternative Music Album, for *Out of Time*, with R.E.M.
1991	Grammy Award for Best Music Video, Short Form, for "Losing My Religion," with R.E.M.
1991	Grammy Award for Best Pop Performance by a Duo or Group with Vocal, for "Losing My Religion," with R.E.M.
2007	Inducted into the Rock and Roll Hall of Fame, with R.E.M.

Buck playing with R.E.M. at the Milton Keynes Bowl, 1995

"It definitely feels to me that if you stay in the studio and tinker with things for that long, you're not really representing who you are, you're just doing this. And everyone I've worked with outside of this tends to feel whoever you are as a person and as a musician comes out more when you're working quickly and taking some chances—you know, and when you take chances, you can fail. But I don't want to make the perfect record, it's not possible."

—PETER BUCK, 2007

BUCKETHEAD

"I like Disneyland. I want to be buried there—parts of me in It's a Small World, Haunted Mansion, and Pirates of the Caribbean, plus parts in Tokyo Disneyland, Euro Disneyland, and Florida Disney World. There are enough bones to go around."

—BUCKETHEAD

Buckethead (born Brian Carroll on May 13, 1969, in Los Angeles, California) is a gifted electric guitarist known for his eccentric professional look, which incorporates buckets as headwear and an identity-obscuring face mask. Held in the highest esteem by guitarists around the world for the quality and speed of his playing, his reluctance to give interviews makes him one of music's most intriguing—and maddening—characters. With a solo catalog nearing thirty albums at last count, Buckethead's output is staggering.

Buckethead started developing a name for himself in guitar circles in the late 1980s; *Guitar Player* magazine noted his "psychotronic, demonic edge." With the Deli Creeps Buckethead assembled a demo and went on to record *Bucketheadland*, initially available only in Japan. The music got the ear of Bill Laswell, a bass player, and together he and Buckethead formed experimental group Praxis, releasing *Transmutation* in 1992, a fine example of Buckethead's ability on the guitar. Buckethead has remained active with Praxis.

Buckethead's first solo release, actually as Death Cube K, surfaced in 1994. He followed up with *Giant Robot* in 1994, which featured Iggy Pop among other guests. *The Day of the Robot*, now a rare collector's item, is Buckethead's third proper release. With his higher profile in the 1990s, Buckethead's music became the sound track to several films and video games. He also struck up a working relationship with actor Viggo Mortensen, with whom he has released several albums.

Buckethead dusted off the Death Cube K anagram for 1997 release *Disembodied*, followed by 1998's *Colma*, an homage to the musician's mother who was battling colon cancer at the time. A year later he scored his most significant hit yet with *Monsters and Robots*; although not quite representing the guitarist's ticket into the mainstream, Buckethead gained further exposure largely thanks to the music video for "The Ballad of Buckethead."

In perhaps his boldest, most mainstream move, Buckethead joined up with Guns N' Roses in 2000. He appears on their 2008 album *Chinese Democracy*, and made several appearances with the band before parting ways in 2004.

In the 2000s Buckethead's solo release schedule seemed to accelerate; the years 2002 and 2004 were especially active, seeing the introduction of three new studio albums each. Buckethead also made his first foray into DVD releases, many of which remain hard to find and contain rare clips from his early career. The year 2007 was a stunningly productive one for the guitarist—he released the gargantuan box set, *In Search of The*, consisting of thirteen separate albums.

Buckethead is also an visual artist—his graphic work graces the covers of several of his albums, and he has issued a handful of standalone paintings, both available only in extremely limited edition.

INSPIRATION

Buckethead's influences are grounded in the mainstream—Angus Young, Yngwie Malmsteen, Michael Jackson—and also the surreal. Chickens and robots feature prominently in Buckethead's aesthetic and a current of giddy, childlike naivety—with just a hint of something darker—runs through his performances and rare press appearances. Buckethead's official press material maintains that he was born into a family of chickens, largely responsible for the way he is today.

In keeping with his schizophrenic embrace of popular culture, Buckethead has also praised basketball pro Michael Jordan, the martial arts, and the Disneyland theme park as important, formative influences on his art.

essential albums

WITH PRAXIS

1992	*Transmutation (Mutatis Mutandis)*
1994	*Sacrifist*
1995	*Metatron*
1998	*Mold*
1999	*Warszawa*
2005	*Zurich*
2008	*Profanation (Preparing for a Coming Darkness)*

AS DEATH CUBE K

1994	*Dreamatorium*
1997	*Disembodied*

SOLO

1992	*Bucketheadland*
1994	*Giant Robot*
1996	*The Day of the Robot*
1998	*Colma*
1999	*Monsters and Robots*
2001	*Somewhere Over the Slaughterhouse*
2002	*Funnel Weaver*
2003	*Bucketheadland 2*
2004	*Island of Lost Minds*
2005	*Enter the Chicken*
2006	*The Elephant Man's Alarm Clock*
2007	*Pepper's Ghost*
2008	*Albino Slug*
2009	*Slaughterhouse on the Prairie*

Buckethead onstage in 2008, masked and wearing a plain white bucket on his head

KURT COBAIN

Kurt Cobain (born February 20, 1967, in Aberdeen, Washington; died April 5, 1994, in Seattle, Washington) was the most visible face of the 1990s grunge movement, a role he attained as the front man of Nirvana. In 1994 Cobain famously ended his own life—but controversy and uncertainty still surround his untimely death. Despite his personal struggles, Cobain is regarded as truly original guitar talent and a rock and roll game changer.

Cobain was reared in a fractured yet artistically supportive family. As a child Cobain demonstrated an interest in music and instruments almost from the moment he was able; he has named the Beatles, the Ramones, and the Monkees as some of his earliest influences.

As a student, Cobain was a reluctant athlete and some-what of a loner—his sympathies for his outcast, less popular peers regularly provoked scuffles and ridicule. In his late teens Cobain started going to punk and rock shows in and around Seattle. With friend Krist Novoselic Cobain formed Nirvana, eventually releasing *Bleach* in 1989.

After becoming a sensation with 1991's *Nevermind*, Cobain found fame a difficult sea to navigate. Striving to maintain the potency of his countercultural, independent stances on such tough social issues as racism and sexuality while fulfilling the demands of his role as one of the world's most famous musicians proved immensely challenging.

Though Cobain had been a long-time drug user, it wasn't until the late 1980s that Cobain began experimenting with harder drugs like LSD and heroin. He started shooting up initially in search of relief from a chronic stomach condition, behavior that quickly turned into a fervent addiction.

By the time Cobain had achieved fame with Nirvana, he was regularly passing out after performances and during public engagements. Wife Courtney Love was something of an enabler, often administering other drugs to Cobain after he overdosed instead of seeking out medical assistance.

Cobain made various attempts at rehab over the years but seemed largely blasé about his drug intake. In March of 1994 Love arranged an intervention with the help of several music industry executives and friends of Cobain. After successfully entering a rehab program in Los Angeles, Cobain had second thoughts and left the facility without any announcement. Ignoring attempts at contact made by Love and concerned family members, he traveled to Seattle, where he was discovered dead near his home a few days later.

Cobain's legacy after his death has taken on an almost mythic quality. His life and music continues to inspire anecdotes, rumors, and squabbles over the stewardship of his music and other life's work. He is universally hailed as a true talent and perhaps the most authentic conduit of early alternative and grunge music—but his appeal is still strong among music fans of all shades. Persistent interest in his life and music resulted in Cobain temporarily passing Elvis Presley on a list of the highest earning dead celebrities in 2006.

Awards and Honors

1995 Grammy Award for Best Alternative Music Performance, for *MTV Unplugged in New York*, with Nirvana

2003 Ranked No. 12 on *Rolling Stone*'s list of the 100 Greatest Guitarists of All Time

Kurt Cobain on the MTV series *MTV Unplugged* featuring Nirvana, 1993. The band released a live album from the recording of the performance, *MTV Unplugged in New York*— the first Nirvana album released after Cobain's death. *Unplugged* received a Grammy Award in 1995 for Best Alternative Music Performance.

"Punk expressed the way I felt socially and politically. There were so many things going on at once. It expressed the anger that I felt, the alienation."

—KURT COBAIN, 1993

NIRVANA

Nirvana formed out of the friendship that started in 1984 between Cobain and bass player Krist Novoselic. While they immersed themselves in the punk subculture of their hometown, Cobain actually started playing drums in a band called the Stiff Woodies, before taking over guitar. Eventually the band locked in a steady lineup and decided to dub themselves Nirvana.

In 1988 Nirvana signed to storied indie label Sub Pop, instrumental in marketing its debut, *Bleach*, which put Nirvana on the underground radar—and on the lips of bands like Dinosaur Jr. and Sonic Youth. After moving to bigger label DGC and recruiting Dave Grohl (later of Foo Fighters) to drum for it, Nirvana released *Nevermind*, its landmark album in 1991, becoming overnight MTV sensations.

Unaccustomed to the spotlight, the band gained a reputation for its unpredictable and sometimes sarcastic live performances. Behavior in the studio was equally erratic—Cobain's drug use and other medical problems slowed down Nirvana's work; a skittish label cobbled together 1992's *Incesticide*, composed of extra tracks and bonus material. *In Utero* followed in 1993, and the band launched a full-scale tour that lasted several months. On the European leg, Cobain attempted suicide after a night of abusing alcohol and pills; the incident was largely covered up and played off as a drug overdose.

After Cobain's death in the spring of 1994, Nirvana continued to release material, mostly compilations of live material. *Nirvana* was released in 2002, the result of a legal struggle between Novoselic, Grohl, and Courtney Love, followed by 2004's *With the Lights Out*. These releases, along with a handful of other box sets sprinkled throughout the 2000s, contained a healthy amount of Cobain's early, unreleased material and other rarities.

Above: Nirvana. From left, Dave Grohl, Kurt Cobain, and Krist Novoselic

Left: Cobain, Novoselic, and Grohl on VH1's *Behind the Music*, 1994

essential albums

1989	*Bleach*
1991	*Nevermind*
1992	*Incesticide*
1993	*In Utero*
1994	*Unplugged in New York*
1996	*From the Muddy Banks of the Wishkah*
2002	*Nirvana*
2004	*With the Lights Out*
2005	*Silver: The Best of the Box*
2009	*Live at Reading*

Above: Cobain, right, onstage with bandmates Novoselic, left, and Grohl, center

Left: Cobain shares a kiss with his wife, Courtney Love, who holds their daughter, Frances Bean, at MTV's Video Music Awards in Los Angeles, California, 1993

COURTNEY LOVE

Cobain and Courtney Love, an actress and fellow musician (with Hole), shared a uniquely public and complex relationship. After meeting in 1989, the two quickly realized that they were kindred spirits, and began regularly using drugs together. They married in 1992, and Love gave birth to their child, Frances Bean, a few months later.

From almost the moment of their union, Cobain and Love were constant tabloid and gossip column fixtures. Facing public scrutiny stemming from their rampant drug use, the young parents saw their daughter taken away by Los Angeles County Children's Services until they could prove their sobriety.

Accused by some as being an enabler, Love has morphed into one of the music world's most famous widows and single mothers. It was Love who led the public display of mourning immediately following Cobain's death, reading aloud from his purported suicide note. In recent years she's raised controversy with the decision to auction off a portion of Nirvana's song catalog, as well as a large number of Cobain's personal effects.

GRAHAM COXON

"I spent a lot of time with people who were eager to conquer the world and make themselves a huge band but I'm really not interested in that nonsense, there's an awful lot more to life than being popular. I think my music's pretty good. It's not the worst, it's not the best but it's doing its job as far as I'm concerned."

—GRAHAM COXON, 2006

Graham Coxon (born March 12, 1969, in Rinteln, West Germany) is a guitar player known for his solo work and his career with established popular British band Blur. He is also a noted visual artist and writer and has worked with other musicians including Pete Doherty and John McCusker, a prominent fiddle player.

Coxon grew up in England and was musically engaged from a young age, at one point appearing on children's television to play the clarinet. While an art student in college he put his talents into several bands, including Seymour, one of his first efforts and the progenitor to Blur.

During Coxon's time with Blur, he branched out as a solo artist for the first time in 1998, releasing *The Sky Is Too High* under his own label. Coxon would follow up with two more records before quitting Blur, and *The Kiss of Morning* was his first effort post-Blur, released in 2002. Two years later his album *Happiness in Magazines* would bring him the greatest success yet, netting an NME award for the effort.

Recent highlights from Coxon's solo career include a live album, *Burnt to Bitz*, released in 2006, and 2009's *The Spinning Top*, a largely acoustic concept album that dropped to effusive praise for its adventurous canvas of sounds.

Coxon is held in high esteem by peers such as Jonny Greenwood of Radiohead and Noel Gallagher of Oasis. Known for using a variety of guitars, including Fenders, Gibsons, and Burns Londons, his signature style is stripped down, yet complex and artistic.

WITH BLUR

Emerging from the rubble of Seymour, Coxon's first attempt at a band, Blur formed in 1989. After scoring a record contract, it concocted *Leisure*, the 1991 album that spawned such hits as "She's So High" and "There's No Other Way."

The 1992 release of the single "Pop Scene" was meant to be a blistering rejection of the prevailing teenybopper culture that it wanted no part of, but few took notice at the time. It wasn't until *Modern Life is Rubbish*, released in 1993, that Blur emerged on the radar of homeland audiences.

By the following year Britain was ready for *Parklife*. Blur's next effort was a chart-topper in the UK, and many of the album's singles were popular in the Unites States, though few Americans seemed interested in the entire record.

Charged by Blur's success, other similar bands, like Oasis and the Boo Radleys, stepped up to the plate, desirous of a piece of the action. Oasis quickly gained ground and its debut gave Blur's *The Great Escape* a grueling run for its money.

Dejected and still without a foothold in the United States, Blur would disappear until 1997, when it released its indie-flavored self-titled album, meant as a jump-start to its fortunes in the United States. Things went as planned, and American fans began taking heed. Coxon put his all into *13*, and the band released a huge commemorative boxed set of its singles through 1999. With *Think Tank* in 2003, Blur experienced its best sales in the United States yet—but Coxon would leave the band, not to return until 2009 with the launch of an enthusiastically received tour.

A Blur documentary and retrospective, *No Distance Left to Run*, was released at the top of 2010.

essential albums

WITH BLUR

1991	*Leisure*
1993	*Modern Life Is Rubbish*
1994	*Parklife*
1995	*The Great Escape*
1997	*Blur*
1999	*13*
2003	*Think Tank*

SOLO

1998	*The Sky Is Too High*
2000	*The Golden D*
2001	*Crow Sit on Blood Tree*
2002	*The Kiss of Morning*
2004	*Happiness in Magazines*
2006	*Love Travels at Illegal Speeds*
2009	*The Spinning Top*

LIVE

2004	*Live at the Zodiac*
2006	*Burnt to Bitz*

Above: Coxon performing with Blur at the 2009 Glastonbury Festival in England

Opposite: Coxon at London's Virgin Megastore, supporting his 2006 solo release

BILLY CORGAN

"Art really is about serving. You want to communicate but there was something about the process of making others happy that somehow was making me feel unhappy. It made me crazy, but I was good at it. It's like you're being rewarded for something that hurts you, but yet everybody is telling you it's a good thing. Then you try to pull that energy back into yourself, you try to make it more about you, and then suddenly you're not making people happy. You're making yourself happy but now that's another form of unhappiness because now you're making other people unhappy. It's taken a long time to get to a place of being OK with it all."

—BILLY CORGAN, 2009

Billy Corgan (born March 17, 1967, in Elk Grove Village, Illinois) is the front man and lead guitarist for the Smashing Pumpkins. After his father bought him a knockoff Gibson Les Paul guitar in high school, Corgan moved to St. Petersburg, Florida, to start a band and pursue a music career. He returned to Chicago after struggling to establish himself. After finding a job in a record store he met James Iha, D'arcy Wretzky, and Jimmy Chamberlin; together, they would form the Smashing Pumpkins, playing their first show in 1988 at Chicago's Metro.

Many were surprised by the success of the band's first two albums, but it was *Mellon Collie and the Infinite Sadness* that would go on to attain seven Grammy nominations and sell almost 5 million copies.

After a tumultuous period of low album sales and conflict stemming from Chamberlin's heroin dependency, the band performed for the last time at the Metro and broke up in 2000.

essential albums

WITH THE SMASHING PUMPKINS

1991	*Gish*
1993	*Siamese Dream*
1994	*Pisces Iscariot*
1994	*Earphoria*
1995	*Mellon Collie and the Infinite Sadness*
1998	*Adore*
2000	*Machina/The Machines of God*
2000	*Machina II/The Friends & Enemies of Modern Music*
2005	*Zeitgeist*

SOLO

2005	*The Future Embrace*

PUMPKINS SMASHED AND MENDED

Corgan's widely-acknowledged reputation as a depressive control freak is well-documented in interviews and through his own electronic missives, posted with frequency on his personal MySpace page after the breakup of the Pumpkins. Several incisive posts in 2004 called out former bandmates from the Pumpkins and Zwan (Corgan's follow-up project), accusing them of being "drug addicts" and "poseurs." Corgan later apologized, going so far as to take out ads in both of Chicago's daily newspapers to declare his openness to a Pumpkins reunion. Founding member Jimmy Chamberlin accepted, and the group's 2007 effort, *Zeitgeist*, found much success. In 2009 Chamberlin departed the band again, and Corgan continued to work on new Pumpkins material with an entirely new lineup of bandmates.

Awards and Honors

1997   Grammy Award for Best Hard Rock Performance, for "The End Is the Beginning Is the End," with the Smashing Pumpkins

1996   Grammy Award for Best Hard Rock Performance, for "Butterfly with Butterfly Wings," with the Smashing Pumpkins

Billy Corgan, left, with Jeff Schroeder, right, of the Smashing Pumpkins, at the Color Line Arena in Hamburg, Germany, 2008

CORGAN'S GUITARS

Never regarded as a virtuoso in the traditional sense, Corgan has received wide praise for his unique guitar playing, as well as his accomplishments as a bassist. Influenced early on by bands like Black Sabbath, Bauhaus, and the Cure, Corgan has also voiced his respect for Jimi Hendrix, Eddie Van Halen, and the members of Radiohead. Apart from his playing, Corgan contributed a series of articles to *Guitar World* magazine in the mid-1990s.

Throughout the years Corgan has been known to play a weird variety of instruments, including a well-used 1957 reissue Fender Stratocaster in the early days of the Smashing Pumpkins. For the Pumpkins' reunion, he adopted a Schecter C-1. In 2008 Corgan designed a Strat to his own custom specifications, crafted to recreate the tone that made the Pumpkins famous in the mid-1990s.

Corgan performing at Den Atelier in Luxembourg, 2007

ANI DiFRANCO

"Having more exposure is kind of a bitter-sweet thing for me, honestly, because it's nice to have a little more job security in life now. Then there's the down side, having a lot of people who don't really know what I do or what I'm about, but who have formed opinions about me based on what they hear in the media. It can be very frustrating and very deflating to be constantly defined and described by other people, so I've stopped reading anything written about me, and I find it much healthier. I just sort of concentrate on what I do and don't worry too much about that."

—ANI DiFRANCO, 1999

Ani DiFranco (born September 23, 1970, in Buffalo, New York) is a singer and guitarist primarily known for her iconoclastic solo work and numerous self-produced albums. Owner of Righteous Babe Records, DiFranco is renowned for her outspoken, independent stances regarding business, politics, and sexuality. DiFranco has released nearly twenty studio albums, as well as nearly as many live albums, plus a handful of EPs.

DiFranco first found her footing in the DIY café culture of her hometown as a teenager, where she studied guitar and began playing gigs. Before the age of 20 DiFranco found herself downstate in New York City, her popularity quickly growing by word of mouth. After recording an extremely personal and unapologetically rough-around-the-edges demo, DiFranco bypassed the corporate recording industry completely by forming her own label, Righteous Babe.

Not a Pretty Girl, released in 1995, brought DiFranco considerable—if not mainstream—success, and since then, her profile has continued to rise along with her output as a musician and a poet.

DiFranco's style is often vaguely categorized as "folk"; however, her many albums showcase a variety of sounds and instrumentations. Her handling of the guitar, though, is always prominent. Lyrically DiFranco's topics gravitate toward the emotional and personal, but her recent albums have tackled "happier" subjects such as motherhood and family life.

Ani DiFranco live at the Kentish Town Forum in London, 2008

RIGHTEOUS BABE

DiFranco has become synonymous with her Buffalo-based independent label, Righteous Babe. Housed inside a handsome Gothic church that the organization saved from demolition, the original building has been expanded to include a performance space and offices for DiFranco's staff—and serves as an informal hub for the surrounding Buffalo community.

The label currently represents sixteen artists, including DiFranco and the earlier recordings of accomplished indie multi-instrumentalist Andrew Bird. Apart from promoting its stable of artists, Righteous Babe has a decidedly political and social mission as well, urging its fans and customers to engage in their communities, support progressive causes that they believe in, find ways to work outside the corporate system and, of course, spread the gospel of DiFranco and her fellow musicians by the tried-and-true method of word of mouth.

essential albums

STUDIO

1989	Ani DiFranco
1991	Not So Soft
1992	Imperfectly
1993	Puddle Dive
1994	Out of Range
1995	Not a Pretty Girl
1996	Dilate
1997	Living in Clip
1998	Little Plastic Castle
1999	Fellow Workers
1999	Up Up Up Up Up Up
1999	To the Teeth
2000	Steal This Movie
2001	Revelling Reckoning
2002	So Much Shouting, So Much Laughter
2003	Evolve
2004	Educated Guess
2005	Knuckle Down
2006	Reprieve
2007	Canon
2008	Red Letter Year

LIVE

2006	Carnegie Hall 4.6.02

Awards and Honors

2003	Grammy Award for Best Recording Packaging, for *Evolve*
2006	Woman of Courage Award, the National Organization for Women

DiFranco is known for using alternate tunings that work with her signature staccato style.

JOHN FRUSCIANTE

"And this whole period of time of gradually working at being a better guitar player and songwriter have gradually led me to the point where I feel I'm doing a clearer representation of the thing that I've been feeling inside me since I was 4 years old."

—JOHN FRUSCIANTE, 2004

John Frusciante (born March 5, 1970, in New York, New York) is the iconoclastic former guitarist of the Red Hot Chili Peppers, as well as a nearly peerless solo artist and composer. Known for his dramatic 180-degree transformation from enthusiastic rock and roll party boy to spiritual and sober artist, Frusciante and his music are studies in contrast and complexity.

Frusciante is the son of classical musicians. Growing up in Los Angeles, the budding virtuoso was inspired by some of rock's more ambitious characters—Frusciante counts Steve Vai and Frank Zappa among his numerous influences. He came of age listening to the Red Hot Chili Peppers, the still-developing band that he would join when he was just 18, after falling in with Flea, the group's famous bass player.

Frusciante's status as a wunderkind was not lost on the older generation of guitar heroes. Frusciante auditioned for idol Frank Zappa, but snubbed the possibility of joining his band because of Zappa's zero tolerance policy regarding substances. Frusciante got involved with the Red Hot Chili Peppers at the right time—*Mother's Milk* was about to transport the band to the height of fame in 1989, but his tenure would abruptly end just two years later.

Exhausted from all the exposure and happy to reclaim a relative level of peace and obscurity after his brief time in the public eye, Frusciante struck up a tentative solo career in the mid-1990s, releasing two albums in 1994 and 1997. Things went south from there, and the former star fell into a chillingly dangerous pattern of drug abuse. But his former bandmates intervened—saving his life, and marking Frusciante's reinitiation into the Red Hot Chili Peppers. The result was the smash hit *Californication*, released in 1999. According to Frusciante, it contains some of his best and most inspired work. Frusciante's winning streak with the Red Hot Chili Peppers continued with 2002's *By the Way*.

Frusciante's output as a solo artist began ramping up during this period, and when he wasn't working with the Chili Peppers, he was feverishly putting the finishing touches on material for a series of new solo albums, including *To Record Only Water for Ten Days* and *Shadows Collide with People*, released in 2001 and 2004 respectively. A veritable slew of albums followed: Frusciante released six solo records or collaborations in the second half of 2004.

With *Stadium Arcadium* in 2006, the Chili Peppers announced an open-ended hiatus; Frusciante is not longer officially part of the band but released his solo effort *The Empyrean* in 2009.

essential albums

WITH RED HOT CHILI PEPPERS

1984	*The Red Hot Chili Peppers*
1985	*Freaky Styley*
1987	*The Uplift Mofo Party Plan*
1989	*Mother's Milk*
1991	*Blood Sugar Sex Magik*
1995	*One Hot Minute*
1999	*Californication*
2002	*By the Way*
2006	*Stadium Arcadium*

SOLO

1994	*Niandra Lades and Usually Just a T-Shirt*
1997	*Smile From the Streets You Hold*
2001	*To Record Only Water for Ten Days*
2004	*Shadows Collide With People*
2005	*Curtains*
2009	*The Empyrean*

Awards and Honors

1992	Grammy Award for Best Hard Rock Performance with Vocal, for "Give It Away," with Red Hot Chili Peppers
1999	Grammy Award for Best Rock Song, for "Scar Tissue," with Red Hot Chili Peppers
2003	Ranked No. 18 on *Rolling Stone*'s list of the 100 Greatest Guitarists of All Time
2006	Grammy Award for Best Boxed or Special Limited Edition Package, for *Stadium Arcadium*, with Red Hot Chili Peppers and Matt Taylor
2006	Grammy Award for Best Rock Album, for *Stadium Arcadium*, with Red Hot Chili Peppers
2006	Grammy Award for Best Rock Performance by a Duo or Group With Vocal, for "Dani California," with Red Hot Chili Peppers
2006	Grammy Award for Best Rock Song, for "Dani California," with Red Hot Chili Peppers
2008	Grammy Award for Best Hard Rock Performance, for "Wax Simulacra," with the Mars Volta

Frusciante at the 2006 Rock in Rio festival in Lisbon, Portugal

A PRECOCIOUS SOUND

Frusciante's talents have been praised for almost as long as he's been playing guitar, and music experts regularly rank him near the top of the pack. Moving from the raw punk sound in his early days, Frusciante's more recent work has taken on new levels of nuance and unabashed emotional color, putting little stock in speed or showy acrobatics. Frusciante has never been afraid of an off-the-mark or downright offensive sound, maintaining that such idiosyncrasies in his sound lend it a certain level of authenticity that many guitarists are afraid to pursue.

A connoisseur of vintage guitars, Frusciante has played a number of axes manufactured by Fender, Gretsch, and Martin.

Frusciante playing at the Telstra Dome in Melbourne, Australia, 2002

NOEL GALLAGHER

essential albums

STUDIO

1994	*Definitely Maybe*
1995	*(What's the Story) Morning Glory?*
1997	*Be Here Now*
2000	*Standing on the Shoulder of Giants*
2000	*Familiar to Millions*
2002	*Heathen Chemistry*
2005	*Don't Believe the Truth*
2008	*Dig Out Your Soul*

LIVE

2000	*Familiar to Millions*

Noel Gallagher (born May 29, 1967, in Manchester, England) was the lead guitarist and songwriter in Oasis, the chart-topping British band he formed with his brother, Liam, in 1991. A lightning rod for the media as well as a notoriously volatile collaborator, Gallagher has earned his reputation as one of contemporary rock's most tempestuous personalities.

Gallagher started playing guitar when he was 13, and toured with the Inspiral Carpets in the late 1980s as a roadie and technician. Gallagher showed interest when Liam started his band, the Rain, which would become Oasis after Noel talked his way into the group as songwriter and guitarist.

Gallagher is famously outspoken, never failing to inflame journalists and fans with a ready-made sound bite or insult for music's most revered acts. His political views have been a source of controversy, also, and more than a handful of fans and members of the music establishment have scrutinized Gallagher's insistent self-positioning as a working-class everyman despite his massive fame, success, and healthy ego.

With a solo career off to a tentative start, Gallagher has not disappeared from the public eye completely—he is currently aligned with the Teenage Cancer Trust and plans to perform for charity in 2010.

Gallagher performing at the Manchester Apollo, 2004

OASIS

With Gallagher in the driver's seat, Oasis recorded a demo and secured a recording deal, producing "Supersonic" in 1994, a moderate hit. Two singles followed, drumming up appetite for Oasis's debut album, *Definitely Maybe*, which was England's fastest-selling debut ever. The band was an overnight sensation in the UK—as much for its music as for the always-contentious rivalry between Noel and vocalist brother Liam. Noel staged the first of many walkouts before the year was through, eventually coming back into the fold to push the band's single, "Live Forever."

American listeners began taking notice in 1995. A tour of the states was well-received, and Oasis released its sophomore album, *(What's the Story) Morning Glory?* in the summer of that year, breaking several records. Set to tour the United States in 1996, Oasis created a huge stir when it cancelled dates across the country, blaming it on the band members' infighting.

A fractured Oasis was not as efficient in the studio as it once was, and it struggled to complete *Be Here Now* in a timely fashion. When it was released in summer 1997, it was their biggest smash yet—almost reaching No. 1 in the United States. The band would retreat from the public view again, throwing its fans a bone in the form of 1998's *Masterplan*, a collection of B-sides.

Bonehead (aka Paul Arthurs, the other guitarist) jumped ship in 1999, eliciting sharp words from Noel. Oasis released its third album, *Standing on the Shoulders of Giants* in 2000, quickly followed by a live collection, *Familiar to Millions*.

Noel Gallagher, right, with brother Liam, circa 1998

Positioned as a back-to-basics comeback album in 2002, *Heathen Chemistry* wasn't the smash Oasis was hoping for—but sales were respectable, and the album contains Liam's first stabs at songwriting, paving the way for his future compositions. Next up was *Don't Believe the Truth* in 2005, featuring temporary drummer Zak Starkey, Ringo Starr's son. Also giving the band's fortunes a boost was *Dig Out Your Soul*, Oasis's latest from 2008. Noel officially left at the end of 2009, and the remaining members adopted the name Oasis 2.0—with a new release slated for the middle of 2010.

Often drawing comparisons to the Beatles, Oasis is certainly Britain's most well-known and important musical export of the 1990s. Its influence has trickled into untold numbers of subsequent bands embracing similar sounds, aesthetics, and ambitions.

Oasis, from left to right: Paul Arthurs, Tony McCarroll, Noel Gallagher, Liam Gallagher, and Paul McGuian

PAUL GILBERT

essential albums

WITH BLACK SHEEP
1985 *Trouble In The Streets*

WITH RACER X
1986 *Street Letha*
1987 *Second Heat*
1999 *Technical Difficulties*
2000 *Superheroes*
2002 *Snowball of Doom*
2002 *Getting Heavier*

WITH MR. BIG
1989 *Mr. Big*
1990 *Raw Like Sushi*
1991 *Lean Into It*
1993 *Bump Ahead*
1996 *Hey Man*
1997 *Live at Budokan*

SOLO
1998 *King of Clubs*
1999 *Beehive Live*
1999 *Flying Dog*
2000 *Alligator Farm*
2002 *Burning Organ*
2002 *Raw Blues Power* (with Jimi Kidd)
2003 *Acoustic Samurai*
2003 *Gilbert Hotel*
2005 *Space Ship One*
2006 *Get Out of My Yard*
2008 *Silence Followed by a Deafening Roar*
2008 *United States* (with Freddie Nelson)

Paul Gilbert (born November 6, 1966, in Carbondale, Illinois) is an in-demand guitar virtuoso as well as an alum of the G3 concert tour. He is widely recognized for his shredding, as well as his work with Mr. Big and Racer X.

Gilbert, who grew up primarily in Pennsylvania, was turned onto the guitar by an uncle. By his mid-teens Gilbert was already a guitar force to be reckoned with—*Guitar Player* magazine profiled him alongside contemporary—and influential—Yngwie Malmsteen in the early 1980s. Adept at self-promotion, Gilbert announced himself to legendary producer Mike Varney, kick starting a relationship that would last much of his career. After moving to Los Angeles to attend music school, Gilbert began his teaching career as well, an outlet he has continued to indulge in to the present day.

Gilbert formed Racer X in 1985 in Los Angeles. Meant as a showcase for Gilbert's ballsy, electrifying style, the band paid tribute to the dramatic style of Judas Priest. Gilbert departed the young band in 1989 to form Mr. Big, even as Racer X was regularly selling out shows. His tenure with Mr. Big would span nearly a decade.

In 1999 Racer X returned with *Technical Difficulties*, which was a hit, especially in Japan. A 2000 follow-up was titled *Superheroes*, with *Getting Heavier* coming out two years later. The band broke up after that album, reuniting for a one-off 2009 show in California, and it still enjoys a high level of popularity in Asia.

In recent years Gilbert has focused his attention on several tribute bands and projects: the band Yellow Matter Custard covers the Beatles, Hammer of the Gods covers Led Zeppelin, and Amazing Journey is Gilbert's homage to the Who. His solo catalog is vast, with releases dating back to 1998, when he issued *King of Clubs*.

Recently Gilbert has released the all-instrumental *Silence Followed by a Deafening Roar* in 2008, his second such effort. An eclectic offering, the album includes Bach's "Prelude in G Major," played in its entirety.

"I'll always be in love with the guitar players of the 1970s because I grew up with them. As much as I'd love to be objective about the new stuff, I'm stuck thinking that Mick Ronson's guitar playing on "She Shook Me Cold" on *The Man Who Sold The World* record is the coolest way to play guitar. Just 'cause that's what I heard when I was 6 years old and that was the seed that was planted."

—PAUL GILBERT, 2008

Gilbert playing at the 2007 G3 tour at Massey Hall in Toronto, Canada

MASTER AND TEACHER

Gilbert's sound is fundamentally rooted in the early rock and roll of the Beatles and the Beach Boys, not to mention Jimmy Page, Jimi Hendrix, and the Ramones. The most obvious aspect of Gilbert's skill is his speed, but he draws on a vast and nuanced pool of influences and sounds to flesh out a truly unique approach to guitar mastery.

A long-time teacher and music theorist, Gilbert has been given forums in the UK's *Total Guitar* magazine and *Guitar Player* in which to discuss instruction and technique. The *Total Guitar* column lasted until 2006, and since then Gilbert has contributed to *Guitar World*.

Like his contemporary Marty Friedman, Gilbert enjoys an outsized reputation in Asia, where his handling of Ibanez axes, among many other guitars, is regarded with special acclaim. The Ibanez Paul Gilbert signature line continues to be updated and improved.

Gilbert demonstrating his skills with a double-neck guitar at the 2007 G3 tour, where he performed with fellow guitar greats Joe Satriani and John Petrucci

JONNY GREENWOOD

essential albums

STUDIO ALBUMS
1993	*Pablo Honey*
1995	*The Bends*
1997	*OK Computer*
2000	*Kid A*
2001	*Amnesiac*
2003	*Hail to the Thief*
2007	*In Rainbows*

SOLO ALBUMS
| 2003 | *Bodysong* |

SOUND TRACKS
| 2007 | *There Will Be Blood* (as composer) |

Greenwood at Heineken Music Hall in Amsterdam, Netherlands, 2006

Jonny Greenwood (born November 5, 1971, in Oxford, England) is a guitarist and composer best known for his work with Radiohead. His passion for electronic and experimental sounds has hugely influenced Radiohead's work since 1997's *OK Computer* and also defines his efforts as a soloist and composer, notably in the sound track to the film *There Will Be Blood* from 2007.

Credited with an "aggressive" playing style that often mandates an arm brace during performances, Greenwood shares guitar duties with fellow Radiohead member Ed O'Brien. Onstage, Greenwood spends a significant amount of time manipulating a nearly infinite array of electronic keyboards, effects pedals, and other devices, including a number of laptops and, from time to time, even a portable radio. Jonny relies primarily on a trio of Fender guitars, each of them significantly customized.

BEYOND RADIOHEAD

Since finding massive success with Radiohead, Greenwood has struck out on his own as a composer. Building on the unexpected, experimental touches he lent to Radiohead's albums, his album *Bodysong* was composed as the sound track to a documentary of the same name by Simon Pummell. Melding otherwise tame string passages with output from an Ondes-Martenot and a rich layering of nearly unrecognizable electronic effects, the album is at once distantly scientific and brimming with life. Greenwood's sound track for *There Will Be Blood*, directed by Paul Thomas Anderson, was infamously disqualified from winning an Academy Award in 2008 because it included portions based on compositions from *Bodysong*.

Above: Greenwood playing with Radiohead in Washington, D.C., 2008

Left: Greenwood has been known to incorporate the bowed guitar technique, popularized in the 1960s by guitarists like Jimmy Page and Eddie Phillips.

"The downside is that people are encouraged to own far more music than they can ever give their full attention to. People will have MP3s of every Miles Davis record but never think of hearing any of them twice in a row—there's just too much to get through. You're thinking, 'I've got 'Sketches of Spain' and 'Bitches Brew'—let's zip through those while I'm finishing that e-mail.' That abundance can push any music into background music, furniture music."

—JONNY GREENWOOD, ON MP3 FILES AND AUDIO QUALITY, 2009

DAVE GROHL

essential albums

WITH SCREAM
1988   *No More Censorship*
1991   *It's Your Choice*
1993   *Fumble*

WITH NIRVANA
1991   *Nevermind*
1992   *Incesticide*
1993   *In Utero*
1994   *MTV Unplugged in New York*
1996   *From the Muddy Banks of the Wishkah*
2002   *Nirvana*
2004   *With the Lights Out*
2005   *Sliver: The Best of the Box*
2009   *Live at Reading*

WITH FOO FIGHTERS
1995   *Foo Fighters*
1997   *The Colour and the Shape*
1999   *There Is Nothing Left to Lose*
2002   *One by One*
2005   *In Your Honor*
2006   *Skin and Bones*
2007   *Echoes, Silence, Patience & Grace*

WITH TENACIOUS D
2001   *Tenacious D*

WITH DAVID BOWIE
2002   *Heathen*

AS PROBOT
2004   *Probot*

WITH THEM CROOKED VULTURES
2009   *Them Crooked Vultures*

Dave Grohl (born January 14, 1969, in Warren, Ohio) is a prolific multi-instrumentalist and singer most recognized for fronting Foo Fighters, the band he formed in 1994 and as the drummer of Nirvana.

A self-taught guitarist, Grohl's exposure to punk music at the hands of an older cousin led him to seriously focus on music as a high school student in the Washington, D.C. suburbs. As a 17-year old, Grohl auditioned to play the drums in a local band called Scream; he got the gig and dropped out of school to tour with the band.

After the sudden disintegration of Scream, Grohl got in touch with Kurt Cobain and Krist Novoselic, members of a fledgling band called Nirvana. After visiting them in Seattle, he joined the band as its new drummer. *Nevermind*, released in 1991, became a smash success, bringing members of the band instant wealth and worldwide fame.

After the unexpected death of Cobain in 1994, Grohl branched out on his own, rounding up a full band to form Foo Fighters. By 2009 the band had released seven successful albums, and Grohl has maintained a frantic schedule with Foo Fighters and a staggering number of auxiliary projects and collaborations.

With the formation of the Foo Fighters, Grohl took center stage as lead guitarist and vocalist, changing roles from his days as Nirvana's drummer.

"I don't really know how to explain it. I think that [my songs] are just the type of songs that I imagine standing onstage and singing for the rest of my life. Each one of them means a lot to me. It's important I have those songs on the set list because they keep me up onstage. I'm not much of a storyteller. I am, but I get tired of the same story after a few spins. I can't really imagine writing an album of urban folk tales."

—DAVE GROHL

GROHL'S RESTLESS TALENT

Grohl is among the few renowned musicians to conquer both the drum kit and the ax. This flexibility has made Grohl especially adept at conceiving his own projects and seeing them through to fruition, not to mention putting him in demand as a drummer and collaborator in some of music's most high profile and successful acts.

Grohl seems addicted to side projects. He brought together a stable of metal vocalists, including Max Cavalera of Sepultura, King Diamond, Conrad "Cronos" Lant from Venom, Lemmy of Motörhead, and Scott Weinrich to record *Probot* in 2004, released to wide-ranging acclaim, with critical consensus dubbing it a "serious" metal album.

As contributing artist, Grohl lent his voice and drum skills to Tony Iommi's *Iommi* in 2000. That decade also saw Grohl appear on albums by Tenacious D, Cat Power, Queens of the Stone Age, Nine Inch Nails, Garbage, Pete Yorn, David Bowie, and Prodigy.

His latest side project, known as Them Crooked Vultures, released an eponymous album in 2009 and made several live appearances that summer.

Awards and Honors

1995   Grammy Award for Best Alternative Music Performance, for *MTV Unplugged in New York*, with Nirvana

2000   Grammy Award for Best Rock Album, for *There Is Nothing Left to Lose*, with Foo Fighters

2000   Grammy Award for Best Short Form Music Video, for "Learn to Fly," with Foo Fighters

2002   Grammy Award for Best Hard Rock Performance, for "All My Life," with Foo Fighters

2003   Grammy Award for Best Rock Album, for *One by One*, with Foo Fighters

2007   Grammy Award for Best Hard Rock Performance, for "The Pretender," with Foo Fighters

2007   Grammy Award for Best Rock Album, for *Echoes, Silence, Patience & Grace*, with Foo Fighters

Grohl, left, with Nirvana band members Krist Novoselic, center, and Kurt Cobain, right

CHARLOTTE HATHERLEY

"I'm happy as Larry because the music is so ace and I not only get to play heavily chorused guitar à la the Cure, but get to play throbbingly fuzzed-up bass, keyboards and twinkly bells."

—CHARLOTTE HATHERLEY, ON GOING ON TOUR WITH BATS FOR LASHES, 2009

Charlotte Hatherley (born June 20, 1979, in London, England) is an up-and-coming guitar and bass talent best known as a part of Ash. More recently she has toured with acclaimed indie artist Bat for Lashes and has her sights set on dominance as a fresh, accomplished guitarist and solo singer/songwriter. In recent interviews, Hatherley has offered up praise for current female indie sensations Fever Ray, St. Vincent, and Ladyhawke, not to mention other influences like Kate Bush and PJ Harvey.

As a London teenager, Hatherley dabbled in the 1990s punk scene, joining forces with Nightnurse, an indie band that enjoyed limited UK chart success. Plucked from obscurity to join Ash by Tim Wheeler, she made her highly visible premiere with the band in 1997.

Ash has always enjoyed status as a darling of the British music press. *Free All Angels* was released in 2001, reversing the band's inevitable slide into financial ruin and raking up rave reviews. *Meltdown* followed in 2004, and Ash's ubiquity was enforced by the selection of several of its songs to appear in popular films and video games.

Over the course of her time with the band, Hatherley proved herself a songwriter, and started hinting at possible future designs on becoming a solo artist. The band fully supported her ambitions and, as members later revealed—were going to ask her to leave at the end of her contract. They bid Hatherley farewell in 2006.

essential albums

WITH ASH
1998	*Nu-Clear Sounds*
2001	*Free All Angels*
2004	*Meltdown*

SOLO
2004	*Grey Will Fade*
2007	*The Deep Blue*
2009	*New Worlds*

Hatherley playing with Ash at London's Virgin Megastore, 1998

SOLO

Hatherley's solo ambitions were given the green light when she was still enrolled in Ash. Her first album shares the name of a song she originally put out with Ash, "Grey Will Fade," in 2001. The full album came to life in 2004, garnering mixed reviews.

Three years later, after her exit from Ash, Hatherley released *The Deep Blue* and embarked on a tour throughout Ireland and her home country. Rubbing elbows with the likes of Blondie and Bryan Ferry, the Grammy-nominated singer of Roxy Music, she also stepped into the role of bass player for electronic act Client. Hatherley's latest effort, *New Worlds*, debuted in 2009, featuring a more assured, polished sound that scored well with tastemakers and the music press, more than hinting at the guitarist's future promise.

Hatherley playing at Thetford Forest in Norfolk, England, 2007

JOSH HOMME

essential albums

WITH THE DESERT SESSIONS
1998 Volumes 1 & 2
1998 Volumes 3 & 4
1999 Volumes 5 & 6
2001 Volumes 7 & 8
2003 Volumes 9 & 10

WITH KYUSS
1990 Sons of Kyuss
1991 Wretch
1992 Blues for the Red Sun
1994 Welcome to Sky Valley
1995 . . . And the Circus Leaves Town

WITH QUEENS OF THE STONE AGE
1998 Queens of the Stone Age
2000 Rated R
2002 Songs for the Deaf
2005 Lullabies to Paralyze
2007 Era Vulgaris

WITH EAGLES OF DEATH METAL
2004 Peace, Love, Death Metal
2006 Death by Sexy
2008 Heart on

WITH ARCTIC MONKEYS
2009 Humbug

WITH THEM CROOKED VULTURES
2009 Them Crooked Vultures

Josh Homme (born May 17, 1973, in Joshua Tree, California) is known for his guitar playing with Queens of the Stone Age, Eagles of Death Metal, Kyuss, and Dave Grohl's Them Crooked Vultures. Although he's earned a reputation for his sometimes snotty rock star attitude—he locked horns with Sharon Osbourne in an amusing exchange—Homme is famously reticent about his guitar technique.

An enterprising Southern California teen, Homme laid the groundwork for heavy metal group Kyuss when he was just 14. He spent a couple of years in the early 1990s performing spontaneous gigs on the road with the band, until he joined up with West Coast grunge rockers Screaming Trees in 1995.

Gamma Ray, the first iteration of Queens of the Stone Age, came about in 1997, debuting its self-titled album the following year. Homme found himself not only playing guitar but also singing in the new band, a career first.

Homme's roots in the American West run deep and inspire much of his body of work. He the started loosely organized music series Desert Sessions in 1997, inviting his favorite peers to jam, play, and regularly release their material. In the last decade Homme has concerned himself with Eagles of Death Metal, a band spawned from the Desert Sessions that has released three proper records. In 2009 Homme made his debut with Them Crooked Vultures, a supergroup formed by the Foo Fighters' Dave Grohl.

Known for his preference for unusual, hard-to-find, or even damaged guitars, Homme has built an impressive collection. He owns several Ovation models, a B.C. Rich Mockingbird, and a handful of rare Gibsons, Matons, and MotorAves axes.

QUEENS OF THE STONE AGE

Under threat from German metalheads Gamma Ray, Homme was forced to give up the name, adopting the moniker Queens of the Stone Age for his new band. Within the band's first two and a half years it released an EP, made its first appearance as an act in Seattle, and released its debut album, *Queens of the Stone Age*. The band's original lineup was largely a recycled Kyuss, and would be subject to significant changes over the course of the next decade. Homme has described the band's sound as repetitive "robot rock," rejecting the obvious "stoner" label frequently ascribed by the press.

QOTSA opened up the new millennium with breakthrough *Rated R*, featuring the contributions of Judas Priest's Rob Halford. The band was formally initiated into the hard rock festival circuit, accepting invitations to perform with the Foo Fighters and the Smashing Pumpkins and at Ozzfest.

Collaborating with Dave Grohl, the band recorded and released *Songs for the Deaf* in 2002, which moved nearly a million copies. Album number four followed in 2005; the band was largely occupied with touring in between releases. The band's profile rose thanks to associations with Billy Gibbons of ZZ Top, a tour with Nine Inch Nails, and a memorable appearance on *Saturday Night Live*.

Amidst some well-publicized tensions and upheaval of its roster, QOTSA succeeded in releasing its fifth album in 2007. The sprawling *Era Vulgaris* was hotly anticipated and featured many past and current friends of the band, including Trent Reznor and Mark Lanegan. A slightly "harder" record, sales numbers were disappointing but reviews were enthusiastic.

Most recently QOTSA is on an unofficial hiatus, given Homme's involvement with several other projects.

Queens of the Stone Age onstage performing at the Eurockéennes rock festival, 2007. From left: Josh Homme, Dean Fertita, and Michael Shuman

"For me, there is music everywhere I turn and what I feel so lucky about is that I get to notice it all. I look at the guitar as a percussion instrument of sorts, because I think I've always been a confused and frustrated drummer."

—JOSH HOMME, 2007

Homme at Liverpool Academy with Queens of the Stone Age, 2007

CHRISSIE HYNDE

"It's not just how they play. It's how they look, how they walk, how they sit. If I see one of my band members walking down the street, as far as I am concerned they represent the band. I hung out with this guy once. He was a songwriter and we used to play this game in the cinema queue. We would stand there and observe people and say, 'What do you think he does?' And, you know, it's nice if you see one of my guys and you're playing that game and you say, 'What does that guy do? Easy. He's in a rock band.'"

—CHRISSIE HYNDE, 2009

Chrissie Hynde (born September 7, 1951, in Akron, Ohio) is a guitarist known as the keystone of the Pretenders and for her moody, contralto singing voice. A champion of progressive causes and, recently, a restaurateur, Hynde has long been a style icon and one of the Fender Stratocaster's most visible wielders.

Hynde spent her early days escaping into the late 1960s and early 1970s music scene of Cleveland, Ohio, where she was exposed to some of her first influences and heroes, including Iggy Pop and Brian Jones. Somewhat of a loner, Hynde signed up for the art school at Kent State. She soon started participating in a series of bands and witnessed firsthand the burgeoning hippie scene, as well as the dramatic Kent State campus shooting, an event that would affect her for the rest of her life.

In 1973 Hynde moved to Great Britain, finding employment at influential music publication *NME*. After a few false starts in fashion and music, the singer returned home to the states just two years later, only to return to Europe almost immediately, settling in London. Hynde struggled through an uncertain period of aborted musical endeavors, associating with many musicians—Mick Jones and Jon Moss, for example—but failing to find a place for herself.

By 1978 Hynde had met a group of like-minded musicians and formed the Pretenders. The self-titled debut would follow the year after, and the band quickly found themselves in a position of influence and popularity.

In her career Hynde has worked with INXS, Morrissey, Eric Clapton, Sheryl Crow, Ringo Starr, and Frank Sinatra.

THE PRETENDERS

With Hynde as the core and sole constant member, the Pretenders emerged from the punk rock scene in London to establish themselves as an elastic band with uncommonly universal appeal. The Pretenders, with Hynde on lead vocals and rhythm guitar, Martin Chambers on drums, Pete Farndon on bass, and James Honeyman-Scott on lead guitar, started playing Kinks covers, including "Stop Your Sobbing," after its genesis in 1978. "Brass in Pocket," one of the band's most recognizable songs was also one of their first singles off their 1980 debut, *Pretenders*. Follow-up *Pretenders II* was more of a critical slow burn, gaining support slowly, though viewed with indifference upon its release.

Success took a rapid toll on the band—by 1982 drug problems shook up the lineup. Just two days after Hynde kicked Farndon out of the band for his substance abuse, Honeyman-Scott died of a cocaine overdose. A year later, Farndon was also dead after drowning in his bathtub following a heroin overdose.

In 1984 the band let loose with *Learning to Crawl*, and another series of new band members came through what was becoming a revolving door. Hynde continued taking a more executive role in the band's output and image, and *Get Close* was released in 1986.

In the 1990s the Pretenders was largely viewed as Hynde's backing band. The Pretenders enjoyed a number of album successes as well as the hit single "I'll Stand by You," released

Hynde playing in Santa Barbara, California, 2007

in 1994. The band would take a hiatus, returning in 1999 with *Viva el Amor*, the first album in a string of three the Pretenders would release over the following decade.

In a poignant 2005 speech marking the band's induction into the Rock and Roll Hall of Fame, Hynde spoke warmly of her late Pretenders bandmates, James Honeyman-Scott and Pete Farndon, subtly lamenting the hefty price the pressures of rock and roll can exact on its practitioners.

essential albums

STUDIO ALBUMS

1979	*Pretenders*
1981	*Pretenders II*
1983	*Learning to Crawl*
1986	*Get Close*
1990	*Packed!*
1994	*Last of the Independents*
1999	*Viva el Amor*
2002	*Loose Screw*
2008	*Break Up the Concrete*

LIVE ALBUMS

| 1995 | *The Isle of View* |

Awards and Honors

| 2002 | Ranked No. 12 on *Rolling Stone*'s 50 Essential "Woman in Rock" Albums, for *Pretenders*, with the Pretenders |
| 2005 | Inducted into the Rock and Roll Hall of Fame, with the Pretenders |

Hynde at the South by Southwest music festival in Austin, Texas, 2006

JAMES IHA

essential albums

WITH THE SMASHING PUMPKINS
1991   *Gish*
1993   *Siamese Dream*
1994   *Pisces Iscariot*
1994   *Earphoria*
1995   *Mellon Collie and the Infinite Sadness*
1996   *The Aeroplane Flies High*
1998   *Adore*
2000   *Machina/The Machines of God*
2000   *Machina II/The Friends & Enemies of Modern Music*

SOLO
1998   *Let it Come Down*

WITH A PERFECT CIRCLE
2004   *eMOTIVe*
2004   *aMotion*

WITH VANESSA AND THE O'S
2005   *La Ballade d'O*

WITH TINTED WINDOWS
2009   *Tinted Windows*

James Iha (born March 26, 1968, in Chicago, Illinois) came to prominence as the songwriter for the Smashing Pumpkins and is currently involved with supergroup Tinted Windows, which features members of Cheap Trick and 1990s pop sensation Hanson.

Iha was a mostly undistinguished student in suburban Chicago when he decided to leave his design studies in college and get serious about his promising career with the Smashing Pumpkins, friend Billy Corgan's band. Iha contributed lyrics and vocals to many of the band's best tracks, including "blew Away" and "Take Me Down," and cultivated a reputation as the more reserved foil to an outspoken and erratic Corgan.

After a decade with the Pumpkins, Iha struck out on his own with the 1998 solo offering *Let It Come Down*. Since then he has preferred to invest himself in a range of side projects and collaborations with other rockers—more or less ignoring recent overtures from Corgan to come back into the Smashing Pumpkins fold.

Iha is a regular featured guest on the releases of both Fountains of Wayne and Ivy. In 2003 Iha lent himself to A Perfect Circle, the prestigious supergroup. With A Perfect Circle, Iha has worked both in the studio and on the road.

A second-generation American, Iha has established an admirable profile in the pop music and fashion scenes within his parents' home country of Japan. He has worked on a number of Japanese projects in music and film, and he remains an important pop producer and collaborator at large, working with names like Michael Stipe, Annie, and Ladytron.

Tinted Windows performed for the first time in 2009 in Oklahoma; S-Curve Records released its eponymous record in April of that year. Iha has hinted at a possible second solo album, but information remains scarce.

CAREER WITH THE PUMPKINS

Iha and Corgan coaxed the Smashing Pumpkins from modest beginnings playing low-budget gigs in the backwaters surrounding Chicago, transforming the band into one of the biggest of the 1990s. With the addition of drummer Jimmy Chamberlin, the Pumpkins moved out of a "sad rock" sound and embraced a more driving, dynamic style.

In 1991 the Pumpkins released its debut album, *Gish*. Already, Corgan was a control freak, angering his bandmates by maintaining ultimate say over what contributions made it onto the final tracks, sometimes stepping in to replay parts himself. Yet all the effort resulted in a warm-up slot on a tour featuring Guns N' Roses, Jane's Addiction, and the Red Hot Chili Peppers. Still success was already wearing the band down; drug use and infighting were taking hold.

Spurred partially by the smash success of Nirvana's *Nevermind*, the Pumpkins worked around the clock to finish its sophomore album, *Siamese Dream*. Though tensions during the recording process nearly tore the band apart, its work was rewarded with hefty sales.

The Pumpkins found success with massive double-album release *Mellon Collie and the Infinite Sadness* in 1995. After a huge tour in support of the album, the band announced it was changing directions and embracing a subtler, electronic sound.

Adore and Machina, released in 1998 and 2000, eventually led to the band's disintegration. Iha did not reunite with the band in 2006.

Awards and Honors

1997   Grammy Award for Best Hard Rock Performance, for "Bullet with Butterfly Wings," with the Smashing Pumpkins

1998   Grammy Award for Best Hard Rock Performance, for "The End is the Beginning is the End," with the Smashing Pumpkins

Iha in 1995. Although Iha is most often celebrated as guitarist for the Smashing Pumpkins, he also contributed as songwriter and vocalist to a number of the band's songs.

"People see me in the context of the band so they ask Billy all these questions. They're already asked all the serious artistic questions to Billy so when they get around to me I make these off-the-wall comments. So people think of me of being mysterious or something. I'm not being mysterious, I'm just making jokes."

—JAMES IHA, 1998

Iha, center, with Smashing Pumpkins members D'arcy Wretzky and Billy Corgan

MICK JONES

essential albums

WITH THE CLASH

1977	*The Clash*
1978	*Give 'Em Enough Rope*
1979	*London Calling*
1980	*Sandinista!*
1982	*Combat Rock*
1985	*Cut the Crap*

WITH BIG AUDIO DYNAMITE

1985	*This is Big Audio Dynamite*
1986	*No. 10, Upping St.*
1988	*Tighten Up, Vol. 88*
1989	*Megatop Phoenix*
1990	*Kool-Aid*
1991	*The Globe*
1994	*Higher Power*
1995	*F-Punk*
1997	*Entering a New Rider*

WITH CARBON/SILICON

2003	*Dope Factory Boogie*
2003	*Sample This, Peace*
2004	*The Grand Delusion*
2004	*The Homecoming*
2006	*A.T.O.M.*
2006	*Western Front*
2007	*The Crackup Suite*
2007	*The Last Post*

Mick Jones (born June 26, 1955, in Brixton, England) is a groundbreaking British punk rocker known for his 1976 founding of—and dismissal from—the Clash. In the last decade Jones has worked under the guise of Carbon/Silicon with Tony James and is an occasional producer. Fans idolize him for his uncanny ability to play across genres and spontaneously master new styles; no two portions of his career output sound the same.

In art school Jones got into the New York Dolls and began lusting after a life in rock and roll. The Delinquents, a glam-flavored outfit he started on his own, fizzled shortly after Jones put it together in the early 1970s. He then moved on to the London SS in 1975. A year later London SS dissolved, and Jones met Joe Strummer. The Clash was soon born.

Jones and Strummer, along with Paul Simonon on bass, Terry Chimes on drums, and Keith Levene on guitar, shot to fame with this first-wave punk rock band.

After his firing from the Clash in 1983, Jones pursued a more funky, eclectic sound with Big Audio Dynamite, a band whose reign would span fifteen years. Jones is currently concerned with Carbon/Silicon, a punk rock duo with a decidedly anti-commercial bent; it regularly releases its work for free online. Its earliest work was rife with samples, and the band continues to tour extensively.

Jones started on a Gibson Les Paul Junior, setting the course for a close relationship with Gibson over the years, though he has been known to pick up a Fender ax, especially during his sessions with Carbon/Silicon.

LONDON CALLING

Under the leadership of Jones, the Clash would emerge from the 1970s as the premiere voice of punk rock—and one of the most influential bands of modern rock and roll.

In 1976 Jones saw a performance by the Sex Pistols, which left quite an impression. Excited by the band's menacing energy, Jones recruited Joe Strummer to join his fledgling band, which, within months, was opening for the very band that inspired its formation. Aided by the press's fascination with the Pistols and the Ramones, the Clash jumped on the chance to sign a hefty record contract in 1977, despite its relative lack of experience. The first result was *The Clash*, released shortly thereafter.

Now tied to a record label with its own ideas, the Clash found itself implored to tone down its sound out of deference to picky American audiences. *Give 'Em Enough Rope* came out in 1978, and a North American tour followed.

The Clash dropped a bombshell with *London Calling* in 1979. With the release of this socially thematic, eclectic masterpiece, the Clash established themselves as titans, with an easily swayed music press in place to quickly perpetuate the new reality. The band entered the 1980s with several singles and the ambitious *Sandinista!*, following up with a stream of more experimental works that were received with a mix of celebration and confusion.

Combat Rock, the 1982 release, gave the world "Rock the Casbah" and "Should I Stay or Should I Go," two of the bands biggest—and catchiest—singles. The album would be Jones's last; he was asked to leave the following year.

The Clash have left a potent political and sonic legacy; consensus exists among critics regarding the Clash's role in crystallizing and immortalizing the sometimes fractured punk movement of the 1970s, tending to reject the most violent and nihilistic impulses often exhibited by its peers.

Awards and Honors

2002 Grammy Award for Best Long Form Music Video, for *Westway to the World*, with the Clash

2003 Inducted into the Rock and Roll Hall of Fame, with the Clash

2007 Grammy Hall of Fame Award, for *London Calling*, with the Clash

As the Clash's influence grew, the public began to dub it as "The Only Band That Matters," a slogan fostered by CBS, the band's label. From left: Nicky "Topper" Headon, Mick Jones, Joe Strummer, and Paul Simonon

The Clash. From left: Paul Simonon, Joe Strummer, and Mick Jones

"We were just playing the music we liked. We took on the music that was actually around us. We never wanted to do the same record twice."

—MICK JONES, 2006

JOHNNY MARR

Johnny Marr (born October 31, 1963, in Manchester, England) cut his teeth as guitarist alongside Morrissey in the Smiths, and more recently he has been connected with Modest Mouse and the Cribs. He is a famous master of Rickenbacker guitars, frequently uptuned during his Smiths career to mesh with Morrissey's higher vocal register.

Inspired by early family music favorites like Marc Bolan, Del Shannon, the Black Velvet Band, and Johnny Cash, Marr took Steven Morrissey up on his offer to start a band and set to putting together the Smiths' first single, "Hand in Glove," in 1983. Marr made headlines as a guitar talent of unusual gifts; he was largely behind the Smiths' intricate, almost impressionistic sound.

After the Smiths broke up, Marr joined Electronic in 1989, and also experienced a stint with The The; he has since moved on from both groups. With Isaac Brock of Modest Mouse, Marr contributed some songwriting to the band's acclaimed 2007 release *We Were Dead Before the Ship Even Sank*, embarking on tour with the band to promote the record.

In the Cribs, a British band formed in 2001, Marr has served as songwriter and guitarist since 2008. The following year's release, *Ignore the Ignorant*, was Marr's studio debut with the group, work of which he is especially proud.

"Things have changed since the late 1980s. People of my generation grew up under the shadow of punk rock, which was fiercely political, and there'd been nothing like it before or since. . . . Actually, it seems that few people under 25 are trying to do anything challenging anymore and it's been left to the older artists to do the experimenting, people like Radiohead and the Pet Shop Boys."

—JOHNNY MARR

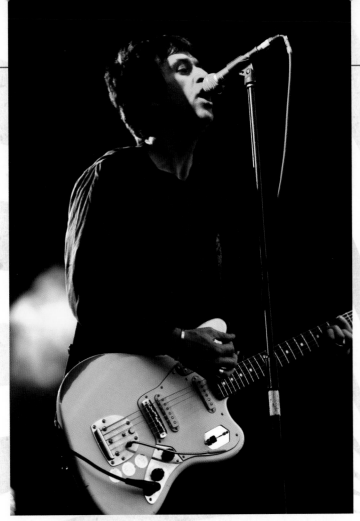

Above: Johnny Marr's deft handling of a Telecaster and the jangly tones of a Rickenbacker gave the Smiths its hauntingly distinctive sonic signature.

Opposite: Marr playing with the Cribs at the 9:30 Club in Washington, D.C., 2010

THE SMITHS

A symbolic and sonic rejection of the fussier, synthesized sounds of the decade, *The Smiths* debuted in 1984, right on the heels of the Smiths' blunt, poetic first single. The band followed up with No. 1 album *Meat Is Murder*. This sophomore effort enjoyed a healthy reign on the charts and guaranteed the Smiths a significant amount of historical relevance—the album is a perennial pick in critics' lists of rock and roll landmarks. *The Queen Is Dead* was placed on an even higher pedestal, selling well in 1986 and continuing to do so today.

With such acclaim came stresses within the group; Marr's relationship with Morrissey had taken on an uncharacteristic chill. Marr would leave in 1987, driven out by Morrissey's shifting musical tastes and ambitions. Legal struggles with the other members of the band related to royalties owed persisted well into the 1990s. Marr has flirted with the idea of a comeback, but Morrissey has independently rejected the idea in several colorful sound bites—despite massive cash offers from concert promoters and pleas from fans.

essential albums

WITH THE SMITHS

1984	*The Smiths*
1984	*Hatful of Hollow*
1985	*Meat Is Murder*
1986	*The Queen Is Dead*
1987	*The World Won't Listen*
1987	*Louder Than Bombs*
1987	*Strangeways, Here We Come*

WITH THE THE

1989	*Mind Bomb*
1992	*Dusk*

WITH ELECTRONIC

1991	*Electronic*
1996	*Raise the Pressure*
1999	*Twisted Tenderness*

WITH JOHNNY MARR AND THE HEALERS

2003	*Boomslang*

WITH MODEST MOUSE

2007	*We Were Dead Before the Ship Even Sank*

WITH THE CRIBS

2009	*Ignore the Ignorant*

The Smiths' legacy is bolstered especially by Marr's guitar playing, and many later groups have cited Marr as a major influence. Noel Gallagher of Oasis and Ed O'Brien of Radiohead are two of his most vocal followers.

Marr and Morrissey are chiefly responsible for the pared-down, monochromatic literary aesthetic that has informed the latest generation of independent, urban rock. The Smiths' tunes regularly appear or are referenced in a wide range of popular culture and media, signifying everything from straightforward 1980s nostalgia to contemporary hipster cred.

MIKE McCREADY

"Early on we decided to keep a lower profile all around to let the music speak for us. It was by design that we mostly used pictures that you could not necessarily see what was going on, and that didn't really focus in on the band, but instead focused in on a theme. This was done to maintain our anonymity a little bit so we could all live normal lives and keep our focus on music."

—MIKE McCREADY, 2005

Awards and Honors

1995   Grammy Award for Best Hard Rock
        Performance, for "Spin the Black Circle,"
        with Pearl Jam

Mike McCready (born April 5, 1966, in Pensacola, Florida) is the lead guitarist and one of the founders of Pearl Jam, a major force in contemporary American rock. He embraces both Gibson and Fender guitars, and his prowess has been recognized by several major music publications.

McCready has been a guitar player and drummer since age 11—he parents raised him on the music of Jimi Hendrix and Carlos Santana. After a few aborted attempts at starting a band after high school, McCready began playing again in earnest while he was living in Seattle. After joining Temple of the Dog, McCready experienced the excitement and chaos of the recording studio for the first time, with his work appearing on the band's 1991 release. With Eddie Vedder, McCready also began laying the groundwork for Pearl Jam, securing a record deal the following year.

McCready has lent his talent to other projects, too. He was a member of the short-lived Mad Season, a band that included John Baker Saunders of the Lamont Cranston Band and Layne Staley of Alice in Chains, both of whom would eventually die from drug overdoses.

During Pearl Jam's reign, the band was invited to back Neil Young on his record *Mirror Ball*, released in 1995; Pearl Jam also supported him on a European tour. In 2000 McCready formed supergroup the Rockfords, which generated a single album before breaking up in 2003.

McCready is a notably instinctive guitarist. He shies away from an emphasis on technique, preferring a more improvisational approach—in his early career, he famously impressed other Temple of the Dog members when he successfully completed playing without the aid of his studio monitors. With a sound inspired by the blues, McCready is also a noted contributor to Pearl Jam's songwriting; his lyrics first appeared on 2006's *Pearl Jam*.

McCready playing with Pearl Jam in Berlin, Germany, 2006

PEARL JAM

One of the most enduring products of the 1990s grunge scene, Pearl Jam came to the forefront with its 1991 release *Ten*. Shortly after its debut, the band found itself the recipient of Grammys and awards from cultural monolith MTV. After the sudden rise to the top, Pearl Jam set to work on *Vs.*, released in 1993 to rapturous reviews and monster sales.

Critical and popular darlings for most of the 1990s, the band, at the height of its popularity, memorably sparred with Ticketmaster over ticket prices, accusing the corporation of unfair business practices. The later half of the decade saw the replacement of several members amidst the releases of *No Code* and *Yield*. Despite its popularity, Pearl Jam had a difficult time rising to the expectations of fans who seemed to desire a large arena tour; members of the band preferred smaller venues and were largely opposed to a permanent life on the road. Pearl Jam faithful got its wish in 1998, when the group worked out their differences with Ticketmaster and once again set to the concert circuit.

The band's latest effort, *Backspacer*, has been lauded—and derided—as a brief, condensed pop record, harnessing an uncharacteristically positive sound.

essential albums

STUDIO ALBUMS

1991	*Ten*
1993	*Vs.*
1994	*Vitalogy*
1996	*No Code*
1998	*Yield*
2000	*Binaural*
2002	*Riot Act*
2006	*Pearl Jam*
2009	*Backspacer*

LIVE ALBUMS

1998	*Live on Two Legs*
2004	*Live at Benaroya Hall*
2006	*Live in NYC 12/31/92*
2007	*Live at the Gorge 05/06*
2007	*Live at Lollapalooza*

Pearl Jam, grunge band icon of the 1990s music scene. From left: Dave Abbruzzese, Stone Gossard, Eddie Vedder, Mike McCready, and Jeff Ament

THURSTON MOORE

"I have an iPhone that has iPod on it, sometimes I'll plug it into the car. But no, I like watching music more than listening to it. I like watching live bands. Looking at records. Touching them. Smelling them."

—THURSTON MOORE, 2009

essential albums

WITH SONIC YOUTH

1982	Sonic Youth
1983	Confusion Is Sex
1985	Bad Moon Rising
1986	EVOL
1987	Sister
1988	Daydream Nation
1990	Goo
1992	Dirty
1994	Experimental Jet Set, Trash and No Star
1995	Washing Machine
1998	A Thousand Leaves
2000	NYC Ghosts & Flowers
2002	Murray Street
2004	Sonic Nurse
2006	Rather Ripped
2009	The Eternal

SOLO

1995	Psychic Hearts
1998	Root
2007	Trees Outside the Academy

Thurston Moore (born July 25, 1958, in Coral Gables, Florida) is the lead guitarist in seminal American punk and rock group Sonic Youth. A contributor to numerous other groups as well as a cultural and aesthetic icon in his own right, Moore is one of the contemporary indie movement's "founding fathers." Moore is a vocal proponent of the Fender Jazzmaster, an instrument that traces its roots to the surf rock of the 1960s.

Raised in Connecticut, Moore had easy access to the punk scene in New York City, where he moved after abandoning the possibility of going to college. He immersed himself in the scene and began playing guitar, leading up to the formation of Sonic Youth in 1981.

Moore is a prolific solo artist and collaborator; his work outside Sonic Youth tends to be instrumental and often borders on the avant-garde. To Live and Shave in L.A., an experimental collective with a wide, rotating membership, claims Moore as one of its members; others include party rocker Andrew W. K.

In 2007 Moore released *Trees Outside the Academy*, his third solo album after 1995's *Psychic Hearts*, and 1998's *Root*, a jarringly experimental project that combined brief clips of Moore's guitar playing with visual art contributed by a number of collaborators.

Sonic Youth

Moore formed the band with Lee Ranaldo and Kim Gordon, later his wife, in 1981. Staking its claim on noise rock, the early band helmed 1981's Noise Festival, providing a stage for its debut as a band to be reckoned with. The EP *Sonic Youth* followed in 1982, with a proper release, *Confusion is Sex*, the following year.

The band stayed largely underground through the mid-1980s, making fans out of college students and members of various urban scenes. *Sister*, released in 1987, brought the band significant mainstream attention, paving the way for *Daydream Nation*, ostensibly the band's breakthrough album. Sonic Youth was rewarded again in 1990 after the major-label release of *Goo*, which netted the band its best sales to that point.

The band rode the alternative current of the 1990s—but not without its own characteristic independent finesse. The band found unprecedented exposure as headliner on the 1995 Lollapalooza circuit. Not long after the band announced a shift with *Washing Machine*, unapologetically embracing even more of a noise rock aesthetic coming off several years of a more mainstream alternative sound.

With the aid of esteemed musician and producer Jim O'Rourke, Sonic Youth started its own label, SYR, in 1996, meant to showcase the band's most extreme work. O'Rourke would go on to become a full-fledged member of the band a few years later.

Meanwhile Sonic Youth maintained a solid release schedule on its main label, DCG, through the 2000s; as of 2009, the band's home has been Matador Records. *The Eternal*, the band's most recent studio release, stands as its sixteenth LP.

Fans and critics revere Sonic Youth for its markedly hands-on approach and fearless exploration of new, undiscovered sounds, especially in the band's early days. With a reliance on open tunings—often to compensate for the suboptimal quality of the members' instruments—the band succeeded from the outset in its quest to introduce the new. Members of Sonic Youth share a kinship with Joni Mitchell, another major proponent of unorthodox tunings.

Above: The current Sonic Youth lineup. From left: Lee Ranaldo, Steve Shelley, Kim Gordon, Thurston Moore, and Jim O'Rourke. Recent work has included a collaboration with Led Zeppelin's John Paul Jones

Left: Kim Gordon and Thurston Moore performing live in Stockholm, 2005

Awards and Honors

2003   Ranked No. 34 on *Rolling Stone*'s list of the 100 Greatest Guitarists of All Time

TOM MORELLO

essential albums

WITH LOCK UP
1989   *Something Bitchin' This Way Comes*

WITH RAGE AGAINST THE MACHINE
1992   *Rage Against the Machine*
1996   *Evil Empire*
1998   *Live & Rare*
1999   *The Battle of Los Angeles*
2000   *Renegades*
2003   *Live at the Grand Olympic Auditorium*

WITH AUDIOSLAVE
2002   *Audioslave*
2005   *Out of Exile*
2006   *Revelations*

AS THE NIGHTWATCHMAN
2007   *One Man Revolution*
2008   *The Fabled City*

WITH STREET SWEEPER SOCIAL CLUB
2009   *Street Sweeper Social Club*

Tom Morello (born May 30, 1964, in Harlem, New York) is best known for his guitar playing with inventive 1990s group Rage Against the Machine, as well as his work with Audioslave and hip-hop influenced Street Sweeper Social Club. The technically accomplished Morello also performs as the Nightwatchman, his solo alter ego.

After his Kenyan father moved back to Africa, his single mother left New York and raised Morello alone in the northern suburbs of Chicago. There Morello's precocious, left-leaning political and social sympathies often bristled with those of his more traditional peers. He took a genuine interest in music, especially metal and punk, during his high school years. After graduating from Harvard in 1986, he shipped off to Los Angeles and started working as a political staffer.

Disenchanted with politics, Morello turned back to music, releasing an album with the band Lock Up in 1989. When Lock Up fell apart in 1991, Morello decided to recruit a fresh lineup, bringing on freestyle rapper Zack de la Rocha, drummer Brad Wilk, and bassist Tim Commerford. The new band,

Rage Against the Machine, signed its first deal in 1992, and its debut album was an overnight smash.

When Rage disbanded, Morello joined Audioslave, a sort of Rage Against the Machine 2.0. With the exception of Zack de la Rocha, Audioslave featured the remaining members of the band, plus Chris Cornell from Soundgarden. Between 2002 and 2007 Audioslave released three albums.

Morello began working solo while still with Audioslave, first performing as folk alter ego the Nightwatchman in 2003. He released his first solo album, *One Man Revolution*, in 2007 and tours regularly. At various points Morello has collaborated with members of the Dave Matthews Band, the Prodigy, the Crystal Method, and Johnny Cash.

His style is marked by a riff-centric attack and extensive use of pedals and other effects. Morello's guitars are many, and almost all of them have been extensively tweaked, modified, and completely reassembled. He often incorporates parts from many models and manufacturers, effectively creating "mutant" guitars that are, quite literally, one of a kind.

Awards and Honors

1997   Grammy Award for Best Metal Performance, for "Tire Me," with Rage Against the Machine

2001   Grammy Award for Best Hard Rock Performance, for "Guerrilla Radio," with Rage Against the Machine

2003   Ranked No. 26 on Rolling Stone's list of the 100 Greatest Guitarists of All time

"Every time I write a song, record a song or step on any stage, I play as if everyone's soul in the room is at stake."

—TOM MORELLO, 2009

Tom Morello onstage performing with Audioslave. During Audioslave concerts, Morello regularly incorporated his unique guitar solos, thrilling the crowd.

RAGE AGAINST THE MACHINE

From the outset Rage was a controversial, defiant band. Its demo got the band signed, and its eponymous first album generated several blistering singles that also served as unapologetic social commentaries.

Internal squabbles delayed a follow-up by a few years, but in 1996 Rage released *Evil Empire*. The record was a hit, though, and the band spent a great deal of time on tour with U2, Green Day, Wu-Tang Clan, and the Roots. *The Battle of Los Angeles* dropped in 1999, followed by covers album *Renegades*—Zack de la Rocha's final record with the band.

After Audioslave, Rage formally reunited in 2007 at the Coachella Festival, leading to a full-scale U.S. tour and several major festival appearances. The band has left the door open for future live shows, but both Morello and de la Rocha have emphatically denied a new album is in the works.

Morello demonstrates his acrobatic flair during a Rage Against the Machine concert at the 2008 Reading Festival in Berkshire, England

DAVE NAVARRO

"We've all been friends for years and years. We've come up in different bands, respected one another, learned each other's songs, hung out and got into a lot of trouble together. That stuff translates. When someone we don't know very well joins us on stage, there's an excitement that we all share. Because every single show is different, we never run into a routine where I'm looking at a set saying, "Oh no, I have the same eight songs to play that I've been playing for the past six months." We never have that stale attitude, because every night is fresh."

—DAVE NAVARRO ON CAMP FREDDY, 2008

Dave Navarro (born June 7, 1967, in Santa Monica, California) is the guitarist of the U.S. bands Jane's Addiction and Camp Freddy. Also noted for his high-profile romantic life and past drug use, Navarro is one of recent music's most recognized stars.

After latching on to Jimi Hendrix's music as a teen, Navarro played in several local Los Angeles bands with friend Stephen Perkins, who hooked up Navarro with an audition for Jane's Addiction. He played a wicked solo, landed the gig, and his playing contributed to the band's quick success. Easy access to hard drugs were becoming a problem for Navarro, though, leading to the band's dissolution in 1991.

Navarro involved himself in several projects in the 1990s, including Deconstruction, a band he formed with old friend Eric Avery, a bassist. After putting out an album in 1994, the band lacked the energy to successfully tour.

The next few years included a stint with the Red Hot Chili Peppers, but Navarro was kicked out of the band in 1998 due to his drug problems. In the meantime Navarro released a solo album, *Trust No One*, and resurrected Jane's Addiction, eking out its final album, *Strays*, in 2003. Most recently Navarro has lent himself to other bands as a contributing guitarist and has moonlighted as an adult film director and Internet radio host.

essential albums

WITH JANE'S ADDICTION
1987 *Jane's Addiction*
1988 *Nothing's Shocking*
1990 *Ritual de lo Habitual*
1997 *Kettle Whistle*
2003 *Strays*
2006 *Up from the Catacombs—The Best Of*
2009 *A Cabinet of Curiosities*

WITH DECONSTRUCTION
1994 *Deconstruction*

WITH RED HOT CHILI PEPPERS
1995 *One Hot Minute*

SOLO
2001 *Trust No One*

WITH THE PANIC CHANNEL
2006 *ONe*

Navarro live with Camp Freddy in Los Angeles, California, 2008

NAVARRO'S STYLE

Through his career Navarro has built a reputation for being an adaptable and versatile guitarist. Unlike many greats, Navarro demonstrates comfort bending his style to suit the music at hand—at various points, he has fused heavy metal, psychedelia, funk, modern rock, and more straightforward, soulful licks inspired by older guitar masters.

Navarro's guitar lineup has varied throughout his career. At this writing he favors an Ibanez RG, finished in white with gold hardware. On stage Navarro is also known to wield a slick-looking white Paul Reed Smith model.

In the Jane's Addiction days, Navarro utilized several distinctive guitars, including a Gibson Les Paul and several custom-finished Ibanez models.

CAMP FREDDY

Camp Freddy is Navarro's rock cover supergroup, established in 2003 with a number of other rock and guitar greats. Members of the group describe it not as a band but as an "occasional happening, a freak of Hollywood nature." The roster is extensive and always shifting; the group's sporadic live performances are known to feature random and sometimes unexpected guests—including such disparate artists as Moby, Macy Gray, actress Gina Gershon, and hip-hop act Cypress Hill. Members of the group also host a radio show from Navarro's home. Two tracks from a possible album have been unleashed on the Internet, mimicking the group's live shows, but no release date has been nailed down.

Navarro playing with Jane's Addiction

ED O'BRIEN

"We've had a tendency to pile on overdubs and tracks and fill everything up. I can't help but feel that we suffered from that. We just piled stuff on. You look to the essence of a great song: you've got great vocals, with lovely lyrics and a great melody, and you've got something that backs that."

—ED O'BRIEN, 2008

essential albums

WITH RADIOHEAD	
1993	*Pablo Honey*
1995	*The Bends*
1997	*OK Computer*
2000	*Kid A*
2001	*Amnesiac*
2003	*Hail to the Thief*
2007	*In Rainbows*

Ed O'Brien (born April 15th, 1968, in Oxford, England) plays guitar in the British band Radiohead. Self-taught, O'Brien's primary role in the band has shifted from rhythm guitarist on its earlier, more "traditional" albums to chief guitarist around the time of *OK Computer* (1997). This shift freed up bandmate and guitarist Jonny Greenwood to focus more on the keyboards, synthesizers, and effects that would, controversially, reshape and reestablish the band's sound from the ground up. O'Brien occasionally provides backing vocals for albums and performances. He's also an accomplished drummer, although his percussion has only made it into one recorded track: "There, There" from 2003's *Hail to the Thief.*

Beyond his full-time gig with the untouchable British band, O'Brien has worked on BBC's *Eureka Street* as a sound track contributor. More recently, he supplied licks on several tracks with electronic act Asian Dub Foundation—featuring Sinéad O'Connor. He also has ties to 7 Worlds Collide, a music charity project helmed by Neil Finn.

Radiohead's members have remained constant since its beginnings. The members originally got together in their schooldays, forming a band called On a Friday. From left: Thom Yorke, Jonny Greenwood, Colin Greenwood, Ed O'Brien, and Phil Selway.

RADIOHEAD

Distinguished by its epic, occasionally dreary catalog and uncanny ability to reinvent itself with every new release, Radiohead is one of the few contemporary bands that has amassed rock star status—and income—while mostly maintaining a loyal fan base and legitimate, indie cred.

Radiohead formed at Oxford University as a student band, initially pursuing relatively lighthearted Britpop/alternative fare. Its first hit was "Creep" in 1992—an emblem of the 1990s, but a song that shares little DNA with the current Radiohead, and one it all but refuses to play.

By 1995 the band had released *Pablo Honey* and *The Bends*, both praised by critics but barely on listeners' radars. After returning home after a tour in support of R.E.M., Radiohead set to work on what is arguably its masterpiece—at least for the largest majority of the band's faithful. *OK Computer* was released in 1997, and was immediately lauded as an sonic manifestation of society's fear and paranoia rushing into a new millennium. With a distinct, more novel sound than the band's previous efforts, *OK Computer* only hinted at what was to come.

In 2000 and 2001 Radiohead released *Kid A* and *Amnesiac* almost back-to-back. *Kid A* shocked most fans with its chilly, unexpected glaze of electronic sounds, obscured vocals and guitars, and instrumental components—but the album is often cited by critics as one of the 2000s' most important releases. *Amnesiac*, made up of material recorded during the same sessions, advances a similar sound, including forays into jazz and experimental percussion.

Hail to the Thief, released in 2003, was a lengthy, more accessible release that brought guitars and other recognizable sounds back to the forefront. Considered by some critics as somewhat of a mixed bag, the album sold well. By now considered among the biggest bands in the world, Radiohead would retreat until 2007, when it unexpectedly announced the completion of *In Rainbows*, which was made available online with a controversial "pay what you wish" policy (a "processing charge" was obligatory). The Grammy-winning record was given a physical release several months later and stands as Radiohead's warmest, most personal effort to date.

Radiohead in the early 1990s. From left: Colin Greenwood, Ed O'Brien, Thom Yorke, Phil Selway, and Jonny Greenwood

Awards and Honors

1997	Grammy Award for Best Alternative Music Performance, for "OK Computer," with Radiohead
2000	Grammy Award for Best Alternative Music Album, for *Kid A*, with Radiohead
2008	Grammy Award for Best Alternative Music Album, for *In Rainbows*, with Radiohead

JOHNNY RAMONE

essential albums

1976	*Ramones*
1977	*Leave Home*
1977	*Rocket to Russia*
1978	*Road to Ruin*
1980	*End of the Century*
1981	*Pleasant Dreams*
1983	*Subterranean Jungle*
1984	*Too Tough to Die*
1985	*Loco Live*
1986	*Animal Boy*
1987	*Halfway to Sanity*
1988	*Ramones Mania*
1989	*Brain Drain*
1992	*Mondo Bizarro*
1993	*Acid Eaters*
1995	*¡Adios Amigos!*
1997	*We're Outta Here!*

Johnny Ramone (born John William Cummings on October 8, 1948, in Long Island, New York) was a founding member and lead guitar player for the influential punk rock band the Ramones.

As a teenager in the Forest Hills section of Queens, New York, Ramone played guitar in a garage band, the Tangerine Puppets, where he met drummer Tomas Erdeli. Described as both a "greaser" and a tie-died Stooges fan, Ramone formed a new band in 1974 with himself on lead, his friend Douglas Colvin on bass and vocals, and former glam rocker Jeffrey Hyman on drums. It was Colvin who came up with the iconic name, the Ramones. When Hyman decided to focus on vocals, drummer Erdeli came aboard.

After groundbreaking gigs at Max's Kansas City and CBGB in 1975, the band's short, fierce songs and "wall of noise" earned it a recording contract with Sire Records. Although it was in the forefront of the new "punk" music scene, its first album barely charted. It was only after a breakthrough appearance at the Roundhouse in London, where the bandmates met members of both the Sex Pistols and the Clash, that the group began to gain momentum. Though the Ramones was never commercially successful, it reinvigorated rock and roll with its high-energy performances and stripped-down songs.

Johnny Ramone's unique playing style, more rhythm guitar than lead, has been described as a "buzz saw," with rapid downstrokes on barre chords. It influenced both the first and second wave of punk artists as well as metal bands such as Iron Maiden and Def Leppard.

Ramone died in Los Angeles on September 15, 2004, after battling prostate cancer.

"We decided to start our own group because we were bored with everything we heard. . . . Everything was tenth-generation Led Zeppelin . . . overproduced, or just junk. We missed music like it used to be."

—JOHNNY RAMONE

Awards and Honors

2002   Inducted into the Rock and Roll Hall of Fame, with the Ramones

2003   Ranked No. 16 on *Rolling Stone*'s list of the 100 Greatest Guitarists of All Time

2009   Ranked No. 11 on *Time* magazine's list of the Ten Greatest Electric Guitar Players

The Ramones in 1979. From left: Dee Dee, Joey, Johnny, and Marky

IT'S ALL ABOUT THE NAME

Douglas Colvin called himself Dee Dee Ramone, which he'd taken from Paul McCartney's early stage name, Paul Ramon. Colvin persuaded his bandmates to adopt the same surname, so Cummings, Hyman, and Erdeli soon went by the monikers Johnny, Joey, and Tommy Ramone—and the Ramones were born. Later members included drummer Marky Ramone (Marc Steve Bell), drummer Richie Ramone (Richard Reinhardt), drummer Elvis Ramone (Clem Burke), and bassist C. J. Ramone (Christopher Joseph Ward).

Filmmakers Michael Gramaglia and Jim Fields delved into the lives of the iconic punk rock band the Ramones in a 2004 documentary called *End of the Century*. From left, Dee Dee, Tommy, Joey, and Johnny in the 1970s

LEE RANALDO

essential albums

WITH SONIC YOUTH
1982	*Sonic Youth*
1983	*Confusion Is Sex*
1985	*Bad Moon Rising*
1986	*EVOL*
1987	*Sister*
1988	*Daydream Nation*
1990	*Goo*
1992	*Dirty*
1994	*Experimental Jet Set, Trash and No Star*
1995	*Washing Machine*
1998	*A Thousand Leaves*
2000	*NYC Ghosts & Flowers*
2002	*Murray Street*
2004	*Sonic Nurse*
2006	*Rather Ripped*
2009	*The Eternal*

SOLO
1987	*From Here to Infinity*
1992	*A Perfect Day (EP)*
1993	*Scriptures of the Golden Eternity*
1994	*Broken Circle/Spiral Hill (EP)*
1995	*East Jesus*
1997	*Clouds*
1999	*Dirty Windows*
2000	*Amarillo Ramp*
2002	*Outside My Window the City Is Never Silent*
2004	*Text of Light*
2008	*Maelstrom From Drift*

Lee Ranaldo (born February 3, 1956, in Glen Cove, Long Island) is a singer, guitarist, songwriter, visual artist, and co-founder of the rock group Sonic Youth.

Ranaldo began performing in New York City, eventually joining the electric guitar orchestra of Glenn Branca. In 1981 he was invited to form a new band with guitarists Thurston Moore and Kim Gordon. Soon after, drummer Richard Edson was added. Sonic Youth, which is considered one of the first "noise" groups, became part of the No Wave art and music scene in New York and was a precursor of the alternative rock movement. Ranaldo helped the band develop the radical alternative tunings for which they were known.

After its debut in London, when its equipment malfunctioned and Moore destroyed it on stage, Sonic Youth received rave reviews from the music press.

Sonic Youth's popularity has spanned more than three decades—from headlining at the Lollapalooza festival in 1985 to the release of their sixteenth album, 2009's *The Eternal*—and they continue to redefine rock music today.

Ranaldo has also collaborated with jazz drummer William Hooker, British rock band the Cribs, and, as half of the duo Drift, has created live installations with improvised music with his wife, experimental artist Leah Singer. Another favorite side project is Text of Light, a group of musicians who improvise to films by Stan Brakhage.

Ranaldo usually plays a Fender Jazzmaster or a Telecaster Deluxe. In 2007 Dutch musical inventor Yuri Landman created the Moonlander for Ranaldi, a bi-headed custom guitar with eighteen strings—six normal and twelve sympathetic.

IN THE DIGITAL AGE

When Ranaldo began to use digital technology in the studio, he quickly pointed out that he was making music, not digital music, and that Sonic Youth was still "plenty analog." He also noted the ways in which digital technology has changed how people listen to music, observing that most songs are now heard in lo-fi through MP3 computer speakers, quite a change from the heyday of the audiophile. Still Ranaldo likes that the Internet has made music more accessible by giving fans exposure to new material and allowing them to download tunes. Ranaldo and his bandmates in Sonic Youth even Twittered updates during the production of their 2009 album, *The Eternal*.

"When I started playing guitar when I was in junior high school, a guitar player showed me some alternate tunings so I could play things like Neil Young songs. I quickly discovered people like the old blues players and even the Velvet Underground, who all played in strange tunings."

—LEE RANALDO, 2010

Awards and Honors

2003   Ranked No. 33 on *Rolling Stone*'s list of the 100 Greatest Guitarists of All Time,

Left: Sonic Youth in 1992. From top, Thurston Moore, Kim Gordon, Steve Shelley, and Lee Ranaldo

Right: Ranaldo's Moonlander guitar

Below: Sonic Youth in 2004. From left, Steve Shelley, Thurston Moore, Kim Gordon, Lee Ranaldo, and Jim O'Rourke

ANDY SUMMERS

essential albums

WITH ERIC BURDON & THE ANIMALS
1968   *Love Is*

WITH THE POLICE
1978   *Outlandos d'Amour*
1979   *Reggatta de Blanc*
1980   *Zenyatta Mondatta*
1981   *Ghost in the Machine*
1983   *Synchronicity*

WITH VARIOUS ARTISTS
1982   *I Advance Masked* (with Robert Fripp)
1984   *Bewitched* (with Robert Fripp)
1994   *Invisible Threads* (with John Etheridge)
1998   *Strings of Desire* (with Victor Biglione)

SOLO
1986   *XYZ*
1987   *Mysterious Barricades*
1989   *The Golden Wire*
1990   *Charming Snakes*
1991   *World Gone Strange*
1995   *Synathestesia*
1997   *The Last Dance of Mr X*
1999   *Green Chimneys*
2000   *Peggy's Blue Skylight*
2002   *Earth & Sky*
2005   *The X Tracks*

Andy Summers (born December 31, 1942 in Lancashire, England) was the lead guitarist for English rock band the Police. After the band broke up, Summers reinvented himself as an ambitious guitar master and turned himself into a successful solo artist as well.

Summers was attracted to jazz and blues in his childhood. His first real gig was with Zoot Money's Big Roll Band, a London R&B group that had some success in the early 1960s scene. After rotating through various gigs in Great Britain and the United States, Summers became a member of the Animals in 1968. He appears on their record *Love Is*.

Settling in Los Angeles for a period, Summers enrolled in a college music program and became a teacher on the side. After going back to England with his bachelor's degree, Summers crossed paths with Stewart Copeland and Sting, his future Police bandmates.

Post-Police, Summers truly came into his own as a groundbreaking solo guitarist, letting loose with a signature sound that incorporated intricately layered effects, unusual techniques, and a style informed by his jazz and classical influences. *XYZ*, from 1987, is Summers' first proper solo release. *The Golden Wire* came out in 1989, kicking off a string of solo releases that would carry Summers through the 1990s.

Summers is, additionally, a photographer and memoirist, and in 2007 Fender immortalized his beat-up 1961 Telecaster with a run of limited-edition replicas.

THE POLICE

Among the most successful rock acts in the world, the Police formed around drummer Stewart Copeland in London, quickly meeting with success and a record deal following a performance of their hit "Roxanne" in 1978. In the band, Summers shined as the Telecaster-swinging provider of epic hooks and a glittering sound that wouldn't be mistaken for any other band's.

Debut album *Outlandos d'Amour* was a hit within a few months, making celebrities out of the band's members—especially Sting, who started getting work as an actor. Even more exposure came with 1979's *Reggata de Blanc* and a subsequent tour would take the Police far from its UK home.

Fans in the United States started paying attention, though, with the 1980 release of *Zenyatta Mondatta*. Within a year the Police were packing Madison Square Garden and quickly set to work on 1981's *Ghost in the Machine*. It released *Synchronicity* in 1983 at the pinnacle of its popularity; the Police was, by now, one of the richest acts on the planet. An unexpected implosion occurred, though, and the band officially broke up soon after.

The Police have reunited in the last two decades for a handful of charity performances and a major appearance together at the 2007 Grammy Awards, which led to a gargantuan reunion tour into 2008.

In addition to "Roxanne," the Police leave behind iconic tracks including "Every Little Thing She Does is Magic" and "Every Breath You Take"—an eternally popular song in its own right, but also given a hit hip-hop treatment via a sample by Puff Daddy in 1997.

Awards and Honors

1980	Grammy Award for Best Rock Instrumental Performance, for "Reggatta de Blanc," with the Police
1981	Grammy Award for Best Rock Performance by a Duo or Group with Vocal, for "Don't Stand So Close to Me," with the Police
1981	Grammy Award for Best Rock Instrumental Performance, for "Behind My Camel," with the Police
1982	BRIT Award for Best British Group, with the Police
1983	Grammy Award for Best Pop Performance by a Duo or Group with Vocal, for "Every Breath You Take," with the Police
1983	Grammy Award for Best Rock Performance by a Duo or Group with Vocal, for "Synchronicity," with the Police
1985	BRIT Award for Outstanding Contribution To Music, with the Police
2003	Inducted into the Rock and Roll Hall of Fame, with the Police

Summers, right, with a shirtless Sting, left, performing with the Police, 1981

Left: The Police in the early 1980s just as the band was bursting onto the music scene. From left: Sting, Andy Summers, and Stewart Copeland

"It accumulates over the years and I've led so many bands of my own now and forced myself into new situations. . . . You would hope that you play better and better—until you just get too feeble to do it anymore."

—ANDY SUMMERS

BERNARD SUMNER

essential albums

WITH JOY DIVISION

| 1979 | *Unknown Pleasures* |
| 1980 | *Closer* |

WITH NEW ORDER

1981	*Movement*
1983	*Power, Corruption & Lies*
1985	*Low-Life*
1986	*Brotherhood*
1989	*Technique*
1993	*Republic*
2001	*Get Ready*
2005	*Waiting for the Siren's Call*

WITH ELECTRONIC

1991	*Electronic*
1996	*Raise the Pressure*
1999	*Twisted Tenderness*

WITH BAD LIEUTENANT

| 2009 | *Never Cry Another Tear* |

Bernard Sumner (born January 4, 1956, in Broughton, Salford, England) is a singer, guitarist, and keyboardist and was a founding member of two influential bands—Joy Division and New Order.

Inspired by a live performance of the Sex Pistols, Sumner formed the group Warsaw in 1976 with several friends from the Manchester area. Renamed Joy Division in 1978, the group at the time consisted of Sumner along with vocalist Ian Curtis, bassist Peter Hook, and drummer Stephen Morris. After its debut EP, "An Ideal for Living," impressed TV personality Tony Wilson, he released its first album, *Unknown Pleasures*, on his own label, Factory Records.

The album, with its opaque, atmospheric sound, was hailed as an important musical step toward the twenty-first century. The band performed live on BBC2's *Something Else* and toured England and Europe. But just before Joy Division's first tour of the United States in 1980, lead singer Curtis, who had been suffering from epileptic seizures and depression, committed suicide. The band's haunting single, "Love Will Tear Us Apart," was released after his death.

Sumner, Hook, and Morris regrouped, forming New Order with the addition of keyboardist Gillian Gilbert. It became part of the New York dance club scene, and with the release of "Blue Monday"—the bestselling 12-inch single of all time—confirmed the band's place as one of the most successful alternative acts of the 1980s.

Sumner and New Order bandmate Phil Cunningham formed Bad Lieutenant, occasionally featuring Morris on drums. Sumner has also performed with Pauline Murray and the Invisible Girls, the Chemical Brothers, and coproduced the band Foreign Press. In 1989, as a side gig, Sumner formed Electronic with guitarist Johnny Marr of the Smiths.

Sumner's favorite onstage guitars are a Gibson SG and a Shergold custom Masquerader.

"One thing we've vowed never to do is repeat ourselves. In the Joy Division days, we weren't aware of such things as your typical verse-chorus-verse-bridge-chorus arrangement. We ended up with some really good songs because we were naive to all of that. "Love Will Tear Us Apart" was a good example."

—BERNARD SUMNER, 2009

Awards and Honors

1988 BRIT Award for Best Music Video, for *True Faith*
2005 Inducted into the UK Music Hall of Fame, for both New Order and Joy Division

Sumner playing with Bad Lieutenant at Digital club in Brighton, England, 2009

GRAVEYARD SHIFT

Sumner's initial concept for Electronic was that it would become his first solo album. He had been taking flack from his New Order bandmates whenever he tried to introduce the synthesizer to their music, so he thought he'd follow the "electronic" muse on his own. As he tells the story, he'd go down to New Order's rehearsal rooms, which were near a graveyard, and work all day on the album and end up sleeping on the floor. He admits it got pretty creepy, there on his own. That was when he invited Johnny Marr to collaborate with him. Electronic's first single—also featuring Pet Shop Boys' Neil Tennant—"Getting Away with It," went on to become a Top 40 hit in the United States.

Sumner with New Order at the 2005 Glastonbury Festival in Somerset, England

PAUL WELLER

essential albums

WITH THE JAM
1977	*In the City*
1977	*This Is the Modern World*
1978	*All Mod Cons*
1979	*Setting Sons*
1980	*Sound Affects*
1982	*The Gift*

WITH THE STYLE COUNCIL
1983	*Introducing The Style Council*
1984	*Café Bleu*
1985	*Our Favourite Shop*
1987	*The Cost of Loving*
1988	*Confessions of a Pop Group*
1989	*Modernism: A New Decade*

SOLO
1992	*Paul Weller*
1993	*Wild Wood*
1995	*Stanley Road*
1997	*Heavy Soul*
2000	*Heliocentric*
2002	*Illumination*
2004	*Studio 150*
2005	*As Is Now*
2008	*22 Dreams*
2010	*Wake Up the Nation*

Paul Weller (born John William Weller on May 25, 1958, in Sheerwater, Surrey, England) is a singer/songwriter who founded both the Jam and the Style Council before pursuing a solo career.

Weller first picked up a guitar at age 11, inspired by such early influences as the Beatles, the Who, and the Kinks. In 1972 Weller formed the Jam with friends Steve Brookes and Dave Waller, first playing bass guitar and then switching to rhythm. Although the Jam was a contemporary of punk bands such as the Clash and the Sex Pistols, it sounded more like the "new wave" bands of the mid 1970s. The group went on to become one of England's biggest bands of the early 1970s, with four chart toppers in the UK.

Feeling the need to perform a broader range of music, Weller announced the end of the Jam in 1982. In early 1983 he formed the Style Council with keyboardist Mick Talbot. The group's mix of pop, jazz, R&B, soul, and folk was a precursor of the jazz/pop revival. The band's singles did well in Great Britain and even charted in the United States. But by 1989 its popularity had faded, and when its label refused to release its fifth album, the group split up.

Weller began touring small clubs as a solo act, combining the jazz/pop of his earlier work with a touch of funk. His first three solo albums, *Paul Weller*, *Wild Wood*, and *Stanley Road*, all charted well, with the latter becoming his most successful album. Weller's subsequent solo albums met with critical and commercial acclaim.

Weller has recorded with Oasis, Death in Vegas, and Dot Nelson, and released an album of covers called *Studio 150*.

"The Jam were a people's band. There was always that feeling at gigs, that we weren't dissimilar to our audience. I was only 21—I was just trying to take everyday subjects and write about things other people weren't writing about—working-class life and culture."

—PAUL WELLER, 2006

TAKING MUSIC OUT OF THE BOX

Weller has never liked the idea of putting music into neat categorical boxes. He feels that all music comes from the same "source," and believes that someone listening to Debussy could easily segue to an album of experimental jazz or a song by Curtis Mayfield. Considering this philosophy, it's not surprising that Weller's own compositions incorporate many musical influences—from blue-eyed soul to German avant-rock. His pioneering mix of psychedelic pop and folk-rock in the 1990s has been called "new furniture seasoned from old wood." In his recent concept album, *22 Dreams*, Weller included a spoken-word piece by Simply Red guitarist Aziz Ibrahim and recorded the sounds of a thunderstorm for the final track, "Night Lights."

Left: Weller in 1998

Awards and Honors

2009   BRIT award for "Best Male Solo Artist"

Weller performing on the Pyramid Stage in Glastonbury, England, 2007

THE JAM

In the late 1970s and early 1980s when other rockers ripped their jeans and then safety-pinned them back together, the Jam donned neat, tailored suits. Nonetheless, this mod revival band kept its working-class roots, writing songs with a political edge. Weller penned many of the group's hits, including "Absolute Beginners," "The Eton Rifles," "Going Underground," and "Town Called Malice." The political stance did, however, lead to complications for the band and for Weller in particular. Urged by a public relations rep to set the Jam apart from other bands in the punk scene, Weller made openly pro-Conservative statements that seemed soft compared to the "angry young men" calling for revolution.

JAZZ, WORLD, AND PROGRESSIVE

Perhaps more than any other genres, these corners of the music world play host to some of the industry's most fearless explorers and visionaries. Unencumbered by the commercial trappings of mainstream pop and rock, these guitarists are, more often than not, simply in it for the music. Running the gamut from self-taught, hands-on craftsmen and masters to fiercely precocious virtuosos and composers, these players are on the forefront of what is new, exciting, and possible in music. Prolific collaborators, insatiable students and historians, and peerless entertainers in their own right, these guitarists challenge boundaries, largely without ego, and are only too happy to invite the rest of us to witness their discoveries.

JEFF BECK

essential albums

WITH JEFF BECK GROUP
1968   *Truth*
1969   *Beck-Ola*
1971   *Rough and Ready*
1972   *Jeff Beck Group*

WITH BECK, BOGERT & APPICE
1973   *Beck, Bogert & Appice*

LIVE
1974   *Live in Japan*
1977   *Jeff Beck With the Jan Hammer Group Live*
2006   *Live at BB King Blues Club*
2008   *Performing This Week . . . Live at Ronnie Scotts*

SOLO
1975   *Blow by Blow*
1976   *Wired*
1980   *There and Back*
1985   *Flash 42*
1989   *Jeff Beck's Guitar Shop*
1992   *Frankie's House*
1993   *Crazy Legs*
1999   *Who Else!*
2001   *You Had It Coming*
2003   *Jeff*

WITH UPP (AS SOLOIST, PRODUCER)
1975   *Upp*
1976   *This Way Upp*

Jeff Beck (born June 24, 1944, in Wallington, England) is a famously accomplished and iconoclastic guitarist primarily associated with the Yardbirds as well as a steady stream of collaborations and solo albums.

An enterprising child, Beck was inspired by technical greats like Les Paul and fell in love with the guitar early on, even making several attempts at building a functional instrument.

One of the three famous Yardbirds alums (along with Eric Clapton and Jimmy Page), Beck joined the group in 1965 to relieve Clapton, put his signature on several tracks, many of which would go on to become some of the band's biggest hits—and parted ways with the group the following year. Beck's short attention span and tendency to depart projects unexpectedly would come to define his career and persona.

Beck bounced from collaboration to collaboration in the late 1960s, teaming up with artists including Rod Stewart in the Jeff Beck Group and Tim Bogert on a record called *Beck Bogert & Appice*.

After a break, 1975 brought Beck major solo success on *Blow by Blow*, a slickly produced jazz-influenced instrumental project. Beck devoted himself to a follow-up effort, the album that would become *Wired*. From the late 1970s until the early 1990s, he contributed to the recordings of an impressive range of artists, including Kate Bush, Mick Jagger, Robert Plant, Tina Turner, and Stevie Wonder.

More recently Beck has output a more experimental series of work, including the 1989 Grammy-winning *Guitar Shop*, as well as a duo of live recordings in 2006.

BECK'S STYLE

Beck is generally associated with the electric guitar, a lifelong pursuit that started before he even really understood the difference between acoustic and electric guitars. Beck's peers laud him for being a "guitarist's guitarist"—he eschews complicated effects and modifications to his equipment, instead concentrating on muscular, hands-on virtuosity. Beck seldom uses a pick and manipulates the guitar's vibrato bar to achieve most of his output.

Beck has played and collaborated with many of the current masters, but he's always been loathe to attach himself to a particular band, scene, or style of playing.

Fender created a custom Stratocaster for Beck in 1991, giving it a makeover in 2004. Constructed of alder and capable of a remarkably wide range of pitch, the instrument was originally available in sea foam green and purple finishes.

Awards and Honors

1986   Grammy Award, Best Rock Instrumental Performance, for *Flash*
1990   Grammy Award, Best Rock Instrumental Performance, for *Jeff Beck's Guitar Shop*
1992   Inducted into the Rock and Roll Hall of Fame, with the Yardbirds
2002   Grammy Award, Best Rock Instrumental Performance, for "Dirty Mind"
2004   Grammy Award, Best Rock Instrumental Performance, for "Plan B"

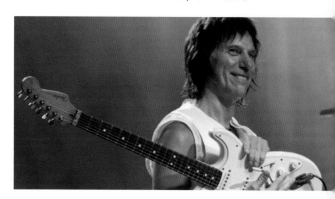

Beck has influenced artists across genres for decades. *Rolling Stone* magazine characterizes "one of the most influential lead guitarists in rock, Jeff Beck has helped shape blues rock, psychedelia, and heavy metal." Here, Beck at the Enmore Theatre in Sydney, Australia, 2009

PATHS CROSSED, PATHS NOT TAKEN

Beck has played with—or almost played with—an outsize assortment of storied bands and legends. In 1965, Beck replaced Eric Clapton in the Yardbirds. A few years later, in 1967, he formed the Jeff Beck Group with Rod Stewart. He was considered as Syd Barrett's replacement in Pink Floyd in 1968, but missed the opportunity as guitarist David Gilmour filled the role. Beck performed on tour with David Bowie in 1973; his performances were, however, not officially released. Then, in 1975, he auditioned to replace Mick Taylor in the Rolling Stones, but the permanent spot in the band was instead given to Ronnie Wood from the Jeff Beck Group, respectively. More recently, Beck rehearsed with Guns N' Roses on tour in Paris in 1992, but couldn't perform with the band due to injury.

Beck performing at the Palais in Melbourne, Australia, 2009

GEORGE BENSON

essential albums

STUDIO

1965	George Benson/Jack McDuff
1965	It's Uptown
1966	The George Benson Cookbook
1968	Giblet Gravy
1969	Shape of Things to Come
1969	Tell It Like It Is
1971	Beyond the Blue Horizon
1972	White Rabbit
1973	Body Talk
1974	Bad Benson
1976	Breezin'
1976	Good King Bad
1977	In Flight
1980	Give Me the Night
1983	In Your Eyes
1987	Collaboration (with Earl Klugh)
1989	Tenderly
1990	Big Boss Band
1993	Love Remembers
1996	That's Right
1998	Masquerade
2000	Absolute Benson
2006	Givin' It Up (with Al Jarreau)
2009	Songs and Stories

LIVE

1978	Weekend in L. A.
1984	20/20
1984	Live in Concert
1986	Live from Montreux
2000	Live at Casa Caribe
2004	Golden Legends Live
2005	Best of George Benson Live

George Benson (born March 22, 1943, in Pittsburgh, Pennsylvania) is a Grammy-winning guitarist and vocalist whose mellow mix of pop, jazz, and R&B became a radio mainstay in the 1970s.

Benson was a guitar prodigy who performed on the ukulele for small change at age 7. The next year he was playing guitar and singing on weekends at an unlicensed nightclub—until the police closed it down. His first single, RCA-Victor's "She Makes Me Mad," was recorded when he was only 10. He recorded his first album, *The New Boss Guitar*, at age 21 with jazz organist and mentor Jack McDuff. After being brought to Columbia by über talent scout John Hammond, Benson released *It's Uptown* with the George Benson Quartet and *The George Benson Cookbook*.

Benson then came under the wing of jazz great Miles Davis, playing guitar on his recording of "Paraphernalia" on the 1968 album *Miles in the Sky*. In 1969 Benson released his personal take on the Beatles, *The Other Side of Abby Road*.

While under contract with Warner Bros. in the mid-1970s, Benson began to reach a wider audience. His 1976 album, *Breezin'*, became a breakthrough LP, going triple platinum, and earning him the Grammy's Record of the Year for "This Masquerade." Two years later he received another Grammy Award for the song "On Broadway," a live performance from the album *Weekend in L.A.*

Whitney Houston later covered Benson's 1977 recording of "The Greatest Love of All," which was made for the Muhammad Ali documentary, *The Greatest*. Benson collaborated with Chet Atkins on "Sunrise," performed on Jack McDuff's *Color Me Blue*, and recorded *Givin' It Up* in 2006 with Al Jarreau.

Benson uses a rest-stroke picking technique similar to that of Gypsy guitar legend Django Reinhardt.

"I listen to other guitar players, yeah. It gives me new concepts and shows me where the instrument is going for the future and it is going some places. There are some musicians who are really putting out a good vibe with new theories. I try and keep up."

—GEORGE BENSON

Awards and Honors

1976	Grammy Award for Best Pop Instrumental Performance, for "Breezin'"
1976	Grammy Award for Best R&B Instrumental Performance, for "Theme from Good King Bad"
1976	Grammy Award for Record of the Year, for *This Masquerade*
1976	Grammy Hall of Fame Award, for *Breezin'*
1978	Grammy Award for Best R&B Vocal Performance, Male, for "On Broadway"
1980	Grammy Award for Best Jazz Vocal Performance, Male, for "Moody's Mood"
1980	Grammy Award for Best R&B Instrumental Performance, for "Off Broadway"
1980	Grammy Award for Best R&B Vocal Performance, Male, for "Give Me The Night"
1983	Grammy Award for Best Pop Instrumental Performance, for "Being with You"
2006	Grammy Award for Best Pop Instrumental Performance, for "Mornin'," with Al Jarreau
2006	Grammy Award for Best Traditional R&B Vocal Performance, for "God Bless the Child," with Al Jarreau and Jill Scott

Benson performs at the Royal Albert Hall, 2006

Benson at the Stowe House, Northamptonshire, England, 2008.

THE TALE SPINNER

After leaving Columbia, Benson wanted to start including vocals in his recordings. He felt that performing songs with a great melody and the right lyrics would allow him to be not only a musician, but also a spinner of tales. He wanted to take listeners, as he put it, "to another place." But record producers were skeptical. It wasn't until Benson signed with Warner Bros. that producer Tommy LiPuma recognized his potential to become the next Nat King Cole. The resulting blockbuster album, *Breezin'*, gave Benson a voice at last.

In 2009, Benson released an album with a title that says it all, *Songs and Stories*. It combines some new material with classics by James Taylor, Smokey Robinson, Lamont Dozier, Bill Withers, and Donny Hathaway. Benson made sure the album would be full of great songs, the kind, he says, that have the capacity to alter reality—for both the listener and the performer.

PACO DE LUCÍA

STUDIO

1965	*12 Canciones de García Lorca Para Guitarra*
1965	*Dos Guitarras Flamencas*
1967	*Dos Guitarras Flamencas en América Latina*
1967	*La Fabulosa Guitarra de Paco de Lucía*
1969	*Fantasía Flamenca de Paco de Lucía*
1969	*Hispanoamérica*
1971	*Recital de Guitarra*
1972	*El Duende Flamenco de Paco de Lucía*
1973	*Fuente y Caudal*
1975	*Paco de Lucía En Vivo Desde el Teatro Real*
1976	*Almoraima*
1978	*Paco de Lucía Interpreta a Manuel de Falla*
1981	*Castro Marín*
1981	*The Paco de Lucía Sextet*
1981	*Solo Quiero Caminar*
1983	*Passion, Grace and Fire*
1987	*Siroco*
1990	*Zyryab*
1996	*Al Di Meola, John McLaughlin, and Paco de Lucía*
1998	*Luzia*
2004	*Cositas Buenas*

LIVE

1981	*Friday Night in San Francisco*
1984	*Live . . . One Summer Night*
1987	*Live Recordings*
1987	*The Paco de Lucía Sextet*
1991	*Concierto de Aranjuez*
1993	*Live in América*

Paco de Lucía (born December 21, 1947, in Cádiz, Spain) is one of the world's most visible and accomplished flamenco guitarists. His talents have translated into a successful career that brings in aspects of classical and jazz styles, and his work has been given center stage through a number of popular films, concert appearances, and collaborations with other artists.

The fifth child of amateur flamenco musician Antonio Sánchez, de Lucía's future in music was all but assured. Before his teens he was performing in front of large audiences and winning prestigious awards, following in the footsteps of his older brother, also a musician. In 1961 he toured as part of dancer José Greco's musical ensemble, and a few years later de Lucía would play on the first of several albums with guitarist Ricardo Modrego.

De Lucía's true solo debut came in 1967 with *La Fabulosa Guitarra de Paco de Lucía*. He would soon go on to establish a productive partnership with singer Camarón de la Isla in 1968, with whom he would record ten albums and tour. De Lucía continued honing his personal style in releases like 1969's *Fantasía Flamenca*, and in 1970 de Lucía made his first appearance at Carnegie Hall.

De Lucía's work through the 1970s was primarily focused on a relatively traditional interpretation of flamenco, but with his guitar trio, including John McLaughlin and Larry Coryell (eventually replaced by Al Di Meola), de Lucía wholeheartedly embraced elements of jazz, first with the 1981 release *Castro Marín*. Billing a new band as the Paco de Lucía Sextet, the guitarist released *Sólo Quiero Caminar* with the help of two of his brothers in the same year. The sextet has released two additional albums.

Siroco, released in 1987, was a return to fundamentals for de Lucía. He would largely concentrate on his own recordings until the reunion of his guitar trio in 1996. Most recently, de Lucía released *Cositas Buenas*; all told, his twenty-first album.

OTHER WORK

De Lucía's work appears in the scores and sound tracks to several ballets and films, including Carlos Saura's version of *Carmen, La Sabina*, directed by José Luis Borau, and a version of *Los Tarantos*, a ballet staged in Madrid in 1986. He also plays in "Have You Ever Really Loved a Woman," the 1995 hit by Bryan Adams that was featured on the sound track to the film of the same name, and contributed a song to Wes Anderson's 2004 film *The Life Aquatic with Steve Zissou*.

Interestingly, de Lucía had no experience sight-reading musical notation until a 1991 concert performance of the epic *Concierto de Aranjuez*, composed in 1939—a nature-inspired work by Joaquín Rodrigo, one of Spain's most acclaimed composers.

De Lucía playing at the 2007 Málaga en Flamenco Festival in Málaga, Spain

"Common sense is limited since it depends on your intellectual capacity. Imagination has no limits, and sometimes my imagination goes against common sense. Sometimes I regret not knowing music, because it's like not knowing reason, technique, mathematics; but the unconsciousness, the ignorance make you fly higher or, at least, make you fly and land on places where reason would not land."

—PACO DE LUCÍA, 1992

Al Di Meola, John McLaughlin, and Paco de Lucía performing in Barcelona, 1980s

Awards and Honors

2004 Grammy Award for Best Flamenco Album, for *Cositas Buenas,* with Javier Limón and Pepe Loeches

AL DI MEOLA

"I have to be [a perfectionist] because the music demands it. It demands that it's played properly. Sometimes, if we get sloppy, I have to point it out right at that moment. If you let the tune go by while you're rehearsing it, by the time you get to the end, you forget the moment where something was really wrong. So, I have to stop the tune. Sometimes I have to continually stop until I get it right. It's frustrating. The thing is, they become better musicians in the course of them hating my guts."

—AL DI MEOLA, 2003

Al Di Meola (born July 22, 1954, in Jersey City, New Jersey) is a contemporary guitar great in the genres of Latin jazz and jazz fusion. He appears with Paco de Lucía and John McLaughlin on *Friday Nights in San Francisco*, one of guitar's best-selling live albums. Di Meola is known for his preference for acoustic modes and his near-impeccable sense of time and meter.

Di Meola spent his childhood listening to the likes of the Beatles, Elvis, and the Ventures. By the time he was enrolled in high school, Di Meola's rigid guitar practice habit was fully formed; he would spend nearly half of any given day in focused isolation.

Entranced by jazz greats Kenny Burrell, Larry Coryell, and Tal Farlow, Di Meola began discovering his own style. One of many illustrious former students of the Berklee College of Music, Di Meola got his first real exposure when legendary jazz pianist Chick Corea asked him to join Return to Forever, his groundbreaking jazz fusion group, in 1974. After

an appearance with the group at Carnegie Hall, Di Meola became a star on the New York jazz scene.

His solo career commenced in the mid-1970s after the dissolution of Return to Forever, and over the course of the decade Di Meola released several Latin-tinged albums, all acclaimed. Paco de Lucía and John McLaughlin joined Di Meola to tour as a trio and released two albums in the early 1980s. During this time, he also worked with Carlos Santana.

In the 1990s Di Meola embraced a world sound, showing it off through his Rite of Strings trio and collaborations with Lucíano Pavarotti, Dave Matthews, Paul Simon, and pianist Yutaka Kobayashi. His latest project, the New World Sinfonia, is a showcase for Di Meola's acoustic guitar work as well as his efforts as composer.

In his early career Di Meola was actually known for his shredding—an approach he has largely dropped in light of his changing musical tastes and ambitions. Ovation and Paul Reed Smith have manufactured Al Di Meola signature models.

RETURN TO FOREVER

Chick Corea, a disciple of Miles Davis, formed Return to Forever in 1971, focusing on a Latin jazz style, which would soon drift in a more rock-influenced direction. Di Meola joined up three years later, vacating his slot at Berklee to take the opportunity. He first appeared on 1974's *Where Have I Known You Before*, a solid success on the charts. The band would do well with the next year's Grammy-winning *No Mystery*, paving

the way for a major label recording contract. *Romantic Warrior* of 1976 was the group's biggest hit yet—but Corea suddenly dissolved the group in order to move in a new sonic direction.

The band—reconstituted at various times throughout Corea's career—leaves behind an important legacy. With groups like John McLaughlin's Mahavishnu Orchestra, Return for Forever is responsible for bringing a sense of the avant-garde and eclectic into the relatively staid realm of jazz during the 1970s. In 2008 and 2009 Corea tapped Di Meola to join him on a reunion tour of the United States and Europe. Remastered versions of the group's best-known albums were released around the same time.

essential albums

WITH RETURN TO FOREVER

1974	*Where Have I Known You Before*
1975	*No Mystery*
1976	*Romantic Warrior*
1983	*Chick Corea with Return to Forever*

STUDIO

1976	*Land of the Midnight Sun*
1977	*Elegant Gypsy*
1982	*Electric Rendezvous*
1982	*Splendido Hotel*
1983	*Scenario*
1985	*Cielo e Terra*
1985	*Soaring through a Dream*
1987	*Tirami Su*
1991	*Kiss My Axe*
1991	*World Sinfonia*
1993	*World Sinfonia II: Heart of the Immigrants*
1994	*Orange and Blue*
1996	*Di Meola Plays Piazzolla*
2000	*The Grande Passion*
2005	*Cosmopolitan Life*
2005	*Flesh on Flesh*
2006	*Consequence of Chaos*
2006	*Vocal Rendezvous*

LIVE

1982	*Tour de Force*
1991	*World Sinfonia Live in London*

Awards and Honors

1975	Grammy Award for Best Jazz Performance by a Group, for "No Mystery," with Chick Corea and Return to Forever

Di Meola performing at the Granada Theater, 2006

ALLAN HOLDSWORTH

essential albums

STUDIO

1976	*Velvet Darkness*
1982	*I.O.U.*
1983	*Road Games* (EP)
1985	*Metal Fatigue*
1986	*Atavachron*
1987	*Sand*
1989	*Secrets*
1992	*Wardenclyffe Tower*
1993	*Hard Hat Area*
1996	*None Too Soon*
1999	*The Sixteen Men of Tain*
2001	*Flat Tire: Music for a Non-Existent Movie*

LIVE

| 2003 | *All Night Wrong* |
| 2004 | *Then!* |

"You have to persist, and out of the sheer frustration of what you've been doing or haven't been doing, you just come out the other side."

—ALLAN HOLDSWORTH

Allan Holdsworth (born August 6, 1946, in Bradford, West Yorkshire, England) is a guitarist, composer, and producer known for his innovative work in jazz-fusion and progressive rock during a career spanning four decades.

Holdsworth's first music teacher was his father, a talented amateur musician, who tutored him in music theory and jazz appreciation. Holdsworth cites Django Reinhardt, Charlie Christian, Joe Pass, Eric Clapton, and John Coltrane as early influences. His journeyman years were spent doing the dance-club circuit and sitting in with jazz saxophonist Ray Warleigh.

Holdsworth's first recording was with 'Iggenbottom in 1969, and in the early 1970s he joined progressive rock band Tempest and played on their debut album. This short stint was followed by collaborations with the Soft Machine, the New Tony Williams Lifetime, Gong, and Jean-Luc Ponty.

In 1977 Bill Bruford, the legendary drummer from Yes and King Crimson, invited Holdsworth to join the new progressive rock bank, UK. But Holdsworth chafed at playing the same solos every night and soon moved on from the group. He next recorded two albums with jazz pianist Gordon Beck, *Sunbird* and *The Things You See*.

Eddie Van Halen brought Holdsworth to the attention of Warner Bros. Records, which released the Grammy-nominated *Road Games* EP in 1983. Holdsworth permanently relocated to Southern California, and in 1992 he set up his own studio— the Brewery—in San Diego, where he produced music for the next eight years. Holdsworth continues to record and tour, and although he has been associated with various bands and performers, it is his solo work that has made the deepest imprint on modern guitar music.

THE PERFECT TONE

This guitar virtuoso is known for the advanced harmonic structure of his compositions, his hornlike sound, and his distinctive playing style, which incorporates slides, hammer-ons, pull-offs, and electronically altered finger-picked chords. In his quest for "the perfect tone," he has turned to the innovations of others—or created his own. For his 1986 release, *Atavachron*, Holdsworth experimented with Bill Aitken's SynthAxe, a guitarlike MIDI controller, and he has continued to use it on his solo recordings. Holdsworth also engineered a number of electronic sound-processing tools, such as the Harness; worked with luthier Bill DeLap creating baritone and piccolo guitars; and designed several custom guitars currently being produced by Carvin.

Recently, personal hardship led Holdsworth to a resurgence in touring and creating new material.

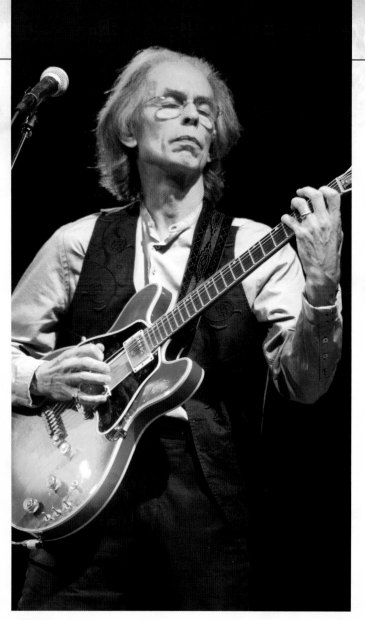

STEVE HOWE

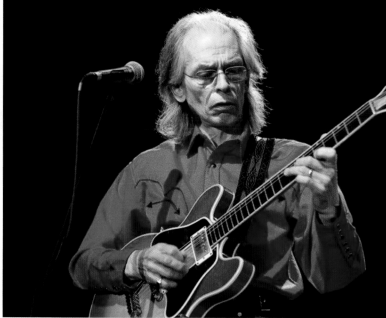

Howe playing with Asia at Volkshaus in Zurich, Switzerland, 2009

"When you start to play off the top of your head, that's when the truth is really known about people."

—STEVE HOWE

Steve Howe (born April 8, 1947, in Holloway, North London, England) is a guitarist/songwriter best known as a member of the British progressive rock supergroups Yes, Asia, and GTR.

Howe came from a musical family and from an early age was exposed to a variety of genres, from Les Paul to brass bands to Tennessee Ernie Ford. He got his first f-hole acoustic guitar as a gift when he was 12 and began playing at local venues. By 1968, he had recorded one album with the psychedelic band, Tomorrow, and another with Bodast.

After declining offers to join Jethro Tull and the Nice—he had hopes of a record contract for Bodast—Howe was invited to replace guitarist Peter Banks of the progressive rock band Yes. With the release of the *Yes Album* in 1971, Howe's blistering guitar, along with Jon Anderson's soaring vocals, Chris Squire's bass, Tony Kaye's keyboard, and Bill Bruford's drums, began to define the group's early sound.

Howe remained with the creative but volatile band throughout the 1970s—watching new members, such as keyboardist Rick Wakeman, come and go—until Yes broke up in 1981. Howe's momentum carried him to Asia, which he formed with John Wetton of King Crimson, Carl Palmer of Emerson, Lake, and Palmer, and Geoff Downes of the Buggles. This iconic band produced two successful albums and several hit singles before Howe left.

Howe then formed supergroup GTR in 1985 with former Genesis guitarist Steve Hackett. GTR's only album went gold before Hackett left to pursue a solo career. In 1988 Anderson, Bruford, Wakeman, and Howe again collaborated, this time on one eponymous album, before rejoining the remaining members of Yes, which some fans now called "Mega-Yes." Howe reunited with the members of Asia in the 1990s and again in 2006 for a twenty-fifth anniversary tour.

essential albums

WITH YES

1971	The Yes Album
1971	Fragile
1972	Close to the Edge
1973	Tales from Topographic Oceans
1973	Yessongs
1974	Relayer
1980	Drama
1983	90125
1997	Open Your Eyes
1999	The Ladder
2001	Magnification

SOLO

1975	Beginnings
1979	The Steve Howe Album
1991	Turbulence
1993	The Grand Scheme of Things
1994	Not Necessarily Acoustic
1998	Quantum Guitar
1999	Pulling Strings
1999	Portraits of Bob Dylan
2001	Natural Timbre
2002	Skyline
2003	Elements
2003	Guitar World
2005	Spectrum
2008	Motif

WITH ASIA

1982	Asia
1983	Alpha
1992	Aqua
2008	Phoenix
2010	Omega

WITH GTR

1986	GTR

WITH EXPLORER'S CLUB

1998	Age of Impact
2002	Raising the Mammoth

Awards and Honors

1982	Best Overall Guitarist, *Guitar Player* magazine
2003	Ranked No. 69 on *Rolling Stone*'s list of the 100 Greatest Guitarists of All Time

Howe at the Headliner in Neptune, New Jersey

GOING IT ALONE

In spite of performing with several of the most famous bands of his era, Howe, like many musicians, felt the need to establish a solo career. *Beginnings* was released in 1975, followed by 1979's *The Steve Howe Album*. Starting in 1991, Howe produced an album nearly every year, including acoustic and progressive entries, as well as a tribute to Bob Dylan. In 1998, Howe's eldest son, Dylan (named for the Welsh poet, not the folk icon), a jazz drummer, joined his dad on the instrumental album *Quantum Guitar*. Both Dylan and younger son Virgil, a keyboardist, performed with Howe on *Elements* under the name Remedy. In 2007 he formed the jazz-oriented Steve Howe Trio, featuring Dylan on drums and Ross Stanley on the Hammond organ.

PAT METHENY

"The challenge of playing is always the same . . . come up with something that has connection to the reality of your own life, and can hopefully manifest into sounds that can inspire things in other people to make them look at their lives differently."

—PAT METHENY, 2003

METHENY'S VERSATILITY

Metheny's embrace of lesser-known guitars and playing styles has made him the subject of much respect and fascination. Following in the footsteps of John McLaughlin and Pat Martino, Metheny is a pioneering user of the twelve-string guitar in jazz music—and his use of alternate tunings is especially notable.

Metheny's work is also colored by the judicious use of the electronic guitar synthesizer, an instrument that experienced the height of its popularity in the 1980s. Other rare Metheny favorites include the Pikasso I, a three-neck harp guitar whose form is said to be inspired by the art of Pablo Picasso.

Pat Metheny (born August 12, 1954, in Lee's Summit, Missouri) is a multiple Grammy-winning jazz guitarist and teacher known for his experimental, instantly recognizable sound with the Pat Metheny Group and as a solo artist. *Zero Tolerance for Silence*, his 1994 album, remains controversial for its overdubbed, improvised electric guitar solos that, to the casual fan, sound more like noise than music.

Born outside Kansas City, Missouri, Metheny followed his older trumpet-playing brother Mike into music; by the age of 20 years Metheny had already studied at Berklee and the University of Miami and made his recording debut alongside Paul Bley and bass player Jaco Pastorius. Metheny has acknowledged an extremely diverse range of influences in his music and style, including jazz player Wes Montgomery, Miles Davis, and the Beatles. He also draws heavily from the traditions of bossa nova and the music of Africa and South America.

Through the 1970s Metheny established himself as a living jazz great, appearing with Gary Burton and Mick Goodrick. In 1976 he recorded *Bright Size Life*, his debut, with Jaco Pastorius and percussionist Bob Moses; their work, too, would receive much praise.

With 1977's *Watercolors* Metheny would launch a long-term collaboration with pianist Lyle Mays and lay the groundwork for the Pat Metheny Group. With many collaborating musicians from the *Watercolors* sessions, Metheny would release the group's self-titled album the following year.

Metheny is most comfortable as a member of a trio or quartet; he has worked with Chick Corea, John Scofield, Herbie Hancock, and Joni Mitchell. His work in the realm of free jazz resulted in *Song X*, a recording in collaboration with Ornette Coleman, the multi-instrumentalist and standard-bearer of the genre. Metheny also counts several well-known Scandinavian musicians among his collaborators, and he has featured numerous female vocalists on his recordings across the years.

THE PAT METHENY GROUP

With the group's second release, *American Garage* in 1980, it achieved mainstream success on the jazz—and even pop—charts. Soon touring and playing for fans on both sides of the Atlantic, Metheny kept innovating with an unusual setup of guitars, synthesizers, pianos, and other effects.

The Pat Metheny Group released a handful of albums in the early 1980s, even teaming up with David Bowie to work on the music for *The Falcon and the Snowman*, a 1985 film starring Timothy Hutton and Sean Penn. The group's popularity surged after this project, and the group's late-1980s releases featured several Latin musicians, including acclaimed Brazilian drummer Armando Marçal.

The group's most experimental work would come in the mid-1990s with a trio of albums, which heavily employed improvisation as well as obscure rhythms and time signatures. Most recently, a revamped version of the group released *The Way Up* in 2005, an improvisatory showcase featuring a roster of up-and-coming musicians from around the world.

essential albums

WITH VARIOUS ARTISTS

1976	*Bright Size Life*
1977	*Watercolors*
1980	*80/81*
1980	*As Falls Wichita, So Falls Wichita Falls*
1984	*Rejoicing*
1986	*Song X*
1990	*Change of Heart*
1996	*Beyond the Missouri Sky (Short Stories)*
1998	*Like Minds*
2000	*Trio 99-00*
2006	*Metheny Mehldau*
2008	*Upojenie*

WITH THE PAT METHENY BAND

1978	*Pat Metheny Group*
1981	*Offramp*
1982	*Travels*
1984	*First Circle*
1987	*Still Life (Talking)*
1989	*Letter from Home*
1993	*The Road to You*
1994	*We Live Here*
1996	*Quartet*
1997	*Imaginary Day*
2002	*Speaking of Now*
2005	*The Way Up*

SOLO

1979	*New Chautauqua*
2003	*One Quiet Night*
2007	*Secret Story*
2010	*Orchestrion*

Awards and Honors

1982 Grammy Award for Best Jazz Performance, for *Offramp*, with the Pat Metheny Group

1983 Grammy Award for Best Jazz Performance, for *Travels*, with the Pat Metheny Group

1984 Grammy Award for Best Jazz Fusion Recording Vocal or Instrumental, for *First Circle*, with the Pat Metheny Group

1987 Grammy Award for Best Jazz Fusion Performance Vocal or Instrumental, for *Still Life (Talking)*, with the Pat Metheny Group

1989 Grammy Award for Best Jazz Fusion Performance, for *Letter from Home*, with the Pat Metheny Group

1990 Grammy Award for Best Instrumental Composition, for *Change of Heart*

1992 Grammy Award for Best Contemporary Jazz Performance Instrumental, for *Secret Story*

1993 Grammy Award for Best Contemporary Jazz Performance Instrumental, for *The Road to You*, with the Pat Metheny Group

1995 Grammy Award for Best Contemporary Jazz Performance, for *We Live Here*, with the Pat Metheny Group

1997 Grammy Award for Best Jazz Instrumental Performance, for *Beyond the Missouri Sky (Short Stories)*, with Charlie Haden

1998 Grammy Award for Best Contemporary Jazz Performance, for *Imaginary Day*, with the Pat Metheny Group

1998 Grammy Award for Best Rock Instrumental Performance, for "The Roots of Coincidence," with the Pat Metheny Group

1999 Grammy Award for Best Jazz Instrumental Performance by Individual or Group, for *Like Minds*, with Gary Burton, Chick Corea, Roy Haynes, and Dave Holland

2000 Grammy Award for Best Jazz Instrumental Solo, for "(Go) Get It"

2003 Grammy Award for Best Contemporary Jazz Album, for *Speaking of Now*, with the Pat Metheny Group

2004 Grammy Award for Best New Age Album, for *One Quiet Night*

2006 Grammy Award for Best Contemporary Jazz Recording, for *The Way Up*, with the Pat Metheny Group

JOHN McLAUGHLIN

"We're really ourselves most naturally when we're being spontaneous with each other, which is the best way to be in life anyway. You know, when you have a family, everybody is spontaneous with each other and sometimes a little brutally honest, but nevertheless it's spontaneous so it cannot really be bad. And that is really my philosophical foundation, if you like, about how groups should be. And maybe this is why I always want great players. I need stimulation, I need them to kick my ass, as it were, and provoke me in some way that will push me to a place that I don't know, that I've never been before."

—JOHN McLAUGHLIN, 2004

Awards and Honors

2010   Grammy Award for Best Jazz Instrumental Album, Individual or Group, for *Five Peace Band—Live*, with Chick Corea

Known also as Mahavishnu John, John McLaughlin (born January 4, 1942, in Doncaster, England) is acclaimed for his contributions to jazz fusion. His influence is wide-ranging—he played on Miles Davis's legendary *Bitches Brew*, and McLaughlin's Mahavishnu Orchestra is an icon of the 1970s.

McLaughlin's career took off in the 1960s as he built a reputation in Great Britain—and eventually, the United States—as an impressive session guitarist. After McLaughlin's migration to the states, he crossed paths with Jimi Hendrix, and together they held a lengthy jam session just before Hendrix's death.

Devotion was released in 1970 and encompassed an impressive spectrum of sounds, melding psychedelic influences with R&B. McLaughlin's follow-up in 1971, *My Goal's Beyond*, took an acoustic approach, infusing the record with Indian and jazz-inspired styles.

Building off *My Goal's Beyond*, McLaughlin folded his electric jazz and Indian obsessions into his new project, the Mahavishnu Orchestra. The group was short-lived, but during its time together the members explored a dizzying array of compositions and styles. The band was reshuffled in 1973, releasing six total albums by 1976.

essential albums

SOLO

1969	*Extrapolation*
1970	*Where Fortune Smiles*
1970	*Devotion*
1971	*My Goal's Beyond*
1978	*Electric Guitarist*
1981	*Friday Night in San Francisco*
1981	*Belo Horizonte*
1982	*Passion, Grace and Fire*
1982	*Music Spoken Here*
1991	*Que Alegria*
1991	*Jazz, Vol. 2*
1994	*After the Rain*
1995	*Guitar Concerto*
1995	*The Promise*
1996	*The Guitar Trio*
1997	*The Heart of Things*
2000	*Remember Shakti: The Believer*
2001	*Saturday Night in Bombay: Remember Shakti*
2003	*Thieves and Poets*
2006	*Industrial Zen*
2008	*Floating Point*

WITH MILES DAVIS

1969	*In A Silent Way*
1970	*Bitches Brew*
1972	*On the Corner*
1974	*Big Fun*
1974	*Get Up with It*
2005	*The Cellar Door Sessions* (recorded 1970)

THE MAHAVISHNU ORCHESTRA

1971	*The Inner Mounting Flame*
1973	*Birds of Fire*
1973	*The Lost Trident Sessions*
1973	*Between Nothingness and Eternity*
1974	*Apocalypse*
1975	*Visions of the Emerald Beyond*
1976	*Inner Worlds*
1984	*Mahavishnu*

POST MAHAVISHNU

McLaughlin continued to explore Eastern music and instruments with Shakti, a group he formed with several noted Indian musicians in 1975. Known for its novel world music approach and exotic, custom-built instruments, the band recorded three albums and toured, but the project was short-lived, breaking up in 1977.

By 1979 McLaughlin's style veered back toward Western styles, the blues in particular. He took up electric instruments for the first time since his early days on *Johnny McLaughlin: Electric Guitarist* and subsequently formed the short-lived groups One Truth Band and the Trio of Doom.

Since the 1980s McLaughlin's repertoire has expanded and diversified. He has continued to collaborate with a range of musicians in different styles, alternating back and forth between acoustic and electric material. Other notable pursuits include his appearance in a film, 1986's *Round Midnight*, as well as his compositional debut with the Los Angeles Philharmonic Orchestra in 1988.

Most recently McLaughlin has continued to experiment with unusual instruments and build on his talents as a composer. He has embraced technology, too—he is the creator of a series of instructional DVDs on Indian music, and he has released live tracks online from one of his latest outfits, the 4th Dimension, in addition to his own solo works.

McLaughlin with the 4th Dimension at Town Hall in New York City, 2007

LES PAUL

"I thought I was out of a job when rock came in. We were told to change and to be less traditional. They used three chords, and not the right chords, and buried the singer! It was another world that you entered into with a riff and rode it, and you needed to turn it up 500 watts to get the sound right. It was rebellion, having something to say with a new beat."

—LES PAUL, 2005

Les Paul (born Lester William Polsfus on June 9, 1915, in Waukesha, Wisconsin; died August 12, 2009, in White Plains, New York) was a guitarist, songwriter, broadcaster, and inventor best known for heavily influencing the development of the electric guitar. Paul possessed a scientific grasp of the guitar as tool, as well as a soulful understanding of music's deep importance and role as entertainment.

During childhood Paul was exposed to the harmonica, banjo, and, finally, guitar. An enterprising innovator early on, he is the inventor of a hands-free device for playing the harmonica—his design prevails today. While a still a teenager Paul moved to Chicago, where he assumed his stage name, befriended guitarist Django Reinhardt, and indulged an interest in jazz music, releasing several early recordings with fellow guitarist Jim Atkins in the mid-1930s. The bulk of his life's creative output would be largely based in country and jazz styles.

After an electrical accident in 1940, Paul moved westward to Los Angeles where he worked with Nat King Cole, Bing Crosby,

and the Andrews Sisters. Around this time Paul also met his second wife, Colleen Summers, a country singer—later known as Mary Ford. They would marry in 1949 and later recorded several popular tunes together. Thanks to Paul's technical wizardry, the multitracked songs featured two versions of her voice in harmony with each other—a groundbreaking studio technique at the time.

Paul made forays into radio and television, too—among his credits: 1950's *Les Paul Show* on the radio and television's *Les Paul & Mary Ford Show*. The pair would divorce in 1962, though. After a period of relative silence from Paul, he reemerged in the 1970s with several releases showcasing new versions of his past tunes, as well as two studio albums he created with Chet Atkins.

Paul became a Grammy winner in 2006 with his collection *Les Paul & Friends*. Active until the very end, Paul's 2009 passing was mourned by multiple generations of musicians and guitar enthusiasts.

PAUL THE ENGINEER

After moving to Queens, New York, in 1939, Paul started building his own guitars—his first instruments, known as "logs," were simple two-by-fours with strings and other basic guitar components attached. Freed from the muffling aspects of early acoustic-electric guitars, Paul's groundbreaking "logs" paved the way for his renowned solid body electric guitars, still built by Gibson.

Paul's influence in the recording studio carries over to this day. The single "Lover (When You're Near Me)" showcased the possibilities of multitracking for the first time in 1948. Paul devised his own apparatus for disc cutting, made with parts from a Cadillac, technology that would be adopted by Ampex to produce the world's first reel-to-reel tape recorder. These innovations have contributed in no small part to Paul's singular role as a father of modern music.

Gibson Les Paul electric guitar

essential albums

1949	*Hawaiian Paradise*
1950	*The Hit Makers!* (with Mary Ford)
1950	*The New Sound*
1951	*Les Paul's New Sound, Volume 2*
1952	*Bye Bye Blues!*
1955	*Les and Mary* (with Mary Ford)
1957	*Time to Dream*
1959	*Lover's Luau* (with Mary Ford)
1962	*Bouquet of Roses* (with Mary Ford)
1962	*Warm and Wonderful* (with Mary Ford)
1963	*Swingin' South* (with Mary Ford)
1965	*Fabulous Les Paul and Mary Ford* (with Mary Ford)
1968	*Les Paul Now!*
1968	*Lover* (with Mary Ford)
1971	*The Guitar Artistry of Les Paul*
1976	*Chester and Lester* (with Chet Atkins)
1977	*Guitar Monsters* (with Chet Atkins)
1979	*Multi Trackin'*
1996	*Les Paul: The Legend and the Legacy*
2003	*California Melodies*
2005	*Les Paul & Friends: American Made, World Played*
2008	*Les Paul & Friends: A Tribute to a Legend*

Awards and Honors

1976	Grammy Award for Best Country Instrumental Performance, for "Chester and Lester," with Chet Atkins
1979	Grammy Hall of Fame Award, for "How High the Moon"
1983	Grammy Award for Lifetime Achievement
1988	Inducted into the Rock and Roll Hall of Fame
2001	Technical Grammy Award
2005	Grammy Award for Best Pop Instrumental Performance, for "Caravan"
2005	Grammy Award for Best Rock Instrumental Performance, for "69 Freedom Special"
2005	Grammy Hall of Fame Award, for "Vaya con Dios"
2005	Inducted into the National Inventors Hall of Fame for the development of the solid-body electric guitar

Les Paul at the Iridium Jazz Club in New York, 2008

JOHN SCOFIELD

John Scofield (born December 26, 1951, in Dayton, Ohio) is a bebop and jazz guitarist considered one of the living masters in that genre. Educated at the Berklee College of Music and now an adjunct professor at New York University, Scofield is responsible for an extensive catalog of solo and collaborative recordings as well as upholding an impressive annual touring schedule.

Scofield grew up in New York City's Connecticut suburbs listening to the masters of blues and rock guitar, taking up the instrument himself at 11 years old. At Berklee he formed networks that would lead him to Chet Baker and Charles Mingus, both of with whom he would record and tour at the beginning of his career in the 1970s.

The year 1977 marked the guitarist's solo debut, *John Scofield*. He would form a well-regarded trio with drummer Adam Nussbaum and bassist Steve Swallow in 1979. A short time later, Scofield met Miles Davis—one of the defining moments of his life and career. The pair collaborated for three years, and Scofield appears on three major Davis recordings;

he has called his time with Davis "an education on a lot of levels."

In the 1980s Scofield continued to release solo work. He also formed the Blue Matter Band with a number of drummers, bass players and keyboardists, a project that resulted in a trio of albums. Going into the 1990s, Scofield would gravitate to a more funk-inspired jazz style of playing, a sound that is apparent on *A Go Go*, his album with Medeski Martin & Wood, the "avant groove" jazz trio.

In the last decade Scofield has partnered with an array of diverse artists. With several guests Scofield honored the repertoire of Ray Charles with a 2004 album, and has performed with former Grateful Dead's Phil Lesh and his band. Scofield continues to appear with Medeski Martin & Wood and released *Piety Street*, an album of gospel music, in 2009.

Scofield is said to spend more than half of any given year on the road. He holds an endorsement deal with Ibanez, the makers of his JSM100—a model based on Scofield's 1981 Ibanez AS-200, his favorite guitar for more than two decades.

SCOFIELD AND CHARLES

Scofield's loving reinterpretation of some of Ray Charles's best-known material, *That's What I Say*, was released in 2005. Featuring a top-shelf list of some of blues' and jazz's most accomplished talent—including Warren Haynes, John Mayer, and songwriter Isaac Hayes—Scofield cherry-picked his collaborators and singers to best serve the track list. With the help of producer Steve Jordan, Scofield selected songs by Charles he felt could be reimagined—"We weren't too reverential about it," he has said.

"I Don't Need No Doctor," "Hit the Road Jack," and "Georgia On My Mind" all make an appearance on the album. Scofield briefly considered the title "Let Sco Get Stoned," a play on the Charles tune, but pulled back against protests from his label.

essential albums

STUDIO

1977	*East Meets West*
1977	*John Scofield*
1978	*Rough House*
1979	*Who's Who?*
1980	*Bar Talk*
1981	*Shinola*
1984	*Electric Outlet*
1985	*Still Warm*
1986	*Blue Matter*
1987	*Loud Jazz*
1988	*Flat Out*
1990	*Time on My Hands*
1991	*Meant to Be*
1992	*Grace Under Pressure*
1994	*Hand Jive*
1995	*Groove Elation*
1996	*Quiet*
2000	*Bump*
2001	*Works for Me*
2002	*Überjam*
2003	*Up All Night*
2007	*This Meets That*
2009	*Emarcy Records*
2009	*Piety Street*

LIVE

1977	*John Scofield Live*
1981	*Out Like a Light*
1987	*Pick Hits Live*
2004	*EnRoute: John Scofield Trio Live*

Scofield performing in Warsaw, Poland, 2004

"You know the old saying: 'Brevity is the soul of wit.' I think that really applies to jazz improvisation. First of all, I don't have tons of technique. If I had tons of technique I would probably play differently. I do have technique, it is my own technique. Louis Armstrong was economical and I love his music as much as any playing in the world. So is B.B. King and Albert King. So is Lester Young, so is Miles [Davis]."

—JOHN SCOFIELD

FRANK ZAPPA

essential albums

WITH THE MOTHERS OF INVENTION
1966   *Freak Out!*
1967   *Absolutely Free*
1968   *We're Only In It for the Money*
1969   *Mothermania*
1970   *Burnt Weeny Sandwich*
1975   *One Size Fits All*

SOLO
1968   *Lumpy Gravy*
1969   *Hot Rats*
1970   *Chunga's Revenge*
1974   *Apostrophe (')*
1971   *200 Motels*
1972   *Waka/Jawaka*
1972   *The Grand Wazoo*
1976   *Zoot Allures*
1979   *Sleep Dirt*
1979   *Sheik Yerbouti*
1981   *Shut Up 'N Play Yer Guitar Some More*
1981   *You Are What You Is*
1982   *Ship Arriving Too Late to Save a Drowning Witch*
1983   *The Man from Utopia*
1983   *Baby Snakes*
1984   *Them or Us*
1984   *Thing-Fish*
1984   *Francesco Zappa*
1985   *Frank Zappa Meets the Mothers of Prevention*
1986   *Jazz from Hell*
1994   *Civilization, Phaze III*

LIVE
1978   *Studio Tan*
1978   *Zappa in New York*
1979   *Joe's Garage: Acts I, II & III*
1981   *Shut Up 'N Play Yer Guitar*
1981   *Tinsel Town Rebellion*
1986   *Does Humor Belong in Music?*
1988   *Broadway the Hard Way*
1988   *Guitar*
1988   *You Can't Do That on Stage Anymore, Vol. 1*
1991   *Make a Jazz Noise Here*
1991   *The Best Band You Never Heard in Your Life*

Frank Zappa (born December 21, 1940, in Baltimore, Maryland; died December 4, 1993, in Los Angeles) was a prolific composer and musician whose work is often impossible to categorize.

Taking an interest in percussion during high school, Zappa developed an early reverence for modern classical and avant-garde composers. Inspired by a diverse set of recordings he began collecting as a teenager, which ranged from jazz and R&B classics to the Latin music of his home in Southern California, Zappa played in various high school bands and began honing his skills as a guitarist.

As a guitarist, beginning with the Mothers of Invention, Zappa was known for his iconoclastic style and his incredible speed. As Zappa grew more comfortable with his playing throughout his career, his album releases tended to focus more and more on his complex, virtuosic solos.

THE MOTHERS

With an initial career spanning an entire decade, Zappa's Mothers of Invention served as a laboratory for the guitarist and composer to hone his eclectic sound and vision.

Though he was not a founding member of the group, Zappa quickly assumed control when he joined as guitarist in 1964. With *Freak Out!* in 1966, the Mothers officially announced its debut and proceeded to tour. Failing to meet its label's sales targets, the band endured a budget cut for their next release but continued to push forward. In 1970 Zappa shuffled the band's lineup, bringing in several new multi-instrumentalists who would the keys to expanding the band's sound. Several diverse and experimental works followed, including a pair of live albums recorded in 1971 and 1972. The reconstituted Mothers would prove to be short-lived; following a fall from the stage while performing in London, an injured Zappa put the group on hiatus.

With Zappa's return in the mid-1970s, it became increasingly difficult to separate his career and musical ambitions from that of the Mothers. Zappa began recording exclusively as Frank Zappa in 1976, leaving the remaining band members a well-known name and a potent musical legacy to maintain.

"The way I state it is this: I am 45 years old, I may play rock and roll music, but I certainly do not consume it. It is not my idea of a good time, nor is country and western, nor is polka music, nor is Las Vegas music, you know. And I find some of these forms incredibly offensive, no matter what they're wearing, or what the lyrics are. I find them aesthetically offensive, but I wouldn't deny anybody the right to listen to them, and I also refute any claim that the lyrics to a song are going to induce antisocial behavior. As if lyrics had that much power."

—FRANK ZAPPA ON CENSORSHIP, 1986

ZAPPA AS COMPOSER

Although Zappa's talent as a guitarist is thoroughly documented across decades of collaborative and solo recordings, it is the role of composer he relished most, a pursuit that occupied the final years of his life and served as an emphatic coda to a varied and lengthy career.

In the mid-1980s Zappa discovered the possibilities of the Synclavier, an early yet complex synthesizer and electronic composition system. With it he was able to achieve a full range of sonic depth, instrumentation and complexity without lengthy or disorganized rehearsals. In 1990 President Václav Havel, a longtime fan, invited Zappa to visit the Czech Republic to serve as a cultural and economic consultant.

Several high-profile European concerts in the early 1990s showcased his classical compositions; Zappa traveled to conduct but was unable to complete the engagement due to recently diagnosed prostate cancer. He passed away the following year at the age of 52.

Awards and Honors

1987	Grammy Award for Best Rock Instrumental Performance, for *Jazz from Hell*
1995	Inducted into the Rock and Roll Hall of Fame
1997	Grammy Award for Lifetime Achievement
2003	Ranked No. 45 on *Rolling Stone*'s list of 100 Greatest Guitarists of All Time

Frank Zappa and band, Memorial Auditorium in Buffalo, New York, 1980

MORE GUITARISTS

Abercrombie, John	Billy Cobham, Jack DeJohnette, Brecker Brothers, solo	b. 1944
Ackerman, William	Solo	b. 1949
Ade, King Sunny	Solo	b. 1946
Akkerman, Jan	Focus, solo	b. 1946
Aldrich, Doug	Burning Rain, Dio, Whitesnake, solo	b. 1964
Aleman, Oscar	Solo	1909–80
Allison, Luther	Solo	1939–97
Almeida, Laurindo	L.A. Four, session guitarist	1917–95
Amigo, Vicente	Manolo Sanlucar	b. 1967
Andress, Tuck	Tuck & Patti	b. 1952
Antoine, Marc	Session guitarist, solo	b. 1963
Asheton, Ron	Iggy Pop, the Stooges	1948–09
Atkins, Chet	The Country All-Stars, the Nashville String Band, solo	1924–01
Bachman, Randy	Guess Who, Bachman-Turner Overdrive	b. 1943
Bailey, Derek	Spontaneous Music Ensemble, session guitarist	1930–05
Baker, Mickey "Guitar"	Mickey & Sylvia, session guitarist	b. 1925
Barbosa-Lima, Carlos	Solo	b. 1944
Barnes, George	Session guitarist, solo	1921–77
Barre, Martin	Jethro Tull	b. 1946
Barrett, Syd	Pink Floyd, Stars, solo	1946–06
Barrueco, Manuel	Solo	b. 1952
Basho, Robbie	Solo	1940–86
Batio, Michael Angelo	Nitro, solo	b. 1956
Batten, Jennifer	Jeff Beck, Michael Jackson, solo	b. 1957
Bauer, Billy	Session guitarist	1915–05
Beach, Reb	Winger, Dokken, Whitesnake	b. 1963
Beamer, Keola	Solo	b. 1951
Bean, Billy	Session guitarist, solo	b. 1933
Becker, Jason	Cacophony, David Lee Roth Band, solo	b. 1969
Belew, Adrian	King Crimson, the Bears, Gaga, session guitarist, solo	b. 1949
Bell, Eric	Thin Lizzy	b. 1947
Bensusan, Pierre	Solo	b. 1957
Bhatt, Vishwa Mohan	Solo	b. 1952
Bhattacharya, Debashish	Solo	b. 1963
Bickert, Ed	Session guitarist	b. 1932
Blackwell, Scrapper	Duo with Leroy Carr, solo	1903–62
Blake, Norman	June Carter, Bob Dylan	b. 1938
Blind, Blake	Session guitarist, solo	1893–33
Bloomfield, Mike	The Paul Butterfield Blues Band, Electric Flag, Al Kooper, solo	1943–81
Boggs, Noel	Bob Wills & the Texas Playboys	1917–74
Bolin, Tommy	James Gang, Deep Purple	1951–76
Bonamassa, Joe	Solo	b. 1977
Bonfa, Luiz	Solo	1922–01
Boon, D.	The Minutemen	1958–85
Box, Mick	Uriah Heep	b. 1947
Boyd, Liona	Solo	b. 1949
Bratta, Vito	White Lion	b. 1961
Bream, Julian	The Julian Bream Consort, solo	b. 1933
Breau, Lenny	CKY Caravan, Three, solo	1941–84
Bresh, Thom	Solo	b. 1948
Bromberg, David	Bob Dylan, Jerry Garcia, George Harrison, solo	b. 1945
Brooks, Lonnie	Session guitarist, solo	b. 1933
Broonzy, Big Bill	Solo	1898–58
Brown, Gatemouth	Solo	1924–05
Brown, Junior	Solo	b. 1952
Brown, Norman	Boyz II Men, Stevie Wonder, solo	b. 1963
Brozman, Bob	The Cheap Suit Serenaders, solo	b. 1954
Bruce, Jack	Cream, Manfred Mann, West, Bruce & Laing	b. 1943
Bruno, Jimmy	Frank Sinatra, Buddy Rish, solo	b. 1953
Bryant, Jimmy	West	1925–80
Buchanan, Roy	Solo	1939–88
Buckingham, Lindsey	Fleetwood Mac	b. 1949
Buckley, Jeff	Session guitarist, solo	1966–97
Bull, Sandy	Solo	1941–01
Bullock, Hiram	Pete Townshend, Eric Clapton, Miles Davis, solo	1955–08
Burrell, Kenny	Stan Getz, Billie Holiday, Johnny Coltrane	b. 1931
Burton, James	Rick Nelson, Elvis Presley, John Denver, solo	b. 1939
Butler, Bernard	Suede, McAlmont and Butler, the Tears, solo	b. 1970
Buxton, Glen	Alice Cooper	1947–97
Byrd, Jerry	Country All Stars	1920–05
Byrd, Charlie	Stan Getz	1925–99
California, Randy	Spirit, solo	1951–97
Campbell, Glenn	Solo	b. 1936
Campbell, Mike	Tom Petty & the Heartbreakers	b. 1950
Campbell, Vivian	Dio, Whitesnake, Def Leppard	b. 1962
Carlton, Larry	Fourplay, solo	b. 1948
Carmichael, Greg	Acoustic Alchemy	b. 1953
Carter, Maybelle	The Carter Family	1909–78
Carthy, Martin	Steeleye Span, The Albion Band	b. 1941
Chad, Dominic	Mansun, solo	b. 1972
Chadbourne, Eugene	Shockabilly	b. 1954
Chaquico, Craig	Jefferson Starship, Starship, solo	b. 1954
Christ, John	Danzig, solo	b. 1965
Christian, Charlie	Benny Goodman Sextet and Orchestra, solo	1916–42
Cipollina, John	Quicksilver Messenger Service	1943–89
Clark, Steve	Def Leppard	1960–91
Clark, Roy	Solo	b. 1933
Clarke, Stanley	Return to Forever, Chick Corea	b. 1951
Cochran, Eddie	Solo	1938–60
Collins, Albert	Solo	1932–93
Collins, Allen	Lynyrd Skynyrd	1952–90
Connors, Bill	Return to Forever, solo	b. 1949
Conti, Robert	Solo	b. 1945
Cooder, Ry	Session guitarist, solo	b. 1947
Copeland, Johnny	Solo	1937–97
Coryell, Larry	Session guitarist, solo	b. 1943
Coulter, William	Orison, solo	b. 1959
Cray, Robert	Solo	b. 1953
Crayton, Pee Wee	Solo	1914–85
Cropper, Steve	The Blues Brothers, session guitarist, solo	b. 1941
Dadi, Marcel	Solo	1951–96
Darrell, Dimebag	Pantera	1966–04
Davis, Rev. Gary	Solo	1896–72
DeGarmo, Chris	Queensryche, Jerry Cantrell	b. 1963
Degrassi, Alex	Solo	b. 1952
DeMartini, Warren	Ratt	b. 1963
Dharma, Buck	Blue Oyster Cult	b. 1947

Diaz, Alirio	Solo	b. 1923	
Dibala, Diblo	Loketo, Matchatcha	b. 1954	
Diorio, Joe	Solo	b. 1936	
Dominguez, Juanjo	Solo	b. 1951	
Donelly, Tanya	Throwing Muses, the Breeders, solo	b. 1966	
Donohue, Pat	Solo	b. 1953	
Drake, Nick	Solo	1948–74	
Duarte, Chris	The Chris Duarte Group, session guitarist	b. 1963	
Duffy, Billy	The Cult	b. 1961	
Eaglin, Snooks	Solo	1936–09	
Earl, Ronnie	Roomful of Blue	b. 1953	
Einziger, Mike	Incubus	b. 1976	
Eklundh, Mattias "I.A."	Freak Kitchen	b. 1969	
Ellis, Herb	Oscar Peterson Trio, Ella Fitzgerald	b. 1921	
Ellis, Tinsley	Solo	b. 1957	
Emmanuel, Tommy	Goldrush, Tina Turner, solo	b. 1955	
Emmett, Rik	Triumph	b. 1953	
Emmons, Buddy	The Everly Brothers	b. 1937	
Entwistle, John	The Who	1944–02	
Escudero, Mario	Solo	1928–04	
Eubanks, Kevin	The Tonight Show Band, the Primetime Band, solo	b. 1957	
Fahey, John	Solo	1939–01	
Farlow, Tal	Red Norvo, Artie Shaw, solo	1921–98	
Farriss, Tim	INXS, solo	b. 1957	
Fats, Hollywood	James Harman	1954–86	
Fernandez, Julio	Spyro Gyra	b. 1954	
Finger, Peter	Solo	b. 1954	
Fisk , Eliot	Solo	b. 1954	
Flatt, Lester	Flatt & Scruggs	1914–79	
Ford, Robben	Charles Ford Blues Band, solo	b. 1951	
Ford, Lita	The Runaways, solo	b. 1958	
Frame, Roddy	Aztec Camera, solo	b. 1964	
Freeman, Russ	The Rippingtons, Mariah Carey	b. 1960	
Fripp, Robert	King Crimson, session guitarist, solo	b. 1946	
Frisell, Bill	Solo	b. 1951	
Frith, Fred	Henry Crow, solo	b. 1949	
Fulson, Lowell	Solo	1921–99	
Funderburgh, Anson	The Rockets, the Fabulous Thunderbirds	b. 1954	
Gaines, Steve	Lynyrd Skynyrd	1949–77	
Galbraith, Paul	Solo	b. 1964	
Gallagher, Rory	Taste, solo	1948–95	
Gallup, Cliff	Gene Vincent's Blue Caps, solo	1930–88	
Gambale, Frank	Chick Corea, Vital Information, solo	b. 1958	
Garland, Hank	Elvis Presley, solo	1930–04	
Garrett, Amos	Stony Plain, solo	b. 1941	
Gatton, Danny	Liz Meyer & Friends, solo	1945–94	
Gaughan, Dick	Solo	b. 1948	
Geissman, Grant	Solo	b. 1953	
George, Lowell	Little Feat, solo	1945–79	
Geremia, Paul	Solo	b. 1944	
Gill, Andy	Gang of Four	b. 1956	
Gillis, Brad	Night Ranger, Ozzy Osbourne	b. 1957	
Ginn, Greg	Black Flag	b. 1954	
Golub, Jeff	Solo	b. 1955	
Goodrick, Mick	Solo	b. 1945	
Goodsall, John	Brand X, session guitarist	b. 1952	
Gorham, Scott	Thin Lizzy	b. 1951	
Gossard, Stone	Pearl Jam, Temple of the Dog	b. 1966	
Graham, Davey	Solo	1940–08	
Green, Freddie	Count Basie	1911–87	
Green, Grant	Blue Note Records, solo	1935–79	
Green, Mick	The Pirates, Van Morrison	1944–10	
Greenwich, Sonny	Charles Lloyd, Hank Mobley	b. 1936	
Grossman, Stefan	Even Dozen Jug Band, solo	b. 1945	
Guns, Tracii	Guns N' Roses, L.A. Guns	b. 1966	
Guthrie, Woody	Solo	1912–67	
Hackett, Steve	Genesis, Quiet World, GTR, solo	b. 1950	
Hall, Jim	Bill Evans, Pat Metheny	b. 1930	
Hammond, John Paul	Solo	b. 1942	
Hanneman, Jeff	Slayer	b. 1964	
Hannon, Frank	Tesla	b. 1966	
Harper, Roy	Nick Harper, Dave Gilmour	b. 1941	
Harper, Nick	Roy Harper	b. 1965	
Harris, Corey	Solo	b. 1969	
Hart, Alvin Youngblood	Solo	b. 1963	
Harvey, P.J.	Solo	b. 1969	
Hayward, Justin	Moody Blues, solo	b. 1946	
Hazel, Eddie	Parliament-Funkadelic	1950–92	
Healey, Jeff	Solo	1966–08	
Hedges, Michael	Solo	1953–97	
Henderson, Scott	Tribal Tech, solo	b. 1954	
Hicks, Tony	The Hollies	b. 1945	
Hoey, Gary	Vinnie, solo	b. 1960	
Hole, Dave	Solo	b. 1948	
Holly, Buddy	The Crickets, solo	1936–59	
Hooker, Earl	Muddy Waters, solo	1929–70	
Hoopii, Sol	Solo	1902–53	
Hopkins, Lightnin'	Wilson Smith, solo	1912–82	
House, Son	Solo	1902–88	
Howe, Greg	Planet X, solo	b. 1963	
Hughes, Brian	Loreena McKennit, solo	b. 1955	
Hunter, Charlie	Disposable Heroes of Hiphoprisy, solo	b. 1967	
Isbin, Sharon	Solo	b. 1956	
Isley, Ernie	The Isley Brothers, solo	b. 1952	
Izmailov, Enver	Solo	b. 1955	
Jabs, Matthias	Scorpions	b. 1955	
James, Skip	Solo	1902–69	
James, Elmore	Solo	1918–63	
Jefferson, Blind Lemon	Solo	1893–29	
Johns, Daniel	Silverchair, the Dissociatives	b. 1979	
Johnson, Blind Willie	Solo	1897–45	
Johnson, Lonnie	Solo	1899–70	
Johnson, Robert	Solo	1911–38	
Johnson, Alphonso	Weather Report, session guitarist	b. 1951	
Johnson, Orville	Session guitarist, solo	b. 1953	
Johnson, Henry	Solo	b. 1954	
Johnston, Randy	Solo	b. 1956	
Johnstone, Davey	Elton John, Alice Cooper, Meat Loaf	b. 1951	
Jones, Mick	Foreigner	b. 1944	
Jones, Steve	The Sex Pistols	b. 1955	
Jones, Adam	Tool	b. 1965	
Jordan, Stanley	Solo	b. 1959	
Jordan, Ronny	The Flaming Lips	b. 1962	
Juber, Laurence	Wings, session guitarist	b. 1952	
Kaapana, Ledward	Hui 'Ohana, solo	b. 1948	
Kaiser, Henry	Solo	b. 1952	
Kane, Raymond	Solo	1925–08	
Kath, Terry	Chicago	1946–78	
Keaggy, Phil	Glass Harp, session guitarist, solo	b. 1951	
Kendall, Mark	Great White	b. 1957	
Keneally, Mike	Frank Zappa, the Mike Keneally Band, solo	b. 1961	
Kessel, Barney	Session guitarist, solo	1923–04	
Khan, Steve	Steely Dan, Billy Joel, solo	b. 1947	
King, Earl	Solo	1934–03	
King, Freddie	Solo	1934–76	
King, Albert	Solo	b. 1923	
King, Kaki	Solo	b. 1979	
Kirtley, Pat	Solo	b. 1952	
Klugh, Earl	Solo	b. 1953	
Kossoff, Paul	Free, Back Street Crawler, solo	1950–76	
Kottke, Leo	Solo	b. 1945	
Kotzen, Richie	Poison, Mr. Big, solo	b. 1970	

Kraft, Norbert	Solo	b. 1950
Kramer, Wayne	The MC5	b. 1948
Kress, Carl	Session guitarist, solo	1907-65
Kubek, Smokin' Joe	Solo	b. 1956
Lagoya, Alexandre	Solo	1929-99
Lagrene, Bireli	Solo	b. 1966
Lalonde, Larry "Ler"	Primus	b. 1968
Landreth, Sonny	Session guitarist, solo	b. 1951
Lane, Shawn	Black Oak Arkansas, Willy, solo	1963-03
Lang, Eddie	Session guitarist, solo	1902-33
Lang, Peter	Solo	b. 1948
Lang, Jonny	Solo	b. 1981
Latimer, Andy	Camel	b. 1949
Lee, Albert	Session guitarist, solo	b. 1943
Lee, Jake E.	Mickey Ratt, Ozzy Osbourne, Badlands, solo	b. 1957
Legg, Adrian	Solo	b. 1948
Lenoir, J.B.	Solo	1929-67
Levene, Keith	Public Image Ltd.	b. 1957
Lister, Aynsley	Solo	b. 1976
Lockwood Jr., Robert	King Biscuit Time, solo	1915-06
Lofgren, Nils	E Street Band	b. 1951
Lofsky, Lorne	Oscar Peterson Quartet, solo	b. 1954
Loomis, Jeff	Nevermore	b. 1971
Lukather, Steve	Toto, session guitarist, solo	b. 1957
Lynch, George	Dokken, Lynch Mob, solo	b. 1954
MacAlpine, Tony	Planet X, Ring of Fire, solo	b. 1960
Mack, Lonnie	Solo	b. 1941
Maghett, Samuel "Magic Sam"	Solo	1937-69
Mahal, Taj	Solo	b. 1942
Malakian, Daron	System of a Down	b. 1975
Malone, Russell	Session guitarist, solo	b. 1963
Mandel, Harvey	Canned Heat, solo	b. 1945
Mangore, Agustin Barrios	Solo	1885-44
Manzanera, Phil	Roxy Music, solo	b. 1951
Maphis, Joe	Solo	1921-86
Marino, Frank	Mahogany Rush	b. 1954
Marley, Bob	The Wailers, solo	1945-81
Martin, Grady	Session guitarist, solo	1929-01
Martín, Juan	Solo	b. 1948
Martino, Pat	Solo	b. 1944
Martyn, John	Solo	1948-09
Marvin, Hank	Cliff Richard, the Shadows, solo	b. 1941
Mascis, J.	Dinosaur Jr., the Frog	b. 1965
Mason, Brent	Session guitarist, solo	b. 1959
Mayall, John	The Bluesbreakers, solo	b. 1933
Mayfield, Curtis	The Impressions	1942-99
McCartney, Paul	The Quarrymen, the Beatles, Wings	b. 1942
McCollum, Robert Lee	Solo	1909-67
McDowell, "Mississippi" Fred	Solo	1904-72
McGeoch, John	Magazine, Visage	1955-04
McGuinn, Roger	The Byrds, McGuinn, Clark, and Hillman, solo	b. 1942
McKay, Al	Earth, Wind & Fire, L.A. All Stars	b. 1948
McMeen, El	Solo	b. 1947
McTell, Blind Willie	Session guitarist, solo	1898-59
Messer, Michael	The Michael Messer Band, solo	b. 1956
Messina, Jim	Buffalo Springfield, Poco, Loggins and Messina	b. 1947
Miller, Jerry	Moby Grape	b. 1943
Milton, Little	Solo	1934-05
Mitchell, Kim	Max Webster, solo	b. 1952
Mo, Keb	Solo	b. 1951
Montgomery, Wes	Solo	1923-68
Montgomery, Monte	Solo	b. 1966
Montoya, Ramon	Solo	1880-49
Montoya, Carlos	Solo	1903-93
Montoya, Coco	The Bluesbreakers, solo	b. 1951
Montrose, Ronnie	Montrose, Edgar Winter Group	b. 1947

Moore, Oscar	Nat King Cole Trio	1916-81
Moore, Scotty	Elvis Presley, solo	b. 1931
Moore, Vinnie	Alice Cooper, solo	b. 1964
Mottola, Tony	Frank Sinatra, Perry Como, solo	1918-04
Mould, Bob	Hüsker Dü, Sugar, solo	b. 1960
Murphey, Matt "Guitar"	Howlin' Wolf, Blues Brothers	b. 1929
Mustaine, Dave	Metallica, Megadeth	b. 1961
Muthspiel, Wolfgang	Solo	b. 1965
Naumov, Yuri	Solo	b. 1962
Navarro, Ken	Solo	b. 1953
Nawahi, King Bennie	Solo	1899-85
Nichols, Roy	Merle Haggard	1932-01
Nico, Doctor	Grand Kalle & l'African Jazz	1939-85
Nocentelli, Leo	The Meters	b. 1946
Nogueira, Paulinho	Solo	1929-03
Nolen, Jimmy	The J.B.'s (James Brown)	1934-83
Nugent, Ted	Amboy Dukes, Damn Yankees, solo	b. 1948
Nyame, E.K.	Solo	1927-77
Oldfield, Mike	Solo	b. 1953
Ostroushko, Peter	Solo	b. 1953
Otis, Shuggie	Solo	b. 1953
Pahinui, Gabby	Session guitarist, solo	1921-80
Paredes, Carlos	Solo	1925-04
Parfitt, Rick	Status Quo	b. 1948
Parkening, Christopher	Solo	b. 1947
Pass, Joe	Session guitarist, solo	1929-94
Pastorius, Jaco	Weather Report	1951-87
Patton, Charlie	Solo	1891-34
Paul, Gayla Drake	Solo	b. 1964
Pauling, Lowman	The 5 Royales	b. 1973
Peña, Paco	Solo	b. 1942
Perkins, Carl	Solo	1932-98
Phelps, Kelly Joe	Solo	b. 1959
Phillips, Steve	Notting Hillbillies, solo	b. 1963
Pisano, John	Session guitarist	b. 1931
Pitrelli, Al	Trans-Siberian Orchestra, Savatage, Megadeth	b. 1962
Pizzarelli, Bucky	The Three Sounds Trio, solo	b. 1926
Pizzarelli, John	Bucky Pizzarelli, solo	b. 1960
Poland, Chris	OHM, Megadeth, solo	b. 1957
Powell, Andy	Wishbone Ash	b. 1950
Powell de Aquino, Baden	Solo	1937-00
Presti, Ida	Alexandre Lagoya	1924-67
Price, Rod	Foghat, solo	1947-05
Quine, Robert	The Voidoids	1942-04
Rabin, Trevor	Yes	b. 1954
Ralphs, Mick	Bad Company	b. 1944
Ramos, Kid	The Fabulous Thunderbirds	b. 1959
Raney, Jimmy	Red Norvo Trio, solo	1927-95
Ranglin, Ernest	Session guitarist, solo	b. 1932
Reed, Jerry	Session guitarist	1937-08
Reed, Lou	The Velvet Underground	b. 1942
Reed, Preston	Solo	b. 1955
Reinhardt, Django	Stéphane Grappelli, Quintette du Hot Club de France, solo	1910-53
Remler, Emily	Solo	1957-90
Renbourn, John	Bert Jansch, Pentangle, solo	b. 1944
Reynolds, Tim	TR3, Dave Matthews Band	b. 1957
Rhoads, Randy	Ozzy Osbourne, Quiet Riot	1956-82
Rhodes, Red	Session guitarist, solo	1930-95
Ricardo, Nino	Solo	1904-72
Rice, Tony	Solo	b. 1951
Richrath, Gary	REO Speedwagon, solo	b. 1949
Ritenour, Lee	Solo	b. 1952
Roberts, Howard	Session guitarist, solo	1929-92
Robertson, Robbie	The Band, solo	b. 1943
Robertson, Brian	Thin Lizzy, Motorhead	b. 1956
Robillard, Duke	Fabulous Thunderbirds, session guitarist	b. 1948

Robinson, Fenton	Session guitarist	1935–97
Rogers, Roy	Solo	1911–98
Rollo, Zoot Horn	The Magic Band	b. 1948
Romeo, Michael	Symphony X, solo	b. 1968
Romero, Pepe	Los Romeros, solo	b. 1944
Romero, Angel	Los Romeros, solo	b. 1946
Ronson, Mick	David Bowie, Slaughter & the Dogs, Ian Hunter, solo	1946–93
Rosenwinkel, Kurt	Solo	b. 1970
Ross, Don	Solo	b. 1960
Rossington, Gary	Lynyrd Skynyrd, Rossington Band	b. 1951
Rotella, Thom	Solo	b. 1951
Roth, Arlen	Solo	b. 1952
Roth, Uli Jon	Scorpions, Electric Sun, solo	b. 1954
Rowan, Peter	Earth Opera, Seatrain, solo	b. 1942
Rush, Otis	Solo	b. 1935
Russell, David	Solo	b. 1953
Rypdal, Terje	George Russell, Jan Garbarek	b. 1947
Sabicas	Solo	1912–90
Sanlucar, Manolo	Solo	b. 1945
Santiago, Joey	The Pixies, Frank Black, the Martinis	b. 1965
Saraceno, Blues	Poison, solo	b. 1971
Schenker, Michael	Scorpions, UFO, solo	b. 1955
Scholz, Tom	Boston	b. 1947
Seals, Son	Solo	1942–04
Seeger, Pete	The Weavers, solo	b. 1919
Segovia, Andrés	Solo	1893–87
Sergeant, Will	Echo & the Bunnymen, solo	b. 1958
Sete, Bola	A Tribe Called Quest, solo	1923–87
Setzer, Brian	The Stray Cats, the Brian Setzer Orchestra	b. 1959
Shamblin, Eldon	Bob Wills & His Texas Playboys	1916–98
Sharrock, Sonny	Solo	1940–94
Shepherd, Kenny Wayne	Kenny Wayne Shepherd Band	b. 1977
Shields, Kevin	My Bloody Valentine, Primal Scream, solo	b. 1963
Shorty, Guitar	Walter Johnson Band, solo	b. 1939
Simmonds, Kim	Savoy Brown Blues Band, solo	b. 1947
Simon, Paul	Simon & Garfunkel, solo	b. 1941
Simpson, Martin	Jessica Radcliffe, solo	b. 1953
Skolnick, Alex	Testament, Ozzy Osbourne, Savatage, Trans-Siberian Orchestra, Alex Skolnick Trio	b. 1968
Slim, Guitar	Solo	1926–59
Smith, Fred "Sonic"	The MC5	1949–94
Smith, Johnny	Solo	b. 1922
Smith, Robert	The Cure	b. 1959
Smither, Chris	Solo	b. 1944
Söllscher, Göran	Solo	b. 1955
Sor, Fernando	Solo	1778–39
Sparks, Tim	Solo	b. 1954
Squire, John	The Stone Roses	b. 1962
Staples, "Roebuck "Pops"	The Staple Singers	1914–00
Stern, Mike	Mike Stern Group, Miles Davis, solo	b. 1953
Stevens, Steve	Michael Jackson, Billy Idol, Vince Neil, session guitarist	b. 1959
Stuermer, Daryl	Genesis, Phil Collins, solo	b. 1952
Sultan, Kenny	Tom Ball, solo	b. 1950
Sweet, Michael	Stryper	b. 1963
Sykes, John	Blue Murder, Whitesnake, Thin Lizzy	b. 1959
Szabo, Gabor	Chico Hamilton Quintet, solo	1936–82
Tabor, Ty	Kings X, Jelly Bean, Poundhound, Jughead, Platypus	b. 1961
Takasaki, Akira	Lazy, Loudness, Ji-Zo, solo	b. 1961
Tarplin, Marv	The Miracles	b. 1941
Tárrega, Francisco	Solo	1852–09
Taylor, Hound Dog	Solo	1915–75
Taylor, Eddie	Solo	1923–85
Taylor, James	Solo	b. 1948
Taylor, Mick	John Mayall's Bluesbreakers, the Rolling Stones, solo	b. 1949
Taylor, Martin	Solo	b. 1956
Taylor, Andy	Duran Duran	b. 1961

Tedesco, Tommy	Session guitarist	1930–97
Thackery, Jimmy	The Nighthawks, solo	b. 1953
Thal, Ron "Bumblefoot"	Guns N' Roses, Bumblefoot, solo	b. 1969
Tharpe, Sister Rosetta	Solo	1915–73
Thayill, Kim	Soundgarden, No WTO Combo, Probot, Dark Load	b. 1960
Thordendal, Fredrik	Meshuggah	b. 1970
Thorogood, George	The Delaware Destroyers, solo	b. 1950
Tibbetts, Steve	Solo	b. 1954
Timmons, Andy	Danger Danger, Ceili Rain	b. 1963
Tolkki, Timo	Stratovarius	b. 1966
Tosh, Peter	The Wailers, solo	1944–87
Touré, Ali Farka	Solo	1939–06
Towner, Ralph	Oregon, Consort	b. 1940
Traum, Artie	Happy Traum, solo	1943–08
Travers, Pat	Pat Travers Band	b. 1954
Travis, Merle	Solo	1917–83
Tucker, Luther	Luther Tucker Band	1936–93
Ulmer, James Blood	Odyssey, solo	b. 1942
Upchurch, Phil	The Phil Upchurch Combo	b. 1941
Van Eps, George	Session guitarist, solo	1913–98
Vaughan, Jimmy	The Fabulous Thunderbirds	b. 1951
Vega, Suzanne	Solo	b. 1959
Verlaine, Tom	Television, solo	b. 1949
Vestine, Henry	Solo	1944–97
Wakenius, Ulf	Solo	b. 1958
Walker, T-Bone	Solo	1910–75
Walker, Joe Louis	Solo	b. 1949
Walsh, Joe	James Gang, Barnstorm, the Eagles, solo	b. 1947
Ward, Robert	Ohio Untouchables	1938–08
Waters, Muddy	Solo	1915–83
Watson, Johnny "Guitar"	Solo	1935–96
Watson, Doc	Solo	b. 1923
Watson, "Wah Wah"	Session guitarist	c. 1951
Webb, Nick	Acoustic Alchemy	1954–98
Webb, Stan	Chicken Shack	b. 1946
West, Speedy	Jimmy Bryant, session guitarist	1924–03
West, Leslie	Mountain, West, Bruce, and Laing, the Vagrants, solo	b. 1945
White, Robert	The Funk Brothers, session guitarist	1936–94
White, Clarence	The Kentucky Colonels, the Byrds, Nashville West, Muleskinner	1944–73
Whitfield, Mark	Session guitarist, solo	b. 1967
Wilcox, David	Solo	b. 1958
Williams, Robert "Pete"	Solo	1914–80
Williams, John	Solo	b. 1941
Williams, Brooks	Solo	b. 1958
Willis, Eddie	The Funk Brothers, session guitarist	b. 1936
Wilton, Michael	Queensryche	b. 1962
Wisefield, Laurie	Wishbone Ash, Roger Chapman	b. 1952
Womack, Bobby	The Valentinos, solo	b. 1944
Wood, Ron	The Rolling Stones, Faces	b. 1947
Wray, Link	Lucky Wray & the Palomino Hands	1929–05
Wylde, Zakk	Black Label Society, Ozzy Osbourne, solo	b. 1967
Yamashita, Kazuhito	Solo	b. 1961
Yepes, Narciso	Solo	1927–97
York, Andrew	Los Angeles Guitar Quartet, solo	b. 1958
Young, Reggie	Session guitarist	b. 1936
Young, Malcolm	AC/DC	b. 1953

INDEX

A

Abbruzzese, Dave 267
Abts, Matt 69
AC/DC 224, 225
Adams, Bryan 293
Adeline Records 40
Adler, Steve 219
Adrian Smith And Project 220
Aerosmith 75, 85, 100, 101, 190, 218
Aikawa, Nanase 195
Airline guitar 129
Alcatraz 208
Alice in Chains 186, 187, 266
Allman Brothers Band 12, 36, 37, 46, 47, 68, 92, 122
Allman, Duane 36–37, 46, 48, 50, 123
Allman, Gregg 36, 37, 46, 47, 68
Allman Joys 36
Altamont 81, 106
alternative music 227–285
Ament, Jeff 267
American Music Awards 189
A&M Records 30, 183
Anastasio, Trey 38–39, 122
Anderson, John 83
Anderson, Jon 298
Anderson, Paul Thomas 251
Anderson, Wes 293
Andrews Sisters 304
Angel, Criss 182
Animals, the 280
Aniston, Jennifer 147
Anno, Paul 213
Anthony, Michael 216
Apollo Theater 70
Arista Nashville 174
Armageddon (film) 101
Armstrong, Billy Joe 40–41
Armstrong, Louis 163
Arrows, the 74
Arthurs, Paul 247
Ash 254, 255
Asia 298
Asian Dub Foundation 274
Asylum Records 140
Atkin, Jim 304
Atkins, Chet 82, 83, 290
Audioslave 270, 271
Augeri, Steve 157
Austin City Limits Music Festival 63

Avery, Eric 272
Avory, Mick 136, 137
Aware Records 146

B

Baby Animals 182
Back to the Future (film) 45
Bad English 156
Badfinger 144
Badger, Pat 183
Bad Lieutenant 282
Baerwald, David 135
Baez, Joan 164
Baker, Chet 306
Baker, Ginger 48
Baldwin, Donny 12
Balin, Marty 81
Band, Alex 112
Banks, Peter 298
Barrett, Syd 66, 289
Bat for Lashes 254
Bauhaus 241
Bayley, Blaze 197
B.B. King Review 20
BB Steal 189
B. C. Rich guitar 204
  Mockingbird 256
Beach Boys 249
Beacon Theater 24
Beale Street Music Festival 27, 33, 76
Beard, Frank 64, 65
Beatlemania 142, 190
Beatles 22, 50, 60, 70, 90, 95, 108, 138, 142, 143, 144, 210, 234, 247, 248, 249, 284, 290, 294, 300
Because They're Young (film) 55
Beck, Gordon 296
Beck, Jeff 19, 27, 48, 64, 96, 101, 110, 116, 196, 209, 210, 288–289
Bellamy, Matthew 228–229
Bell, Marc Stev3, 277
Belmont University 174
Benno, Marc 30
Benson, Brendan 129
Benson, George 290–291
Berklee College of Music 102, 124, 146, 294, 300, 306
Berry, Bill 230
Berry, Chuck 42–45, 70, 104, 224
Bertinelli, Valerie 126
Bettencourt, Nuno 182–183
Betts, Dickey 37, 46–47, 68
Big Audio Dynamite 262
Bill DeLap 297
Bill & Ted's Excellent Adventure (film) 183
Bird, Andrew 243
Bishop, Elvin 12–13
Bitch 205
Black Eyed Peas 53
Blackheart Records 74

Blackmore, Ritchie 92, 184–185, 196
Blackmore's Night 184, 185
Black Rock Coalition 215
Black Sabbath 193, 202, 203, 241
Black Velvet Band 264
Blade, Wayne 185
Bley, Paul 300
Blind Faith 48, 51
Blondie 76, 255
Bloomfield, Mike 32
Blue Army 100
Blue Balls Festival 141
Blue Ridge Rangers 140
blues 11–33, 42, 63, 113, 142, 143, 157, 164, 177, 186, 224, 280
  blues rock 289
Blur 238, 239
Bo Diddley Beat 15
Bogert, Tim 288
Bolan, Marc 264
Bonehead 247
Bonfires and Amplifiers Tour 175
Bonham, Jason 96
Bonham, John 96, 99
Bon Jovi 110, 111, 201
Bon Jovi, Jon 111
Bonnaroo 21
Bono 56, 57, 230
Boogie Nights (film) 13
boogie rock 140
Boo Radleys 239
Borau, José Luis 293
bossa nova 300
Bowie, David 30, 58, 84, 119, 253, 289, 301
Bown, Andrew 59, 109
Brakhage, Stan 278
Bramhall, Doyle 30
Branca, Glenn 278
Branch, Michelle 112
Brewers Droop 82
British Invasion 106, 138
Britpop 118, 275
Brock, Isaac 264
Broken Arrow 54
Brooker, Gary 121
Brookes, Steve 284
Brooks, Garth 68
Browne, Jackson 30
Bruce, Jack 48, 120
Bruford, Bill 296
Bryan, David 111
Buck, Peter 230–231
Buckethead 232–233
Budokan 95
Buffalo Springfield 130, 154
Buggles 298
Bumbershoot music and arts festival 74, 171
Burke, Clem 277
Burnett, Chester. *See* Howlin' Wolf
Burns London guitar 238
Burr, Clive 196

Burrell, Kenny 294
Burton, Cliff 201
Burton, Gary 300
Bush, Kate 254, 288
Butler, Geezer 203
Butterfield, Paul 12, 210

C

Cacophony 194
Cadillac guitar 15
Cain, Jonathan 156, 157
Caldwell, Bobby 33
Camarón, de la Isla 292
Camp Freddy 272, 273
Cantrell, Jerry 186–187
Capricorn Records 92
Carbon/Silicon 262
Carey, Mariah 214
Carlos, Bun E. 95
Carlton, Larry 173
Carpenter, Mary Chapin 83
Carr, Eric 193
Carroll, Brian. *See* Buckethead
Carter Family 160
Carter, June 160, 161, 162
Carvin guitar 297
Casady, Jack 81
Cash, Johnny 160–163, 164, 264, 270
Cash, Roseanne 168
Castillo, Randy 211
Castronovo, Deen 156
Cat Power 253
Cavalera, Max 253
CBGB 77, 215, 276
CBS Records 113
Celestial-Smith, Mathew 121
Chamberlin, Jimmy 240
Chambers, Martin 259
Charles, Ray 306, 307
Charlie's Angels (film) 101
Cheap Trick 74, 94, 95, 260
Cherone, Gary 126, 183
Chess Records 42
Chicago Blues Festival 21
Chimes, Terry 262
Chinmoy, Sri 113
Chitlin' Circuit 70
Christian, Charlie 296
Chuck Berry: Hail! Hail! Rock 'n' Roll (film) 44
Clapton, Eric 16, 19, 21, 24, 27, 30, 36, 37, 48–51, 68, 70, 78, 96, 110, 119, 122, 126, 144, 147, 154, 156, 161, 209, 258, 288, 289, 296
Clark, Dick 55
Clark, Gilby 219
Clark, Steve 188
Clash 14, 227, 262, 263, 276, 284
classical music 248, 280, 285
Clayton, Adam 56, 57
Cobain, Frances Bean 237
Cobain, Kurt 234–237, 252, 253

Coe, David Allan 68
Coghlan, John 109
Coleman, Ornette 300
Cole, Nat King 291, 304
Collen, Phil 188–189, 221
Collins, Phil 51
Colosseum II 90
Coltrane, John 296
Columbia Records 32, 139, 146,
    160, 164, 290, 291
Colvin, Douglas. See Ramone,
    Dee Dee
Commerford, Tim 270
Concert for Bangladesh 144
Constanten, Tom 80
Conundrum 170
Cook, Paul 74
Copeland, Stewart 38, 280, 281
Corea, Chick 294, 295, 300
Corgan, Billy 202, 240–241, 260,
    261
Cornell, Chris 270
Coryell, Larry 292, 294
Cosmopolitan magazine 228
Costello, Elvis 178
Cotton, James 12
country music 143, 159–179, 186
Cow Palace 115
Coxon, Graham 238–239
Cox, Terry 171
Cray, Robert 30
Crazy Horse 130
Cream 27, 48, 50, 70, 120, 126,
    218
Creedence Clearwater Revival
    140, 141
Cribs, the 264, 278
Criss, Peter 192
Crook, Bill 175
Crook Custom Guitars 175
Cropredy Festival 179
Crosby, Bing 304
Crosby, David 130, 154, 155
Crosby, Stills and Nash 154
Crosby, Stills, Nash and Young 155
Cross, Christopher 78
Crossroads Guitar Festival 169
Crouch End Festival Chorus 139
Crow, Sheryl 134–135, 169, 258
Crüe Fest 211
Crystal Method 270
Cummings, John William.
    See Ramone, Johnny
Cunningham, Phil 282
Cure, the 241
Currie, Cherie 74, 77
Curtis, Ian 282
Cybernauts 189
Cypress Hill 273

D
Daft Punk 229
Dale, Dick 52–53
Daltrey, Roger 116, 118, 119

Dave Matthews Band 24, 68, 270
Davies, Dave 136–137, 138
Davies, Ray 136, 137, 138–139
Davis, Miles 295, 300, 302, 306
Dead Weather 128, 129
Death Cube K 232
Death in Vegas 284
Decoding Society 214
Deconstruction 272
Deep Purple 92, 93, 184, 185, 196,
    208, 216
Def Jam 205
Def Leppard 188, 189, 276
de la Isla, Camarón 292
Deli Creeps 232
Delinquents 262
Del-Tones 52
de Lucía, Paco 292–293, 294
Densmore, John 86, 87
Derek and the Dominos 48
Derek Trucks Band 122, 123
Derringer, Rick 33
Desert Sessions 256
DeVille, C. C. 190–191
Diamond Lie 186
Di'Anno, Paul 196
Dickey Betts and Great Southern
    46
Dickey Betts Band 46, 68
Dickinson, Bruce 197, 213
Diddley, Bo 12, 14–15, 44
DiFranco, Ani 227, 242–243
Di Meola, Al 292, 293, 294–295
Dinosaur Jr. 236
Dio, Ronnie James 203
Dire Straits 82, 168
Dirnt, Mike 41
Dixie Dregs 92
Doherty, Pete 238
Donegan, Lonnie 142
Donovan 96
Doors, the 86, 87
Double Trouble 30
Downes, Geoff 298
Downing, K. K. 222, 223
Dozier, Lamont 291
DramaGod 182
Drama Kings 174
Dream, the 183
Dream Theater 102, 103
Drift 278
Dryden, Spencer 81
Dunlop 59
DuVall, William 187
Dylan, Bob 55, 129, 144, 145,
    161, 164–165, 170, 299

E
Eagles 166, 167
Eagles of Death Metal 256
Earth 150
Earth, Wind and Fire 24
Easton, Sheena 151
Eddie Howell 90

Eddy, Duane 54–55
Edge 56–57, 99
Edson, Richard 278
Ed Sullivan Show (television series)
    14, 64, 87, 142
Edwards, John "Rhino" 109
Electromagnets 78
Electronic 264, 282, 283
electronica 215, 229
electronic file sharing 201
Elektra Records 211
Ellington, Duke 84
Elvin Bishop Group 12, 13
EMI Records 213
Endless Tour 60
Entwistle, John 116, 118, 119
Erdeli, Tomas 276
Eric Johnson Group 78
Erlandsson, Adrian 204
ESP guitar 111, 200
    KH—20 199
Esquire magazine 147
Eureka Street (television series) 274
Evans, David. See Edge
Everly Brothers 42
Exodus 198
Extreme 182

F
Fairport Convention 178, 179
Falcon and the Snowman (film) 301
Falcones 62
Family Band 24
Farlow, Tal 294
Farm Aid 130
Farndon, Pete 259
Favored Nations Records 124
Felder, Don 166–167
Fender guitar 31, 53, 93, 127, 238,
    245, 250, 262, 266
    Dave Murray signature model
        212
    Jazzmaster 268, 278
    Number One 31
    Stevie Ray Vaughan Signature
        model Stratocaster 31
    Stratocaster 31, 47, 67, 72,
        111, 120, 146, 179, 184,
        196, 209, 212, 241, 258,
        289–290
    Stratocaster Rosewood 79
    Stratocaster Sunburst 62
    Telecaster 47, 108, 168, 190,
        265, 280
    Telecaster Deluxe 278
    Tribute series 31
Ferrington, Danny 179
Ferry, Bryan 255
Fertita, Dean 257
Fever Ray 254
Fillmore East 12, 32, 37
Finn, Neil 274
First Act guitar 62
Fishman, Jon 39

flamenco guitar 86
Fleetwood Mac 16, 58, 90, 91, 101
Fleetwood, Mick 16, 17
Flowers, Brendon 41
Fogerty, John 54, 140–141
Fogerty, Tom 140, 141
folk music 92, 159–179, 224, 230,
    284, 285
Folsom Prison 161
Foo Fighters 236, 252, 253, 256,
    257
Forbes, Doug 59
Ford, Mary 304
Ford, Tennessee Ernie 298
Foreign Press 282
Forrest Gump (film) 54
Fountains of Wayne 260
Fourth Dimension 303
Fowley, Kim 77
Fox, Jackie 77
Fox, Michael J. 45
Framptone 59
Frampton, Peter 58–59, 92
Frankenstrat 127
Freddie Mercury Tribute Concert
    for AIDS Awareness 183
Free Form Funky Freqs 214
Frehley, Ace 192–193
Frey, Glenn 167
Friedman, Marty 194–195, 249
Frost, Bernie 108
Frusciante, John 244–245
Fulson, Lowell 30
Fulton-Webb amp 79
funk 215
Furay, Richie 130, 154
Fur Peace Ranch 81

G
G3 tour 102, 124, 208, 216, 248,
    249
Gallagher, Liam 246, 247
Gallagher, Noel 41, 238, 246–247,
    265
Gamma Ray 256, 257
Garbage 253
Garcia, Jerry 60–61, 81
Gary Moore Band 90
Garza, Henry 62–63
Garza, Jojo 63
Garza, Ringo 63
Gathering of the Vibes 25
Geary, Paul 183
Genesis 298
Gershon, Gina 273
Gers, Janick 196–197, 213, 221
Gibbons, Billy 64–65, 257
Gibson guitar 17, 56, 64, 80, 93,
    99, 123, 127, 200, 238, 256,
    266
    Blueshawk 23
    Cara 192
    Country Western 134
    development with Les Paul 305

ES—335 157
ES—355 23
Explorer 57
Flying V 137, 198
Hummingbird 134
Les Paul 16, 17, 37, 68, 91, 101,
    140, 157, 192, 218, 240,
    273, 305
Les Paul BFG 91
Les Paul Goldtop 47, 220
Les Paul Junior 262
Les Paul Standard 65
Little Lucille 23
Lucille 23
Pearly Gates 65
SG 37, 47, 50, 188, 224, 282
Gilbert, Gillian 282
Gilbert, Kevin 135
Gilbert, Paul 248–249
Gillan, Ian 185, 196
Gill, Vince 168–169, 174
Gilmour, David 66–67, 103, 178,
    289
Girl 188
Girly Sound 148
glam rock 262, 276
G&L guitar
    Cantrell Rampage 186
Glover, Roger 93
Goddard College 39
Gogmagog 196
Golliwogs 140
Gong 296
Good Morning America (television
    series) 50
Goodrick, Mick 300
Gordon, Kim 269, 278, 279
Gordon, Mike 39
gospel 14
Gossard, Stone 267
Gov't Mule 68, 69
Graham, Bill 37
Grand Ole Opry 174
Grant, Amy 169
Grateful Dead 14, 38, 60, 68, 69,
    80, 306
Gray, Macy 273
Greatest, the (film) 290–291
Greco, José 292
Green Day 40, 271
Green, Peter 16–17, 90, 91
Greenwood, Colin 274, 275
Greenwood, Jonny 238, 250–251,
    274, 275
Gretsch guitar 15, 245
    Chet Atkins 6120 55
    Country Gentleman 142
Grohl, Dave 202, 236, 237,
    252–253, 256, 257
grunge 234
GTR 298
Guild guitar 137
guitar
    double-necked guitar 99, 249

eighteen-stringed guitar 278
resonator guitar 123
twelve-string guitar 144, 300
seven-string guitar 124
pedal steel guitar
slide guitar 25, 144 25
Guitar Hero video game 53, 78
Guitar Player magazine 54, 93,
    232, 248, 249
Guitar Slim 19
guitar smashing 116, 119
Guitar World magazine 202, 241
Guns N' Roses 215, 218, 232, 261,
    289
Guthrie, Woody 164
Guy, Buddy 18–19, 21, 30, 42, 48,
    50, 122, 147, 224
Guyton, Andrew 89
Gypsy guitar 290
Gypsy Sun and Rainbows 70

H
Hackett, Steve 298
Hackford, Taylor 44
Hagar, Sammy 126, 216
hair metal 211
Halford, Rob 222, 257
Hall & Oates 153
Hamer guitar 214
    Phantom GT 223
Hamilton, Tom 100
Hammer, Jan 156
Hammer of the Gods 248
Hammett, Kirk 198–199, 201
Hancock, Herbie 147, 300
Hanson 260
Hard Day's Night, A (film) 145
Hardline 156
hard rock 181–225
Harris, Emmylou 83
Harrison, George 54, 59, 142–145
Harry, Debbie 76
Hart, Mickey 60
Harvard University 176, 270
Harvey, PJ 254
Hathaway, Donny 291
Hatherley, Charlotte 254–255
Have Gun—Will Travel (television
    series) 55
Have, Václav 309
Hayes, Isaac 307
Haynes, Warren 46, 68–69, 122,
    307
Hazlewood, Lee 55
Headon, "Topper" 263
Heaven and Hell 202
heavy metal 137, 181–225, 289
Heil, Bob 59
Hendrix, Jimi 19, 48, 62, 64, 67,
    68, 70–73, 90, 101, 110, 120,
    137, 150, 154, 198, 199, 200,
    208, 212, 220, 241, 249, 266,
    272, 302
Henley, Don 167

Herd, the 58, 59
Herrera, Raymond 204
Hetfield, James 103, 200–201
Highwaymen, the 161
Hill, Dusty 64, 65
hip-hop 153
Hobbs, Randy Jo 33
Holdsworth, Allan 296–297
Hole 237
Holly, Buddy 42, 164
Hollywood Rose 218
Homme, Josh 256–257
Honeyman-Scott, James 259
Hooker, William 278
Hook, Peter 282
Hooters, the 153
Hot Tuna 80
Hour Glass 36
Houston, Whitney 290
Howe, Dylan 299
Howe, Steve 298–299
Howe, Virgil 299
Howlin' Wolf 26, 27
Hudson, Saul. See Slash
Humble Pie 58
Hurricane Katrina 14
Hutton, Timothy 301
Hyman, Jeffrey 276
hymnal music 14
Hynde, Chrissie 139, 258–259

I
Ibanez guitar 124, 194
    AS—200 306
    JSM100 306
    JS signature series 217
    Paul Gilbert signature line 249
    RG 273
Ibrahim, Aziz 285
Iha, James 240, 260–261
Ike and Tina Turner 28, 141
Ike Turner & the Family Vibes 29
Imperial College London 89
indie music 227–253
Internet radio 272
In the Pink 183
INXS 258
Iommi, Tony 202–203, 253
iPod 268
Iron Maiden 196, 197, 205, 212,
    213, 220, 276
Isley Brothers 70
It Might Get Loud (film) 99
iTunes 153, 157
Ivy 260

J
Jackie Brenston and His Delta
    Cats 28
Jackson, Alan 174
Jackson guitar 188, 194
    Dinky 220
Jackson, Michael 189, 218, 224,
    233

Jackson, Ronald Shannon 214
Jades, the 130
Jagger, Mick 84, 104, 106, 107,
    215, 288
Jam, the 139, 284, 285
Jam Band 100
James, Elmore 28, 123
James, Rick 150
James, Tony 262
Jane's Addiction 261, 272, 273
Jansch, Bert 170–171
Japanese television 195
jazz 113, 142, 143, 173, 278, 280,
    284, 285, 287–309, 290
Jeff Beck Group 288, 289
Jefferson Airplane 80, 81
Jefferson Starship 12
Jeffersons, the (television series) 84
Jennings, Waylon 161
Jethro Tull 201, 298
Jett, Joan 74–77
Jimi Hendrix Experience 70, 72
Joan Jett and the Blackhearts
    74–75
Joe Perry Project 100
Johanson, Jai Johanny 37, 47
John Mayall & the Bluesbreakers
    16, 48
John Mayer Trio 147
Johnnie Johnson Trio 42
"Johnny B. Goode" (song) 45
Johnny Cash Show (television series)
    163
Johnny Winter And 33
Johnson, Brian 225
Johnson, Don 46
Johnson, Eric 78–79, 92, 216
Johnson, Robert 50
Jolie, Angelina 148
Jonathan Winters Show (television
    show) 87
Jone, Mick 262–263
Jones, Brian 106, 258
Jones, John Paul 96, 99, 269
Jones, Mick 258
Jones, Steve 74
Jordan, Steve 307
Journey 156, 157, 182
Joy Division 282
J-pop 195
Judas Priest 205, 213, 222, 223,
    248, 257
Junior Wells Band 18

K
Kansas 94
Kantner, Paul 80, 81
Kato, Nash 149
Kaukonen, Jorma 80–81
Kaye, Tony 298
Kent State 130, 258
Kerrang! magazine 228
Khan, Chaka 173
Khan, Nusrat Fateh Ali 123

Killers, the 41
Kimmel, Jimmy 205
King, Albert 30, 50, 90, 137
King, B.B. 12, 14, 17, 20–23, 33, 36, 48, 50, 62, 64, 70, 82, 112, 147, 174, 214, 224
King Crimson 296, 298
King Diamond 253
King, Freddie 48, 50
King, Kerry 204–205
Kings of Rhythm 28, 29
Kinks 96, 119, 136, 137, 138, 139, 259, 284
Kirwan, Danny 17
Kiske, Michael 220
Kiss 85, 94, 110, 111, 190, 192, 213
Kitade, Nana 195
Kizart, Willie 28
Knights, Dave 121
Knopfler, Mark 82–83, 168
Kobayashi, Yutaka 294
Konk studio 137
Kooper, Al 32
Kramer guitar 111
Kravitz, Lenny 84–85
Kreutzmann, Bill 60
Krieger, Robby 86–87
Kristofferson, Kris 83, 161
Kroeger, Chad 112
Kyuss 256

L
LaBrie, James 103
Ladyhawke 254
Ladytron 260
Laguna, Kenny 74–75
Lamont Cranston Band 266
Lancaster, Alan 109
Landman, Yuri 278
Lanegan, Mark 257
Lange, Mutt 189
Languedoc, Paul 38
Lansing, James B. 53
Lant, Conrad "Cronos" 253
Laswell, Bill 232
Late Late Show (television show) 182
Latin music 113
Leadon, Bernie 166, 167
Led Zeppelin 27, 85, 96, 99, 101, 198, 218, 248, 269
Lee, Geddy 207
Lee, Tommy 210, 211
Legends of Rock 'n' Roll concert 44
Lemmy 253
Lennon, John 22, 63, 95, 142, 143
Lesh, Phil 38, 60, 69, 80, 122, 306
Les Paul Show (television series) 304
Levene, Keith 262
Liberto , Vivian 160
Life Aquatic with Steve Zissou, the (film) 293
Lifeson, Alex 50, 206–207

Liggins, Jimmy 29
Linkin Park 229
LiPuma, Tommy 291
Liquid Tension Experiment 102
Little Richard 44, 64, 164
Live 8 concert 66
Liverpool John Moores University 89
Living Colour 214
Living Loud 92
Lock Up 270
Lollapalooza 269, 278
London SS 262
London Symphony Orchestra 108
Lord, Jon 93
Los Angeles Philharmonic Orchestra 303
Los Lonely Boys 62
Love, Courtney 235, 236, 237
Lovefixer 195
Lovin' Spoonful 60
Lowdens guitar 179
Lydon, John 41, 124
Lynne, Jeff 145
Lynott, Phil 90
Lynyrd Skynyrd 37

M
Machine Head 204
Mack, Lonnie 137
Madison Square Garden 154, 281
Madonna 84
Mad Season 266
Mahavishnu Orchestra 113, 295, 302
Make Some Noise Project 63
Malmsteen, Yngwie 208–209, 233, 248
Manassas 154
Manson, Hugh 228
Manzarek, Ray 87
Marçal, Armando 301
Margolin, Bob 26
Marquee Club 96
Marriott, Steve 59
Marr, Johnny 264–265, 282, 283
Mars, Mick 210–211
Martin, Dewey 130
Martin, George 95
Martin guitar 79, 111, 245
    D—35 162
Martino, Pat 300
Mary Kaye Trio 64
Mason, Nick 66
Matador Records 148, 269
Maton guitar 256
Matsuura, Takeomi 195
Matthews, Dave 38, 294
Max's Kansas City 276
Mayall, John 21, 48
May, Brian 88–89, 182
Mayer, John 50, 123, 146–147, 307
Mayfield, Curtis 285

Mays, Lyle 300
McCarroll, Tony 247
McCartney, Paul 54, 142, 143, 277
McConnell, Page 39
McCready, Mike 266–267
McCusker, John 238
McEntire, Reba 169, 174
McGuian, Paul 247
McKagan, Duff 219
McKernan, Pigpen 60
McLaughlin, John 113, 292, 293, 294, 295, 300, 302–303
McShee, Jacqui 171
McVie, John 16, 17
Medeski, John 24
Medeski Martin & Wood 24, 306
Megadeth 194, 195, 200, 204, 205
Meisner, Randy 167
Melody Maker magazine 51
Mercury, Freddie 88
Mercury Records 111
Merseybeat 142
Metallica 198, 199, 200, 201
Metheny, Pat 300–301
Metropole Orchestra 125
Michaels, Bret 190
Mills, Mike 230
Mingus, Charles 173, 306
Minneapolis sound 151
Mitchell, Joni 130, 172–173, 269, 300
Mitchell, Mitch 70, 73
Moby 273
Modest Mouse 264
Modrego, Ricardo 292
Molina, Ralph 130
Monkees 234
Monterey International Pop Festival 81
Montgomery, Wes 300
Montreux Jazz Festival 29, 30
Moon, Keith 116, 118
Moonlander guitar 278, 279
Moore, Gary 90–91
Moore, Thurston 268–269, 278, 279
Morello, Tom 270–271
Morissette, Alanis 176
Morrison, Jim 87
Morrissey 258, 264, 265
Morris, Stephen 282
Morse, Dave 92
Morse, Steve 92–93, 103, 185
Mortensen, Viggo 232
Moses, Bob 300
Moss, Jon 258
Mothers of Invention 308, 309
Mötley Crüe 210, 211
Motor Ave guitar 256
Motörhead 218, 253
Mourning Widows 182
Moving Sidewalks 64
MP3 files 251

Mr. Big 248
MTV 102, 111, 128, 148, 150, 153, 187, 189, 201, 219, 235, 267
Mullen, Larry Jr 56, 57
Murray, Dave 212–213, 220, 221
Muse 228, 229
M.U.S.E. 177
Music Man guitar 93, 102
Music Rising 56
MusicYo guitar 111
Mustaine, Dave 195, 198, 200, 201, 204, 205
My Morning Jacket 198
MySpace 153, 241
Myung, John 103

N
Napster 201
Nash, Graham 155
Nashville (television series) 174
National Music Museum 23
Natural Born Killers (film) 54
Navarro, Dave 272–273
Nazz 152
Neil, Vince 211
Nelson, Willie 62, 161
Network 40
New Order 282, 283
Newport Jazz Festival 71
Newsted, Jason 201
New Tony Williams Lifetime 296
New World Sinfonia 294
New York Dolls 262
New York University 190, 306
Nice, the 298
Nielsen, Rick 94–95
Night, Candice 184
Nightcrawlers 30
Nighthawks 68
Nightnurse 254
Nightwatchman 270
Nine Inch Nails 253, 257
Nirvana 187, 234, 235, 236, 252, 253, 261
NME magazine 107, 228, 258
Noise Festival 269
noise rock 269
North Mississippi Allstars 24
Notting Hillbillies 83
Novoselic, Krist 234, 237, 252, 253
No Wave 278
Nunez, Joe 204
Nussbaum, Adam 306

O
O2 Wireless Festival 129
Oakley, Berry 37, 46, 47
O.A.R. (Of a Revolution) 24
Oasis 41, 238, 239, 246, 247, 265, 284
Oberlin College 148
O'Brien, Ed 250, 265, 274–275
O'Connor, Sinéad 274
On a Friday 274

Ondes-Martenot 251
One Truth Band 303
Ono, Yoko 95
Orbison, Roy 145
Orbital 198
O'Rourke, Jim 269, 279
Osbourne, Ozzy 201, 202, 205, 208
Osmond, Donny 189
Ovation guitar 111, 256
    Al Di Meola signature model 294
Oxford University 275
Ozzfest 257

P

Paco de Lucía Sextet 292
Paganini, Niccolò 208
Page, Jimmy 19, 27, 48, 96–99, 110, 116, 182, 249, 251, 288
Paice, Ian 93
Paisley, Brad 174–175
Palmer, Bruce 130
Palmer, Carl 298
Paramounts, the 120, 121
Parfitt, Rick 109
Parker guitar 214
Parkpop Festival 135
Parton, Dolly 169
Pass, Joe 296
Pastorius, Jaco 300
Pat Metheny Group 300, 301
Paul Butterfield Blues Band 12, 13
Pauline Murray and the Invisible Girls 282
Paul, Les 54, 288, 298, 304–305
Paul Ray & the Cobras 30
Paul Reed Smith guitar 115, 194, 273
    Al Di Meola signature model 294
Pavarotti, Luciano 294
Pearl Jam 266, 267
Peavey guitar
    Wolfgang Special 127
Penn, Sean 301
Pentangle 170, 171
pentatonic scale 39
Perfect Circle, A 260
Perkins, Stephen 272
Perry, Joe 100–101, 110
Perry, Steve 157, 182
Peter Green and Friends 16
Peter Green's Fleetwood Mac 16
Peter Green Splinter Group 16, 17
Petersson, Tom 95
Petrucci, John 102–103, 216, 249
Pet Shop Boys 264, 283
Petty, Tom 145, 162
Phair, Liz 148–149, 176
Phillips, Eddie 251
Phillips, Sam 20
Phish 38, 39
Phoenix, Joaquin 162

Pikasso I guitar 300
Pineda, Arnel 156, 157
Pinhead Gunpowder 40
Pink Floyd 66, 67, 119, 289
Plant, Robert 96, 99, 288
Poison 110, 190, 191
Police 75, 280, 281
Ponty, Jean-Luc 296
Pony Canyon Records 208
Pop, Iggy 232, 258
pop music 15, 133–157, 284, 285, 290
Praxis 232
Precious (film) 84
Preisner, Zbigniew 67
Presley, Elvis 54, 70, 82, 90, 130, 160, 235, 294
Preston, Billy 144
Pretenders 139, 258, 259
Prince 84, 150–151
Prince and the Revolution 150
Princess Bride, the (film) 82
Procol Harum 120, 121
Prodigy 253, 270
progressive music 287–309
psychedelia 289, 298
Psycho Motel 220
Pulp Fiction (film) 53
Pummell, Simon 251
punk rock 118, 227–253, 262
Pure Prairie League 168
Purple Rain (film) 150
Pye Records 139

Q

Q magazine 45, 228
Quaife, Peter 136, 137
Quarrymen 142, 143
Quatro, Suzi 74, 77
Queen 75, 88, 94, 101
Queens of the Stone Age 64, 229, 253, 256, 257

R

Racer X 248
Raconteurs 64, 128, 129
Radcliffe College 176
Radio City Music Hall 67, 103
Radiohead 238, 241, 250, 251, 264, 265, 274, 275
Rage Against the Machine 229, 270, 271
Rain 246
Rainbow 184
Raitt, Bonnie 169, 176–177, 178
Ramone, Dee Dee 277
Ramone, Johnny 276–277, 277
Ramones 77, 227, 234, 249, 263, 276
Ranaldo, Lee 269, 278–279
Randolph, Robert 24–25
R&B (rhythm and blues) 11–33, 37, 48, 177, 280, 284, 290, 308
RCA-Victor 139, 290

Redding, Noel 70, 73
Red Hot Chili Peppers 244, 261, 272
Red Special guitar 89
Reed, Jimmy 12
Reeves, Greg 155
Reid, Vernon 214–215
Reinhardt, Django 82, 290, 296, 304
Reinhardt, Richard, 277
R.E.M. 230, 231
Remedy 299
Renbourn, John 171
Return to Forever 294, 295
Rey, Alvino 59
Reznor, Trent 257
Rhythm & Blues Foundation 177
Richards, Keith 77, 104–107
Rich Hippies 68
Rickenbacker guitar 142, 265
Riders of the Storm 86
Ridley, Greg 59
Righteous Babe Records 242, 243
Rihanna 182
Riot Grrrl 75
Road Crew 218
Robby Krieger Band 86
Robinson, Smokey 291
Robin Trower Band 120
Rocha, Zack, de la 270, 271
rock and roll 14, 15, 34–131
Rock Band video game 41
"Rocket 88" (song) 29
Rockets, the 130
Rockfords, the 266
Rock of Love (television series) 191
rock opera 41, 119
Rodrigo, Joaquín 293
Rolling Stone magazine 32, 45, 48, 116, 289
Rolling Stones 14, 27, 60, 93, 96, 100, 101, 104, 106, 118, 149, 201, 215, 289
Romeo Blue. *See* Kravitz, Lenny
Roots, the 214, 271
roots music 143
Rose, Axl 218, 219
Rossi, Francis 108
Roth, David Lee 124, 126
Roundabout 185
Roundhouse 276
Roxy Music 255
Rubin, Rick 204
rumba 15
Runaways, the 74, 77
Rundgren, Todd 152–153
Rush 206, 207
Russell, Leon 144

S

Sabo, Dave 110
Sacred Steel gospel 24
Sambora, Richie 110–111
Sam Phillips 29

Sánchez, Antonio 292
Santana, Carlos 63, 94, 112–115, 156, 198, 266, 294
Satriani, Joe 78, 102, 124, 198, 208, 216–217, 249
Saturday Night Live (television series) 101, 150, 257
Saunders, John Baker 266
Saura, Carlos 293
Schecter guitar
    C—1 241
Schenker, Michael 198
Schon, Neal 156, 156–157
Schroeder, Jeff 241
Scofield, John 300, 306–307
Scorpions 111
Scott, Bon 224
Scream 252
Screaming Trees 256
S-Curve Records 260
Selway, Phil 274, 275
Septic Death 198
Sepultura 253
Serious Moonlight Tour 30
7 Worlds Collide 274
Sex Pistols 41, 74, 124, 263, 276, 282, 284
Seymour 238, 239
Shakey, Bernard 130
Shakti 303
Shankar, Ravi 142
Shannon, Del 264
Shawkat, Alia 77
Sheer Greed 189
Sheila E. 151
Shelley, Steve 269, 279
Shergold guitar
    Masquerader 282
Shirley, Jerry 59
Shorter, Wayne 173
Shuman, Michael 257
Simmons, Gene 126, 192, 193
Simonon, Paul 262, 263
Simon, Paul 294
Simply Red 285
Simpson, Jessica 147
Simpsons, the (television series) 118
Sinatra, Frank 258
Sinful 183
Singer, Leah 278
Sire Records 276
sitar 144
Sixx, Nikki 210, 211
Skid Row 90, 91
skiffle 139, 142, 143
Skillings, Muzz 215
Slash 218–219
Slayer 204, 205
Slick, Grace 81
Sly and the Family Stone 24, 150
Smashing Pumpkins 240, 241, 257, 260, 261
Smith, Adrian 197, 213, 220–221

Smith, Chad 216
Smiths, the 264, 265, 282
Snakepit 218
Social Distortion 77
Soft Machine 296
Some Kind of Monster (film) 199
Sonic Youth 236, 268, 269, 278, 279
Sonovox 59
Sorum, Matt 219
soul 157, 284, 285
Soul SirkUS 156
Soul Stew Revival 122
Soundgarden 270
South by Southwest music festival 149, 259
Southern acoustic 27
Southern rock 47, 92, 174
Spears, Britney 147, 179
Spectres 109
Spectrum, the 153
Spencer, Jeremy 17
Spider-Man (film) 186
Squire, Chris 298
Squires, the 130
Staffell, Tim 88
Staley, Layne 186, 187, 266
Stanley, Paul 192, 193
Stanley, Ross 299
Starbucks Hear Music 173
Starkey, Zak 247
Starr, Ringo 50, 142, 144, 154, 247, 258
Status Quo 109, 140
Steele, Andrew 59
Steeler 208
Stella guitar 157, 176
Steve Howe Trio 299
Steve Morse Band 92
Stewart, Kristen 77
Stewart, Rod 288, 289
Stiff Woodies 236
Stills, Stephen 154–155, 166
Stills, Steven 130
Sting 280, 281
Stipe, Michael 230, 260
Stone Free 212
Stooges 276
Stradlin, Izzy 219
Stratocaster. See Fender guitar
Stratton, Dennis 221
Street Sweeper Social Club 270
Streisand, Barbra 169
Strummer, Joe 262, 263
St. Vincent 254
Style Council 284
Sub Pop 236
Sumlin, Hubert 26–27, 50
Summer of Love 81
Summer of Sam (film) 13
Summers, Andy 280–281
Sumner, Bernard 282–283
Sundance Film Festival 77
Sun Records 20, 29, 160

Super Bowl 101, 150
Super Session 32
Supro Ozark guitar 70
Surreal Life, the (television series) 191
Swallow, Steve 306
Sweet Children 40
Swift, Taylor 174
Synclavier 309
SynthAxe 297

T
Tadeschi, Susan 122
Taj Mahal 36, 177
Talbot, Mick 284
talk box 59
Tamaki, Nami 195
Tangerine Puppets 276
Tarantino, Quentin 53, 218
Taylor, Billy 130
Taylor, Gary 59
Taylor guitar 111
Taylor, James 130, 291
Taylor, Mick 106, 289
Teenage Cancer Trust 246
Tejano 63
Telecaster. See Fender guitar
Temple of the Dog 266
Tenacious D 253
Tennant, Neil 283
Text of Light 278
Them Crooked Vultures 253, 256
There Will Be Blood (film) 251
Thin Lizzy 90, 91
Thomas, Kristen Scott 150
Thomas, Mickey 12, 13
Thomas, Rob 112
Thompson, Danny 171
Thompson, Linda 178
Thompson, Richard 178–179
thrash metal 198, 204, 215
Ticketmaster 267
Tinted Windows 260
Tipton, Glenn 222–223
Tokyo Metropolitan Symphony Orchestra 125
To Live and Shave in L.A 268
Tomorrow 298
Tom Petty and the Heartbreakers 162
Tornadoes 228
Torres, Tico 111
Total Guitar magazine 228, 249
Townshend, Pete 49, 70, 116–119
Toxic Twins 100
Transatlantic Records 170, 171
Traveling Wilburys 145
TR-i 153
Trio of Doom 303
Triple Threat Revue 30
Trower, Robin 120–121
Trucks, Butch 37
Trucks, Derek 122–123
Turner, Ike 28–29

Turner, Tina 28, 288
Twang Machine 15
Twitter 147, 279
Tyler, Steven 84, 100, 101

U
U2 21, 56, 57, 162, 230, 271
Ulrich, Lars 200
Under the Cherry Moon (film) 150
Underwood, Carrie 174
University of California-LA 86
University of Chicago 12
University of Miami 92
University of Southern California 201
University of Vermont 39
Urchin 212, 220
Utopia 152

V
Vai, Steve 102, 124–125, 216, 244
Valens, Ritchie 62
Valory, Ross 156
Van Halen 74, 124
Van Halen, Eddie 50, 126–127, 182, 192, 241, 296
Van Halen, Wolfgang 126
Varney, Mike 208, 248
Vaughan, Jimmie 30
Vaughan, Stevie Ray 19, 24, 27, 30–31, 50, 51, 62, 146
Vedder, Eddie 266, 267
Velvet Revolver 218, 219
Velvet Underground 279
Vendetta 210
Venom 253
Ventures 294
VH1 Save the Music Foundation 147
VH1's Behind the Music 236
VH1's Storytellers 162
Vincent, Vinnie 193
Voodoo Lounge World Tour 105

W
wah-wah pedal 72, 199
Wakeman, Rick 298
Walk the Line (film) 162
Waller, Dave 284
Ward, Christopher Joseph 277
Warlocks 60
Warner Bros. Records 78, 145, 290, 291, 296
Warsaw 282
Washburn Guitars
  Nuno Bettencourt N4 182
Waterman, Dick 176
Waters, Muddy 18, 28, 32, 33, 42, 70, 104, 106
Watts, Charlie 106
W. C. Handy Blues Award 19
Webber, Andrew Lloyd 119
Weinrich, Scott 253
Weir, Bob 60

Weller, Paul 284–285
Wembley Arena 41, 44, 49, 83, 207
West, Sandy 77
Wetton, John 298
Wheeler, Tim 254
Whiskey a Go Go 87
White, Bukka 20
White Horse 210
White, Jack 99, 128–129
White, Meg 128, 129
White Spirit 196
White Stripes 128
Whitford, Brad 101
Who, the 96, 116, 118, 248, 284
Wicked Lester 193
Wilbury Records 145
Wilk, Brad 270
Williams, Hank Jr 64
Wilson, Barrie James 121
Wilson, Danny 130
Wilson, Tony 282
Winter, Edgar, 32, 33
Winter, Johnny 32–33, 68, 122
Winwood, Steve 51
Withers, Bill 291
Wolf Pack 26
woman tone 50
Wonder, Stevie 84, 288
Wood, Ron 106
Woodstock 70, 81, 112, 118, 154
Woodstock '79 154
Woody, Allen 69
Woody's Truck Stop 152
world music 123
Wretzky, D'arcy 240, 261
Wu-Tang Clan 271
WWVA Jamboree (radio program) 174
Wyman, Bill 106

Y
Yardbirds 27, 48, 96, 218, 288, 289
Yellow Cloud guitar 151
Yellow Matter Custard 248
Yes 296, 298
Yohimbe Brothers 214
Yorke, Thom 274, 275
Yorn, Pete 253
Young, Angus 224–225, 233
Young, Malcolm 224
Young, Neil 130–131, 154, 155, 161, 266, 279
YouTube 157

Z
Zander, Robin 95
Zappa, Dweezil 182
Zappa, Frank 70, 124, 125, 244, 308–309
Zimmerman, Robert. See Dylan, Bob
Zoot Money's Big Roll Band 280
ZZ Top 64, 111, 200, 257

CREDITS

ABBREVIATIONS USED

SS = *Shutterstock*; Wi =*Wikipedia*

Front Matter
3 Starstock/Photoshot 4 Danilo Moura/SS 4 Starstock/Photoshot 5 Ryan Rodrick Beiler/SS 6 Nick Elliot/Starstock/Photoshot 7 Starstock/Photoshot 8 Starstock/Photoshot

Blues and R&B
10 Danilo Moura/SS 11 Masao Nakagami/Wi 12l Photofest 12r Photofest 13 Photofest 14 UPPA/Photoshot 15 Mark Obstfeld/Starstock/Photoshot 16 Grenville Charles/Starstock/Photoshot 17l Sposato/Wi 17r UPPA/Starstock/Photoshot 18 WpN/Photoshot 19 Will Rose/Starstock/Photoshot 20 Robert Fullerton/SS 21 Starstock/Photoshot 22 Roland Godefroy/Wi 23 Tim Holt /Starstock /Photoshot 24 Nrbelex/Wi 25 Michael Eckmann/Wi 26 WpN/Photoshot 27 WpN/Photoshot 28 uppa.co.uk/Starstock/Photoshot 29 Sergei Bachlakov/SS 30 Epic Records 31 farrell71/Photobucket 32 Photofest 33l Photofest 33r WpN/Photoshot

Rock and Roll
34 Andrey Zyk/SS 35 Starstock/Photoshot 36 Photofest 37bl Ed Berman/Wi 37tr Photofest 38 WpN/Photoshot 39 WpN/Photoshot 40 Photoshot 41bl Face to Face /Starstock/Photoshot 41tr Photoshot 42 Grenville Charles/Starstock/Photoshot 43 WpN/Photoshot 44bl UPPA/Photoshot 44br Starstock/Photoshot 45l Grenville Charles/Starstock/Photoshot 45r Masahiro Sumori/Wi 46 Simone berna/w 47bl PAETEC 47 Photofest 48 Starstock/Photoshot 49 fattkatt/Wi 50l WpN/Photoshot 50tr Alan Davidson/Bandphoto/uppa.co.uk 51bl Starstock/Photoshot 51tr Starstock/Photoshot 52 Photofest 53bl Mike Burns/Wi 53 Photofest 54 UPPA/Photoshot 55 Uppa.co.uk/Starstock/Photoshot 56 Ryan Rodrick Beiler/SS 57bl Chris Sansenbach (Kurisu)/Wi 57r Bandphoto /Starstock/Photoshot 58 Andrew F. Kazmierski/SS 59 Starstock/Photoshot 60 Carl Lender/Wi 62 WpN/Photoshot 63 WpN/Photoshot 64 Photofest 65bl Gibson Guitar Company 65c Gibson Guitar Company 65r Photofest 66 deep_schismic/Wi 67bl deep_schismic/Wi 67c Gary Lee/Starstock/Photoshot 67tr WpN/Photoshot 68 rossmckillop/Wi 69 Carl Lender/Wi 70 Photofest 71l Photofest 71r Photofest 72t Photofest 72br UPPA/Photoshot 73bl Photofest 73tr Photofest 74l SS 74br Joe Mabel/Wi 75bl WpN/Photoshot 75tr SS 76bl Joe Mabel/Wi 76r Lindsey T/Wi 77 WpN/Photoshot 78 Photofest 79tl Photofest 79r WpN/Photoshot 80 Steve White Photos/SS 81l SprayPaintStencils.com 81r Starstock/Photoshot/Band Photo/uppa.co.uk 82l Starstock/Photoshot/Bandphoto/uppa.co.uk 82r Starstock/Photoshot/Band Photo/uppa.co.uk 83br aherrero/Wi 83tr Nick Lewis/Starstock/Photoshot 84 Bandphoto/Starstock/Photoshot 85l Bandphoto/Starstock/Photoshot 85l Ian Gavan/Starstock/Photoshot 86 Notimex/WpN/Photoshot 87 Elektra 88 Starstock/Photoshot 89 Carl Lender/Wi 90 David Fowler/SS 91l David Fowler/SS 91r Starstock/Photoshot 92 Andy Bradshaw/Starstock/Photoshot 93 Nick Soveiko/Wi 94 Carl Lender/Wi 95 Photofest 96 Dina Regine/Wi 97b Jim Summaria/Wi 97t David Wimsett/Starstock/Photoshot 98l Starstock/Photoshot 98l Ian Gavan/Starstock/Photoshot 99b Starstock/Photoshot 99t Starstock/Photoshot 100 WpN/Photoshot 101b Rob Rubio/Wi 101t daigooliva/Wi 102 Ferenc Szelepcsenyi/SS 103 Ian Gavan/Starstock/Photoshot 104 Andy BradshawStarstock/Photoshot 105l Photofest 105r Machocarioca/Wi 106 Photofest 107l Starstock/Photoshot 107r WpN/Photoshot 108 Jason Havord/Photoshot 109l Kev Meredith/Wi 109r Jason Havord/Photoshot 110 Nick Elliott/Starstock/Photoshot 111 Rosana Prada/Wi 112 Mark Obstfeld/Starstock/Photoshot 113 Shutterstock 114 Regis Martin/WPN/Photoshot 115l Shutterstock 115r David Gans/Wi 116 Photofest 117 Photofest 118l Photofest 118r Photofest 119l Photofest 119r Photofest 120 Doug James/SS 121 uppa.co.uk/Starstock/Photoshot 122 Xophersmith/Wi 123l Carl Lender/Wi 123r Xophersmith/Wi 124 Slavko Sereda/SS 125l Slavko Sereda/SS 125r Vento di Grecale/Wi 126 uppa.co.uk/Starstock/Photoshot 127bl Carl Lender/Wi 127m Henning Ihmels/Wi 127tr Wi/Alan Light 128 Starstock/Photoshot/Bandphoto 129l Frida Borjeson/Wi 129r Fabio Venni/Wi 130 Photofest 131b Andrea Barsanti/Wi 131t Andy Bradshaw/Starstock/Photoshot

Pop Music
132 mashe/SS 133 Photofest 134 WpN/Photoshot 135l Fred Kamphues/SS 135r Scott Taylor/Starstock/Photoshot 136 Matt Gibbons/Wi 137l uppa.co.uk/Starstock/Photoshot 137r uppa.co.uk/Starstock/Photoshot 138 Yves Lorson/Wi 139 ultomatt/Wi 140 Imagebrokers/Photoshot 141 Imagebrokers/Photoshot 142l Photofest 142r 6strings/Wi 143 Photofest 144 David Hume Kennerly/Wi 145 Photofest 146 Scott Taylor/Starstock/Photoshot 147l Nancy Rivera/Newscom/Starstock/Photoshot 147r Scott Taylor/Starstock/Photoshot 148 Lana/Wi 149l Bandphoto/Uppa.co.uk/Starstock/Photoshot 149r WpN/Photoshot 150 Photofest 151m WiscoBoy91/Wi 151r Photofest 152 Jean-Luc Ourlin/Wi 153 Carl Lender/Wi 154l WpN/Photoshot 154r Bob Sanderson/Wi 155 Atlantic Records 156l Claus-Dieter Jurkat/Photoshot 156r Matt Becker/Wi 157 Ian Gavan/Starstock/Photoshot

Folk and Country
158 Brian Weed/SS 159 Photofest 160 Photofest 161l Photofest 161r Photofest 162l Photofest 162r Photofest 163 Photofest 164 Photofest 166 Photofest 167 Elektra Asylum Records 168 Vince Clements/SS 169 Truejustice/Wi 170 Joe Mabel/Wi 171 Joe Mabel/Wi 172 uppa.co.uk/Starstock/Photoshot 173 Capannelle/Wi 174 Pete Souza/Wi 175l WpN/Photoshot 175r minds-eye/Wi 176 John Edwards/Wi 177l Sam Jones/Big Hassle 177r David Gans/Wi 178 6tee-zeven/Wi 179 Dxede5x/Wi

Hard Rock and Metal
180 Eky Chan 181 Photofest 182 VorlonX/Wi 183 uppa.co.uk/Starstock/Photoshot 184l Photofest 184r Photofest 185 Nick Soveiko/Wi 186 Shutterstock 187l Jason Havord/Starstock/Photoshot 187r the baldy/Wi 188 Ian Gavan/Starstock/Photoshot 189 Andy Bradshaw/Starstock/Photoshot 190 Matt Becker/Wi 191l WpN/Photoshot 191r Weatherman90/Wi 192l Photofest 192r Photofest 193 Photofest 194 Shadowgate/Wi 195 Shadowgate/Wi 196l Joel Cofre/Xinhua/Photoshot 196r adels/Wi 197 Narcis Parfenti/SS 198l Starstock/Photoshot 198l Michael Schofield/WPN/Photoshot 199 Photofest 200 Shutterstock 201l Photofest 201r Kreepin Deth/Wi 202 uppa.co.uk/Starstock/Photoshot 203 uppa.co.uk/Starstock/Photoshot 204 WpN/Photoshot 205l Cecil/Wi 205r Suelen Pessoa/Wi 206l Bandphoto/Starstock/Photoshot 206r Vince Clements/SS 207 Bandphoto/Starstock/Photoshot 208 alterna2/Wi 209l alterna2/Wi 209r alterna2/Wi 210 WpN/Photoshot 211l J Almasi / Starstock /Photoshot 211r Photofest 212 Narcis Parfenti/SS 213 Photofest 214 WpN/Photoshot 215bl WpN/Photoshot 215tr WpN/Photoshot 215 Mario/Wi 216 Girish Menon/SS 217l Girish Menon/SS 217r Tim Holt/Starstock/Photoshot 218 Photofest 219l Starstock/Photoshot 219r Photofest 220 adels/Wi 221l Narcis Parfenti/SS 221r Photofest 222 Tim Holt/Starstock/Photoshot 223l Narcis Parfenti/SS 223r Photofest 224 Starstock/Photoshot 225l Matt Becker/Wi 225r Band Photo / uppa.co.uk/Starstock/Photoshot

Alternative, Independent, and Punk
226 GrungyBit/SS 227 Dodo/Wi 228tl Slavko Sereda/SS 228bl Starstock/Photoshot 229bl Starstock/Photoshot 229tr Moses/Wi 230 Starstock/Photoshot 231bl Starstock/Photoshot 231tr Starstock/Photoshot 232 Foxtongue/Wi 233 Foxtongue/Wi 234 Photofest 235 MTV/Photofest 236tl Photofest 236bl MTV Networks/Photofest 237bl MTV/Photofest 237tr Photofest 238tl Starstock/Photoshot 238bl Tim Holt / Starstock / Photoshot 239 Starstock/Photoshot 240tl SS 241bl Schnékert/Wi 241tr Starstock/Photoshot 242 Starstock/Photoshot 243tl B1179_123218_0002.jpg 243br Starstock/Photoshot 244 WpN/Photoshot 245bl Bandphoto/Starstock/Photoshot 245tr WpN/Photoshot 246tl Starstock/Photoshot 246br Dean Grear / Bandphoto /Starstock/Photoshot 247bl Photofest 247tr Photofest 248 Roberto Scorta robescor@alice.it/Wi 249bl Vinod Sankar/Wi 249tr Vinod Sankar/Wi 250tl Hardtoexplain/Wi 250br Michell Zappa/Wi 251br Michell Zappa/Wi 251tr Sandstein/Wi 252 SS 253tl SS 253br Photofest 254 Scott Taylor/Starstock/Photoshot 255l Nick Elliot/Starstock/Photoshot 255r uppa.co.uk/Starstock/Photoshot 256 Paul Crowther/Starstock/Photoshot 257l Rama/Wi 257r Paul Crowther/Starstock/Photoshot 258 Starstock/Photoshot 259b WpN/Photoshot 259t Jslonaker/Wi 260 Sry85/Wi 261l Photofest 261r Tiffany Bauer/Wi 262 nikolai36/Wi 263l Photofest 263r Photofest 264l Andrew Sturmey/Starstock/Photoshot 264r David Holmes/Wi 265 Andrew Sturmey/Starstock/Photoshot 266 Lrheath/Wi 267l deep_schismic/Wi 267r Photofest 268 Stig Nygaard/Wi 269b Anders Jensen-Urstad/Wi 269t Photofest 270 Mark Obstfeld/Starstock/Photoshot 271l Ian Gavan/Starstock/Photoshot 271r Shutterstock 272 Shutterstock 273l Shutterstock 273r Dooley Productions/SS 274l Laura Sylvester/Wi 274r Kollision/Wi 275 Photofest 276 WpN/Photoshot 277l Photofest 277r Photofest 278 Delgoff/Wi 279br Photofest 279l Photofest 279mr Yuri Landman/Wi 280 WpN/Photoshot 281l Photofest 281r Photofest 282 Andrew Sturmey/Starstock/Photoshot 283l Richard Harding/Starstock/Photoshot 283r Andrew Sturmey/Starstock/Photoshot 284 Bandphoto/uppa.co.uk/Starstock/Photoshot 285l Bandphoto/uppa.co.uk/Starstock/Photoshot 285r Will Rose/Starstock/Photoshot

Jazz, World, and Progressive
286 David Hernandez/SS 287 Andy Bradshaw/Starstock/Photoshot 288 WpN/Photosho 289l Mandy Hall/Wi 289r Mandy Hall/Wi 290 Face To Face/Bandphoto/uppa.co.uk/Starstock/Photoshot 291l Nick Lewis/Starstock/Photoshot 291r Andy Bradshaw/Starstock/Photoshot 292 montuno/Wi 293l montuno/Wi 293r Stoned59/Wi 294 Reservoirhill/Wi 295 chascar/Wi 296 Photofest 297 Photofest 298l WpN/Photoshot 298r Ueli Frey/WI 299 Andrew F. Kazmierski/SS 300 Mattia Luigi Nappi/Wi 302 WpN/Photoshot 303 WpN/Photoshot 304 Thomas Faivre-Duboz/Wi 305b Thomas Faivre-Duboz/Wi 305t M.E. Mulder/SS 306 Rdrozd/Wi 307 Michael Hoefner/Wi 308 Photofest 309 Eddie Berman/Wi

Cover
f Bob Gruen (bobgruen.com) b Brandon Blinkenberg/SS